Twisted Visions

ALSO EDITED BY MATTHEW EDWARDS
AND FROM MCFARLAND

*Klaus Kinski, Beast of Cinema: Critical Essays
and Fellow Filmmaker Interviews* (2016)

*The Atomic Bomb in Japanese Cinema:
Critical Essays* (2015)

*Film Out of Bounds: Essays and Interviews
on Non-Mainstream Cinema Worldwide* (2007)

Twisted Visions

Interviews with Cult Horror Filmmakers

MATTHEW EDWARDS

McFarland & Company, Inc., Publishers
Jefferson, North Carolina

LIBRARY OF CONGRESS CATALOGUING-IN-PUBLICATION DATA

Names: Edwards, Matthew, 1978– editor.
Title: Twisted visions : interviews with cult horror filmmakers / Matthew Edwards [editor].
Description: Jefferson, North Carolina : McFarland & Company, Inc., Publishers, 2017. | Includes index.
Identifiers: LCCN 2017020687 | ISBN 9781476663760 (softcover : acid free paper) ∞
Subjects: LCSH: Horror films—History and criticism. | Motion picture producers and directors—Interviews.
Classification: LCC PN1995.9.H6 T95 2017 | DDC 791.43/617—dc23
LC record available at https://lccn.loc.gov/2017020687

BRITISH LIBRARY CATALOGUING DATA ARE AVAILABLE

ISBN (print) 978-1-4766-6376-0
ISBN (ebook) 978-1-4766-2814-1

© 2017 Matthew Edwards. All rights reserved

No part of this book may be reproduced or transmitted in any form or by any means, electronic or mechanical, including photocopying or recording, or by any information storage and retrieval system, without permission in writing from the publisher.

Front cover: Joanna David as Angela Paradise in the 1984 cult film *Sleepwalker* (Saxon Logan)

Manufactured in the United States of America

*McFarland & Company, Inc., Publishers
Box 611, Jefferson, North Carolina 28640
www.mcfarlandpub.com*

Dedicated to my parents
for their continued support of my writing career
and all aspects of my life

Acknowledgments

This book would not have been possible without the help of my family and friends and the interviewees and contributors who participated in this book. I would like to thank Marcus Stiglegger and Johannes Schönherr for contributing their brilliant interviews. It has been a pleasure working with again and an honor to have them in this collection. I would also like to thank all the interviewees.

I would also like to express my gratitude and thanks to David Geevanathan for the superb translations of the Higuchinsky and Yoshihiko Matsui interviews from Japanese to English. Without him, it would not have been possible to undertake such an in-depth interview with these directors.

Thank you also to my Mum and Dad and my brothers Paul, Mark and Daniel for their support during the production of this book and with my writing. Thank you to Doug and Rosemary for listening to me witter on about these crazy horror films. Special thanks also to Mimi the cat, to my nieces Lily, Poppy, Naomi and Eliza, and to Mandy and Kate. Thank you also to Patrick Prescott for his support in my writing endeavors and for continuing to spread the word about my books.

Last but not least, a huge thank you to my wife Johanna for her love and support during the writing of this book and for allowing me to watch hours and hours of horror cinema and to spend time transcribing the interviews. Without her, the book would not have been completed.

Table of Contents

Acknowledgments — vi

Introduction — 1

1. *A White Dress for Marialé* and *Nightmares in a Damaged Brain*
   AN INTERVIEW WITH ROMANO SCAVOLINI — 5

2. *Schalcken the Painter*
   AN INTERVIEW WITH LESLIE MEGAHEY — 17

3. *Alice, Sweet Alice*
   AN INTERVIEW WITH ALFRED SOLE — 28

4. *Savage Weekend* and *Schizoid*
   AN INTERVIEW WITH DAVID PAULSEN — 39

5. *Drive-In Massacre*
   AN INTERVIEW WITH STU SEGALL — 54

6. *Don't Go in the House*
   AN INTERVIEW WITH JOSEPH ELLISON — 63

7. *Alone in the Dark* and *The Hidden*
   AN INTERVIEW WITH JACK SHOLDER — 82

8. *Sleepwalker*
   AN INTERVIEW WITH SAXON LOGAN — 99

9. *Gritty Streets*
   AN INTERVIEW WITH BUDDY GIOVINAZZO
   BY JOHANNES SCHÖNHERR — 106

10. *The Death King*
    AN INTERVIEW WITH JÖRG BUTTGEREIT — 123

11. *Born of Fire*
    AN INTERVIEW WITH JAMIL DEHLAVI — 137

12. *Noisy Requiem*
    AN INTERVIEW WITH YOSHIHIKO MATSUI — 142

Table of Contents

13 *Dark Waters*
  An Interview with Mariano Baino — 153

14 *Aswang*
  An Interview with Barry Poltermann — 165

15 *Uzumaki*
  An Interview with Higuchinsky — 175

16 *Late Bloomer*
  An Interview with Gō Shibata
  by Johannes Schönherr — 180

17 Outside Peering In
  An Interview with Dante Tomaselli — 188

18 Horrific *Offspring*
  An Interview with Andrew van den Houten — 206

19 *Jug Face*
  An Interview with Chad Crawford Kinkle — 217

20 *The Last Will and Testament of Rosalind Leigh*
  An Interview with Rodrigo Gudiño — 228

21 *Off the Beaten Path*
  An Interview with Scott Schirmer — 236

22 *Headless*
  An Interview with Arthur Cullipher — 247

23 Visions of *German Angst*
  An Interview with Michal Kosakowski
  by Marcus Stiglegger — 254

Index — 267

Introduction

To those less receptive to the joys of the horror film, or "Twisted Cinema," I have always found it difficult to articulate the immense enjoyment that one can derive from these movies. Mainstream Hollywood cinema relies on the flamboyant and movies laden with special effects, star names and huge budgets. Commerce and entertainment are now its driving principles, as opposed to genuinely trying to communicate with its audience. In Hollywood, the marketing of the movie has become more important than the quality of the film. If a film executive has 30 seconds of decent high-impact footage to make a trailer to entice punters into multiplexes, then that is deemed a success. Raking in the dollars, making a profit is the name of the game in any cinematic venture, but in Hollywood, profit comes at the expense of the "art-look-tone-mood" of the film itself. Hollywood uses the mono-form as its cinematic blueprint. The images and sounds are presented in such a frenzied and bombastic manner that it stifles an audience's ability to process what they're watching. Rapid editing, its use of sound and music to dictate the mood and feelings of the audience, and the conventional approaches to narrative, camerawork, lighting and direction, have all contributed to a standardization of what is deemed "normal" or "accepted" practices in filmmaking.

For this reason, over time I have become more disillusioned with mainstream cinematic fare and I have sought to find films and filmmakers from a European or "world perspective" to connect with. I have looked toward directors such as Abel Ferrara, David Lynch, Werner Herzog, Béla Tarr, Andrei Tarkovsky and Peter Watkins, toward Japanese, Russian and New Wave Eastern European films in order to find solace. Yet it isn't just art house cinema that resonates with me, because I have always found solace in exploitation, horror, Hong Kong action and trash cinema. Positioned at the other end of the cinematic spectrum, these horror-trash filmmakers, often maligned (by those who can't comprehend a cinema other than the mono-form dished out to them by Hollywood and mainstream media corporations), have sought to stick two fingers up to the establishment and make films that don't fit into the neat little packages they're expected to fit into. Horror cinema has always been at the forefront of this vanguard, pushing boundaries, experimenting and challenging audiences.

These films not only entertain, they provided scares, thrills and genuine horror while articulating themselves in ways opposed to the mono-form in artistic and unconventional ways. They set out to communicate with the audience our darkest fears and utilize different cinematic tropes or approaches to get their messages across. John Carpenter (*Halloween*, *The Fog*), Sam Raimi (*Evil Dead*), Dario Argento (*Suspiria*), Mario Bava (*Blood and Black Lace*) were able to create new, exciting films that made audiences sit up and take note. Films with their own unique identities. Films that scared us shitless.

My love of horror developed at an early age from being terrified by Karl Freund's *The Mummy* (1932) before progressing onto the Hammer horror films. By my teens I had discovered the Italian *giallo* and American slasher films before splintering off to enjoy all facets of the horror genre, soaking up plenty of twisted and off-the-wall pictures in between, while immersing myself in the legendary horror magazines *Rue Morgue*, *Fangoria* and *The Dark Side* and the now defunct U.K. publications *Fear* and *Shivers*. They provided my horror fix and introduced me to new films and filmmakers. My parents helped feed this love of horror in myself and my three brothers by allowing us to rent 18 and over films (similar to the NC-17 rating in the U.S.) from rental outlets and purchasing controversial classics films like *Henry: Portrait of a Serial Killer* and *Man Bites Dog* from high street stores. (The thing that always makes me laugh about us watching violent crazy films like this is that my dad was a police sergeant and it was illegal for underage children to watch them! My Dad bought *Henry: Portrait of a Serial Killer* for me during his lunch break when patrolling the streets of Bath. I still find it amusing to think of my dad in his police uniform buying *Henry: Portrait of a Serial Killer*!)

From this love of the genre, and my own interest in interviewing film directors, I decided to put together an anthology covering a wide spectrum of horror cinema for fans who enjoy strange and offbeat cinema. The people within these pages have been chosen because I feel that they have contributed significantly to the genre and their films have strayed away from the mono-form and standardized practices as their goal was to make something truly original, terrifying, gross, experimental or groundbreaking. Films that were created for horror-exploitation fans, giving them what they couldn't get from the big studios. Inside you will hear stories of the hardships these filmmakers endured to realize their visions. The graft, the setbacks, the vicious attacks from the mainstream press who ridiculed and censored some of their films upon their initial release. You will find *giallo*-slasher movies, '70s British televisual horrors, psychological horrors, necrophilia, Islamic horrors, weird and twisted Japanese cinema horrors, surrealist horrors and interviews with some of the brightest independent horror moviemakers working today, like Dante Tomaselli and Scott Schrimer.

In this collection, 23 horror directors—some rarely interviewed in print or in English—speak candidly about their cult-classic horror films and the process of distribution. The interviews, conducted in just under two years (from September 2014 to June 2016), are previously unpublished and specifically intended for this anthology. The interviews have been collated and ordered into year of release, from the mid–70s to the present day. This approach will show how the horror genre has changed over the past 40-odd years and how filmmakers have built on the legacy of others to create their own original visions.

Inside you will find interviews with Romano Scavolini of the video nasty *Nightmares of a Damaged Brain* and rare interviews with Joseph Ellison, director of the wonderful *Don't Go in the House*, and David Paulsen of the lost slashers *Savage Weekend* and *Schizoid* fame. One of my greatest delights was tracking down and interviewing the great Stu Segall of the amazingly nutty *Drive-In Massacre* and in securing an interview with Yoshihiko Matsui of the radically twisted *Noisy Requiem*. Interviewing Mariano Baino, director of one of my all-time favorite horror films *Dark Waters*, and Jack Sholder of the brilliant *Alone in the Dark* and *The Hidden* were also privileges. All the filmmakers included are ones I admire because they have made films that I love and enjoy and wish to share with other horror fans. They are renegades of cinema, defiant of the constraints and practices dictated by Hollywood-mainstream cinema. They are filmmakers who march to the beat of their own drummer, creating twisted visions that are deeply personal expressions of what they want to communicate to their audience. Without them, the magic of cinema would have died a long time ago.

The interviewers: This author conducted 20 of the 23 interviews herein.

Two of the interviews (9 and 16) were conducted by **Johannes Schönherr**, a freelance writer who joined the anarchist Kino im KOMM cinema collective in Nuremberg after his arrival in the West and became involved in setting up American underground shows. He is the author of *Trashfilm Roadshows: Off the Beaten Tracks with Subversive Movies* (Headpress, 2002) and *North Korean Cinema: A History* (McFarland, 2012).

Interview 23 was conducted by **Marcus Stiglegger**, a professor of film studies and vice president at the DEKRA media school, Berlin. He is a visiting professor at Clemson University and a lecturer at universities in Germany, Austria, and Poland. His publications include *Nazisploitation! The Nazi Image in Low-Brow Cinema and Culture* (Continuum, 2012) and *David Cronenberg* (Bertz + Fischer, 2014).

1

A White Dress for Marialé and *Nightmares in a Damaged Brain*

An Interview with Romano Scavolini

Film director Romano Scavolini is synonymous with the amazingly warped 1981 slasher flick *Nightmares in a Damaged Brain* (aka *Nightmare*) that caused such a stir in the U.K. upon release that it was banned and its distributor sentenced to 18 months in prison for refusing to cut one second of footage. Oh the absurdity of the BBFC (British Board of Film Classification) and its moral crusading, though perversely, Hollywood-mainstream cinema seems to be able to get away with a lot worse these days which strikes of hypocrisy.

The Director of Public Prosecutions, was set up to help local authorities identify "obscene films" that they believed were in violation of the *Obscene Publications Act of 1959*. The DPP drew up a list of 72 films of so called "video nasties" and this was made public in June 1983. As a result of the DPP list, and what constituted obscene material from one authority to another, Parliament passed the Video Recordings Act in 1984 which stated that all video releases had to appear before the BBFC for certification and approval for release. Many films were banned or cut heavily. Of the 72 films, 39 were successfully prosecuted under the Obscene Publication Act and these included *The Driller Killer*, *Cannibal Holocaust*, *I Spit on Your Grave* and many more. Many of these film were later released in the UK, albeit with cuts. Such has the nature of censorship changed in the UK that most of these films are now available to own uncut by the BBFC.

Interestingly, of the 72 films on the original DPP banned list, *Nightmares in a Damaged Brain* was the only one that saw the distributor prosecuted and spend time behind bars.

This genre classic, featuring gory decapitations and ax-wielding mayhem, centers on schizophrenic loner George Tatum (Baird Stafford), who undergoes a series of drug tests at a local hospital. Haunted by violent images of his childhood, he escapes from the hospital and heads back to his Florida home. Violent memories resurrect themselves in George's fractured psychosis, urging him to kill again. This kickstarts a brutal killing spree that intensifies as the repressed images from his childhood are pushed back into the forefront of his conscience. *Nightmares* is considered by some in the horror fraternity to be a bona fide genre classic which taps into the scummy New York vibe of that era.

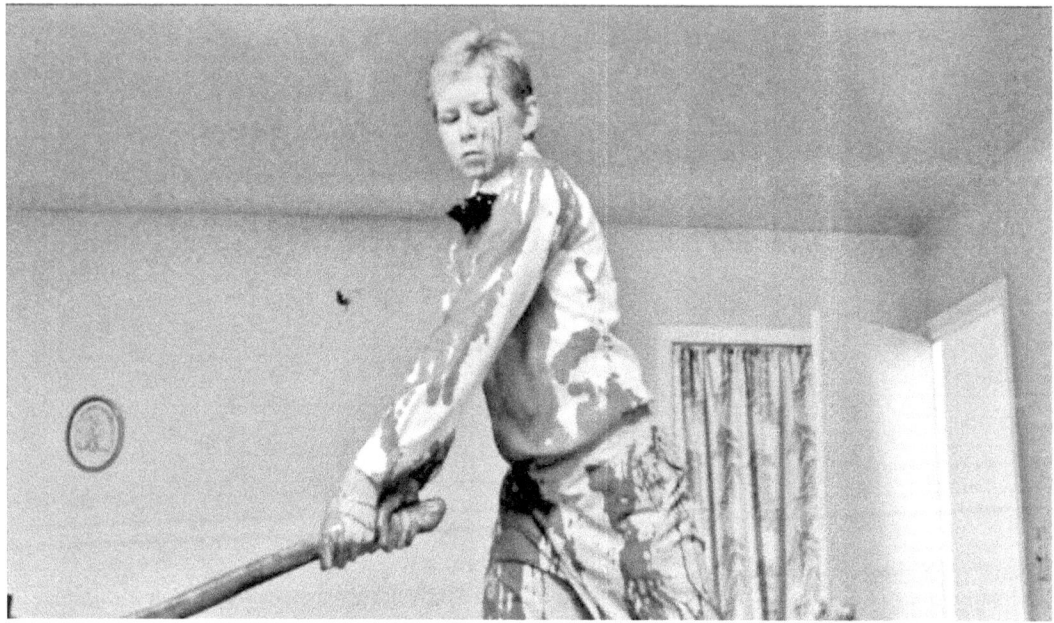

Little George (Scott Praetorius) goes Nutzoid with an ax in *Nightmares in a Damaged Brain*'s violently grotesque ending (courtesy Romano Scavolini).

It's a controversial shocker full of sleaze, nudity and a general haze of exploitation and explicit splatter. Small wonder the film has found widespread acclaim in the horror community.

What is less known about Scavolini is that he directed one of the most underrated *giallo* films to emerge from Italy, the wonderfully haunting *A White Dress for Marialé*, starring Evelyn Stewart and Ivan Rassimov. As a child, Marialé sees her father murder her unfaithful mother and her lover (who dies heroically by twisting naked in the air in a pirouette with his penis exposed as it flaps about against his thigh) before turning the gun on himself. Ten years later a traumatized Marialé lives in a dilapidated castle with bully husband Paolo (Luigi Pistilli), who keeps her confined to the place by sedating her. Marialé invites friends over, much to her husband's annoyance; her guests include her former lover Massimo, arguing couple Semy and Gustavo, and hedonistic free-loving trio Mercedes, Joe and Sebastiano. When touring the castle, the group discover strange outfits in an underground crypt, including the white dress Marialé's mother was wearing when she was killed. Putting on these outfits kicks off a passionate masquerade dinner and a wild, surreal and flamboyant orgy, fueled by alcohol and their perverse desires. When the dust settles, all is not what it seems as one by one the guests are picked off by an unknown murderer. It is left to the viewer to untangle the threads and guess the identity of the killer in the midst. A superb *giallo*, *A White Dress for Marialé* is visually arresting, atmospheric and surreally horrifying. This unsung Euro-horror is a critique of male violence and oppression towards women and '70s hedonism. It's surprising that such an accomplished film has slipped by many *giallo* fans.

In March 2016, I had the pleasure of interviewing Romano Scavolini about his two seminal contributions to the horror genre. I thank him for being interviewed for the collection and for sharing his memories and experiences on the making of these genre classics.

Matthew Edwards: *How did you get involved in film?*

Romano Scavolini: My professional experience is more extensive than just writing and directing *A White Dress for Marialé* and *Nightmares in a Damaged Brain*. Before directing *A White Dress for Marialé* I did more than 50 short films and documentaries. During that time, at the age of 18, I went to Germany working as a stevedore on the Neckar River which crosses the city of Stuttgart, and while working, during the weekends, I wrote, directed, acted and produced my first film *The Ravaged One*. It took 18 month to finish shooting the film and then I returned to Italy, where I established myself in Rome. I had to wait 'til 1964 to shoot my first short film *The Quiet Fever* while in the meantime the only copy of my first film, *The Ravaged One*, became lost in the cellars of a New York post office. *The Quiet Fever* won numerous prizes worldwide as a powerful essay on human violence with the commentary of five poems by Dylan Thomas.

Finally in 1966 I made my first (second in my count) professional full-length feature, *Blind Fly*, considered a controversial pictorial analysis of aimless violence brought on by the central character's lack of motivation and purpose in life. The film was obstructed and censored by the Italian government and "banned forever." Nonetheless, the film made the rounds of major international festivals, eluding the government order hidden inside Diplomatic Luggage. The film promoted me to the ranks of a "cult" filmmaker. The next year I wrote and directed *The Dress Rehearsal* [1968], a "Joycean" film exploring multi-faceted aspects of the making of film through innovative editing and structure, and then I realized "a non-film" or, if you prefer, "a voluntary abandoned project in the making," titled *Entonce* [1969]. Then I thought that my experience as a filmmaker was at an end, and I went to Vietnam as a freelance photographer (I voluntarily surrendered to the idea of not bringing with me a film camera but only two still cameras) in order to "be physically there" where I could see with my own eyes the real horror of modern time. I was wounded, hospitalized in a South Vietnamese camp and, when released, I returned to Rome. I continued to survive but only as a D.P. on various "genre" films, even working with Gideon Backman on a "special" on Federico Fellini. Then I started my own production company [Lido Film Company] and after a while I was almost forced to write, direct and produce a number of films on a broad range of subjects such as *A White Dress for Marialé*.

You have spent time as a photographer and documentarian in war-torn regions such as Vietnam. How has this experience shaped you as a person and would you say it shaped your cinematic vision in any way?

The experience in Vietnam, like any other experience of horror, can never relate to the experience that you live witnessing the same horror depicted in a movie. While in a theater, the viewer knows that what he sees is fiction; the horror which has a real-life spectator has a radically different consequence in your consciousness. Although it is inevitable that in the theater the spectator identifies with the images on screen, in real life all the existential parameters collapse. In Vietnam, as in any other human tragedy, "being there" is [means] everything; while watching a movie, it is pure "appearance." The fact is that while at the movies, unconsciously, in every viewer co-exist two different entities that assist to the show immersed in the darkness of the theater. The first one is the viewer who "sees" the film. The second entity is the one who "observes within" the reactions of the first one. This event did not take place in real life. Because the emotions that the spectator feels when he witnesses real horror "stain" his consciousness in a completely different way as when watching a movie. In short, while watching a movie, the spectator enters in a state of "hypnagogic" consciousness, a state of semi-hypnosis that is closer to a state of a dream which is different from the waking state. In the theater the viewer is immersed in a sort of schizophrenic state of mind which ends as soon as the lights of the theater turn on. My experience in Vietnam has been the typical experience of those who were transferred dramatically and suddenly from his living room watching the news on television on the war in Vietnam to the front line of the same war. And to answer your question, I must say that my experience of the Vietnam War did not affect at all my choices while making a film. Quite the contrary: In *Nightmares in a Damaged Brain*, for example, the scenes of horror I did emphasize them just because I was always conscious of the fact that the "viewer" is a "atypical" witness of all kind of violence as they appear on screen. The viewer of a horror movie, even though he identifies with what he sees, he knows that at the end what he saw did not even stain the screen, but they will go away as a dream that vanishes on awakening. The front line of the war in Vietnam never vanished from my consciousness; it is there every day as a "continuum" in space and time, reminding me that I was "immersed flesh and blood in the horror."

I consider A White Dress for Marialé *[aka* Spirits of Death*] one of the most underrated Italian films of the '70s, along with* Footprints on the Moon *[1975, directed by Luigi Bazzoni]. How did you become attached to the project?*

A White Dress for Marialé is an atypical project of my filmography. The fact is that I had previously produced a film with my brother Sauro, and I was in debt, a lot of money. I had no ongoing project which was able to cover my debts, so I agreed to direct, photograph and also execute the production of the film with an associate of mine. This is the reason why I have often said that the film is not mine. The screenplay they submitted to me was really terrible. It was written by two B movie scriptwriters and the cast had already been decided. In order to direct and photograph the film, I asked to rewrite the screenplay, but I was only allowed if I agreed to not delete or make changes to the existing characters. They gave me two weeks to rewrite it. I rewrote the full screenplay but didn't sign it, because the two writers denied me this. The budget was contained; therefore I had to make a number of choices to carry it out, trying [to avoid selling out] entirely, but rather, doing everything to make it a horror film of a high standard. Not only did I rewrite the script to the extent that the production had imposed upon me and manage the photography, but I was also the camera operator and I only had a three-week shooting schedule.

You state that you weren't initially thrilled with the script, in that it was a more conventional horror film. What changes did you make?

Right now I do not remember exactly the scenes I had rewritten, but I can assure you that the script that I was given to read had to be thrown in the trashcan. It was not my kind of story, and all the tragedy that took place in that castle was very far from my taste. I remember that I tried to instill in the plot a kind of "psychoanalytic" dimension by acting on the central character of the film, and by opening the movie with a flashback in which Marialé , as a child, witnesses the murder of his mother by his father. This single scene has characterized all the changes that I later made to the script.

Talk us through the production of the film. Did you experience any technical challenges or difficulties?

As I told you, I have held various positions: from the executive producer to the rewriting of the script, direction of the photography and also the cameraman. I had to do all

Luigi Pistilli as the abusive husband Paolo in *A White Dress for Marialé*, who drugs and keeps Marialé prisoner in his family castle before the explosive and nightmarish finale that inevitably ends in bloodshed (courtesy Romano Scavolini).

this in three weeks. The first decision I made was to pre-light all the interiors so that I could be free to move the camera 360° without limits. To be able to run safely without repeating too many slates meant that I was able to spend many hours with the actors. We did rehearsal after rehearsal of all the scenes scheduled for the day. Consider that for more than half of the film, the group of actors was always in front of the camera. Rehearsals for hours with the actors, and choreographing their movements, allowed me to stay physically behind the camera and shoot in controlled time even complex scenes. Many people do not know this, but I shot the film in widescreen format using a perforations system that was used at the time in Italy called "2P." I used a camera whose shutter was "modified" to impress "half frame" of a full 35mm at a time. Half of a 35mm frame impressed is equal a rectangular image similar to a 16:9 format, which was then converted into CinemaScope format only in post-production. Today the film is released on Blu-ray and I can tell you that at least, photographically, it's absolutely top quality.

The opening, when Marialé's father shoots his unfaithful wife and her lover in the woods, and Marialé is forced to watch, is sublime. I thought that sequence was beautifully shot and edited. Were you pleased with the way you realized this scene?

    I consider the opening scene very important because all the tragedy that overshadows the whole plot sheds a significant light on everything else. Marialé witnesses the murder of her mother but also her father's suicide, not seen but perceived throughout the sequence. I wanted to open the film with idyllic images … the lovers flirting under the shade of an ancient tree while the light of the sun wraps around the romantic scene as a painting of Degas. Then the arrival of the car, the soft steps of the woman's husband in the grass, then the shot. I asked the young actor to die spouting into the air like a wounded fawn. I did not want a double homicide with blood, but only two red spots on the woman's dress. She's still fully dressed and apart from the nudity of the young lover, she had always taken a very pure attitude.

Another fantastic sequence is when the characters converge inside the underground chamber with the mannequins. That scene oozes style and atmosphere and a real sense of foreboding horror. How did you set about visualizing it?

Among all the props that enrich the film, Marialé's dress occupies the most important place. The film's title clearly states it: Marialé's dress is the central core of the story. With this in mind, I thought that the [clothing] of Marialé's mother but also other clothing and customs, could assume a meaning. With this in mind, I created the sequence in the basement filled with dummies because I wanted to specifically point out that Marialé had developed her illness throughout the years by creating a whole imaginary world to surround herself with imaginary people (dehumanized dummies) who wear clothes that could have been those of her mother 40 years before. Her guests are inclined to visit the castle 'til they go down to the basement. Meanwhile, one guest, hidden among the dummies, wears one of the dresses and has assumed the frozen posture of a dummy. This sequence has offered me the chance not only to describe one aspect of Marialé's syndrome, but also to start the sequence (which I consider the best of the film) of the orgiastic-blasphemous "last dinner" in which, wearing various clothes found in the basement, all the guests, (to the exclusion of Marialé's husband) make themselves up, each of them assuming the mask of their own idiosyncrasies.

The film is seemingly a deliberate clash of cultures. You have this new era of hippie free love and hedonistic attitudes juxtaposed with the gothic castle setting. The film is seemingly about the death of the free love generation. What was your angle on the film?

Your comments before the question implies what you think about the cultural and narrative structure of the film. But this film has only offered me the opportunity to highlight the corruption of the morals, the idiocy of mankind, the ambiguity of all passions, the lack of compassion, the dominance of greed, the sexuality lived as pure blasphemous vice, and ending without offering any positive final. In fact, the film was violently opposed by the Vatican, and though it was very successful at the various openings, it was withdrawn from circulation by the distributor [who was] fearful of judiciary complaints.

Talk us through the feast-masquerading orgy scene. How did you direct the actors in that sequence?

The orgy, or better to say "the Last Supper" in blasphemous-key, represents the best part of the entire film. I set out to design the scene as a series of long sequences with the movement of the actors accompanied by a song that I loved very much, played by a pop group called Iron Butterfly, entitled "In a Gadda da Vida" (which in post-production was re-arranged by Fiorenzo Carpi). As I said earlier, I choreographed the entire sequence with all the actors repeatedly, then I placed the camera on a three-wheeled platform that was free to be moved by two technicians and I shot the series of sequences while the camera was dancing with the music.

I loved Semy's [Shawn Robinson] underwater death in the film as she is repeatedly bludgeoned in the swimming pool.

While the entire film was shot in a castle in Rome's suburbs, to shoot underwater we were forced to move to a sound stage with a pool that had portholes for filming purposes. Shawn Robinson was an extraordinary professional and in that sequence she worked with a great disposition although she was forced to stand in the water, at night, for a few hours. In addition to the pool sequence, we also shot in studio the sequence of the "scorpions." Those are very peculiar animals and needed to be treated under the supervision of an expert on tropical insects. Their venom can be deadly.

Composer Fiorenzo Carpi and conductor Bruno Nicolai's score is truly magnificent and one of the best the giallo genre has to offer. Were you pleased with it?

Few people know that the "theme" of *Marialé* was chosen (I do not know by whom) to accompany the first flights of the Concorde: one with a French flag from Paris and the other with the English flag, from London, January 21, 1976. Fiorenzo Carpi's score is still unmatched today. I followed the whole process until the recording in the studio with the orchestra conducted by Bruno Nicolai.

You have stated that you wish it didn't belong on your own filmography. Do you still feel this way? Personally, as I stated earlier, I consider it to be a brilliant piece of filmmaking.

Thanks very much. I consider myself an author and as such I consider only those films that I've written from the first page to the last. After the writing comes the realization, and most of the time what has been written does not correspond 100 percent to what has been imagined. Each author has always two films to come to terms with: One is what he imagined to shoot and the second is what he is able to translate into images. It is increasingly the case that the two films never fit together. But the reasons are too long to engage in this type of explanation now. *Marialé* is one of three films in my filmography, which I did not conceive, imagine, create, write, etc. The film does not even belong to the genre I love, that of stories that I feel close to my sensibility. But I consider myself a professional and as such I think that *A White Dress for Marialé* is a good packaged product for the market and if there are people out there that appreciate it, then I am satisfied.

How was A White Dress for Marialé *received critically in Italy? Are you surprised that the film has become a cult film in both America and Europe, since its release on DVD?*

The film was instantly a box office success and well received by critics attentive to its revolutionary content. But as soon as the film hit a large audience, it was violently criticized by the Vatican and by a bigoted and hypocritical religious people who asked that the film be withdrawn from the theaters as it was in contempt of religion and morality. So it was withdrawn by the distributor. In Italy the movie is practically unknown even if there are various requests for it to be released again. I don't really care.

You returned to the horror genre with the infamous slasher film Nightmares in a Damaged Brain. *This film has been the subject of a lot of controversy, especially in Great Britain, where it was labeled a video nasty and banned until recently. The original distributor in the U.K., David Grant, was thrown in jail for 18 months for refusing to edit one second of violent footage! How did you feel about the censorship of your work and the treatment of the film in the U.K.?*

When it all happened, I was involved in another project and I received the news about David Grant and all that mess as a "second-hand" event. I knew for sure that Margaret Thatcher had reunited her cabinet urgently in order to ban *Nightmares in a Damaged Brain* in the U.K. And also that hundreds of VHS copies of the film were seized by the police before it could be sold underground. A strange fact remain: After more than 20 years, it was a British distribution company that was the first to re-release *Nightmares in a Damaged Brain* on DVD, making a lot of money by selling it over the Internet. Soon after, Code Red in the U.S. managed to find 35mm copies of the film and set about rebuilding the original movie based on my script, before digitally regenerating the parts still not damaged before releasing *Nightmares in a Damaged Brain* into the market in its "full version."

You wrote the script for Nightmares in a Damaged Brain. *Where did the initial idea stem from?*

To be honest, my intent was to not just shoot a horror genre film. I wrote a plot inspired by a true story that I read in an American weekly mag, *Time* or *Newsweek*, I don't remember which. There was an editorial denouncing some experiments that the CIA had done on human subjects, namely prisoners and mental patients, who were administered a powerful drug in order to study how those drugs would alter their behavior. Reading about these kinds of "guinea pigs" experiments affected me deeply. So I decided to use that editorial as a base to develop a plot. The plot was chosen among hundreds from an executive of a new company looking to produce a low-budget film. I had already forgotten the plot I wrote, when I got a call from Goldmine. They wanted to know who I was and if I was available to sell the story or to direct the film myself and also to write the screenplay. It all happened very quickly. I took a flight to Cocoa Beach in Florida, where I had friends, and I wrote the screenplay in 15 days. I returned to New York on the last flight from Orlando while John Watkins, a Goldmine executive, was waiting for me at the airport to read the screenplay right away as I got off the plane.

To shoot the film in Cocoa Beach, a small Florida town, was a great experience. The crew was composed entirely of people from New York with whom I had made a strong and sincere friendship during my early years in the U.S. All of them had a strong desire to work on an independent film and build up a career. Many other people, eager to help us out, were

Old Continental VHS Sleeve of *Nightmares in a Damaged Brain!* proclaiming "not suitable for children," as it might turn them into ax-wielding maniacs!

found on the spot. For a small provincial town, a film crew represents a rare opportunity: a little taste of Hollywood maybe, or, above all, to get out of the isolation that characterizes the typical American towns. For three weeks we were the focus of the curiosity and attention of the population. The last day of shooting coincided with the beginning of the Christmas holidays, so we tried to work hard, 13, 14 consecutive hours, just to finish and move back to New York for the holidays. Every day the dailies were sent to the lab in New York, but I could see the rushes only two or three days later. If I was not happy about something, I surely had no time to reschedule some shooting. I had to be 100 percent on top of my game and I could not afford to make a single mistake. But I believed a lot in my script even though I wrote it in 15 days. Meanwhile, in New York, news started going around saying that there was a horror movie in production in Florida unlike any other in the genre. David Jones, Goldmine's producer, excited by these voices, decided to increase the budget in order to give me the opportunity to add those scenes that I felt were weaker and to strengthen the story with sequences that I had deleted because we considered them too expensive to shoot. I believe that this fact alone was a turning point for the movie from the point of view of its latent power.

Nightmares in a Damaged Brain oozes pure sleaze and filth, and is aesthetically in total contrast to the stylized and beautifully choreographed A White Dress for Marialé. *Did you deliberately employ such a documentary and grungy look in order for it to suit the script?*

Every story needs to be told with its own style to be successful. The Anglo-Saxon or European cinema offers more space to the author than the American one, especially regarding the aesthetic. Even the Anglo-Saxon editing is slower than that of American cinema. There is a big difference between the camera's point of view in an American film from that of an Anglo-Saxon or, if you prefer, European. In fact, all the major American directors "would" (or like to be) be more European. But Hollywood does not allow an American author to be himself. For the American film industry, a movie is a product and just that. For us, Europeans, a film is not only entertainment but also art, culture, poetry, painting, etc. I realized *Nightmares in a Damaged Brain* was trying to tell a story and not just to hit the stomach of the viewers. To hit the spectator's stomach, you need to tell a story that has its roots in reality, not in fantasy. The massacre of the father and mother by the young Tatum is not the explosion of a mental disorder but flows from the inability of him to "understand" that his parents love to have sex through sadomasochistic practices. And when the story reaches its peak, the viewers understand precisely how things are, because what sets in motion the whole tragedy is not only the ambiguity of feelings and emotions but the eternal conflict between "to be" and "to appear." *Nightmares in a Damaged Brain* is in fact a fierce dream that flows out of a conscience unable to accept "the sense of guilt." In my film there is no hope, because the real and final message is that we are all at the mercy of our demons.

The film has garnered further notoriety through the inclusion of Tom Savini on press material stating that he worked on the special effects. I understand he merely acted as a consultant.

On this issue, I have only one comment to make: Darryl Ferrucci, Ed French, Johanne Hansen and Robin Stevens took care only of prosthetic effects [the head of Tatum's father, the head of the beheaded mother, a part of the back and spine and severed arm of the nanny]. They didn't make the effects but realized only the "dummies" and they are credited as: "special effects makeup artist and special effects makeup assistant" and they did this in New York. But Tom Savini oversaw the making of the prosthetic, and he was all the time on the set for monitoring and directing all the master special effects sequences in the film, from the beheading of the mother and then the father by young Tatum. There are several slides showing Tom Savini on the set teaching the young actor who played Tatum how to hold and swing the ax in the air and how to hit the head of his mother and then behead his father. These facts are incontrovertible and I never understood why Tom Savini has denied having worked on the set for *Nightmares in a Damaged Brain*. The only logical explanation that I know for sure is that his refusal to put his name in the headlines of the film was money. He asked the production for more money whose amount was considered excessive for his role. On the web there are even rumors that the film had gone over budget. It's false. Like I said in my answer to a previous question, David Jones of Goldmine decided, completely autonomously, to increase the budget of the film so that he could give me the opportunity to improve some sequences.

I will tell you a story about the film which few people know: David Jones had full faith in me to the point that he accepted—after my request—to re-assemble all the negatives and re-edit the movie two consecutive times, because I asked him and because I refused the first two editors after they showed to me how they edited the film. After two denials, finally John Watkins, the executive in charge of the production, decided to call Robert Margisson to cut the film, and Robert was my choice since the beginning. But because John Watkins didn't want me to have "the final cut," he decided to hire two different editors to cut *Nightmares in a Damaged Brain*; but because in my opinion they failed, David Jones decided to come to my terms. And with that, I hope to close the debate once and for all. I can only add that the film's success has disturbed some wild independent filmmakers in New York. I was wrapped up for years by an obsessive jealousy and envy, a bitterness and resentment that I did not deserve because I had only had success with a low-budget horror movie while in Los Angeles there were at least 100 horror films that grew moldy in the majors' basements!

One of the interesting elements of your film is that you try to humanize the killer, George. I feel the film elicits a degree of sympathy for his character.

Tatum was a victim of a secret CIA bio-experiment. His life was turned upside down. He was not a bad guy. He was suffering from a mysterious syndrome artificially inoculated into his system because of those experiments. Why should not I have a special eye on this man?

The death scenes are wonderfully gruesome and explicit. Did you feel you were pushing the boundaries of cinematic violence at the time?

I will tell you another story. Before being distributed, a copy of the film was required for projection at Warner who definitely wanted to cut all the so-called "splatter" scenes. Then came forward Universal, which, after the projection, made the same requests. David Jones called me up over the phone asking me what was my attitude towards these requests. I told him that if he accepted the cuts, the film would be a total failure. The strongest scenes had to remain uncut because the film should be a scandalous event. The American spectators had never seen anything like what I had decided to get them to see when I realized *Nightmares in a Damaged Brain*. It was my firm intention to cross all limits imposed by the Anglo-Saxon puritanism and present to the audience a gruesome decapitation of a couple by their very young child in order to touch the deepest chords of the viewers. If David Jones had agreed to cut those scenes, he would have killed the film. David agreed and resisted the demands of both Universal and Warner. Finally the film was released with three "X"s (like pornography) in 117 New York theaters, distributed by a small and unknown local distribution (21st century), but all theaters were controlled by Universal, without the logo, because all majors do not put their logo on a movie to be released with three "X"s.

Talk us through the wonderful finale and the filming of the decapitation of George's father's lover. That scene, for many horror fans, is cinematic gold!

The whole scene of the final decapitation had occupied us for nearly a week. We had five of Tatum's father's prosthetic heads and five prosthetic heads of the mother. We studied all scenes with a storyboard made with small mannequins. I first decided how to choreograph the events taking place inside the room. Then, with Gianni Fiore the D.P., we choose 36 different positions of the camera in order

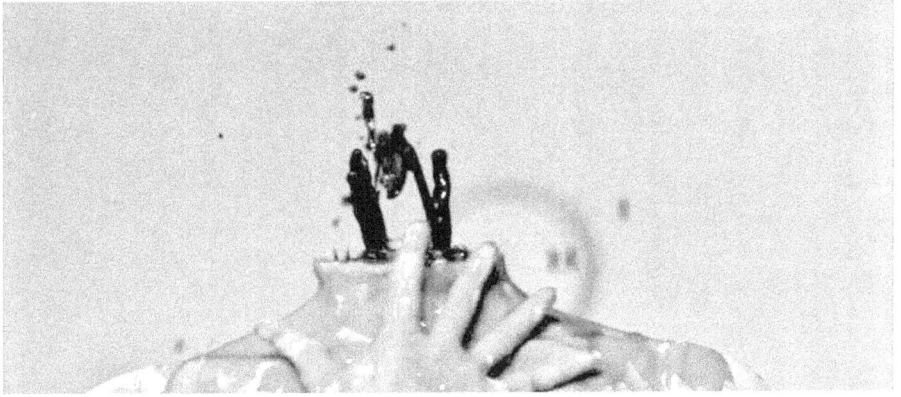

Top: 21st Century Distribution Corporation's iconic promotional poster of *Nightmares in a Damaged Brain*, aka *Nightmare*. *Bottom:* Bloody decapitations galore in Romano Scavolini's brilliant brutal video nasty *Nightmares in a Damaged Brain*! (courtesy Romano Scavolini).

to have an explosive cinematic editing of the entire sequence. Then we moved to implementation. The hardest thing was not to realize the beheading of Tatum's mother but how could we get the hatchet—wielded by the young Tatum—splitting literally in the middle of his father's head while he was begging and screaming to his son. The hatchet that enters the frame, and which cuts in half the man's head, was being maneuvered by Tom Savini! Tom Savini also maneuvered the blood pumps to spill out from the trunk of the decapitated woman!

What are your thoughts on the films over 35 years later?

Your readers will judge if I have been up to the task. I would not want him/her to believe that I tried to escape from this adventure. During the past decades in which *A White Dress for Marialé* and *Nightmares in a Damaged Brain* were made, my profession has experienced enormous changes. I have crossed various stages of life and spent years of absolute rigor; I lived like a vagrant moving from one continent to another by writing and dreaming explosive films that I never managed to realize. I accept a certain amount of curiosity on my filmography, but with irony. The film industry is full of authors far more important than I.

One thing is certain: I never tried to make films for the masses, but for a mature viewer with the critical ability to sit in the dark of a movie theater and watch what happens on the screen with a certain detachment. A cold spectator who observes the film as an object without identifying with it. I do not care to be rewarded and admired. If due to *Nightmares in a Damaged Brain* some say I am a "monster" [*The New York Times*' Janet Maslin said this when *Nightmares* was released in New York], then I accept to be considered a monster and to be placed in that painful human dimension with my huge and glaring contradictions between what I have been and what they believe I am. Answering your questions and to appear as having a life and having a story to tell, will be impossible. The needs behind any interview are subtle and insidious but I hope that your book will be successful.

That said, I am thrilled. I still am, at how, after so many years, these little films, especially *Nightmares in a Damaged Mind*, have made their nest in millions of viewers' minds.

2

Schalcken the Painter

AN INTERVIEW WITH LESLIE MEGAHEY

Saved from obscurity by the British Film Institute, *Schalcken the Painter* is a film barely known outside of its native Britain and those interested in British televisual horror of the '70s and early '80s. A loose adaptation of J. Sheridan Le Fanu's chilling ghost story of the same name, this exquisitely shot horror film effortlessly weaves documentary with fiction to create a stunningly terrifying picture based on the work of real-life seventeenth century Dutch painter Godfried Schalcken. Exploring the notions of greed, art and commerce, director Leslie Megahey tells the story of Schalcken (Jeremy Clyde), an aspiring young painter who is the favored pupil of his master Dou (Maurice Denham). Schalcken is besotted with Dou's kindly niece Rose (Cheryl Kennedy) and longs to marry her. When a specter named Vanderhausen appears, demanding to purchase Rose for his wife for a casket of gold, Dou agrees; to Dou, the shiny coinage is worth more than his niece. Aghast at the prospect, Rose implores Schalcken to elope with her but he too has now been blinded by commerce and merely informs her that he will buy her back when he has made his fortune. Rose is spirited away and Schalcken is made to pay for his spineless decision in a shocking and disturbing finale.

Essentially a tale focusing on the glory era of Dutch painting, the film is a critique of the treatment of women, who were merely seen as objects for sexual gratification or to be lusted over, and an attack on bourgeois materialism. The film shows how women are dehumanized as merely tools for trade—whether paid off for marriage or a commodity to buy for sex—or to be stripped, scrubbed and painted nude for the male voyeuristic eye to admire. What is interesting about the film is that the male characters are universally unlikable; the only strands of decency, or characters with pure morals, are the female characters. Yet their voices, desires, wants are crushed by the greed and selfishness of men.

When Megahey first presented his script to the BBC in 1976, the head of the Music and Arts Department was reluctant to assign him the directorial responsibilities on the picture, instead advising him that he should relinquish them to Lawrence Gordon Clark of *A Ghost Story for Christmas* fame. Refusing, Megahey sat on his script for three years, by which time he had assumed control of the popular arts program *Omnibus* for the BBC. Commissioning his own script with some German co-funding, Megahey put the film into production, opting to shoot entirely in studio and by employing a docu-drama style. With minimalistic dialogue and visually sumptuous set design that captured the feel and look of seventeenth century Holland, the film was aired on December 23, 1979, to widespread acclaim. With its stylized tableaux that capture the essence of the Dutch painters of the era and how they worked and loved, the film at times is like an arts lecture with fictional strands mixed in. Then the emergence of the ghost sets in motion a nightmarish chain of events that wrong-foots the viewer as we hurtle towards its ghastly and genuinely unsettling and deeply unnerving conclusion.

In February 2016 I telephoned Megahey and interviewed him about this lost classic. I thank him for the generous amount of time he gave up to be interviewed for this collection.

Matthew Edwards: *How did you get involved in television?*

Leslie Megahey: I started at the BBC as one of their general trainees, the magic ticket into television where you started producing and directing straight away. I started off in radio drama, producing and writing plays, in my early twenties, before moving into television. I happened to be in the right place at the right time when the new Music and Arts Department was launched and they were open to highly individual filmmakers, unlike today at the BBC, which is more presenter-led programming. Back then they were into originals, they had Ken Russell, and Huw Wheldon was the presiding genius. We were encouraged to try stuff out. So I ended up in the Arts Department and ended up there for 20 years and had the most wonderful time making the films that I wanted to make, which was glorious. I can depress any young director these days by saying how free and easy it was back then [*laughs*]!

I was eventually made the editor of the art-based *Omnibus* series, along with *Arena*, which was on BBC 2. Then I took over the show and that's how I came to make *Schalcken the Painter*. Prior to *Schalcken the Painter*, I had made other films about artists. I had made drama-documentaries, unlike what we see today where they insert a scene of someone dressed up as an artist. When we did our docu-dramas, we tried to find a real core for the film; a real stage for the action for the film. We often focused on a period in an artist's life or a theme, a thematic device. It is hard to explain, without showing the films. They were really different and we were encouraged to be experimental. It was a wonderful time.

The British Film Institution unearthed Schalcken the Painter, *didn't they? It was considered lost.*

Yes, you are right. It disappeared. The BBC, I had a funny feeling, didn't ever want to repeat the film. I am not absolutely certain [why], but I think it was due to the nature of the film surprised a new generation. I know that when the BBC put out a series of ghost stories on DVD by Lawrence Gordon Clark [editor's note: the brilliant BBC series *A Ghost Story for Christmas*, M.R. James and Charles Dickens adaptations made between 1971 and 1978] and Jonathan Miller's *Whistle and I'll Come to You* [another sublime adaptation of James' work, made for *Omnibus* in 1968], they didn't put out *Schalcken the Painter*. I had long since left the BBC, and I can only assume that someone either didn't like it or thought it was too slow [*laughs*]. Then the BFI rang me out of the blue—and the BFI is very good at following serious film blogs and actually acting on what people want to see, because there was quite a few strands on *Schalcken* and what had happened to the film— and said they wanted to release it on DVD. At first the BBC said they didn't have a copy of the film, making up a weird excuse that they didn't have it, and then the BFI found a really good print in their own archive, which they must have got from the BBC in 1979.

So the BFI were able to restore and bring the visuals and the black levels back to real life. They did a wonderful job on the film.

Where did you get the idea from? I understand you adapted the short story by Sheridan Le Fanu.

It is quite a convoluted story. What happened was that I had worked on our early art films about Goya with a film editor called Paul Humfress, who was a brilliant filmmaker. He was very hip and co-directed *Sebastiane* [1976] with Derek Jarman. He was a very imaginative film editor as well. I said to him, "At some stage we have to stop making drama-documentaries and adhere to the absolute truth as we see it and make a drama-documentary that goes bad and becomes something else." We were always trying to mess and subvert form. So this idea when art films go bad came up and the most obvious direction was to turn the docu-drama into a gothic horror film or a ghost story.

Meanwhile, Paul left to make films in Amsterdam and he sent me through the post a book of Sheridan Le Fanu's ghost stories. Because there was no Internet in those days, and because the book was his friend's copy, he typed up the whole book for me on an old Remington typewriter! He said, "I think this might be the story that we are looking for." It is about a real artist, so it starts off as a documentary and you can be true to the period, and then it turns into the most chilling and horrific story. I read the book and I was so inspired that I was up all night writing a screenplay in my flat in Notting Hill. I wrote the first draft, which was very short as it had no real dialogue in it.

How did you adapt his story?

First of all, I wrote this first draft which was pretty much adapting the story and changing Le Fanu's narration so that it was more contemporary, or sayable, so you know that an actor can say it well. Generally, I pretty much kept close to the original story in the first draft. Then later, I started adding a lot of scenes which bolstered up the main themes of the story: that everything was for sale, commerce; even the woman being for sale through the greed of her uncle and the lackadaisical attitude of her lover. So I added these scenes, particularly the scenes in the brothel, and I went to the Hague in the Netherlands to look at their Schalcken archive. They have a reproduction of almost every painting that Schalcken ever painted. I actually went to the Hague after I had written all these extra scenes and I found, because I had sort of based them on Dutch art, that Schalcken had virtually painted the scenes that I had written! It was uncanny and somehow a meeting of souls. So the finished script and film is very true to the original story but with a lot of my own additions that hopefully most people won't even notice. The bit that is most obvious is that the film keeps trying to go back to being a documentary, in spite of itself. It keeps failing as all these horrible things kept overtaking the documentary side of the film. Generally it is pretty true to Le Fanu's original work. Since leaving television, I have always gotten into trouble with film producers when writing various scripts, especially in America, for sticking too closely to the original books. Goodness! If it is a good book, then you should stick to that and not what's in my fevered imagination!

I understand that after you wrote the script, the BBC wanted Lawrence Gordon Clark to direct.

My boss at the time, who was the head of the Arts and Music Department, wanted Lawrence to direct the film because he was a drama director. He had already made his foray in drama and with the *A Ghost Story for Christmas* films. He had made a big success of them and my boss at the time thought I had written the screenplay because I just wanted to. He thought it was a great script and wanted to make the film, and he put it to me as a question of who I wanted to direct it: Lawrence Gordon Clark? I quickly said no and I think that's what held the film up, because he probably thought I was being too cocky when I said that I wanted to direct it [*laughs*]! So it didn't get made for a couple of years 'til I became the series editor of the *Omnibus* series. The series was known for producing the best television ghost story ever, Jonathan Millers *Whistle and I'll Come to You*. Jonathan had done that initially as a documentary. This is especially true of the first shot in that film. The first shot has a voiceover that doesn't tell you about the Michael Holden character, who you are seeing, but about M.R. James. That was Jonathan's lip service to it being a documentary and he did that a decade before I made *Schalcken the Painter*. It is a wonderfully made film. He made it for a previous editor of *Omnibus* and when I became series editor I thought I am going to do that and I made my own film.

So you were given a lot of freedom to make the programming and content that you wanted.
   Yes, it was absolutely extraordinary. You couldn't have made *Schalcken the Painter* on a basic *Omnibus* budget, even though it was shot with a modest budget and it happens all in one set. So what you had to do as the boss of the series was to go out and on the behalf of directors, or in this case myself, find co-producers. This was done in the most relaxed way. I went to lunch with a German producer and I took with me a list of projects which people wanted to do, which was written on the back of an envelope. Like Christopher Burstall wanted to do Graham Greene [*Graham Greene—The Hunted Man*, 1968], and my German producer would agree and simply ask how much money we needed. I would say some astronomical sum, like £30,000, which was a huge amount of money in those days. He would say okay. Then I would go down the list and say that I wanted to make a film about a real-life painter called Schalcken and then it turns into a ghost story. I thought he may not want it as it wasn't a formal documentary but he was intrigued by it. I asked for a set amount of money and he agreed to it! We didn't even have any treatments for these films, they were simply ideas! But that's how it was done. Then you rang some chap in the BBC, I think it was called BBC Enterprise at the time, which was the commercial sales department of the BBC, and you would tell him that you had done this deal. He would sigh and then have to draw up a contract. So it was a kind of nirvana.

How much did the film actually cost?
   The budget estimate form shows what they called an "above the line" cost of £68,969, and a "below the line" of £54,769. It's the above-the-line cost that the BBC actually paid in cash—actors' fees, film stock, extras, action props, copyright in reproductions of the paintings, etc. The below-the-line costs are staff and other items who belong to the BBC, or are on BBC salaries, therefore being paid anyway, e.g., crew, costume and makeup designers, set designers and builders, etc.

It is amazing you could be so experimental and post-modern at the BBC during this period. If you think about all the hoops you have to jump through now to get anything green-lit, it is astonishing the freedoms you had at the time and you were able to go off and make these extraordinary pieces of work.
   It is extraordinary to me. I know a number of marvelous documentary filmmakers who today struggle to get any work. They can't get any work from these commissioning editors. When they do propose something, they are asked to submit a script for the docu-

mentary they want to make which is ludicrous when you are making a film about real life which may be shaped by an idea or a theme and not a script!

The quality of filmmakers I worked with back then was staggering. We didn't ask them for a full script, we would ask for half a page if we felt we needed to get co-production or to help sell the idea to the BBC controller. Most of the time, if I wanted to make a film—and this was before I started running *Omnibus*, where I could commission myself—I would go to either the editor of a series, or the head of department, and tell them my idea, like, for example, I want to make a film about Gauguin and the point of the film is Gauguin's art in the Southern Seas wasn't paradise but a place that was being raped by Westerners and Western ideas, and in a weird way Gauguin was part of that. I wanted to build a South Seas island on a sound stage in Ealing Studios and I would shoot the whole thing there. That would be the pitch. There was nothing written down. If I was there on a lucky day, and my last film had been good, the commissioning editor would say, "Okay, go and work out a budget. Sounds good." You would go away, work out a budget and get it approved. As soon as that happened, you were utterly on your own. You produced it, directed it and wrote it on your own. You got the designers and you hired your favorite cameraman and editors, you shot it and edited it, and only when you had finished editing the film would you show people the rough cut. I showed the BBC pretty much the final cut. As long as there wasn't anything dreadful in it in terms of offensive political, sexual or religious content, then that would be it. No one else would see it until it got aired. It was staggering. By the time we reached the '80s, when I was in my forties, I was making films that I wrote, produced and directed that nobody saw 'til they were transmitted. The only time I ever referred them to a superior officer, for example, was if I knew there was something contentious in the film that needed to be checked out in case it got the BBC in trouble. I went through whole films with no one looking at them unless they asked to have a look. It was another world but now sadly that is gone.

Talk about the production design of the film.

That was all designed by a wonderful production designer called Anna Ridley, who went on to become a director in her own right. We worked together with the cameraman, John Hooper, and the three of us said that this whole film is going to happen inside one house. I wanted to shoot it at Ealing, so it all had to be built as I didn't want to go over to Holland and have all the horrors of trying to lay tracks in creaky little rooms. So we built the rooms partly to fit the camera. If we wanted to dolly through a door, which we did quite often due to those Dutch interiors…. Like for example when you see a door through a door. We actually took a dolly into the studio and we measured it and Anna designed the doors accordingly. It was done with that kind of precision.

What sticks out in my mind is the dolly shot when the model is brought in…

Yes, that's right. You are looking from the living room into a small back room. There is a line of models that are brought in and she is picked out and stripped and scrubbed up and turns into this completely wonderful and glowing woman. And the only character that feels alive in the film is Rose, who is played by Cheryl Kennedy. She is the character that gives the film some life and warmth. In the middle, for a moment, because Schalcken's paintings around that time felt "dead" as they lacked any warmth or humanity, they just painted their subjects classically, I thought it would be wonderful to have this glowing and wonderful model and Schalcken turn her warm flesh into this cold, knock-it-out-and-slog-it type of painting. In a sense, that character Lesbia (played by Val Penny), to my mind, is the only other genuine warm and sensual thing in the film itself, other than Rose. That was really important. As everyone remarks, it is a pitiless film. It is a pitiless story.

What I like about the film is that all the characters seem as dead as the life objects that Schalcken is painting.

Exactly. They are connected with them quite closely and Dou [Maurice Denham] is always connected with his money and Schalcken is connected with his life objects.

Did you convey that idea to the actors to get the performances you were looking for?

They usually don't need it. Maurice Denham, who is a stalwart of British movies, and a great actor, got it from the script. I had to do very little work with any of the actors, including John Justin who plays the death figure of Vanderhausen. He pretty much turned up on set and had worked the character out. He worked out the voice, that stance and that stare. He was a great actor. He had been a handsome movie star in his early days in the 1940s. Jeremy Clyde [who played Godfried Schalcken] complained once or twice that the only thing he was given to go on in the script was that he later went on to become a rather morose and grumpy individual [*laughs*]. It worked because the male characters turn into vipers and it is Rose that acts like a human being.

In the film, Schalcken begins to admire Vanderhausen and sells his soul for money and materialism. That is basically the crux of the film.

Jeremy Clyde as Godfried Schalcken in Leslie Megahey's *Schalcken the Painter* **(1979).**

Yes, he joins the game. There is a moment when he has the chance to make a choice. One assumes that is when the contract with Vanderhausen is exposed and it became clear that it was going to go through and Schalcken cravenly doesn't do anything. I added that in, the part where he pathetically says that he will buy back the contract when he can afford to. That is not how you talk to a woman who is stolen from under your nose and who you are in love with. You would run away with her!

John Justin as the evil specter Vanderhausen in *Schalcken the Painter* (1979).

It demonstrates how much he has become consumed with the idea of wealth.

Precisely. He wants his master to become wealthy and he is visited by Rembrandt, who is a role model to all the students there. Presumably, in that instant he makes up his mind that that is going to be his life.

For all his artistic pretensions, when the second wealthy man visits Schalcken, he initially claims that he is not in it for the money...

You are right and then he is commissioned to paint that ghastly picture, which really exists. The girl with a doll is a real painting by Schalcken. How terrible is that? That scene is played exactly like the very first time when Vanderhausen appears. You have the same noise—the creak of the floor—you have the same low ominous orchestral sound on the soundtrack—that low hum—and he comes in out of the shadows. It might almost be another visitation but it turns out to be a slightly buffoon-like, wealthy man.

The film still has documentary elements in it as you are condemning that era. So the narrative flips backwards and forwards from a drama to a documentary in its own strange way.

Yes it does. I think the documentary keeps trying, in my view, to assert itself and take us back on some kind of even keel. And possibly, may even take us back to a comfortable world of historical fiction. In a sense, you can dramatize their lives and they can be funny, successful, tragic or absolutely horrible or diabolical but you are just dramatizing their lives. And that will be it. It is all over. I had this view that if the documentary kept trying to bring us back rather cruel analysis of the facts, then the drama would become really terrible and disturbing. I always used to say to people when making it that it is a film where nothing happens for about half an hour; then what does happen is the worst thing in the world. I still feel that to an extent. And the documentary keeps trying to pull it back by being objective, by saying this happened, that happened, and critiquing the painting, leaving the film slightly cold. Then it's as if the documentary loses its nerves and the drama takes over and it isn't cold any more. It is absolutely horrible now. I genuinely wanted people to be disturbed by something that otherwise might have been an interesting matter-of-fact documentary.

There is a haunting stillness about the film, especially at the start, which ultimately feeds into the shocking ending.

I am glad you say that because when you watch your work, you think whether or not you went too far. It is still disturbing to this day.

I think you led up to the ending well. You are never sure what is happening. It feels like a strange documentary and then suddenly descends into horror. This is helped by the performances which are so "unreal." Then when the specter or ghost appears, things start to slowly unravel.

That was absolutely my intention. Sometimes you do things in an irrational way. When I was making the film, I never considered that the documentary aspect would be trying to pull itself back into the film and that the drama must take precedence and the documentary must not, or it must lose its way. I never thought that. That's just what I was doing. It is only recently, with this newfound interest in the film, that I have seen what is happening in the film. When you make the film, you are planning the shots, directing or writing; you don't sit down and articulate what you are doing. When the film came out, it got fantastically nice reviews, but they were all television reviews. They weren't in-depth enough and didn't have anything to do with content and meaning. It wasn't until the BFI released the film a couple of years ago that the people started writing thoughtful essays on the film, which has been great.

How did you approach the visual stylization of the film?

Similar to what you said about "stillness." I was looking for a kind of stillness we had all seen in Dutch art of that time. When I say "we all," I mean myself, John Hooper and Anna Ridley. So that was where the look came from. John's lighting was extraordinary. I don't think people realize that as other people have since done that kind of thing, like Peter Webber in the film about artist Johannes Vermeer, *Girl with a Pearl Earring* [2003]. So the visual stylization was built up through that stillness and the silence, but broken with something unnerving, ominous or with something funny, before returning to that stillness. So gradually you are building up this lighting that is so pristine and beautifully modulated. You can see that on the wide shots. Even on the surface of a wall you will see how the light and the paintwork modulate so that it resembles a Vermeer painting. It is done with such skill by John's lighting and Anna's design. Then that stillness is broken with something that is so left-field, and so completely wrong. That's when things start to, as you put it, "unravel."

I protest always that the film was not a technical exercise to see how well John Hooper could light the film to resemble a painting. That was not our intention. There was something more disturbing about the pristine quality and beauty of the sharp vertical and horizontal lines and so on, it is about the disturbance of that calm.

The film is based on one painting by Schalcken, though I am unsure if it really exists.

Le Fanu describes the painting at the beginning of his story and says there is a man in seventeenth century dress and he has a sword which he is in the act of drawing and then there is a woman, with a candle, with an arched smile. And in the darkness, in a bed behind the woman, there appears to be some form. I never found that painting. I found paintings with each element in it but I never found the actual painting, and a very talented artist painted the picture for me which we used in the film.

The film condemns the treatment of women, doesn't it?

It is the tragedy of the film that anything can be bought or sold, even a young woman. And Schalcken allows that to happen. Everything is for sale.

I think that is what is truly horrifying about the film.

I agree now with people who say that the film is almost unwatchable. I find it quite shocking and I know what's going to happen!

You kind of feel a bit sorry for Schalcken at the end of the film, despite his behavior throughout.

I do think that Schalcken becomes quite sympathetic and pitiful towards the end, even though he never shows any real regret for his actions. Yet I get the feeling, when he confronts Rose at the end, and the way he paints the painting at the end, with that little lie he puts into it, which I added into the script—the observation from Le Fanu—that he told this lie. In the film he faints when confronted with the mess he has made of his life, and the necrophilia scene, when Schalcken sees Rose straddling the deathly Vanderhausen in the vault. But he lies in the painting that he tried to confront it, with him drawing his sword. That is a pathetic ending in a pathos kind of way.

That last scene is quite unexpected and shocking. Did you think at the time that you might have to get that referred to higher echelons at the BBC?

I can't remember though I probably did, especially with the nature of that scene. Interestingly, that scene, and the film, didn't cause any real fuss which you would normally have. I had no papers ringing me up, or the audience research department telephoning me to say they had 3000 complaints. I was actually in Rome when the film was shown on BBC television. I heard no complaints but then Ken Russell received a lot of problems for his Grand Guignol films, like *The Devils* [1971]. Yet I received none. I always found this quite interesting as I find the last scene in *Schalcken* a more terrible thing to confront than anything Ken did [*laughs*]!

What I find interesting is that, on what was perceived as a highly respected arts program on terrestrial television, you were able to include this scene along with the full frontal nudity.

I encountered no objections or problems. This was the '70s so everyone was quite relaxed about it. I think I mentioned to the BBC controller that there was going to be some nudes in the film but the only time I was admonished was when there were male and female nudes and I was warned to be careful of moving male nudes! But now people mention that the nudity from Val Penny was only included to show a bit of tit and ass. The end sequence with Cheryl Kennedy naked, you can't really class that as nudity as it is in no way sexual. It is more disturbing, frightening and animal-like. She did it brilliantly, and if I recall, she opted to do it that way. She pulls her dress halfway up, and not all the way off, so it's not a strip scene, and then she goes onto the bed before she takes her dress off fully.

It is almost as if she is taunting Schalcken.

Yes, asks for his purse, then throws his money on the ground and then fornicates with the specter. I don't think the moment with money is in the original story but an element I added to the film. She is more or less saying, you wouldn't have to pay for this, like the other prostitutes Schalcken is seen with, if he has stepped in to stop her being sold. It is a very confrontational scene and rather unpleasant ending!

I thought the way you experimented with the sound and image in the film was very interesting.

Yes, it was. I tweaked up the sounds, like the sound of the money or the sound of the writing when Dou is signing the document to give Rose away. Tweaking up these nasty and scratchy sounds gets under your skin more, I think. They are aggressive. There is also that low hum when Vanderhausen appears. But there is only one point where I think the music actually underlines the point of the scene and that's when Rose comes back from the dead. You get this urgent harpsichord and this adds to the energy of the scene. It is used ironically at the end of the film when Rose is on the bed with Vanderhausen. There is this sweet little harpsichord theme, which is not the music you would expect when a man is having the most horrible nightmare in his life and the woman he loves is making love to a devil figure! That sweet little theme of music, I think, makes that scene even more frightening.

I liked the narration. I thought that worked.

Oh, good. That is Le Fanu shot through that, although slightly altered to suit the voice. Charles Gray is wonderful. He had a fabulous, cynical voice. The rhythms of the narration are Le Fanu's. I kept them, even when I made up the narration. I felt it was important to keep the rhythms because they inject that mordant humor. That is all him, dear old Sheridan.

The narration doesn't give you too much historical fact but snippets for those who are unfamiliar with the period or the painter.

Actually, all the historical facts in the film are perfectly true. But after a while, the film gives up on it and descends into a horror film. Once you start looking into these lives of people in a less than straightforward historical docu-drama way, you discover something that is truly terrible about the theme. Once that happens, then facts go by the board.

I understand that the film was broadcast in the slot that was traditionally reserved for A Ghost Story for Christmas.

The transmission was Sunday, December 23, 1979, starting at 10:50 p.m. If the film is 70 minutes, that means it would have finished bang on midnight.

Was the reaction to the film positive?

Yes it was, especially the press reaction. For a couple of weeks after the film was broadcast, I received a number of good reviews in the newspapers and magazines that had rounded up the Christmas viewing. A lot of them stated that the film was the highlight of the festive season and how good the film was. I don't think you would get that today, people saying that the highlight of their Christmas was a frightening, unpleasant and terrifying ghost story [*laughs*]! One of the recent reviews of the film has said that it was too cold and chilly for Christmas and that they were surprised that the film went out in the Christmas Eve slot.

I disagree with that. I think it is ideal entertainment for Christmas.

What, to upset people before Christmas as they eat their mince pie [*laughs*]! I suppose most of Lawrence's *A Ghost Story for Christmas*es were M.R. James adaptations and set in Victorian Britain, so it lent itself to that idea of oil lamps, log fires, etc. Some of his films are very frightening but they do have a Christmassy feel to them, whereas *Schalcken the Painter* starts off cold and ends cold.

Vanderhausen reminds me of a Dickens visitation.

[*Laughs*] A bit like Marley's Ghost! I always found Marley frightening as a child. Thinking back to what you said earlier, I am wondering whether the BBC refusing to show the film again with the other Christmas ghost stories was due to the fact that they found it too chilling.

You certainly couldn't make this film now, especially at the BBC.

No. Not content-wise nor with that stillness or length. You would have someone on your back the whole time telling you to cut there, cut there. It would need a much tighter storyline. You couldn't make a film like *Schalcken the Painter* these days with the fast-paced editing and the way contemporary drama is mounted. Older films have a quality where they say, "Make of this what you will." I left the BBC when the new regime led by Michael Jackson came in. I knew my days were up as I knew the days of the kind of filmmaking I was used to were over. That autonomy that the filmmaker once had was completely over. It seemed to me that the writing was on the wall so I accepted a job elsewhere. I suspect that had I not left then, I would have been shoved out into the wilderness. *Schalcken the Painter* wouldn't be made now nor would any of my films I made in the '70s and '80s.

3

Alice, Sweet Alice

An Interview with Alfred Sole

Alfred Sole's *Alice, Sweet Alice* (a.k.a. *Communion*, 1976) is one of the most overlooked and neglected slasher films to emerge out of the golden era of horror cinema. The brutal film begins in spectacular style with the murder of a young Brooke Shields during her first communion. With a plethora of stylish kills and scary thrills, it is surprising that the film has fallen somewhat into the cinematic abyss. *Alice, Sweet Alice* is essentially a taut psychological horror film woven around a story of sexual tension and Catholic repression, that possessed all the ingredients to become an instant classic; but it has never received as much attention as the more infamous masked killer films such as *Halloween* and the *Friday the 13th* series. Inspired by the work of *giallo* directors, *Alice, Sweet Alice* predates its more famous American counterpart films and shares more of a common thread with the pantheon of splatter slashers that were making the rounds in the Italian horror scene of the '70s.

Of Italian descent, Alfred Sole was clearly influenced by his Italian counterparts and his stylishly shot and brilliantly edited film evokes moments from the best of the aforementioned masters of Italian *giallo*, yet transported to New Jersey. Where *Alice, Sweet Alice* differs from its more violent *giallo* counterparts is that the violence is less explicit and more implied. This makes the horror more horrific—yet when the violence does arrive it still packs a powerful punch.

I spoke to Alfred Sole in September 2014, during a break in the filming of the hit television series *Castle* (he's the show's production designer).

Matthew Edwards: *Would you tell me about your background and how you got involved in the film industry?*

Alfred Sole: I was living in New Jersey and I was really in love with film and I couldn't figure out how to get into the movie business. I used to read *American Cinematographer* and think, "How do they do this?" At that time, I was working as a designer/architect and I got myself a Bolex and started making short films. Eventually, I wanted to make a feature but I couldn't get the money for that. So I read that Francis Ford Coppola had got started in the X-rated movie industry and at the time I thought, well, I'll make an X-rated movie. I figured if I could do that, I could go on and make some other films and give my career some kind of kick-off. So that's what happened and I made *Deep Sleep* in 1972.

You took a route similar to Driller Killer *[1979] director Abel Ferrara, who started his career with* Nine Lives of a Wet Pussy *[1976].*

We didn't have film school back then. We didn't have film courses at colleges and universities. So it was different when I was getting started.

You are best known for your brilliant horror film Alice, Sweet Alice. *Where did the inspiration come from?*

I saw Nic Roeg's film *Don't Look Now* [1973] and I was blown away by it. I was always a fan of Hitchcock and when I was a kid I loved the Dracula and Frankenstein movies—I'm a big fan of vampire movies and I've gone to see every vampire movie ever made [*laughs*].

The iconic image in Alice, Sweet Alice *is the masked murderer in the yellow raincoat and the transparent creepy mask, so I can see the connection with Roeg's* Don't Look Now.

Yes, the yellow slicker was a nod to *Don't Look Now*. I just love that movie and I think it is incredible.

You co-wrote the story with Rosemary Rivto.

She used to teach English literature at the local university and she was my neighbor and we would always talk about films. She was a Catholic and we would talk about the Catholic Church, religion and stuff like that. Then we started talking about films and theater and I discovered she had a great love of horror films. At that point I had started writing the script and mapping out my idea and I asked her whether she wanted to help me write this. She said, "Yes, let's do it." So we would meet on weekends and we co-wrote the script.

How did you finance the film?

What I did was approach one of my architect clients and to other people who I knew could help raise the money. Then I started asking friends and neighbors. I asked my family and cleared my life savings and re-mortgaged my house. It was one of those scenarios where money kept on coming in slowly and we kept starting and stopping shooting throughout the film's production. But my family was really supportive and my mother cooked for the crew, my neighbors chipped in; everyone was just so kind and supportive of me that we eventually got it made. But we did have a lot of problems during the making of the film. Linda Miller slit her wrists and tried to commit suicide. All kinds of crazy things like that happened during the production.

The film was shot in New Jersey and utilizes some excellent locations and beautiful architecture. Was that an important part to get right for you, especially when working on a low-budget horror film?

The masked killer of *Alice, Sweet, Alice* **in her yellow rainslicker (courtesy Alfred Sole).**

That was really important. When I was writing the script, I had all these locations already worked out in my head. I was working in Paterson, I knew the city very well, and I was aware that the city was turning all these factories into lot spaces. I was working for the wife of the mayor and I was going around to all these abandoned buildings and opening these doors to these places that had been empty for years. Through this process I had all my locations ready for when we came to shoot *Alice, Sweet Alice*. All the locations are in Paterson, New Jersey. The church where we filmed was actually a chapel in a local hospital and they were nice enough to let us shoot there.

Alice, Sweet Alice is infamous partly for the casting of Brooke Shields in her first role. How did you come to cast her?

I saw Brooke Shields' picture in a magazine. I think it was *Vogue* or something similar. She was 12 or 13 at the time and an up-and-coming model. I tracked down her parents in New Jersey and spoke to her mother and she agreed to do the picture. They loved the idea. It is great that Brooke Shields was in the film. When her career skyrocketed, it really helped our film and it was re-released again under the title *Holy Terror*. She was terrific and delightful to work with and really supportive. We were very lucky to have her in the movie.

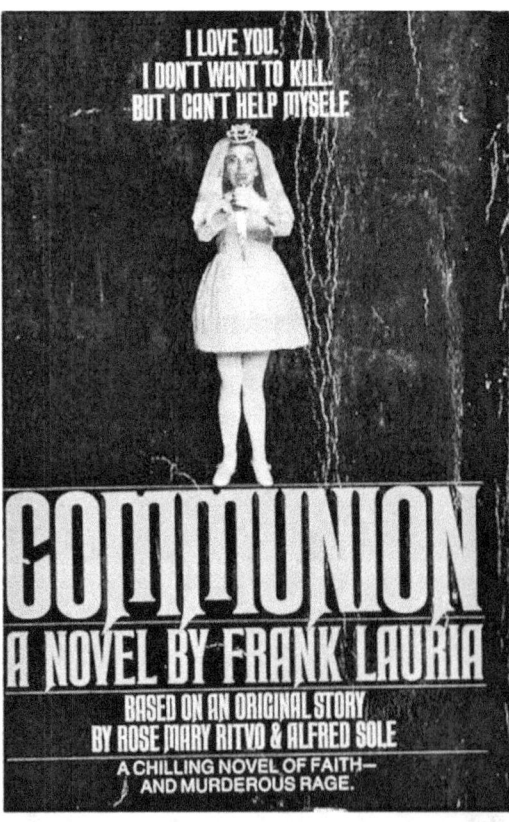 

Cover of novelization of Alfred Sole's film by Frank Lauria, going under the title *Communion*. The film was also known as *Holy Terror*, as shown in this promotional poster that tried to cash in on Brooke Shields's fame (courtesy Alfred Sole).

How did you come to cast Paula E. Sheppard in the role of Alice?

I had a friend who was an actor and he was living in New York, and he was working with Andre Gregory. Andre Gregory at that time was teaching acting classes and so he invited me to go up to Connecticut for a weekend because he was there performing a play. I went up and while he was rehearsing, I took a walk and I happened to walk into a rehearsal dance class. And there she was dancing! When I saw her, I said, "That's her. That's Alice!" So I started talking to her and she thought I was a little wacky [*laughs*] and I told her about this movie I was writing and that I wanted her to be in it. And she was looking at me as if to say go away but eventually it happened. She was terrific in the role but obviously she was much older, I think she was 18 or 19 at the time. On set she was supportive and always listened to my direction and what I wanted to do. She got it. She was great and I was really lucky with her and everyone. Except for my cameramen, that was my big disaster.

I understand you went through a number of different cameramen during the filming and that you had a very problematic shoot.

We had at least six cameramen. I was hiring out of New York, and we were interviewing people and trying to find people who would work for practically no money. It seemed that I was getting a little bit of an attitude from them because "I'm in the business," "I know what I'm doing," "You've never done this before," "You're a novice, go away." I knew that filmmaking was like a car and with the right training, you know exactly where everything goes and how it starts and how the engine works. I applied the same principle to film, simply through reading film books. I was watching so many movies. I watched them without the sound to see how they were cut and how long scenes were. I remember taking a stopwatch and timing individual scenes. I knew exactly what I wanted. It was one of those moments where I really felt secure in what I wanted but insecure in what I was doing. But I knew where I wanted my camera, I had all my locations picked out, storyboards, and I really did all my homework. I just loved what I was doing.

The visual style of the film remains constant throughout. Are you proud of that achievement?

I am. You don't realize that when you are doing it. I am very proud of that movie and I'm surprised and so happy that people are still watching it. I'll tell you a quick story: I work now as a production designer on the television show *Castle*, and there is another show coming in and I was talking to their production designer who knew the film and he was telling me that he just got off a feature film where the director said, "I want this movie to look like *Alice, Sweet Alice*." I was like, wow. I am very proud that it is regarded so highly.

I have been trying to get the negative of the film. You see, the only way I was able to make prints of the film was through a print of the movie that was never shown in theaters. That was the only way I could make copies. The sad thing is, I can't locate the original negative as I would love to go back and re-time it and re-master it. The negative does exist but no one seems to be able to track it down.

You said earlier that the production was beset with a number of problems. What happened?

The biggest problem I had during the filmmaking was with some of the actors because they were New York actors and they were doing me a favor. It was a big issue. I was having problems with Linda Miller who I clashed with to the extent where we developed hostility towards one another, but we have since put that aside and made up. We get along better now. On set, she was really difficult to work with, though. A real nightmare. She could be very difficult and I remember I was living in fear that she wouldn't turn up to work today or she would say "I'm not going to do your movie." There was that kind of craziness going on. Then she cut her wrists during filming and came in screaming when we were shooting a scene. We had to shut down production. I thought, "This is it. We are never going to finish this movie." Luckily the cuts weren't that deep and she returned to complete the film. Then I ran out of money and I had to shut down the production for several weeks 'til I could raise more money. I initially had $25,000 but that soon went. There was no production office. I had no trucks to get the equipment and actors to locations. I had so many logistical problems, too. But people always came out and helped me, which was wonderful. Every low-budget filmmaker has the same story on how hard it is.

One of the film's strengths is that you elicit great performances from the cast, especially the female actors. Linda Miller, Mildred Clinton, Paula E. Sheppard and Jane Lowry are all fantastic in their respective roles, aren't they?

Linda is an excellent actor; they all are. I would spend time interviewing people and finding people and then they would commit before dropping out and I would think, "Oh, Jesus, we're never going to get this movie made." Luckily, someone else would come along. At the time, I was going to see a lot of theater in New York and I was hanging out at the theater when actors came out. There was one actor called Geraldine Page, a famous theater and film actor, and I wanted her to be in the movie. I wanted her to play Mrs. Tredoni. One day I waited outside the theater—I think she was starring in a Neil Simon play—and I stopped her, I talked to her and I gave her the script. She later called me and said she read the script and it was terrific, but she passed on it. But that's what I was doing, I was looking for people by going to Broadway shows or small theater pieces and that's how I got people attached. Alphonso DeNoble [Mr. Alphonso] I already knew. He was someone I met a long time ago in New Jersey. As you probably know, he used to work in a graveyard and dress up as a priest.

An interesting facet of the film is that the family unit is seen as broken and hostile towards one another with various characters suffering from some sort of psychosis. The sibling rivalry between Karen and Alice is brilliantly handled, which builds up tension from the get-go. Was this your intention?

Yes. I'm Italian and I have aunts and uncles who always seem to have some sort of drama in the family. That was kind of reflective of my youth and being involved in those dramas with my aunts and uncles arguing amongst each other. So that's where the inspiration came from. The character of Mrs. Tredoni came from the lady who lived next to my grandmother in the rectory of a Catholic church. She was the priest's wife and she looked after the rectory; she was Mrs. Tredoni. She was this strong-willed woman and you had to talk to her in order to talk to the priest. She ruled everything and that woman lived next to my grandmother. That's where the inspiration came from.

The scene where the masked killer kills Karen during her communion is a fantastic piece of filmmaking. It is edited so poetically. How crucial was editor M. Edward Sailer in the success of the film?

Edward was very crucial in the success of the film. First of all, he had the patience of a saint. We didn't have a lot of takes and he would look for bits and pieces and create things; he would flip the film around and extend scenes by double printing. He showed up every day with me. Edward is an amazing editor and I still see him today. He works for Paramount now. He is an amazing, talented man.

In another superb scene, Dom is attacked in the stairwell in the abandoned building. Did you achieve the knife falling into the handrail on the first take?

I knew that location as I had been in the building several times and I wanted to use it in the film. When I was there, I saw the separation of the stairs and the landing and I said, "Let's try this." So we kept on dropping the knife and dropping the knife until it landed perfectly [*laughs*]. But everyone was very patient with me. It is very hard to get people to rally around you, especially when you are up against people who have been in the business a long time and have a bit of an attitude. I try not to surround myself with people like that any more.

You have said that you are an ex–Catholic. How did your Catholic upbringing shape the film?

Totally! Having a grandmother who lived next door to the rectory; it just goes without saying that when you are a Catholic in the '70s and the church is controlling people, you couldn't get divorced and I always questioned all that stuff. But I always loved the ritual of the Catholic Church: take my body, take my blood. It's so primitive. It's so ingrained in you. I also liked the films of Fellini who was always taking a pop at the Catholic Church.

The film also deals with themes such as sexual repression.

I felt that was a really important part of Linda Miller's character [Catherine Spages]. A lot of people don't pick up on the scene where Alice and her mother talk in the schoolyard just after she has had her period. She's a troubled child, a big kid, but no one really wants to love her. That was really important to me that there was this really good kid that no one wants to love because she is not pretty; she's not as pretty as her sister.

Post-production, you sold the film to Allied Artists who insisted on a title change. I understand you dislike the title Alice, Sweet Alice *and prefer the title* Communion.

What happened was that we originally sold the picture to Columbia Pictures and I was in seventh heaven. They were going to release a paperback book to coincide with the picture. I was riding high on a feeling that I was going to Hollywood, "This is it, I've made it." They had wanted a couple of changes to the ending which I was fine with. They didn't know it but I would have changed a lot more if they had asked, as long as they took my idea and got it out there into theaters. They were so nice to us and I remember going up to their offices in New York City and seeing the Academy Awards in glass cases. I was thinking, "I'm in heaven, I'm going to have an orgasm here!" I was going into meetings and talking about the book and I thought, "This is really cool. I can't believe this is going to happen."

Then they sent me to California to make the changes. However, the deal fell through because of our producer on the film, Richard Rosenberg. Now, towards the end of the film I didn't have enough money to complete it so Richard Rosenberg came into my life. He was a lawyer from New Jersey who I knew and he got involved and raised the rest of the money. I had to sign everything over to him to finish the movie. What happened was, when he was making the deal with Columbia Pictures, they were interested in buying the film for the amount that it cost. However, Rosenberg was over-inflating the cost of production and they found out, so they dropped the film like a hot potato. They didn't like him and they didn't want to go near him. So because of that, they dropped the film. I found this out later when I finally had a chance to talk to Columbia.

So I got a phone call from him when I was in California saying that Columbia dropped the film because it was too violent and they didn't want the film any more. This was not true. When I came back from California, I discovered it had been dropped because Columbia had been double-crossed when he inflated the costs in the budget when he was negotiating the deal. Time went by and he contacted Allied Artists and struck a deal. I didn't have anything to do with it. They weren't particularly interested in the movie as it was seen merely as a throwaway film to them. It was Allied Artists' decision to have a name change. They had some other names and I got involved in that because they refused to use the name *Communion*. They argued that no one would go and see a movie called *Communion*. They were absolutely adamant about that. I remember I had no choice in that, so I eventually came up with the name *Alice, Sweet Alice*. I was not happy with that.

So you always refer to the film as Communion?
Yes. Yes I do.

Upon release, how was the film critically received?
In England it got rave reviews. Film critic Colin Paolo wrote about it at length and did a great review of the film. The distributor flew me over to England to do some publicity for the film, largely due to Colin's review. I met him and we became friends. That's where it all started. In America the film was received poorly. It opened up in California and the film critics hated the movie, especially *The L.A. Times*. They didn't get it; they didn't get the Catholic stuff. They tore the movie apart and that was it. The film never got a chance to establish itself. Their review killed it.

Did you encounter any censorship problems?
I encountered no problems other than the violence. That was always a big issue, nothing else. Nothing about Alphonso's relationship with Alice; there was nothing about any of that stuff relating to the pedophilic landlord.

When it was released on DVD and video in the U.K., it was cut by three seconds for the Tartan DVD release in 1998 and then by eight seconds in 2003.
Are you serious? I didn't know that. Why?

A cut was made due to animal cruelty. The BBFC stated, "A cut was required [due] to [the] sight of actual animal cruelty (in this case a kitten swung around by the neck) in accordance with BBFC Guidelines and Policy." It was released uncut by 88 Films in 2014.
The kitten was never harmed at all and it was just the camera angle that made it look so violent. I'm relieved to hear that it has now been released uncut.

What is your view on film censorship?
I totally disagree with any kind of censorship. It always amazes me that they always censor sex but never violence. We don't censor anything any more, especially when it comes to violence. I'll tell you a story about the staircase scene in *Alice, Sweet Alice*. I went to see an Italian movie about gangsters and we were making the film at the time. I was in the theater watching this movie and these mobsters were shooting these guys with machine guns, bam, bam, bam. There was no reaction from the audience, who were very quiet during the shooting and violence. Then suddenly one of the guys spits in the other guy's face and you heard a gasp from the audience. I was shocked and it somehow pushed

3. Alfred Sole

Norwegian VHS sleeve of *Alice, Sweet, Alice*.

a button on me. I realized that people don't know what it is like to be shot with a bullet but they do know if you bang your hand or stub your toe or someone spits in your face, those are things that an audience can relate and connect to. So I did the idea of the staircase differently. Initially I was going to have the masked lunatic stab the aunt in the hips but I changed it to the foot, because I felt the audience would relate to that more. So I switched it and we got a great reaction from that. And people actually think they see a lot more than they actually do. It's an idea I got from reading about Hitchcock. People think they see more than they actually do and think it is more violent than it really is. That's how that came about. I was very proud of that scene and how that turned out. It's one of my favorite scenes in the movie. We filmed that scene in Paterson and I love the narrow steps and when she is screaming outside in the pouring rain … yeah, I love that scene.

Was Alice, Sweet Alice *inspired stylistically by the giallo films of Bava [*Blood and Black Lace, *1964], Argento [*Deep Red, *1975], Lenzi [*Eyeball, *1975] and Fulci [*Don't Torture a Duckling, *1972]? It shares a connection with these films. Or is that just coincidence?*

Yes, I was inspired by those films which I was watching at the time. You had to be. All those masters were making these kind of films at the time. I loved horror movies since I was a kid. I remember the first horror movie I ever saw that really grabbed me was *Les Diaboliques* (1955). It was the editing and the cutting of this French movie that blew me away and the beginning of the illusion of horror for me.

I don't enjoy some of the horror films of today. I don't go to the cinema to watch films like *Saw* [2004]. That doesn't interest me. There is no illusion in these films, just graphic violence like we're going to cut your fingers or your head off and that's it. And that's not scary. People are immune to this violence now. They don't respond. I'd rather watch a bad B-movie that is fun and is so bad it is good.

Your film is a testament to the idea of "less is more." I would argue that your film is not overtly graphic and violent, compared to what is available today.

No it is not. In fact, in the film my neighbor made me that knife. I didn't have a special effects person so my neighbor made that knife for me and we used it in the film. We only had one knife and we had to treat it with kid gloves and if we lost that knife, we were in deep trouble. You can actually see the separation on the blade, it is really that obvious. So what we did was shine a lot of light on the knife blade itself so that it killed the separation when it collapsed.

How did you create the promotional poster?

We shot that ourselves. I remember taking the picture. I found the paper bag, the mask, the knife and the doll. It was all done in my basement.

Iconic promotional artwork of Alfred's sole infamous cult slasher, *Alice, Sweet, Alice* (1976) (courtesy Alfred Sole).

Alice, Sweet Alice predates slasher films and masked maniac films such as Halloween *and* Friday the 13th. *Do you think your film has influenced other filmmakers or is it natural for horror filmmakers to borrow from each other?*

I remember going to see those movies and I was in Hollywood at the time trying to get into film. I think it is natural that we are influenced by one another. Something touches us. We all watched Hitchcock, the old black-and-white horror films like *Dracula* and *Frankenstein*. Directors are also influenced by the films of their generation—based on what they saw when they were growing up. You get inspired by that. The love of cinema and the genre.

*Post–*Alice, Sweet Alice, *you made a couple of other pictures. Would you tell me a bit about them and your work on the television series* Castle?

After *Alice, Sweet Alice,* I went Los Angeles and I finally I got to make a movie called *Tanya's Island* [1980] and later a comedic slasher film called *Pandemonium* [1982]. It wasn't a great experience for me. I came from New Jersey and I was totally in awe of everyone in the entertainment business. Going to Hollywood and making a Hollywood film was totally petrifying. I went to work each day terrified. I felt like a fish out of water. I did the best I could but I wasn't that good at comedy. The only fortunate thing was that I used to go to the Groundlings Theater where people like Paul Reubens [Pee-wee Herman] and Phil Hartman came out of. So I went to them right away and asked them for their help [on *Pandemonium*]. They helped me out. Paul was cast in the lead and all the other guys has bit parts in the film. It was crazy. I was killing Eve Arden, of *Grease* fame, with a fart. She was one of the biggest stars in the world and I was killing her with a fart! This is not the kind of movie I wanted to make. I did everything I could to make it successful. I swung the camera round, I turned it upside down. I was doing all these tricks to make it as funny as I possibly could. I wasn't used to a big crew and producers. I wasn't ready for that. It was out of necessity as I couldn't get a job as a director. After that film, I couldn't get a job so I moved into working as a production designer.

Initially I worked with Paul Monette; he was my writing partner for over ten years. We wrote a lot of scripts and books. We got a good reputation for being good ghost writers. We wrote for Movie of the Week, we wrote *Hotel*, we wrote an episode of *Thirtysomething*, we survived. We did okay. Sadly Paul caught AIDS and that ended the partnership. He got too sick to continue any more. I was surviving by doing design work and visual work for different people. I was lucky when a friend hired me as a production designer on a Movie of the Week she was working on, and that started my career as a production designer. Now I work on *Castle*, which is a great show. I get to build a lot of sets. I get to build at least four or five sets each episode, which is great. So I am totally happy. But I am still a frustrated film director! But I am very thankful for my current career.

Do you think you will ever get behind the camera again?

No, I doubt it. The only thing I really want is for my cousin Dante Tomaselli to remake *Alice, Sweet Alice*. That would be a major dream come true for me. Can you imagine that? Dante is someone who I love and who is so talented. If that ever happens, I will be on Cloud Nine. It would be fabulous.

His work is great. What films of his do you particularly admire?

I like all of them. He has such great production values. I admire him because he makes the kind of movies that he wants to make. His storylines are not always my favorite but he makes movies that he wants. I think because of my situation in Hollywood, where I made a big movie and I was caught up in the Hollywood machine, I respect Dante so much for remaining true to himself. If I could change one thing, I wish I never came to Hollywood and stayed in New Jersey making the films I wanted to make.

He's very true to his vision, isn't he?

He's very true. I adore Dante because of that. He has such talent. His production values are amazing and he does that with no money. He creates such amazing stuff. I have this fantasy where he directs a remake of *Alice, Sweet Alice* and I work as the production designer. I said to him, "You can direct it and it will be your baby, but I want to be production designer! You can't fire me."

I would like the film to be a remake as opposed to *Alice, Sweet Alice 2*. I would want him to do it again using the same story and set in the same period. I would want him to give another vision or take on that story. I'm not a fan of sequel films as I believe they don't work. I've been approached before and I have always said no. I don't have a story in my head. A couple of people have contacted me with new scripts but it has never got off the ground or I said, "Let's not." But I would like to see a Dante version with his spin on it. It's out there. Let the gods decide. I know Dante is working very hard to do it. We will see. He's amazingly talented. He just needs his break. I like the way he remains true to his vision.

There's a wider issue at play. Now there are too many voices. Look at the show I work on! Ten or fifteen producers work on the show. Everyone has something to say. You can't have that. But television is different. The writer or creator is the king and not the director. But I'm pleased for Dante. He is so passionate about his movies and the films he wants to make.

Alice, Sweet Alice *is now remembered as one of the classic horror films of all time. Are you surprised by this?*

I'm amazed and really grateful that people are still enjoying the film. I'm pleased that people are still watching it. It makes me feel terrific. I am so pleased it is constantly finding a new audience.

4

Savage Weekend and *Schizoid*

An Interview with David Paulsen

The name David Paulsen will be familiar as a writer, producer and director of the hit prime time television shows *Dallas, Knots Landing* and *Dynasty* that gripped audiences throughout the '80s. Prior to his involvement in these shows, Paulsen was responsible for two cult slasher-horror films that seem a world away from the feuding Ewings and the cattle-ranching land of Southfork. He directed *Savage Weekend* (1979), a criminally underrated masked killer flick that has astonishingly sunk into cinematic oblivion. A year later came the brilliantly odd *Schizoid* (1980) starring the madly unpredictable Klaus Kinski and Craig Wasson.

Savage Weekend tells the story of recently divorced Marie. She attempts to escape from her abusive ex-husband Greg for some quality time upstate with new boyfriend Robert, who owns a lakeside summer house. Tagging along is Nicky, Marie's flamboyant and extroverted gay friend, and Shirley and Jay. The promiscuous group quickly gets down to indulging in their carnal desires. This backwoods community is home to local weirdo Otis (played brilliantly by William Sanderson), who takes a dislike to these city slickers and harbors resentment towards Robert, who has hired him to restore a boat to its former glory. Otis' desire to get to even stems from his anger that his father was the original owner of the boat and he feels his heritage is being snatched away from him by these arrogant New York jumpstarts. Otis has a checkered past and one that hints towards violence and murder. Soon, the vacationers become the target for a deranged masked lunatic intent on dispatching the whole lot of them. There's a clever build-up, concentrating on the characters' charms and flaws, and then Paulsen goes for the jugular in the last third as panic and terror is unleashed upon the group. Who is the murderer in their midst? Paulsen keeps you guessing up till the final frames.

Savage Weekend missed its target audience on its first run and this travesty is partly down to the poor distribution the film received by Cannon Films. It was shown in its wrong aspect ratio which meant that boom mikes appeared in shots and the film looked technically amateurish. Because of this error, *Savage Weekend* was maligned by audiences, ridiculed and relegated to a footnote in many slasher-horror filmographies. But when it's presented in its correct aspect ratio, what you have is a genuinely frightening and tension-filled slasher with a decent story and interesting subplots that are nicely tied together at the film's conclusion. *Savage Weekend* deserves to be better known; trust me, in time it will be hailed as a hidden gem of '70s horror cinema and posited as a lost classic of the slasher genre. Once it gets going, and the savagery goes up a few notches, there is a lot to keep horror buffs engaged. While the gore is pretty low, there are enough chainsaws, bale hooks, machetes and table saws that are turned on the innocents in this gritty flick.

In contrast, *Schizoid* reached a wider cinematic audience primarily due to the star-studded cast of B-movie favorites Kinski, Wasson, Donna Wilkes, Marianna Hill and Christopher Lloyd. In *Schizoid*, a therapy group becomes the target of a sadist hell-bent on killing all its female members. As the bodies begins to pile up, advice columnist Julie (Hill) receives threatening letters and realizes that she is next on the scissor-wielding maniac's

"You have been chosen. You are doomed. Prepare yourself for… *Savage Weekend*." Fun promotional poster to this lost and underrated slasher/thriller.

list. Is it the creepy therapist Pieter Fales (Kinski), who seems to have an unhealthy relationship with his patients, so much so that once he has bedded them they end up dead? Is it Fales' daughter (Donna Wilkes), who seemingly shares an unhealthy relationship with her father and is resentful of his romantic involvement with Julie? Could it be Julie's estranged husband (Craig Wasson) or the oddball maintenance guy (Christopher Lloyd)?

What is noticeable about *Schizoid* from the get-go is that it was clearly intended as a psychological thriller as opposed to a standard schlocky stalk-and-revenge flick. Paulsen's script is testimony to this as it acts as a framework to present a series of flawed characters, each capable of committing heinous murderous acts. Paulsen asks us to play detective and unmask the real killer. His script also asks the audience to put aside preconceived notions of the actors and characters, for if not, their own prejudices will cloud their judgment in rooting out the fiend. This psychological aspect is still evident in the film but, like the killer's victims, it has been butchered by the scissors of the Cannon Film Group who saw crazed killer tropes associated with the script as a means to cash in on the slasher craze. After being re-edited to resemble a more formulaic slasher, the film failed to click with horror fans or with cinemagoers looking for a standard thriller. For the former, the lack of gore and low-death count was a deficiency, while its gruesomeness proved too strong for mainstream cinemagoers. The film was left to wither and fade into obscurity.

Despite the re-editing, *Schizoid* remains an interesting addition to the slasher genre and one that has its own allure. This is primarily helped by Paulsen's solid direction and handling of the cast. He elicits strong performances from the cast, most notably Marianna Hill, Donna Wilkes and Flo Lawrence who are excellent. Added to this is the sprinkling throughout the picture of a number of inventive and stylish kills, including a memorable scene of the scissor-wielding killer claiming a victim in a hot tub and Lawrence's character being dispatched by the killer on a chain link fence. Lawrence had this to say about this excellent sequence during an interview with her about *Schizoid*:

> In the scene I am supposed to die at the hands of the killer, at the end of being chased. The director decided that he would play his role so that I wouldn't be at risk of getting hurt. In the scene I get off from work late at night, after dancing in the topless club; I don't have a car and I'm running to catch a bus and there is someone following me. It gets freakier and freakier and I'm running down a back alley. There is nowhere to get away from my pursuer and nowhere to hide. I have been chased down a dead end alley and you see me trying to climb up a chain link fence as a last ditch effort to get away. I get knifed with the scissors and you see me sliding down the chain link fence with my hand still grabbing at the loops of the chain link. It was a wonderful scene, I totally trusted the director with the scissors and what happened in the scene was believable enough so that all the crew clapped when it finished. That's fun!

Klaus Kinski is decidedly creepy throughout the film, and although flat during excessive talkie scenes, he becomes a bulging-eyed beast when asked to cavort with the female cast. Lawrence details the problems she encountered on set with Kinski:

> My first bit of work on the film was with Klaus Kinski. I was excited and nervous and so on. Nowadays there is so much nudity and sexuality in films, it is almost a given that you don't even question it. At the time, the one reason I justified doing the film was that I was, quote unquote, a Wellesley graduate, which is a very erudite and extremely wealthy and snooty school for women on the East Coast in the States. So my part was a Wellesley graduate who was a topless dancer. So I thought one justified the other. So I actually went down to the airport, to a place called the Jet*strip*, and watched the topless

Kiva Lawrence recoils as the scissor-wielding maniac strikes the hot tub again in David Paulsen's cult classic slasher *Schizoid* (courtesy David Paulsen).

dancers, because I was very nervous to do that. I think they had a closed set for me. I was a topless dancer even though I had, as you will probably remember from the film, stockings, panties and a garter belt. So, I do my little topless scene and then I come off stage and into my dressing room. I have a kimono on and I start counting the money I had made while dancing. In the mirror I see Kinski, which the camera picks up, Kinski is hiding behind a water cooler and I turn around and say my first lines, "You always surprise me." Those were the lines. Then Kinski starts grabbing me and touching me in places that he had no business touching me. My acting chops went out the window, I should have slapped him, but I was just so shocked and no one yelled "Cut" at that point. I guess it was a split decision in that moment on my part that I at least maintain my professionalism so I stayed in the scene. Kinski was way out of line. I don't think we shot that over and I think that scene is in the film also in the moment of what was going on. Two or three days later, Kinski had the gall and audacity to call me up and invite me to go to lunch. I told him, "What you did to me on the set, do you realize that I could go to Screen Actors Guild and tell them what you did, and you would never work in this country again?" And Kinski said, "I'm sorry, I was very tired and just got off the plane. I'm sorry." Blah, blah, blah. I also did some group scenes with Kinski, because he played a therapist. I think that was about it.

I told Marianna Hill what happened to me with Kinski, so that she could be prepared in case he tried anything … like an aggressive assault. I think Kinski was rough on Donna Wilkes, who plays Kinski's daughter in the film, she might have had a lot of black and blue spots on her. I think Donna Wilkes did get along with him regardless of any rough handling. Kinski presented her with some perfume as I recall. I don't feel like I am being too harsh regarding Kinski.

In the aftermath of allegations of rape by Pola Kinski towards her father, the plot strand that sees Kinski's Dr. Fales adopt a seemingly unhealthy relationship with his daughter Alice will be uncomfortable viewing for some. In the beginning of the film, we see Dr. Fales ogling his naked daughter as she emerges from a shower. In another scene, Dr. Fales, in a fit of rage, violently manhandles his daughter, ripping her blouse and

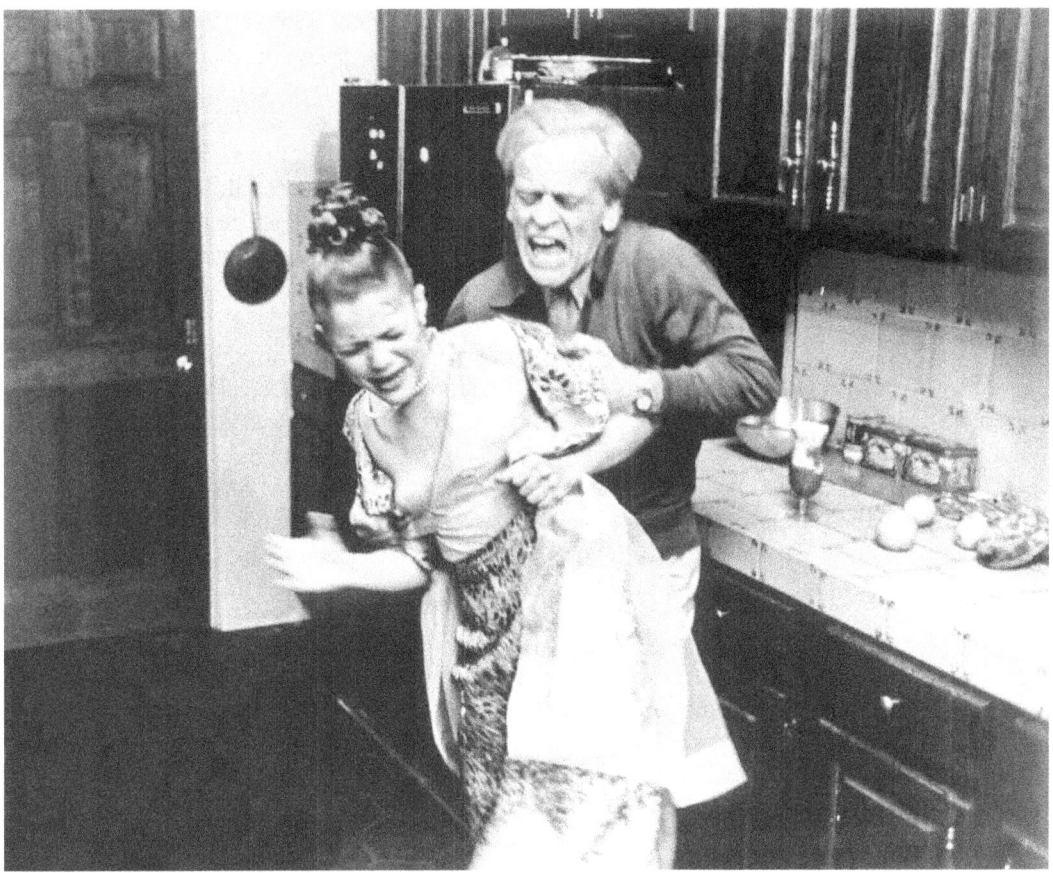

Dr. Pieter Files (Klaus Kinski) manhandles his daughter (Donna Wilkes) in *Schizoid* **(courtesy David Paulsen).**

revealing her breasts. Fales is presented as a violent, egotistical man who may or may not be involved in an incestuous relationship. In terms of narrative, Paulsen here creates a complex man—one who is qualified to offer therapy to others, but who clearly is in need of it himself. Could the killer be Dr. Fales or is he merely displaying other depravities that became all too real in his own life?

Schizoid is a gritty slasher cum psychological thriller with a nod to the European *giallo* films and the critically lauded masked killer of *Halloween* and *Friday the 13th*. It deserves to be better known by the horror fraternity. Audiences forgiving its lack of gore will be rewarded with a bastard slasher with enough trashy elements and stylish kills.

In September 2015 I had the pleasure of interviewing director David Paulsen in relation to both films.

Matthew Edwards: *Would you tell me a bit about your background? You were the writer, producer and director of the hit show* Dallas.

David Paulsen: *Dallas* and *Dynasty*, with a year out to do *Knots Landing*. That was in the '80s. Then in the early '90s I ran a production company for ABC-TV International out of Europe and ended up co-creating a show for it. It was called *Dangerous Curves*. That all happened after I had made *Savage Weekend* and *Schizoid*.

How did you get involved in the film and television industry?

Well, I started off trying to be an actor. I got a few jobs, off-Broadway, summer stock. Not much. At one point, knowing I needed to pay the rent, a friend helped get me some crew work on TV commercials and documentaries. I did some sound work with him, grip work, some editing, and then, by a stroke of pure luck, Lee Strasberg happened to see me in a piece I acted in for a director friend at the Actors Studio and cast me in a Chekhov play he was directing on Broadway with what was basically an all-star cast except for me. Which put me back into the acting world. I did two plays at the Aldwych in London, I was at Chicago's Second City Company for about half a year, did some work in Europe.

In the early '70s, with an equal amount of serendipity, I was hired by the Israeli producer Menahem Golan to write the English lyrics for an Israeli musical film he was making. The script and lyrics had been written in Hebrew and then translated into English. He was going to double-version it, scene for scene—Hebrew and English. Well, when he saw what I did with the songs, he asked me to rewrite the entire script—in English—which they then translated back for the Hebrew version. Strange convolutions. That was a picture named *Kazablan* [1974]. It was the first of half a dozen or so I ended up writing for him. One of which I directed.

How did you get from there to making Savage Weekend?

Savage Weekend came about when a guy who'd committed to finance my directing another script I'd written suddenly got cold feet. We were all set to go, but a week before the first day of shooting he backed out, said he couldn't risk the kind of money he'd committed to. It wasn't much by film standards but it was a lot for him. He offered to put up a much tinier amount, I think it was about $20,000, and asked if we could do something with that. I had never directed a picture at that time and was dying to. I thought about it; I figured all we could do with that measly amount of cash was either something pornographic, which held no interest for me, or something in the horror genre. At least we could develop a story for something like that. So he put down a small deposit for me to write a story and promised to put up the rest, up to $20,000 when I was finished. We'd get the rest of the money elsewhere. Which is what happened. My wife and I spent a couple of weeks at a friend's place in East Hampton and I wrote *Savage Weekend*.

Where did the original idea come from?

You remember the hook-in-the-foot scene? Well, I was out on a lake fishing with a buddy of mine the year before. The hook on his line had dropped into the boat. He jerked it up to cast again, not realizing that the damn thing had slipped under my bare foot. Needless to say, that smarted. Took me quite a bit of hacking to get it out. But that incident gave me the initial idea. For the film. I didn't know where I was going to go with it, but I put together a bunch of characters and developed a story. At the time, these horror-slasher type films weren't that popular. I don't even think *Friday the 13th*, had been done.

How did you begin?

I just thought I'd think up how many different ways I could kill people deliciously, and put them all into a movie. [*Laughs*] What came out was *Savage Weekend*, which we shot about six months later. It took me calling in a pot load of favors from friends I'd worked with in the industry—director of photography, associate producers, other crew people, an editor. On the basis of the script, I was able to scrounge up a little more cash.

A bloody end to David Gale in *Savage Weekend* **(courtesy David Paulsen).**

Not much, but we got labs and equipment houses to put up their services. I made a deal with Screen Actors Guild so that union actors could work deferred plus a small percentage of producer's gross. The whole thing was done for about $58,000 plus the deferments. It was a hellish shoot but that 58 grand got us to cut a work print which we could show and eventually sell.

Why was it "hellish"?

Two reasons mainly. First, I was a novice director. I'd never done a feature before. And then, well ... my partner, who had put up the initial funding, was supposed to be producing. And he had no idea what he was doing. Because it was such a minuscule-ly budgeted film, we had to do everything we possibly could ourselves. That meant transportation, housing and feeding cast and crew and he didn't know how to do that hands-on stuff. The producer should have been the tougher guy, the person to say *no* when necessary. Not the director. You really need somebody strong in there, and John just wasn't the person to do it. So I ended up having to be the bad guy as well as the good guy director-writer. That's always difficult, even on the best of shoots when you are paying people actual money. We weren't and every day I was terrified somebody would walk. Which would cost us the film.

How long was the film shoot?

I think around 18, 20 days, something like that. Sadly, looking at the movie again after so many years, I cringe at things that would have been so easy to fix, so easy to improve if I'd only known a little more. For example, the whole pace of the film. I needed more close-ups, more cutaways, shots to cut to make things move faster. I just didn't have enough time to get them because we were shooting so fast. Our director of photography was a man named Zoli Vidor; a wonderful guy. He was considered one of the best commercial D.P.s in New York at the time. He worked on the film as favor to our friendship, but he was used to shooting 30-second commercials that had higher budgets than we had for our whole film. Some of his cinematography is gorgeous. But the time it took really cost us! Interiors weren't so bad, but when we were doing exteriors we were at the mercy of upstate New York clouds, which we discovered came in like waves. That nude scene with Caitlin O'Heaney (credited as Kathleen Heaney) and Devin Goldenberg? We were setting up the shot when suddenly there was an ocean of clouds on the horizon, and they were coming in fast. "Whoa," I'm hollering, "let's get that shot quick." But Zoli's saying, "I can't shoot yet! Clouds!" "Fuck the clouds," I hollered! "I need the scene." I yell to the actors: "Kathleen, lie back. Devon, get your clothes off. Quick! Lie down! On top of her! But look calm! Look calm for Christ's sake. Kathleen, you too!" Then, after they were done: "Okay, get up, Devon! Cloud cover's coming. Pull your pants up. Good! Okay, wander out now, Dev. Great. Nice and easy. Zoli, did you get it?"

Zoli cursed and muttered under his breath. [*Laughs*] He was so pissed off. But time was flying. There are a number of sections that would have been so easy to improve if we'd only had an extra hour or so to get some proper cutaways.

It is interesting that you mention the pace of the film. Some viewers have said that the pace of the film is one of its strengths, in that Savage Weekend *takes its time in setting up the characters and atmosphere before going for the jugular in the final third. This sudden descent into violence and terror makes the film more horrifying.*

Yeah, I read that in the reviews you sent me. I have to tell you, I was astonished. You asked me what could have been improved. For one thing, the fight scenes could have used more voice work. Shouting, screaming, general ad-libbing. It would have been great if I had been able to get it on location but I couldn't—too many sound problems and too little time. I needed a day in a studio with the actors just screaming and voicing concerns. Couldn't get it. No money. Even at the opening, when the girl is running away. I should really have whipped up the sound. Built some real terror into it.

The start reminds me of Deliverance *[1972], especially with the music.*

I did all the music in Israel with a prominent Israeli composer who was a friend of mine. I wrote the song at the end of the picture, "Upstate Man." Not the music, someone else wrote that, but I wrote the lyrics. I thought it turned out well.

In some versions of the film, the boom microphone is frequently visible. Was this due to the film being presented in the wrong aspect ratio?

If I remember correctly, what happened was we knew the mics were getting into the picture but the film was supposed to be released with bands top and bottom to frame it properly. We were shooting for a wide angle ratio of 2.85 to 1. But at the time, remember, this was 1976, we didn't have the means to frame it wide like that in the camera. That was to be done in the printing. But it wasn't. When I screened the first print, I was horrified. We were showing it in a small theater in Cannes, during the season of 1977. I saw those mics and thought, "Oh my God! The lab didn't re-frame it. " So my wife and I took a roll of silver gaffer's tape, pasted it across the top and bottom of the projector, and stood next to the projector in the projection room adjusting the frame as each new reel came up. Golan-Globus, who released the film, assured me that the problem would be taken care of before release, but it wasn't. When I downloaded it and watched it on my wide TV screen, the mics don't show at all. On the version you sent me, which had a square screen [not the correct aspect ratio], you see them. And that's what some reviewers [of *Savage Weekend*] have commented on. Appropriately.

The film has received a lot of criticism in some quarters for the "gratuitous nudity." I find this criticism unfair for it is the sexual tension and relationships between the characters that ultimately help define them in the film.

For me, the nudity was never gratuitous. There was a fair bit of it; that's the kind of film we were making, but compared to films we've seen since, frankly, it's even a bit tame.

Christopher Allport is great in the role of Nicky. You rarely see a gay character in one of the leading roles in a horror film. Was it is your intention to bring something different to the story?

You know, I wrote it in two weeks. I wanted some interesting costumes and I wanted to sex up the film a bit. I thought Christopher did well. A number of viewers didn't understand why Shirley was trying to seduce him. But that was a misreading of their scenes. She wasn't really trying to seduce him! His character was gay, flamboyantly so. I just wanted to get some interesting music into it so I had them dance in costume. They were screwing around—being sexy without being sexual. And while that was going on, the scenes were punctuated by shots of the killer in a horrific mask coming into the house. Besides giving it music and color, it was a way of building up the tension. Christopher was a very good actor. He died in a skiing accident [Author's note: Allport, and two other people were killed during a freak avalanche in the San Gabriel Mountains, northeast of Los Angeles, on January 26, 2008.]

I loved the scene in the bar when he confronts the homophobic punks.

Again, no time for me to get enough close-ups. Another scene we had to shoot in half a day. I'm surprised it turned out as well as it did. The two guys he was fighting were not actors, they were crew guys.

William Sanderson is brilliant as the unhinged local, Otis. He brings a tragic sense of insanity to his character. Were you pleased with his performance?

I was thrilled with his performance. The part I'd envisioned was a man in his sixties but when Billy came and auditioned, he was so good I stopped looking for anyone else. And he was a joy to work with. Over the years he has become a friend. In fact, when he was doing the *Newhart* [1982] show, he'd be invited onto late night talk shows. Several times I learned he credited me with having created the role of Larry he was playing on *Newhart*. He did play Larry like Otis, except he played Larry for comedy and Otis was anything *but*. Although, come to think of it, I guess we managed a few laughs.

The death scenes in the film—were you satisfied with how they turned out?

They work, but they could have been more terrifying. The girl on the saw, for example. Once established, I should have cut back to her more often. Just a couple times more would have made an important difference. We could have had the audience screaming. At the end, when Otis turns out to be "the hero" so to speak, the girl should have been fleeing. She should have been trying to get as far as she could from the men. All just stuff I didn't know how to do very well then.

When we first showed it in Cannes, the audience was full and they loved it. They were so involved in it, they were screaming—which, frankly, shocked the hell out of me. Much of the process of doing it was fun. I mean that in the sense that you come up with an idea and you shoot it—close-ups of knives or saws or needles going into what looks to be flesh. But then, after you put it together and you see it with an audience, especially one that likes that kind of thing … holy hell! My wife and I left that theater in Cannes, she pulled me into a bar for a few shots of whisky. Middle of the afternoon. I was shocked by what I had created. I'm speaking of the violence. I'm not a violent person.

The scene where the identity of the killer is revealed: Were you pleased with the way that scene turned out?

I had written that scene entirely differently. It was a much longer scene. When he rips the mask off, in his manic frenzy, he starts telling her the story of what he feels brought him to his madness. He acts out his whole backstory in the closed room with her when she knows he's murdered her friends and is in terror for her own life. He describes what happened to him when he was working with his boss in a crazy sort of way. I wanted you to see his madness with a much more internal dynamic, something we had not seen before. Unfortunately, the scene went on and on and it wasn't well done. It took months for me to realize that I had to cut it to what you see now. That was painful. It was like cutting off my arm fingers first, then wrist, then elbow. I was trying to keep as much as I could, but finally I bit the bullet, so to speak. I saw that all we needed was to get to where he turns his head, we see his sweaty, glassy-eyed face. We see he is nuts. Cut! So I did. But by doing so, I was also cutting the film's running time which needed to be a certain minimum length. So losing that big chunk cost me the ability to make trims in other scenes that would have helped the film to move faster.

Savage Weekend *has become somewhat a cult slasher film in some circles. Did you ever expect this?*

Expect it? Never. I'm astonished. [*Laughs*] It is, though, nice to know that the film has received some positive reviews.

How did Schizoid *come about?*

On New Year's Eve 1980, I think it was, I learned that producer Menahem Golan was in L.A. So I gave him a call. I hadn't seen him for two or three years. He told me on the phone he'd just bought Cannon Films and needed to produce three low-budget films right away. Did I have any ideas? If so, he'd let me write and direct one. I said I didn't have one at the moment but that I would by tomorrow morning. So I spent the night thinking shit up.

Next morning I went to his office, pitched him half a story I'd come up with. He liked it, commissioned me to write it and put a production together. The only two things he insisted on were: One, I'd need to be shooting by the 4th of March (this was the 17th of January, mind you). Two, I needed to use Klaus Kinski. Golan had a contract with him.

So I wrote this next script in about two weeks and called it *Schizoid*. I remember I was dictating it to a typist whom Menahem had sent to work with me. She was typing on an IBM Selectric—this was in February 1980. Well, suddenly we're hit by a major, major, major thunderstorm. All the electricity in the apartment went out—lights, everything. All power! Luckily I had an old Hermes manual in a closet. I pulled it out, dropped it on the young woman's desk, put a match to a couple of candles and we kept going by candlelight.

Were you apprehensive about working with Kinski?

No. I mean, I knew the kinds of characters he'd played in the past and that audiences would assume the one he was doing for me would be similar, so I decided to do a twist on that. I made him a psychiatrist, a psychotherapist, to create some doubt in the minds of the audience as to whether he was in fact going to be the killer—as people figured that he, Kinski, most likely would be.

Would you talk through your first meeting with Klaus Kinski? What was he like?

Quite pleasant. He was staying at the Beverley Wilshire. I went to meet him. We talked. He quite liked the script when I showed it to him. And he was quite pleased to learn, in the course of conversation, that my wife was French and that I spoke French. He did too, of course, and later he used that—spoke only French with me—on the set. I guess he wanted to hold himself apart from the rest of the cast and crew, make himself a little more special … as though he really had to. He rarely ever said anything to me in English when anyone else was around. Actually, we got on exceptionally well. There were a couple of occasions when he got a little Kinski-ish, but by and large, we worked well together.

I hear the female cast members had a hard time with him.

Yeah. He wasn't well liked by the women on set. They were afraid of him. And you could see why. So I had to step in a couple of times when he got a little outrageous. Protect them from him. We did get into one blow-up when were shooting a bedroom scene with Marianna Hill. Marianna was mostly nude and he was Klaus Kinski. That was a difficult scene to shoot and not at all pleasant for Marianna but she handled it intelligently. Klaus went over the top a few times but Marianna was very strong throughout.

Were you impressed with Kinski as an actor?

Oh, he was an exceptional talent. And he was perfectly professional. Except for a handful of tantrums, he did his job. There wasn't much in the script for him to display his "genius" or whatever. And I must say I was concerned that he was a little slow and that we might have done better had I been able to speed him up. But apart from that, working with him was fine.

The film has an impressive cast. Were you given free autonomy to cast roles as you saw fit or were some actors already contracted to Cannon Films?

As I mentioned, the film was put together in an instant and I had to employ Klaus Kinski because he was contracted to Golan. I was writing the script and casting at the same time. We put out calls in Los Angeles and my casting director was very good in getting people attached. I didn't know Craig Wasson at the time. I did want Christopher Lloyd in the movie. I had seen him in *One Flew Over the Cuckoo's Nest* [1975] and I loved his face and I wanted him in the picture. Donna Wilkes was a good actress and looked much younger than her age. She was very pretty and seemed the best fit for the part of Alison. Marianna Hill was the same—very, very pretty. Again, I didn't know her work, but she did an audition and I chose her. I saw a lot of actors in a short space of time and I had to come up with the answers very quickly.

Having only two months to prepare for the film, were you given much time to shoot?

Our schedule was 24 days. I saved the last two days for connectors, shots to do without the cast that would have linked the film in the way that I had written it. There was a certain depth to the film as written that was far better than the way it was cut. However, Golan cut off the last two days of shooting from the budget at the last moment. The film needed that small stuff I was scheduled to shoot and record but he wouldn't allow it.

Obviously that impacted the film.

It impacted it greatly. This was a film that was not just a slasher. We had a pretty strong story having to do with the psychology of the killer. At one point, which you don't see now [in the final edit], you see the police pointing their guns at the killer who is hiding behind a piece of cardboard with a fierce drawing on it. The killer was mad, utterly mad. That didn't come out. Golan re-cut it from the direction I had it moving and turned it into a slasher film.

Were you frustrated with how the film turned out?

I had worked with Golan since the early 1970s and after we did this movie I didn't speak to him for eight years. I was livid. We had a screaming match and that was the end of it.

How did you choose the locations for the film?

I wrote the script knowing that I would be terribly limited both in budget and locations. So I sought locations as I was writing and wrote to them. Much of the script was shot in the offices of Golan-Globus. We decorated them and re- and re-decorated them. We were able to shoot late at night and all the fight sequences could be filmed there, so I adapted my script to take advantage of that. We found that beautiful house which we used for Kinski's character and made good use of that. Apart from that, we didn't travel around too much as we had so little time and shockingly little money. We shot the film for about $350,000. I did have a very good production manager. Chris Pearce had worked for Coppola, then later went on to work with Golan-Globus.

Was Schizoid *a difficult film to shoot with so many big personalities?*

No. In that respect it was easy. *Savage Weekend* was a terribly difficult shoot! I didn't have any fun on that film. It was awful. With *Schizoid*, I vowed that whatever happened, I would have fun. I would enjoy the shoot and I would make it enjoyable for the cast and crew. And I did. Everyone enjoyed it. We had some difficult personalities. I had no problem with Klaus. When he was working with me, he was fine. Craig Wasson was something else.

Flo Lawrence has stated that she felt so frightened of Wasson on set and his unpredictability. She told me in an interview that during her death scene you stepped in and acted as the knife-wielding maniac.

I think I donned the killer's coat and performed the kill on Flo's death scene. And I was the guy who jumped out of the window and chased Craig down the alley, shouting at him.

Was Craig Wasson difficult on set?

He worked well with me but I know he had problems with other actors and crew. There was some ugliness that took place. I don't want to say too much except that Klaus once took me aside and told me that Craig was crazy [*laughs*]! And if anybody knows crazy, Klaus Kinski knows crazy! Craig was a good actor but I think his personal problems helped stultify his career.

Donna Wilkes has gone on record saying that during the final death scene, she accidently stabbed Wasson for real with scissors and he ended up in the hospital.

I have a vague, but only a vague recollection of that! I also have a recollection of the fight scene between Craig and Klaus Kinski. If I recall correctly, the fight got very severe. By that point, neither liked the other. I recall Klaus getting whacked on the head and we had to take him to the hospital!

I never considered this film to be a "slasher" film. It was intended as a story with a

The mad genius Klaus Kinski with Flo Lawrence in *Schizoid* (courtesy David Paulsen).

fair bit of violence in it. When I wrote it, I saw it as a psychological film and I set it up so you did not know who the killer was. I wanted the audience to suspect Kinski. I gave him the name Fales, which can be read as *fails or phallus*. That was deliberate [*laughs*]. I wanted you to suspect Chris Lloyd as well. I set up a variety of killers.

When editing the film I got to thinking about the film *High Noon* [1952]. (No quality comparison intended, for sure.) But when *High Noon* was first shown, my understanding is that nobody cared for it. Then the editor convinced the director to do one more little thing: shoot the clock as it closed in on noon which would give the film a clear sense of time itself closing in. And it worked. Those clock shots tied everything together. So when the end comes, you are geared up for it.

I thought about that when I wrote *Schizoid*. I had certain small links in the film that would have made that very, very clear. What I was trying to show was the madness of this young man, who seemed perfectly normal, perfectly fine, who was just a bit disturbed because of a thing or two that happened in his life. Yet he went bananas! That's what I was trying to achieve and I feel certain I would have had Golan not stepped in. He brought in an Israeli film director friend of his and had him cut it as if it was a slasher. *Schizoid* was never intended to be that.

Schizoid is what it is. But I would have liked it to be the best it could have been. The psychological aspects were important to me. Craig Wasson was playing a character we see slowly going mad. It was disappointing, of course, to see that casually tossed aside.

There is a strange father-daughter relationship between Donna Wilkes and Klaus Kinski's characters in the movie. What prompted you to explore such a dark subject?

I'm not sure "explore" is the right word. I think my intention was to use the relationship to show two sides of a complicated man who is hit by the emotions of his daughter's jealousy of her father's attraction to other women. I also wanted to show the character's home life and the dangerous qualities within him, especially the scene when he watches her in the shower. And of course I wanted the audience to suspect that Donna could also be the killer.

Did Yoram Globus and Menahem Golan do much to promote the film?

Zero. No promotion whatsoever. It played in a few theaters and then died. I hated what they had done to the movie so I essentially turned my back on it. I was astonished

Promotional material for *Schizoid* (courtesy David Paulsen).

when you contacted me and sent me some of the positive reviews! I am pleased that people are talking about the film and that they like it.

As a stalk-and-slash movie, are you proud of what you achieved with Schizoid? *What aspects of the film are you proud of and what would you change now, if you had the chance?*

I re-watched the film for this interview and I'm glad I saw it, because unless my mind has gotten more feeble than I thought, it's not nearly as bad as I thought it was years ago. It moves. It has a good bit of tension. Not much blood but that was a choice. Some of the acting is pretty good. Craig Wasson, Klaus, Richard Herd, Chris Lloyd, Flo Lawrence and Donna Wilkes especially.

Regrets that I have, in seeing it again, are that I had so little time, I was generally forced to go with takes that I knew could be better, but lack of time and money forced us to move on. And some of the dialogue, which wasn't bad, if I say so myself, was either swallowed up in Klaus' accent or buried amid the softness and frequent poor sound quality. I'm sure it sounds better on a bigger screen. I hope the DVD sounds better because much was lost in the YouTube version that I saw.

Dutch VHS cover of *Schizoid*.

Sound is a big issue. I had scheduled an audio session for the actors to come in and do some extemporaneous vocal work—shouts and screams and panting during their runs. Vocal stuff we didn't have time during the shoot to improvise. Those and the pickup shots I've mentioned were extremely important. But Golan stupidly yanked the plug. We're also missing good sound effects. Better music would have helped as well. But those things were done after I had gone.

I'm not satisfied with the ending. It all comes together structurally but I'm missing an emotional closing. Had I had more time to reflect when writing to think of a proper ending scene, I would have. And had I had a just little more time during the shoot, all would have come out far better. That said, it ain't too bad, a discovery that surprises the hell out of me.

5

Drive-In Massacre

An Interview with Stu Segall

During my teenage years, I embarked on my own filmmaking career with my three brothers: I directed and starred in a plethora of *giallo-* and slasher-inspired films on a camcorder appropriated from our parents. Such was the prowess of my acting ability that my brothers scrawled on the credits, "Ham supplied by Matt." My shoddiness in front of the camera was matched by my shoddiness behind, as demonstrated through a number of yawn-inducing yarns that included *Butcher Mansion* and *Blood Is Red*, the latter about a crazed scientist who believes not all blood is red, hence goes on a murderous rampage to prove his hypothesis right. Fortunately for the cinematic community, and the wider horror world, both have been lost to the ether or taped over with an episode of *CHiPs*.

What does this interlude have to do with *Drive-In Massacre*? The British Board of Film Classification had left all the violent gory deaths intact, and uncensored. So I used one of the grisly deaths in *Butcher Mansion* —the infamous decapitation scene—so that I could make it more viscerally violent. Our special effects budget stretched to 99p (around $1.25) which consisted of fun blood and a giant syringe so we could squirt the fake blood into our faces. Despite the footage from *Drive-In Massacre*, *Butcher Mansion* remained and as formulaic and clichéd as the films it was desperately trying to emulate. When I mentioned this to *Drive-In Massacre* director Stu Segall, he was so pleased that he said, "Well done! I am glad someone would use something from it. That makes it more special."

For many horror fans, *Drive-In Massacre* is a special film as it brings back memories of a certain time and place in their lives, or the drive-ins of yesteryear. It's one of the zaniest movies, or non-movies, ever! The flimsy premise sees a homicidal maniac undertake a brutal killing spree at a California drive-in. Despite its patrons being cut up, or having their heads detached from their torsos, the customers continue to show up, and arrogant manager Newton Naushaus refuses to shut down the operation as he has bills to pay! It's up to a couple of hapless cops who dress in drag to catch the killer. Is it local sex pest Orville the resident dunce? Grimy, an ex-carnival performer? The mad manager? Thrown in for good measure is a knife-wielding maniac in a local warehouse who yips and yells for ten minutes before being shot! The twist ending will have you screaming in your (car) seats in wild horrifying delirium!

With a jumble of styles and continuity lapses, pedestrian scenes padded out to make up the running time that contrast suddenly with scenes that zip along, wildly erratic

Drive-In Massacre original promotional poster artwork. Filmed entirely in Gore-Color! (courtesy Stu Segall).

acting and hilariously clunky dialogue, the film should be a bona fide disaster. Yet it is not. It is an endearing mess with enough stylish kills to keep the gore-hounds happy and situations that will leave you in stitches. Take for example the cops swinging around the murder weapon—the samurai sword—moments after it has slaughtered some unfortunate soul. It is 75 minutes of weirdness where insults are flung about just as frequently as the killer's sword.

As Segall details in the interview that follows, there was no time, nor budget, for reshooting scenes or imposing a degree of visual flair into the proceedings. When working close to the bone like Segall and his team were doing, it was fly-by shooting.

The film was primarily exhibited in drive-ins where it freaked out a lot of the kids, as many feared losing their heads when they reached out of the car to get their audio headset. The film's marketing gave us this glorious line: "Warning: The Red Stuff on Your Hot Dog May Not Be Ketchup!"

Drive-In Massacre is a brain-exploding movie best served with a six-pack or bottle of whisky to get you into the spirit of the proceedings. Viewers wanting something akin to *Citizen Kane* may as well jog on now. On the other hand, those with a sympathetic heart will get a kick out of chopped-off rubber heads bouncing around the screen while insults and threats issue from the actors who have cranked up their performance to "ham" (my acting skills are well suited to this film).

A barrel of crap or the demented work of a genius? You decide. I'm opting for the latter. With that in mind, I tracked down the genius of this work. Stu Segall proved to be a true gentlemen and an absolute pleasure to speak to. While *Drive-In Massacre* was his only foray into the world of horror, he has found fame elsewhere for a number of critically acclaimed sex films, the most famous being *Insatiable* (1980) with Marilyn Chambers. I spoke to Mr. Segall in September 2015 and about *Drive-In Massacre* and the production history and filming of this cult classic shocker that still entertains and delights audiences the world over, 40 years after its initial release.

Matthew Edwards: *Would you tell me a bit about your background and how you got involved in the movie business?*

Stu Segall: From 1967 to 1970, I was a private investigator. I worked for a detective agency in Beverly Hills. I did what private investigators do, though far less dramatic than they make it on television [*laughs*]. It was a very interesting job. Through circumstances, I met a fella who was a makeup artist who worked in the "nudie business," as they called it back then. The "nudie business" were films where the girls were naked and the guys wore underwear. So it wasn't anything near pornography but it was probably considered it at the time. My friend invited me to the set to give him a hand on some gals working on the film. He needed an extra pair of hands. I said, "I don't know anything about the movie business." He told me not to worry and that he would take care of it. So I went with him and spent my first day with him on the set putting body makeup on very large-breasted women [*laughs*]! It was like a Russ Meyer movie! So that was my first foray into moviemaking and one thing led to another, and I ended up working with various different crews that made these type of low-budget nudie movies. It really didn't fall into pornography, which I would later go into.

You are fondly remembered for directing one of the zaniest horror films of the '70s, Drive-In Massacre. *You had made adult pictures prior to this. What prompted you to switch hemispheres into the world of horror?*

About six months into my filmmaking career, I thought that it was pretty simple stuff and that I could do this. Now, I never had a background in cinema, but I got into the adult business and produced and directed a bunch of softcore sex movies. My partner Marty Green had a deal with a theater group that wanted to make a bunch of R-rated movies. So what we did was make two feature-length R-rated features and I took two softcore adult movies and made them into R-rated movies by reshooting 20 minutes of each picture. We did all of this at one time. So within 14 days—which was our shooting schedule—we did *Drive-In Massacre*, a movie called *C.B. Hustlers* [1976] and we did a couple of others. [Editor's note: The other films were most likely *The Spirit of Seventy*

Sex and Young Students, both made in 1976.] It was quite a project! We were all young and in our twenties. We worked 20-hour days, every day 'til we got it done and then we would fall apart! So basically that is how *Drive-In Massacre* came to be, in that my business partner told me we had to make some R-rated features. So we came up with some ideas and just got going. We only had a few bucks—and very little money to shoot the movies. The crew consisted of around eight or nine guys and gals. Everyone did a little bit of everything and we went out and made those movies. And *Drive-In Massacre* was the best received out of all the movies we did because of its subject matter.

Where did you get the initial inspiration from?

It came from an idea I had. Drive-ins had grown up as a great place for a date and you could make out and hopefully get laid in the back of your car. We were all pretty much out of high school, and drive-ins were the place to go socially. I thought, "What could be more frightening?" because everything you have to do in a drive-in involves sticking your head out of the car window and to get that speaker to bring it in! So that was the premise: When you go to grab that speaker, you are going to lose a limb!

John F. Goff and George "Buck" Flower are credited with writing the picture and they star in the film.

They were two good friends of mine, back in the day. They were also actors and writers. Both worked on a lot of low-budget movies. So both of them wrote the screenplay for me and both starred in the film, too. John Goff was one of the cops and he was the crazy guy!

He was the crazy guy with the machete in the warehouse!

Yeah … well, he was supposed to have been [*laughs*]!

The scene with Flower as the machete-wielding maniac seems almost like a scene from another film when it appears suddenly in the picture. It did seem that this was shot later. Is that correct, or was this part always envisaged in the original script?

That is very, very perceptive on your part. I'll tell you how that happened. The only professional on the crew was a gal who was in the union. The rest of us were non-union and mostly low-budget filmmakers who worked on films with little or no money and had very little experience. But what we did have was the energy and zeal to make movies. *Drive-In Massacre* was shot on film. It was on 35mm. We had no video playback at that time. It was strictly load and shoot. Anyway, the girl who was the script supervisor, I had given her the four scripts and a breakdown of how we were going to shoot it. And we had a day off scheduled four days into the shooting on the movie. It was a day of no shooting. Two or three days into the shooting, the girl came up to me and said that we had a problem: "I've timed this out and *Drive-In Massacre* is only going to be 60 minutes." I said, "That's impossible." She said, "No," and I was like, "Holy shit." I realized that we had to write another day's work into the movie and we had to do it on the only available free day in our schedule. So I went to "Buck" and said, "You need to write a scene that lasts about ten minutes!" So he wrote that scene of him sulking in the warehouse. I got permission to shoot in the warehouse from my brother-in-law, but because it was a running business we could only go in and shoot at night. So starting at six at night, we shot until about six or seven in the morning. We milked that scene so we could get an extra ten minutes to insert into the picture. Everything else was pretty much shot as we wrote it. We loaded the camera, shot the scene and moved on. We didn't have time to get into the scene and cover it properly. Some of the scenes are really long for a reason: because we needed to boost up the running time. If I'm not mistaken, to be a feature film we needed 75 minutes. The script supervisor had timed the film out at 63 minutes. So we all panicked, wrote in a new scene and shot it. That's how it happened and you picked up on that very well.

It kind of works, though, as the film throws another red herring into the proceedings.
There are times we did things in *Drive-In Massacre* that didn't make any sense but it didn't make a difference. We had these movies pre-sold.

Talk about the production of the film.
We used the same cast in every movie so we couldn't double-bill these pictures as you would see the same actors in the other movies. *C.B. Hustler* had some of the same cast as *Drive-In Massacre* had. Consequently we had to put out the films separately, otherwise the audiences would get bored. And when you make movies like that and at that pace on 35mm, that is some achievement. It was a lot of fun to make, though sometimes the art suffers as a result because you don't have the time. We didn't have the time or budget for retakes. We had to go and be out of certain locations at certain times. We had to shoot most of the film at night before the sun came up. We shot the film in Hollywood. Part on stage, part in a warehouse in the San Fernando Valley, and we found a drive-in in California.

Was there much money in the budget for special effects?
We hired a guy to do the prosthetic heads that were going to be severed in the film and the day we needed him, he showed up and did a horrible job. And so we never used his stuff. I was sitting there thinking, "Oh my goodness, we've got to cut this guy's head off and we don't have a prosthetic head to complete the shot." So I sent one of the crew members down to the market to get me a banana squash. So we got this banana squash and put a wig on it attached to a stand, and I was off-camera with a sword. When the guy stuck his head out of the car to get the speaker, we intercut the decapitation shot of the banana squash and then cut to the severed head rolling into the frame. That's how we did it. Also with the prosthetic heads, I asked the crew guy to get some cow brains and we scooped out the banana squash and put the cow brains in! So when we cut the head off, the brains were supposed to spill out. I don't know if it ever came out but I remember we needed the brains to make it look more authentic. We mixed them with loads of fake blood and it was fun to do, despite the fact that it was cold and freezing. We didn't have any heaters but we had to make things up on the spot because things failed. When you are in the middle of nowhere, you have to make things work because we didn't have the resources to go back and reshoot. So that's what we did!

You have to remember that I did all these movies at one time. I worked with an editor and we cut those four movies. I was done with the project mentally because we had to make them so quick. My partner Marty did the marketing of the one-sheets, so if you see the one-sheets there is a word in it, "dysfunctional," and it is spelt incorrectly. That was done in error. However, we had already printed 500 one-sheets. I wasn't going to change it as that would cost too much money. So it went out like that. But my partner Marty was really good at marketing. He is also in the movie, making out with his girlfriend, and he who gets stabbed through the neck. So we killed him off straight away!

I love the poster, warning those with severe emotional disorders or chronic coronary dysfunctions to avoid the picture! That was a great piece of marketing, similar to successful marketing employed by Herschell Gordon Lewis on his films.

I don't know who Herschell Gordon Lewis is. I have to say that I didn't pay homage to anyone because I didn't have any cinematic history. I was not an aficionado of movies and I was not a film junkie who could dissect a film and talk about it. I've never been like that. In those days, we all worked from our own brains and not so much tried to emulate someone else's style because we didn't really know that. There were certain people who were immersed into the intelligentsia of the business, but I certainly wasn't one of them. I was more of a mechanic. I don't denigrate myself by saying that. Some people are very artistic. I had a little bit of that in me, but I always directed movies as a producer. When you do that, the production usually fails. I mean that from a low-budget film standpoint and not a film directed and produced by Michael Bay, who makes these massive hits. I am referring to down-and-dirty films where you have five days to shoot it. Where you shoot under these conditions, lots of things go by the wayside. As a low-budget producer, you have to think, "What is the quickest and cheapest way that we can shoot this scene?" It may not be as cinematic as if you put the camera elsewhere and made it look nice, the overriding factor was time. So consequently, when I directed I always directed as a producer, and most times the work suffers because of it, because you are thinking more about money than the film as an art form. There are some people who only think about the art and they don't care because it is not their money. We had to make sure we worked within our budgets.

So what kind of budget were you working with on Drive-In Massacre?

We made the four movies for $15,000. No money! And remember we shot on 35mm film and that included sending it to the lab to be developed, made into dailies and editing. When you figure in those costs and with how much we actually had to make the films, then it was peanuts! We paid the crew, locations and lunch, which was usually sandwiches kindly made up by one of the crew—it was very, very low-budget. I doubt you could make a movie, let alone four of them, for that cost today. We had no money to really milk a scene and edit it effectively. We literally had to get through five pages at one location, then seven pages at another. It was more of a mechanical process to get the movie done and the artistry was relegated out of it.

Now that I know the ridiculously low budget, it is even more impressive that the film has lasted all these years.

You're right. It has always been mind-boggling. I have always heard that *Drive-In Massacre* has always been well-received in the United Kingdom, simply because it was. And I could never understand why that was the case. I'm very flattered and I think it's great. I feel bad that I didn't put more effort into it to make it better [*laughs*]!

Robert E. Pearson was great as Austin Johnson. How did he wind up in the film?

We were all of the same low-budget family. Robert was a very good film director. He made some very good movies [*The Devil and LeRoy Bassett*, 1973]. He was older than a lot of us. What was strange was that one day he woke up blind. In the middle of the night, his retinas detached and when he got out of his bed and walked to his window, because he knew where it was, he thought it was five a.m. He couldn't see anything. He was stone dead blind. Now, he was like that for years and he was a film director and writer. I knew him for a while, but we didn't stay in touch, because I went in another direction into the T&A business. I always wondered what happened to him. He did do some incredible things. One day he was in a Jeep traveling to the set of a movie he was directing and the guy he was traveling with fell asleep at the wheel and he hit the gear shift knob and locked up the transmission and they flipped the car. I think the other guy died and Bob got broken up pretty badly. They put a cast on Bob's arm and he went straight from the hospital to the set and carried on directing and shooting, after all this drama. He was quite a guy! He was a good actor and did well in *Drive-In Massacre*, though a little over the top. [Editor's note: Pearson passed away in 2009. Prior to his death he became a successful painter, a feat even more impressive in that he had been suffering from Parkinson's disease and was clinically blind in his right eye and legally blind in his left. He was also color-blind.]

My favorite performance was that of Douglas Gudbye as Germy. He came across to me like Stan Laurel but with a psychopathic glint in his eye!

I love the way these names came about [*laughs*]! That was a good one. I can't remember his real name. He had just quit Douglas Aircraft to follow his dream to become an actor, and this was the first movie that he did. His [screen name] was Douglas Gudbye to say goodbye to his previous employer! I don't recall what happened to him after we made *Drive-In Massacre* and *C.B. Hustlers*. I don't believe we went through a casting director. We cast it within our wide group of non-union folks. We didn't have a casting director because we couldn't afford one. We did everything in house. We asked favors from guys we knew, like "Buck," who wrote and starred in the film. We just used all our friends, who happened to all be wannabe actors. This was nearly 40 years ago. We were all dumb, young and energized to do these things.

There is a real punk ethic to making of the film.

You are right. You had to really love what you were doing as you had to put so much time and effort into the making of the film. Every day we worked 20 hours. We literally worked and slept on that movie.

From a directorial standpoint, were you pleased with the way you shot the film? At times the camera is very static, at other times there is a verve and immediacy, like the chase seen with Orville, the town's bumbling sex-addict?

I haven't seen the movie in a long time but I think we shot one day in the rain and the next day the sun came out! So at one point he is running in the rain and he rounds a corner and the sun is out!

Were you pleased with the way you filmed that chase scene?

I certainly have creative thoughts in my mind but I don't get hung up on them. They don't stop me from pushing the narrative forward. We tried to make it look as good as it can and I was always receptive to new ideas on the film set. I wasn't precious with the film like some directors can be. It was very organic and if someone came up with a great idea, we would roll with it. I have creative abilities in me but I am not the most talented director. I would say that I was a talented producer. I don't direct any more because I was never really crazy about doing it in the first place. I know my strengths.

Another clever element was the credit sequence, which announced the film as if you were at a drive-in. Again, that was a clever piece of marketing, especially as your intended audience would primarily see the film in such a venue.

That was an interesting idea that we used in the movie and it was very fitting for the movie. It saved us a bit of money to do it that way. It certainly wasn't thought up in post-production as we simply didn't have the time or means to do that because we didn't have the money. Everything was financially driven in those days. We had a certain amount of bucks and there was no going over the budget as there was simply no more money to be had.

What was the reaction from people who saw it in drive-ins? Did they find it unnerving?

I had to ask my partner this, as I never actually followed up on this. I had given the movie to the distributor and I had moved on to the next project, as I was also working in distribution alongside my work in production. I understand that the film played in hundreds of drive-ins and apparently there were a few drive-ins that didn't like the movie because it kept the kids in the car. They were too afraid to get out of the car to get popcorn! They complained about that. This happened in a number of theaters where they didn't sell many refreshments when they played that movie. That was an unintended consequence of what we did. But that made sense as the audience believed what they were looking at and were scared.

Upon release, how was the film received critically and commercially?

Do you want to know the truth? I don't know. I imagine it was so-so, based on the obvious flaws in it. But again, it had a few moments that the audience liked. I never read up on the critiques relating to *Drive-In Massacre*. It never made much difference to me. It was a project; it was a business deal. I certainly cared about what I was making—you just can't crank these things out and not give a damn—but I never followed reviews, and no one ever said anything to me, so I assumed that it was responded to as well as it could for a movie of its type. Over the years I have been contacted by various companies in the U.K. wanting to release the film, which is very flattering. 88 Films is putting out a new version with digitally re-mastered picture and a host of new features.

I have only ever done one horror film. All the other vehicles have been sexy T&A and then I got into television in the mid–80s. Now all the television that I do is pretty much action-adventure, shoot-outs, car chases, etc. So horror wasn't really my thing. I was a fan of the films of Wes Craven and John Carpenter and some of our crews crossed paths, and they were real aficionados of their craft and they had more money to work with than I did. We just shot *Drive-In Massacre* straight from the hip and we didn't analyze too much what we were doing. Intuitively I knew it would work. It was instinctive and when we edited and cut it together, we were proved right. I am pleased that 40 years later people still want to release it, view it and write about it. I am proud of the worst movie ever made! I am proud of the people who worked with me on the film and the effort they put into it. If for some reason my directorial inexperience didn't come to the fore, they still took on the idea and tried to make something great. We never approached it that we were making a piece of crap. We tried to do the best we could with the limited amount of money that we had. Unfortunately, the picture was money-driven, not artistically. When we made the film, we never got any accolades and we simply went on to the next project. My company name at the time was the Movie Manufacturing Company. That's what we were doing. We were manufacturing movies. Not to demean them, but we were cranking out so many at the time that it became somewhat like a factory. We made three or four movies at the same time. One day you would shoot one movie and the next another, on the same set you shot the day before. It was a nightmare. Fortunately, the girl who saved me was the script supervisor because she had her shit together. I had no production manager, no first assistant director. I had myself and my cameraman who was also the camera operator. So I had a tiny crew. We had gals who did makeup and wardrobe but I paid them all in cash and kept going. We didn't have any of the things you need now to make a production work.

And yet the film lives on when so many bigger-budgeted films have sunk into obscurity. Partly through companies in the U.K. like Vipco, we were able to get our horror fix through titles like Drive-In Massacre *which were not butchered by our draconian censorship board at the time. Viewers associate these films with a fondness that recalls a particular part of their lives.*

I do too and the film makes me think of my career and how much I learned making that movie. Every day you make a movie, you learn something new that day forward. It was a tremendous background to be when making low-budget movies during the '70s. There were extremely creative people working in the industry with really creative ideas all trying to raise the finance to make their pictures. We had a lot of laughs making the pictures. We laughed all day! We had fun doing it because we knew what we were making was outlandish and having it played in theaters is remarkable considering we shot and exposed it on 35mm. I feel really blessed as it allowed me to continue in the business and do a number of different productions.

You also made the film Insatiable *with Marilyn Chambers, which was shot in the U.K.*

I flew to London because she was performing there near Piccadilly Circus. I hired a local camera crew and I shot a load of footage and I put my passport up to rent the equipment and we got busted for shooting near Buckingham Palace! It was fun.

6

Don't Go in the House

AN INTERVIEW WITH JOSEPH ELLISON

Joseph Ellison has two feature credits to his name, the fun rock'n'roll teen drama *Joey* (1986) and the unforgettable "video nasty" *Don't Go in the House* (1979), a film of relentless horror that leaves an indelible mark on your retinas. It is a brilliantly grim and disturbing film that viewers will find hard to forget. Yet, astonishingly, that is just exactly what happened to Ellison's debut shocker. Misunderstood, dismissed and forgotten, the film was left to languish on the fringes of the genre where it has been ostracized primarily because it didn't fit in with the "rollercoaster ride" horrors that exploded during the slasher boom of the late 1970s and early '80s. While *Friday the 13th* was rich in visceral thrills and deliberate cheap scares, *Don't Go in the House* refused to adhere to these conventions. Instead it's a psychological study of pathological murder from deranged protagonist Donny. Audiences expecting a fun horror flick were instead delivered a deeply unsettling and brutal film that was graphically violent and yet artistically shot, edited and directed with a stylized mastery that audiences at the time didn't appreciate. The film was also wrongly attacked for being misogynistic which serves to show how misunderstood the film was upon release. Co-written by Ellison's wife Ellen Hammill, the film only shows one female death in graphic detail and had many female crew members working behind the scenes. It is a film that is less concerned with exploitation and gratuitous violence than with commentating on the nature of child abuse and psychological trauma.

The film centers on Donny, a psychopathic loner who has suffered a lifetime of physical abuse from his sadistic mother. Via flashbacks we see the punishment meted out to poor Donny. We witness the emotional bullying and the horrors of having his arms burned over a stove. The scars and psychological trauma have left Donny psychotic, disturbed and dangling on the precipice of sanity. Donny works at an incinerator plant where a co-worker accidentally catches fire; Donny can only stare at the flames instead of coming to the man's aid. When he is derided as a sicko by his boss, this is our introduction to the warped psychosis of our protagonist. Returning home to the creepy secluded mansion of his mother, he is pushed into insanity when he finds his mother has died. As the voices in his head take hold of his fragile mind, Donny unleashes a reign of violent terror with his hatred and rage directed towards all women who he believes are responsible for the abuse he suffered at the hands of his mother. Carefully selecting his targets, Donny first picks up his victims in his truck before braining them and stringing them up naked in a specially built metal room. Here, Donny extracts his revenge by dousing the women in gasoline before burning them with a flamethrower. We see the first victim scream in agony as she goes up in flames in a shockingly explicit sequence that has to be seen to be believed. As the charred corpses begin to stack up in his home, and Donny is tormented by his mother's rotting corpse, Ellison propels us deeper into Donny's damaged psychosis and off-kilter reality. The horrors of his childhood and his actions finally catch up with him in the film's excellent finale.

One can view *Don't Go in the House* as more than a mere psychological horror or exploitation film as the film reveals how young children can be deeply traumatized by their upbringings through psychological and physical abuse, impacting on their ability to function normally in society. This endless cycle is brilliantly captured by Ellison and depicted wonderfully in the film as Donny's mother's terrifying puritanical wrath and torture of her son is the root cause of Donny's psychopathic tendencies and misogynistic world-view in later life. In a way, the film implies that such "monsters" are a product of their early-life experiences which can shape and define them as adults and lead them down a path towards evil. Ellison elicits a certain degree of sympathy for the killer. In some regards, his mother is equally the "monster" of the film as she has defined and nurtured the creature that Donny has become. One can see Donny as a victim to some degree, but Ellison refuses to glorify his actions or deflect the blame for his murderous actions

Donny's POV as he watches his co-worker "Ben" burn in *Don't Go in the House* (courtesy Joseph Ellison).

Priest runs from house after being hit with Donny's flamethrower in *Don't Go in the House* (courtesy Joseph Ellison).

away from him. Ultimately, rightly or wrongly, Donny is still responsible. While audiences can view Donny as a victim to some degree, that does not excuse his behavior or his murderous impulses. What Ellison presents to his audience is a depraved and vile character with no redeeming factors. In a way his killing-spree is made even more sickening by the fact that the women who fall prey to him are wholesome and gentle. This makes their deaths even more repellent and detaches the audience further from Donny, making him wholly unlikable and repulsive. The death of Kathy Jordan is testament to this idea. In the film she offers Donny nothing but kindness, yet he abuses this kindness in the most heinous of ways whereby she is literally stripped of all her decency, chained up and cruelly burned alive. The burning of these women is an attack on their physical beauty. This marks Donny as one of horror's most sadistic killers.

Another facet of the film that deserves analysis is the way that Ellison pays close attention to the movements of the corpses when they come back to life. Instead of having them stagger zombie-like, Ellison stylizes their movements and actions in a manner that is reminiscent of early German Expressionist cinema, akin to that seen in *The Cabinet of Dr. Caligari* (1920) and *Nosferatu* (1922). Like those seminal films, he achieves this terrifyingly stylized effect by using low angles and shooting upwards at the "monsters," similar to what Murnau did in *Nosferatu*, in particular the legendary shot of the vampire on the *Demeter*. Their otherworldly movements imbue the film with a surrealistic element that makes the scenes with the corpses creepy and frightening.

Partly due to Stephen Thrower's in-depth text on *Don't Go in the House* in N*ightmare USA* (Fab Press), the film seems to have risen like a phoenix from the ashes. The film is now widely considered by scholars to be one of the best films from the heyday of slasher cinema. *Don't Go in the House* is a true masterwork of the genre and one of the most terrifying, disturbing and stylish horror films of the last 40 years. In April 2016 I had the pleasure of interviewing Joseph Ellison about his film and its lasting impact.

Matthew Edwards: Don't Go in the House *is one of my favorite horror movies.*

Joseph Ellison: Thank you. What is interesting is that I wasn't much of a horror film fanatic. I mean, I felt they were helpful in showing some terrible things about humankind.

I agree. Actually, I would class your movie as more of a psychological horror film.

Yes, it really is. Though a few have said that the justification was nailed on. It wasn't, it was really intrinsic to the story and it was that reason why I approached it. I should tell you that I didn't set out to make a horror film. What happened with me was, when I met my girlfriend Ellen, who was to become my wife, I was location scouting, doing some production work for a friend of mine. I had started writing a script, a wholesome story about overcoming adversity, and it wasn't going anywhere, and to be honest it wasn't particularly good. I wasn't the best writer in the world and this script had a heroic ending and was more of a social commentary. It certainly was not a horror film. When I couldn't get any money to produce that film, I was working on the movie *To Fly* [1976]—which was perhaps the first major IMAX-formatted film—for the Smithsonian Air and Space Museum. I was very proud to be working on that and I had just moved to Hollywood from New York to work on mixing it at Todd-AO. While in Hollywood I realized that I wouldn't be able to raise the money I needed to make my feature. It was frustrating. Ellen asked me, "What are we going to do now?" We were out of luck, out of ideas, and I said, "We'll go back to New York and make a horror film." She said, "You're crazy!" I came to this realization because there were only two types of movies you could make on a low budget that could be released in the theaters and stood any chance of getting a real audience. That was either a sexy comedy where you showed some nudity, which I wasn't interested in and refused to do—I guess I'm kind of a prude [*laughs*]—or the other way which was to do a horror film! I felt if I could find something that was "classic horror" that was visually exciting, then I could get into it and approach it as an artist. I was interested in Gothic and Expressionist horror and had studied German Expressionist filmmaking from the early days of film, which had a lot of entries in the horror genre. Films like *The Cabinet of Dr. Caligari*, *Nosferatu*, even Murnau's *Sunrise* [1927]—which isn't a horror film. I was really taken with early German silent cinema and a lot of it was either horror or suspense. So I guess I glorified the idea and went back to New York to find the sickest script I could find and make a horror film out of it.

Joe Masefield at the time was a film editor who worked in a suite of production offices where I worked. He had an idea which sounded promising. I think he brought in a treatment the next day and it was in a blue plastic binder. The treatment was called *The Burning Man*, and right away it had a visual effect on me. I thought of fire and ice. Then on reading it, I felt the treatment had some amazing stuff in it. It made sense on some level. It was basically a story of a really scarred young man who had been burnt by his mother on a stove for punishment as a child. When I read it, a couple of things rang a bell. I had been doing a lot of sound work and I thought I could use this experience in the film by using sound to enrich the piece. Then I could bring other qualities to the film from the other skills that I possessed. So I was excited by that prospect and that I had a control of the visuals. I felt I could make this work with the tools I already had.

How did you set about raising money?

I approached a few people and I remember one guy, who was a stranger to me, said, "You are here asking me for money. I'm a businessman and I've raised money for my projects. I am going to tell you what they told me: If you can't raise money from your own family and friends, then you can't raise money from anybody. You should be telling people what's in it for them and why it is a good idea. And if it's not a good idea, you will be able to determine that." I thought that was good advice. So I decided to approach people that I knew and ask them. I did think [the proposed movie] was good idea and that people would want to see it. An unusual, very sick horror film. This kind of movie was filling theaters across the country then. Eventually I went to friends and family and I would look them in the eye and say, "I am going to make this movie and if I am alive when it's finished, you will have your money back." I put it that way to them. I knew there were dangers I wasn't aware of yet. I was smart enough to know that but dumb enough to not let it stop me. I was positive of that despite the advice from everyone like: "Don't start making the film until you have the money to finish it." Or, "Make sure you have a distributor before you shoot anything." All good advice but I never would have done anything. My friends, family and even a few strangers could tell I wasn't kidding and was a do-or-die kind of person. Still, most said "No!" [*Laughs*]

The budget was around $250,000, correct?

Well, yeah, but we didn't spend anything like that amount. All we ended up with was around $100,000 in cash and we got plenty of deferments as some people were willing to wait, even though we might not be able to ever pay them back. Some just wanted to be involved. Others wouldn't do anything without being paid. They had been around filmmaking long enough to know how the distributors make it impossible to get any profits out of a film.

Ellen and I drove around in my pick-up truck every weekend to Staten Island, New Jersey, upstate New York, to look for locations. It was hard as most places weren't suitable, and when we *did* find a good location, we didn't have the cash to secure it or they didn't want us bothering them. They thought we were just kids or that we were going to rip them off. Actually, in hindsight, I could have done things this way or that, but I do think my naiveté was a saving grace in the making of this movie. Although I didn't have all the answers, I was moving in the right direction. And when we turned a corner that gray day in Atlantic Highlands, New Jersey, we both gasped. This was it! A dilapidated Victorian mansion at the top of the hill, a frightening mess. We had to have it. We walked in and there was barely a place to step. Furniture, car parts, engine blocks and carburetors! I recognized an Alfa Romeo valve cover. It was an indoor junkyard. Under the junk? Inlaid polished hardwood floors. The man of the house liked it just the way it was but when we told his wife that our crew would have to move everything off the floors and up to the hidden attic, she said "Wonderful." He balked. We offered to put it all back the way it was but she said, "No! That's all right. Just leave it all up there." We offered them what we could. They seemed thrilled to have it.

But we had some really weird goings-on in that house. For one thing, no heat in zero degree weather. A prop glass of water on the night table froze solid during a dinner break one night. The man of the house got tired of having an entire film crew in his home *all the time.* Who wouldn't? But I did have to disarm him one night as he pointed a loaded rifle at me and others. As I alluded to before, you would've had to shoot me to get me to abandon this project.

But you needed that passion to get the film made. You had so many obstacles in your way from the get-go. You had to raise the money yourself. Without that passion, the film would have never happened.

Exactly.

How did you set about casting?

The most important casting job was the lead. After that, you had to have people who were believable but there were no *tour de force* supporting acting roles.

I understand that lead actor Dan Grimaldi was offered the part after you had seen him in an off-Broadway play.

That's true. Dan and I were good friends but I didn't plan it that he was going to play that role. He was dying to do it but I didn't really see him as the character. I was much more interested in the actor being a skinny blond guy, with a quivering look, someone who was easily undone by themselves. Dan wasn't that type. But what I found instead in Dan was the guy who works in the incinerator. He is just an average American guy. Nobody knows what's going on between his ears. He told me a year or so later that someone approached him outside the theater where *House* was playing and said, "I feel like that sometimes." Danny said it really gave him the creeps.

Johanna Brushay plays the first victim, the kindly flower shop owner Kathy Jordan. She was brilliant in the film, giving such a terrific and sympathetic performance. Did she have any reservations about appearing naked in the film while tied up and burned alive?

She loved taking her clothes off, she was a Playboy Bunny! Ellen took good care of her—Johanna was her friend. She just had fun making the movie.

Talk me through the filming of "the metal room" scene. Did you find it difficult to shoot that knowing that you had to be deliberately explicit as audiences would be expecting this?

The scene had to be explicit as the story, script and, yes, market demanded that it be. It took months of research and tests to make that work. It was extremely difficult but simple in design. There were two stages and a 45-degree glass. It reflected the fire but also showed the other non-fire stage. The fire stage had a dummy that could be moved to match the actresses' movements. Meanwhile, the actress screamed and moved on the other stage a hundred or more feet from the flames. Looking through the lens of the Arri 35mm, the effect came together. My brain believed *twice* that we were actually murdering our actress. I had to glance up to make sure that my eyes were deceiving me. Yep, she was fine. That effect is completely believable.

Some viewers find Kathy's death sequence the most repulsive, yet I find the second death scene more terrifying. It's is a masterful example of sublime editing and beautiful shot composition. For me personally, it is the most horrifying element of the film for the audience now sees that Donny's kindness is a façade for his homicidal tendencies. When we see her climb into the pick-up truck to the next shot of her smoldering corpse, it is a moment that ranks alongside the best of the genre.

I wanted the first death scene to be very explicit and uncomfortable for the audience. I wanted it to be really upsetting. I made that scene with a vengeance. I wanted the first murder to be: "You want this, you really want this? Well, here you are." In part it was a personal statement that I didn't really want to do a horror movie but it was also a B movie and it had to deliver where a studio couldn't or wouldn't. Studio movies in those days were not delivering movies that were so horrific or explicit, as they were the studios. They didn't do that. They didn't have to. They had a higher budget and didn't need to. It was left to the independents to show the underbelly of filmmaking. I gave everything for that scene. There it was for everyone to gawk at. I think the reason you like that scene so much, and that it works so well for you, is because you already have the explicit death to the nth degree, and you have seen what happens to these people. So here you are watching the set-up and we could have gone into the nuances of that but I didn't see the need for it. I felt I would be wasting our time. I think had we shown her murder, then it would have been gratuitous. That is not the point of the scene. The point of the scene is to show he has become a serial killer. It's what he lives to do. Why bother getting into the nuances?, this is not what the movie is about. I could have done that and we could explored whether they were or not "worthy" of being murdered like some of the slasher movies. There are a lot of things that could have been done differently but that's not how this film was constructed.

You were right in not showing the explicit death again. You say it all so perfectly in the way you edit that scene. I found it more horrifying that when she got into the pick-up truck, we knew the fate that would befall her. Sometimes you don't have to show the horror. In my mind, it was horrifying enough.

Exactly. In fact, you get the introduction to who this man is and why he acts in this way. Yes it is a little linear and perhaps too straightforward and open, but on the other hand it is set up and there it is, this is what you can expect from him. So the point becomes: Here he is, here is what he is doing, what's going to happen and how is it going to work itself out? It's more dramatic irony than mystery. Clearly we are not going to watch hours and hours of him killing people. What I was interested in was where this was going and how it was going to resolve. So this is the second step in that sequence. It is not Hitchcockian, is it? Hitchcock would say, "You want to know if she is going to be saved or not." Hitchcock favors suspense verses shock. And he's of course right. But in our case, it was shock. There is no suspense here. Once she steps into the car, her fate is sealed. I have set it up in that way by virtue of the first murder. And now he has a collection of these people. His new friends! And *that's* when the suspense begins, I believe.

If you ask me, the most frustrating part of the final product is that a lot of the footage of him talking to the women, and their responses—I had them talking to him and you could hear their responses—it is missing now. We cut it down because too many people were saying that the picture was too long. It wasn't falling in with the type of horror films that people were watching in those days. It wasn't a rollercoaster or adventure ride for a date. It was a dark and disturbing psychotic experience and there was no time for some of this unnecessary exposition. That's what a lot of people felt. At the time, we were running out of money and trying to get the picture finished. We needed to get the money back to our investors and we needed to meet deadlines to show the film at festivals. You start to make decisions based on other things, aside from pure aesthetics. Ellen and I would have fights because I wasn't finishing scenes on time and over things she didn't think worked in the film. We never argued at all, and all of a sudden we were clashing over the movie. We were crazy about each other and we never had had an argument but now we were arguing constantly. She would say, "You're only going to have half a movie!" To which I replied in my youthful grandiosity, "Well, it's going to be a beautiful half a movie!" She'd say, "You'll never get it finished if you work like this." She was a natural as a producer, despite having no experience of working with a crew, and she helped get the film done—her background was in the art world where she oversaw the production of famous artists' prints of their originals. But she knew nothing about how to get a film completed. She stepped in when Joe Masefield backed out. She said, "Who is going to produce this movie now?" I said, "You are!" She did a great job but it came at a cost of a certain flavor of our relationship, which is a shame. On the other hand, she did such a great job that we managed to finish the movie. A whole movie, titles, music and all.

Another reason for the way we truncated that death scene wasn't just budgetary. I wanted to move to the next phase of this film. You have the trauma of Donny's mother's death, and then his reaction to that, before his devolving into complete insanity. He had evidently been deeply disturbed for many years—they call him a sicko at work, and we have that scene at the beginning where he stands by and watches someone burn. He is a disturbed person to begin with, from what he had been through, and now he is losing his mind completely, so what he is going to do with these corpses? How is he going to interact with them? I wanted to move the film forward and get on to that part. I also wanted to develop the interaction between the corpses and Donny, and how that worked, which is pretty bizarre [*laughs*]! But I really miss what you didn't see and what you don't know even exists which are these incredible conversations with the women, and he kisses one of them. It is an example of fun and inventive filmmaking, like the bit when he slaps one of the corpses for laughing at him, or the POV of the corpse in the rocking chair, which suggests this may be real. Some people have argued with me about that, saying the point is that Donny is crazy. It is his POV, how could you do that? He's the one that is crazy! It isn't really true if a corpse is looking at him. "What a stupid argument," I thought. First of all, it's only a movie and yes, it is an insane world, and yes, these corpses are alive, the whole thing is upside down and crazy. I suppose I stole from Carol Reed, my hero. Everything was off axis in *The Third Man* [1949] because the whole deal, the whole world was crooked. It didn't have to be from Harry Lime's point of view or Holly Martins' point of view, the world was that way. I thought this was a similar thing in that the whole world was crazy.

I love that POV shot. Did you have to fight to keep that in the final cut or did you have the artistic freedom to keep it in?

I was the last word on everything. If I had to go and work loading trucks, I would have done it to pay my investors back, as I wanted to pay everyone back. That's how I raised the money, therefore I had no boss, per se. My bosses were time constraints, lack of money and a desire, a necessity to pay people back and to get the movie out. So reality was my boss. For me, it was a question of how I could get this done properly. I also wanted to make something that was valid and worthy. So I tried to be objective as well as subjective. I guess my objectivity became my boss too, which can hurt you. You can end up doing the wrong thing to try to please all of the people. And as I was saying before, when you have a movie which isn't a rollercoaster ride, a movie that's not just entertainment, a movie that disappoints people, it is too bad! When the film opened, you had *Friday the 13th* in the multiplexes on one screen and *Don't Go in the House* on another. You had the kids screaming and hugging each other when watching *Friday the 13th*, but they weren't screaming and hugging each other when watching *Don't Go in the House*. They were sitting there in absolute horror. They were disturbed and upset. This was not a good date movie!

We ran out of funds several times. Once I had to dub a kung fu film into English right in he middle of post. The negative's at the lab, the work print's sitting in a cutting room and I don't have money to pay an editor. Eventually I paid the editor from my earnings and other money I could raise. One person who was in a lot of financial trouble, needed his money back urgently. That's a story I don't wish to talk about here, as it is an amazing, frightening story—more frightening than the movie! Anyway, I managed to handle the situation and nobody was hurt. Everyone got their money back but what happened to make this movie was really stunning. It is a miracle it got done. Put it this way, when I told my investors that I would repay them if I was still alive, I didn't intend that as a melodramatic statement. It was an accurate assessment and a truthful disclosure and that was a reason why they might not be paid back. But I was alive and all the investors were paid back when it was over. *Don't Go in the House* made money so I was able to pay everyone back from the receipts of the film. That is a miracle because you don't get paid on independent films. Whenever you don't get paid a salary, or up front on a movie, you

Don't Go in the House's **Producer Ellen Hammill pointing at the word "pray" on a phone booth while director Joseph Ellison phones for dollars (courtesy Joseph Ellison).**

don't get paid. Some people thought I got rich, which is ridiculous. I made what would average out to be a salary for a while and payback for my personal money (earnings, really) that I put in. But when the film made "millions," even some good friends thought I was getting paid "millions." Baloney. The distributor was making the money. If I hadn't gone on to make another movie, and indeed loaded trucks again as a stagehand and Teamster which is where I started in "show biz," I wouldn't have had anything.

You talked about the death sequences and the parts where Donny befriends the girls that he kills, I feel that one of the areas the film succeeds in is that you care about the victims, which is not always the case in horror films. This makes the killings even more shocking. Was it your intention to make the girls all likable and sympathetic characters?

Very much so. The tendency in horror films is that the girls are punished for having sex with their boyfriends. That became part of the style, part of the genre. You've got these naughty girls having sex, doing what they are not supposed to be doing, and that's one justification for why they get killed. In *Don't Go in the House*, it makes no sense whatsoever. They certainly don't deserve to be killed. Who deserves to be murdered by a psycho? I don't see that. I didn't intentionally set out to make them likable, but they were nice people who would help you out. Still they are burned alive.

I think this element makes the film frightening as it seems so true-to-life and there is a reality about the killer and the victims.

Thank you. I agree, but I will also say that it's linear and you could say that he was burned by his mother so he burns his victims. So often a person who is treated that way is a victim. I did a lot of research and one critic accused me of having some cheap justification for the exploitation by having the child abuse theme in the film. I have to say that a lot of work was done to study the effects of child abuse on people and what happens to them as a result and how they respond. Some do respond as the victimizer. There are small touches that are missed in my film. An example is when one of the girls runs for the bus. We went to an awful lot of trouble to put an advertisement on the back of the bus, which you will barely see unless you pause or freeze-frame the film and blow it up big, which shows a picture of a child with a tear, having cried, and it says, "It shouldn't hurt to be a child." I don't know if you are familiar with that campaign, but it was hugely successful here in the U.S. and that was the phrase. It became a classic. We tried, and failed in many cases, to infuse that theme of child abuse into the film. Of course, the last scene does that with the little boy, when we see the woman overacting while trying to wash up her kitchen and having her child not listening to her, and she slaps the dog shit out of him. We then see that the boy hears imaginary voices talking to him, to imply that the circle of abuse continues. It is true and it does happen. For some people, it was perhaps too realistic.

Also, it was my intent that the killer was not someone to emulate or to find glamorous. On the contrary, you see him as a coward, aside from the lucky punch he gives that guy in the parking lot and knocks the guy out—that bit is a little silly and audiences tend to get a laugh out of it because it is such a lucky punch and not realistic at all. But the fact is, it was intended to not show Donny as a powerful and an attractive murderer who is sexy in any way. Vampires are sexy, we all know this as there is this sexy theme that they are attractive and they woo and seduce their victims. Certainly this was nothing like that. This was supposed to be a cowardly and disturbed person who needed psychiatric help.

There is nothing likable about Donny at all. You can sympathize with the character and understand that his upbringing has shaped him. That central theme of young children being deeply traumatized by their upbringing through psychological and physical abuse which then impacts on their ability to function normally in society is very true.

I can understand why some viewers may sympathize with Donny, and see him as the victim, and you should, but you also see him as a person who needs to be stopped. He is so far gone and is in need of psychiatric care. There is nothing sexy about him.

The film implies that these monsters tend to be a product of their early life experiences and how this shapes and defines them into adulthood and this leads them down the path towards evil. That's the way I read it, and I am not justifying his actions, but you see this so many times—I believe kids don't set out to be bad. Were you looking to explore this idea?

Yes, most definitely. We factored this into the movie. We studied it and talked about it. We read about it. There was no internet at the time, but we called experts and got reports about it. We studied this concept in depth and it was an important part of the movie. We wanted it to be accurate as it was the background to this monster. It's a bit like when Bruce Banner gets exposed to radiation and turns into the Hulk, this little boy is exposed to extreme brutality and becomes a monster as a result. There are stories of people like Jeffrey Dahmer, and other mass murderers, mutilators, who don't seem to have an excuse for their crimes. The people who adopted these children had no such stories to tell, and didn't do anything to these kids. They claimed nothing was done to them, and they are shocked when they find out as there were never any problems. Yes, of course, it doesn't have to be neat and dressed up like a package. But we wanted to have this element in the film.

The killings in the metal room seem to have a cinematic connection to Psycho *[1960]. Was that intentional?*

A lot of people compared my movie to *Psycho* because of that scene and other elements. Of course, I wasn't imitating *Psycho.* How could I have? They are very different movies and I don't claim to be Hitchcock. But I will say that the metal room scene was influenced by the shower scene. It is in the original treatment. Structurally the scene also appears at roughly the same time as the shower scene does in *Psycho.* Like *Psycho,* it is an explicit scene—obviously ours more so, as it was a different time and era—and I felt when you were making a B movie that you had to deliver certain things. In Hitchcock's case, he made the film in black-and-white, of course, because of that scene.

I understand that the charred corpses were played by dancers.

First of all, I did a lot of work studying how to achieve the makeup on those charred corpses. There were many different ways to do that, and I did a lot of research, and I ended up using the image of a charred G.I. sticking out of the turret of a Sherman tank during World War II as my inspiration. In terms of personnel, that was easy for me. I hired women from the Harkness Ballet, whom I had worked with before. They were young trainees who were thrilled to be in a movie. God, they were troupers! They were only 18 or 19 years old, and they had no idea what they were in for. Do you remember the dream sequence where the corpses jump out of the hole at the ocean? Well, those girls were in that hole—which took us all day to dig, by the way—*all* day. It was frozen ground, as it was one of the coldest winters for over 100 years. It was unbelievably cold. And we shot that scene in January and they came leaping out at Donny. There were a

Rise of the corpses in the horrifying finale of *Don't Go in the House* (courtesy Joseph Ellison).

couple of things that I knew about them: one was that they didn't have to talk but, two, they did have to move in a special way. Also, they had to be troupers and dancers are troupers! They were strong and did all their scenes without a single complaint. They were wonderful. To this day, they have my admiration.

The visual style of the film is sensational. Beautifully framed composition shots give way to Expressionist angles or titled camera that seem to further enforce the notion that the world-view of the protagonist is warped. When Donny is interacting in the world, everything seems normal, but as soon as he steps into his home the visual feel of the film changes and becomes otherworldly.

There was nothing subtle about the way I approached the visual style and I wasn't trying to be. It was clear that he was insane and that's the way he saw the world and things. And of course it was great fun shooting in that way.

The visual look seemed inspired by German Expressionism.

The film was, to an extent, but the Carol Reed films were more of an influence with the off-angle shots. Someone once said that they would buy Carol Reed a level for Christmas so that he could keep his camera straight. Some find that approach to filmmaking over-the-top, or too obvious … baloney! It is fabulous, fun and what filmmaking is all about. Very few people bothered to do it and if you did, you would have to be very careful how you cut the movie and how you set it up. There are lots of things to be concerned about when you shoot a film in that manner.

Some critics can be very snobbish towards horror cinema and cannot see the clever aesthetics at work. I actually believe that Don't Go in the House *was ahead of its time, hence now it is being re-evaluated by film scholars as a classic of horror cinema.*

What, my film? Wow, that is wonderful to hear. I really appreciate that. This isn't just my ego, but I did feel at the time that people weren't getting the picture. I felt very frustrated when the movie came out because people were just comparing it to films like *Friday the 13th*, but I don't really know what *Friday the 13th* has, other than the standpoint of this rollercoaster ride of murder, that mine doesn't. I see the value of *Carrie* [1976], and that is a very smart film. I don't see *Friday the 13th* in the same light as I do *Carrie*. But it certainly was a successful franchise with an "all-powerful" killer.

Director Joseph Ellison directing the epilogue scene of *Don't Go in the House* **(courtesy Joseph Ellison).**

I actually think your film is better and more stylishly shot.

This is going to sound terrible but I totally agree with you [*laughs*]. Oliver Wood shot *Don't Go in the House*, and he is one of the best cinematographers in the world. [Editor's note: Wood went on to work on *Die Hard 2* (1990), *Face Off* (1997), *The Bourne Identity* (2002), *The Bourne Supremacy* (2004), *The Bourne Ultimatum* (2007), *Anchorman 2: The Legend Continues* (2013) and *Ben-Hur* (2016).] He is quite a talent. When I met him, I had already hired another D.P. but he wasn't really interested in shooting the movie so I was glad when that person left for California. I was free to hire Oliver. He and I are still good friends, despite my leaving the business. Ellen often says that I should have just shut up and gone ahead and made slasher-type films, that they wanted me to make, but I refused because they wouldn't let me do it my way. I just didn't see the sense.

I can understand why you didn't want to pursue those types of films as some slasher films follow the simple formula of a bunch of college kids getting killed by a masked killer. THE END!

You have just written one, now go ahead and make it [*laughs*]! And I had an offer of such a movie and I turned it down. Ellen is certain that if I had done that, then my whole film career could have taken off. I did have another idea for a movie called *Scary Movie*, because I didn't want to make a horror film, but one that was a send-up of horror films. That was the title and the concept! Ellen and I wrote an entire script and registered it with the WGA. Honestly! I had William Morris wanting to sign me but they couldn't get anyone interested in my idea. They never did it so I was really infuriated, which was a shame. Decades later I see my idea making hundreds of millions as a franchise. Oh, well…

Where did you find the asbestos suit that Donny wears in the film?

Amazingly enough, I grew up looking at that asbestos suit in a window of a nearby store. They dressed a mannequin outside the store wearing it. Kaufman's Surplus, which was on 42nd Street, if I recall. And they had cartridge boxes and Army and Navy surplus gear. I saw that suit when I was a child and they never sold it. It was used by the Navy to put out fires on board ship. Of course they have stuff made of Nomex now, so it's less clunky. Asbestos is not good for you!

I understand Dan Grimaldi kept it after filming.

Yes, we gave it to him. We thought he had earned it!

After you had finished filming, how did you set about marketing the feature?

It was really episodic. The first step was to screen it for a small independent distributor that I knew. It wasn't fully finished at that point. It was roughly edited, not mixed, just work track, and we hadn't added in all the sound or effects. The distributor fell asleep 20 minutes into the film and started snoring loudly. We all thought, "Oh my God, oh my God." It was a really depressing afternoon. But that particular distributor always fell asleep during screenings. After that we were unsure with what we had. We screened it next for Paramount; by then, we had a finished composite print. We brought it up ourselves with our two ICC shipping cases. Ellen and I sat outside the screening room in the waiting area as they were watching it. When you're not sophisticated, you do crazy things. After the showing, they came out and said, "Oh, you're still here!" I said, "Yes, we were going to take the print with us, unless you need it?" And they said, "Who else have you shown it to?" and we said, "No one." They said, "We would be interested in hearing what other

In a steel room built for revenge they die burning ... in chains. Apex's VHS video sleeve of *Don't Go in the House*.

people think." They didn't know what to make of it! They were shocked and they didn't know what to do with the nudity in the film. It was so much fun seeing their reaction. They were so shocked and upset by it. And instead of saying, "Yes, we want this movie and we will pay anything you want, here's five million dollars," instead we got this confused and bemused look from them which implied, "What are you still doing here?" They said to us that they would be interested in hearing what other people think of the movie and "feel free to come back" once you have shown it to some other distributors. Isn't that an amazing reaction?! But that's what the industry is like. When you get all these big shots who don't know what to make of something, then they miss it. Nobody ever got fired for saying no to a movie but on the other hand, if they are missing something, and this is a new trend, then they like to be there. So they wanted to know what other distributors thought of the film and then wanted us to go back to them before making any deals. That's what they were saying.

So who ultimately picked up the film?

We had no offers and we were terrified. We had the movie finished, titles and everything. We had shown it to a couple of other distributors after Paramount who said "No thanks." Remember, I owe all these investors their money and vendors as well; the sound houses, etc. It was a frightening place to be. I didn't know where to go with this. Then a couple of independent filmmakers in New York told me what I needed to do was take it to Milan and hang out. I had an agent who I had re-done a lot of movies for, the ones Tarantino likes, and I would re-write the script and dub them into English. Kung fu and karate movies, Italian horror and action films, etc. I went to him and told him that I had this horror film. He paid for me to ship him a print. Once he saw it, he said he would be happy to represent the movie. He would set up screenings at MIFED in Milan. He set up one screening in October of 1979 and one or two people said to us that we would get a U.S. distributor in Milan. "You will be one of the few American movies there and you will get people's attention." I went there—even though we were completely out of money. A friend of mine was a waiter at the Ginger Man in New York. I used to leave him huge tips when things were going well, and I was completely broke and we would go in there for a steak dinner and he would cross out the tip amount and give me and Ellen a steak to split and a bottomless gin glass for me on the rocks. Ellen didn't drink. Then happily hand me a bill for $19.98. He was supposed to invest in the movie but his wife wouldn't let him, so this was his way of helping out. That was the shape we were in. We didn't even have any food money! Another friend of mine lent me money so I could go to Milan and try to sell the film, but he wanted to come too. I said he was more than welcome. So we all went to Milan and our screening was on Thursday (MIFED was one week long) and we start hanging out and my agent started doing deals with all kinds of people. He sold the rights to Argentina for $5000, who knows what for Sri Lanka! I could see actual deals being made and I was thinking "Oh my God, I can actually pay some people." For a while I had thought I might not be able to sell it to anyone. Now I felt the tide was turning.

    We went into the screening room and people started coming in and the theater started filling up. It was full. So we left, to allow more people to see it. Outside, we saw more people filing into the theater and our agent was acting like a Japanese conductor on a subway. He was pushing people inside and was trying to close the doors behind the people going in. They all watched the entire movie, bar two people from Sweden because they couldn't have violence and nudity in the same film. They could have violence and they could have nudity, but not both together! That was explained to me by these two blond guys. When the film was over, the screening room doors burst open and I had about 20 people running at me. I used to do work for Bob Shaye in those days, dubbing Sonny Chiba films for his company, and he was in there. And he said, "Can we talk later?" So he walked away and I was being pulled by people from all over the world, from Italy, Germany, America and people from the big independent distributors. As I was standing there talking to a friend of mine from Rome, a principal in a production company, my agent came over to me and said that he wanted me to talk to a Mr. Montoro but I had no idea who this was, so I carried on talking. Suddenly he grabbed my arm and he guided me over to meet Mr. Montoro and his associate, who was very interested in my movie. We went for lunch and proceeded to talk about the film and they said they wanted to change the title from *The Burning* to *Don't Go in the House*. He said, "I am looking for a movie to put that title on. I have the title and a campaign and I am ready to go. I know just what to do with this film and how to sell it and make a lot of money for you." He said the film was very well done and finished properly. He said he wanted it! I said, "Thank you, Jesus!" This was unbelievable. Finally, somebody was going to help us get out of the hole and we could pay people and maybe have some money left over." We were so relieved and excited. I had an offer from Film Ventures. Soon I was getting other offers, though Bob Shaye didn't have enough money. That's funny to think of now, as he went on to create the big version of New Line Cinema. We thought we had a great deal, though I refused to give Film Ventures anything other than U.S. and Canadian rights. And thank God I did because otherwise I would have been completely ripped off. The only money I ever saw from Mr. Montoro was the advance and then when he needed the footage for TV. I withheld that until he gave me some more money so I could pay the IRS and the production companies. Thank goodness there were other sales being made where I could pay off the investors and the deferments we had.

When we walked into the sound company where I had mixed the movie, the owner said he was amazed! He was amazed with two things: He was amazed that we got the money and amazed that we had paid him and he didn't have to chase us for it! People thought we were stupid. People thought our honesty was moronic! I thought, "Are we doing something here that we shouldn't?" We were paying our bills. The interesting thing is that I don't think they actually liked us succeeding. I got the impression that they would have preferred it if we had failed. There is something very sick about it in that they would have preferred it if you had failed. While some others thought we had made *millions* and Ellen and I were hoarding it all for ourselves. That was hard to take. We tried to give *more* than we had to. I guess they have conspiracy theories. *Variety* says "$10M." We must've gotten at least a million of that, right? Ridiculous! We couldn't get another dime out of the distributor.

During the making of the film, we bought the rights to a disco song that became a big hit, "Struck by Boogie Lightning" by L'Ectrique. We wanted to get "Disco Inferno" by the Trammps but that was too big. Regarding "Boogie Lightning," we got near to the end of wrapping up the picture. We were mixing in the studio and the engineer put on this song and Ellen and I thought, "Oh my God, where have you been hiding this? This belongs in the movie. We want this music." I listened to the other tracks and they were much better than the tracks that I had recorded for the film. So we ended up using a mixture of both, as some of our tracks were good. We bought them and the deal was no money up front, but I forget how much (but a lot) on first day of release. Well, when the movie opened, we called them up and we had to remind them of who we were. "We made the movie *Don't Go in the House* which we used your music in…!" They didn't know who the hell we were!

We opened the movie on Memorial Day, which is a huge weekend. There are a lot of big movies that open up on that day. So we had to remind them we had a deal and that we had to pay them and where to send the check. They laughed hysterically and thought it was a joke! The guy said that we had restored his faith in human nature. So he told us his address and Ellen sent him the check for the music. This is the reaction we got when we were successful! No one was expecting us to be and nobody was expecting to get paid.

What was the general reaction to the film from cinemagoers?
We went from theater to theater and you could hear a pin drop. There wasn't a sound. When the movie opened up in New York, we drove around and went to the Bronx. There was a huge line outside the cinema, and only two movies showing, and Ellen jumped out of the truck and asked them what film they were waiting to see and they said *Don't Go in the House*. They were waiting for our movie! There were plenty of people going to see it but there was nobody yelling or screaming when watching it. I remember

one night I was sitting next to three girls who had gone to see the film and when it was over, after the shot of the little boy with tears in his eyes, as the credits rolled, one of the girls, who was almost in tears herself, said, "Oh, that was awful!" I took that comment to heart. I still remember it almost 40 years later. Now I sort of know what she meant. It wasn't a critique of the movie I don't think so much as she thought it was terrible, the abuse these children had to endure and what it did to them. The whole thesis of the film. I think that's what she meant and I am not flattering myself. I don't think she meant it as the film was awfully made, a terrible piece of crap movie. There were people who did think that, by the way. "Lurid junk" was what one reporter called it. Some didn't see any art in the movie whatsoever. They didn't think it was artistic but merely exploitation. I knew that without that scene in the metal room, I might not have gotten a release. The

Brilliantly creepy German poster artwork of Joseph Ellison's *Don't Go in the House*.

picture might not have gone out. To bring in an audience, the explicit nature of that scene was important. In order for them to see your movie and not Steven Spielberg's, you better give them something they can't get in a Spielberg picture. Spielberg isn't delivering scenes involving naked women being burned in a metal room! For a while I was ashamed of the movie and I didn't want my daughter to see it. I was always worried it would turn people into psychotic killers! That's pretty silly to consider. Now, compared to the movies that are released today, this is tame. There are torture movies that the studios are putting out now.

What further film projects were you offered?

Exactly the type that I never wanted to make. Slice-and-dice they used to call it, for laughs. It wasn't funny. But I wanted to do that comedy. And when it came out so many years later after I had shopped it all over town, it made me remember vividly why I had left that world.

I thought it would really be horrible to leave filmmaking. It's been my redemption. I've been able to write and produce more original music and support my family from my "day job." But I wouldn't trade the experience and challenge of making *Don't Go in the House* for anything!

The film is now considered a classic of its genre with high profile fans such as Quentin Tarantino.

I do have mixed feelings. I never wanted to make suffering entertainment. When I go to shows or the cinema and we see people being shot, hurt or murdered, we don't want to watch that. It's not my thing. We'd rather watch a sensitive drama. I comfort myself with the fact that people are seeing what I thought was my artistic expression in this movie. It is very important that this is recognized. I really did feel those juices flowing and I want the readers to know that I wasn't simply making an exploitation piece to make money. This was an expression of my artistry and I wanted people to recognize that. Yes, sure, it was a low-budget film that we sold and made some money on, but the idea was that it was art. That's what I wanted people to see.

7

Alone in the Dark and *The Hidden*

AN INTERVIEW WITH JACK SHOLDER

Jack Sholder is one of the most underrated genre filmmakers of the last 30 years. With an impressive résumé that includes such classic horrors such as *A Nightmare on Elm Street 2: Freddy's Revenge* (1985), the cult favorite action-crime flick *Renegades* (1989) and the blinding genre-morphing science fiction horror classic *The Hidden* (1987), he should be a bigger name in the horror community. What is a bigger travesty is that his debut feature, the brilliant 1982 slasher film *Alone in the Dark*, has slipped into obscurity, despite it being technically superior and scarier than some of the humdrum horror films widely available and talked about by horror fans. The film, starring cinematic legends Jack Palance, Donald Pleasence and Martin Landau, revolves around a quartet of homicidal psychopaths who escape from their mental institution during a blackout and set about hunting down their psychiatrist. While the violence is more restrained than other slasher entries, this gem is rich in atmosphere, black humor and a foreboding sense of the macabre as our deranged pack of murderers slip back into the real world only to find that they are not as crazy as those who are on the outside. Peppered with a series of visceral death scenes and startling jumps, *Alone in the Dark* is a low-budget slasher that those in the horror fraternity looking for something different should seek out. But what marks the film is Sholder's characterization of his psychopaths, humanizing them while offering a damning critique on society, and asking who is truly sane in this crazy world.

In December 2015 I had the pleasure of speaking to Sholder. He talked in depth about *Alone in the Dark* and the award-winning *The Hidden*, in which Kyle MacLachlan plays an FBI agent, teamed with homicide detective (Michael Nouri) as they hunt an alien parasite that possesses human life forms as it goes on a violent rampage in L.A.

Matthew Edwards: *You are best known for your work in the horror genre.*

Jack Sholder: Honestly, I am not a big horror film fan. Basically, I wanted to be Jean Renoir. I always considered myself a humanist filmmaker and one who was influenced by the French New Wave. I never saw myself as someone who directed horror films. I had a long association with New Line Cinema. I started out cutting trailers for them and I was best friends with the guy who ran the company, a gentleman called Robert Shaye. At that point they had primarily been involved in distribution but not film production. They understood the youth market so well that they thought if they could make a low-budget horror film, they could clean up. This was around the time of *Friday the 13th* and *Halloween*. So I came up with the idea of *Alone in the Dark* and they said fine. It was always my plan to direct films. I had written scripts but they were influenced by the French New Wave in the '60s. I saw this as a chance to direct so I concocted a story inspired by a giant blackout that happened in New York City, where I was living. We had no power for three days. There were these stories that during the blackout, people started looting. Now it is commonplace, but back then, it felt as if society was breaking down.

I was also inspired by R.D. Laing, a Scottish psychiatrist who wrote extensively on mental illness. His point was that people who were psychotic had merely adjusted to a crazy world. That struck me as a wacky idea. So, all those things inspired the script of *Alone in the Dark*. It is definitely a slasher film. It is more than a conventional horror film. Actually, *Alone in the Dark* is very similar to *Straw Dogs* [1971], in that it has a guy trapped in a house with a band of people outside. I have to say that *Straw Dogs* didn't influence me at all when I was writing it. So I had this incentive that if I could come up with a good enough story in that genre, I might be able to direct my first feature film. That's basically what happened.

You were the editor on Tony Maylam's controversial slasher The Burning *[1981]. How did working on that film help you when directing* Alone in the Dark?

It helped me a lot because I had seen a bunch of horror films. I went with Robert Shaye to watch the first *Friday the 13th* movie. That film made a lot of money. So I had an understanding of the genre and how these films worked. Also, as a kid I used to watch the creature features on television, like *The Mummy* [1932] and *Frankenstein* [1931]. You know, the old-fashioned horror movies. *The Burning* was a highly original idea at the time: a psychotic murderer in a summer camp. No one had thought of that one before! It was an attempt by the filmmakers to figure out everything that made money in horror films and put them all into one script. While editing the picture, I learned a lot about building scares and how to build suspense and tension. I also learned the difference between suspense and surprise.

After editing The Burning, *did you tweak your own script?*

I had written the script for *Alone in the Dark*, which they liked, but they weren't able to raise the money. Then I got the job editing *The Burning*. After working on the movie, I really felt that I knew the genre so much better and I went back and rewrote the script, taking what I had learned during the editing of that film. It was basically the same but it had a lot more scares and better suspense and tension. Whether it was due to the rewrite, or that things just fell into place, a year later the movie got funded.

What were the major differences in the scripts? I have read elsewhere that the initial premise included the Mafia.

My original pitch was that a bunch of psychotic and criminally insane people escaped from a mental hospital in New York City during a blackout and were rounded up by the Mafia after they terrorized people in Little Italy. It is similar to Fritz Lang's *M* [1931], where all the criminals decide that the child molester is hurting business so they all band together to capture him. It is a film that I knew well so if there was anything I stole from Lang, then it was probably that element. Before I ever wrote the first draft of the script, New Line Cinema said it was too expensive to shoot this idea. They couldn't afford to shoot it in New York so they advised me to set it somewhere else. So basically, the script that I first wrote and the script that I ended up directing, I honestly couldn't tell you the difference. The latter was simply scarier and a lot tighter.

Did you just work as editor on The Burning *or were you on set during the production?*

I worked just as the editor. You know the scene with the canoe? Well, I have always considered myself a very good editor. I have won an Emmy for my editing. I have always felt that if there was one thing I was really good at in this life, it would be editing. So I edited that scene together and thought it was really good. However, the Weinsteins, who had never made a movie before, started their meddling with the editing right with their first film. They said that scene was too short and I said that I used all the footage that I had. They still said, "It's too short. You need to stretch it out more." So I went back and found some footage which I could use to make it longer. Still they weren't happy! They said I had to stretch it out even more! So I ended up stretching out the scene using almost every bit of footage that we had, as they approach the canoe. Once the guy with the hedge clippers pops up, I don't think I changed a lot. You have a bunch of campers having a good time and there is this empty canoe that they are paddling towards. Everyone in the audience knows something bad is going to happen. The more you can stretch that out, the better, as it builds suspense.

In fact, the scene in *Alone in Dark* in the bedroom when the knife comes through the bed, New Line Cinema wanted me to make that scene shorter. They said, "Why would

Rank Video VHS sleeve of *Alone in the Dark*.

she stay on the bed? She would just jump off." I said, "Yeah, but if she did, we wouldn't have a scene." So I resisted all their attempts to make it shorter and actually when we screened the film, that was the most effective scene.

I agree. She is so terrified that she is rooted to the bed…

I have read a lot of horror scripts which people have sent me. Most of them are garbage. They just have these various beats that they just want to happen and connect them up. For example, the scene with the woman on the bed, I actually thought about that and why the character remains there. A lot of horror scripts don't consider this. As you rightly say, in *Alone in the Dark*, the character is frozen with fear. She doesn't know what will happen if she jumps off the bed. I was trying to play on that as well because as a kid I think I saw an episode of the *Twilight Zone* with an alien creature under the bed. I used to worry that something was under the bed. I knew there wasn't but if you asked me to dangle my foot off the bed, I wouldn't have done it! I used to tuck the sheets in. So I was trying to get in touch with the idea of the monster under the bed.

I think that worked as audiences can relate to the idea of the bogeyman under the bed. I consider it one of the scariest elements of the film as it plays on our own fears. Can you talk us through how you filmed that scene?

In that scene we had to change a few things. Firstly, the average thickness of a mattress is around nine inches. Realistically, if you stuck a knife up through a mattress, only the last inch would come through. Obviously we had to make the knife protrude more! In fact, no one has ever questioned that. I figured out where I wanted Carol Levy, the actor who played Bunky, to go. If I recall correctly, when the knife comes up through the mattress, she retreats back. This makes her go farther from the edge of the bed and harder for her to jump off. I had to decide where I wanted the knife to come up and chunks were cut out of those areas so that the knife could easily come up.

I used a wide-shot to film Bunky's death. As I recall, [actor] Erland van Lidth, who played Ronald "Fatty" Elster, literally picked Levy up by her neck! Levy was a dancer and van Lidth was very strong. He had been on the Olympic wrestling team and an incredible weight lifter. He was able to pick up Levy very easily [*laughs*]!

You assembled a great cast for the picture. How did you get so many famous names?

I don't recall whether Donald Pleasence was my idea or the studio's. I was in awe of Donald Pleasence. I thought he was one of the great actors. I had seen him in Roman Polanski's *Cul-De-Sac* [1966] and he was exceptional in that. I thought he was a brilliant actor and I was thrilled to get him. As for Jack Palance, the producer suggested him, which I thought was great. Then Martin Landau's agent called us. I guess he was in a low point in his career and he needed to make some money! I said, "Great!"

Palance actually agreed to do the film on the assumption there would be no night shooting, and the producer had assured him there wouldn't be any. *Alone in the Dark* … no night shooting! [*Laughs*] At the same time he had done a pilot for a television show called *Ripley's Believe It or Not*, where he was the host. They wanted him to go to Florence to shoot some footage for that show but we had a contract with him and we held him to that. We insisted that instead of going to Florence that he went to New Jersey [*laughs*]. So he wasn't a happy camper being stuck on our low-budget movie.

What were they like to work with individually?

Donald Pleasence was the first one to show up on set and on my second day we had a scene with him. So I met him and we rehearsed the scene and I watched it and my mind went completely blank. So I said, "Uhhhh, let's do that one more time. Let's rehearse that again." We did it again and he was great. I gave him some small direction and he said, "Okay," and I thought "Wow! He is actually listening to me." So after that, things went pretty well. That afternoon we also shot the scene where he first meets Dr. Potter in his office. That went well so I was feeling pretty good. And then Landau and Palance showed up. At the end of the first day's shooting, Rob Shaye came up to me—and Rob can have a bit of a devilish streak in him sometimes—and he said, "I met Jack Palance today. He is really angry. He is really mad that he has to be here. We were walking down the street and someone recognized him and [Palance] almost punched the guy in the mouth!" I literally had a panic attack. I was supposed to go and have dinner with Martin Landau at that point, so literally went into a liquor store and bought a bottle of liquor and got into a taxi [*laughs*]. I tried to drink to calm my panic! I specifically remember the dinner with Landau because I ordered consommé as it was the only thing I could eat.

The following day I had a scene with Palance. I woke up the next day thinking, "I am the director, I am not taking any shit from this guy. It is my set and I need to carve out my territory." I met him about midday. We were shooting in the mansion that served as Pleasence's mental hospital. It was a beautiful mansion and they had put Palance in the largest room and bought him loads of flowers. You had to walk about 20 feet across the room to get to him. It was like having a meeting with Mussolini. I informed him there was two scenes to shoot that day, both with dialogue, one being the scene where he walks with Dr. Potter and says the line, "We're not crazy, we're just on vacation." He said he couldn't possibly do that scene because no one had told him that he had to do it. It had three pages of dialogue and he had a hard time remembering his lines so he couldn't do that. Then that night we were shooting the scene where they escape and kill somebody. Palance said he wasn't going to do the scene because he didn't believe in violence! [*Laughs*] That's how we started off.

What did you say to that?
I told Jack that we had to shoot the dialogue scene and that we had to shoot it on that day. I said we would shoot it in the afternoon which would give him three hours to work on the dialogue. I suggested we shoot it in little pieces so he could remember the dialogue. As far as killing the guy, I told him we are not even discussing that. I told him we would shoot the first scene at four o'clock. So four o'clock rolls round and he did it in one take and he was fantastic. I said, "Wow, that was really good." He said, "You're full of shit." But that was his way. And then we broke for dinner and I went back to his room and had a friendlier conversation. I discovered he loved opera and I knew a bit about it and we talked. Then I said, "As far as the scene tonight, I'd like to discuss your character, but as far as the script goes, you have to kill the guy. That's just the way it is." And he said, "Why? Why does my character have to kill the guy?" I said, "Well, you need to make the audience know that you are capable of murder." He turned and stared at me and said, "They'll know." And he was right! You just had to look at his face and you knew. It was one of the great lessons that I have learned about filmmaking. There was also a line in there about "Fatty" being big and strong and he said. "You don't have to say that. Just look at him. You never want to state the obvious."

Jack's character was clearly the guy in charge. So I said, "Someone has to die in order for them to get the car." So Jack said, "Get the fat guy to do it." I said, "Let me think about it." So I went over to Robert Shaye—and you are supposed to follow the script, that is part of the deal—and I said "Listen, Jack doesn't believe in violence and doesn't want to kill anyone. He wants 'Fatty' to do it. Is that okay with you?" He said, "Sure, I don't care." So that's what we did.

Landau was a real sweetheart. At that time he was married to Barbara Bain, who would occasionally come to the set. When the film was over, we stayed in touch and he was something of a mentor to me. He helped me out a lot with working with actors. I went on to work on two other features with him, *By Dawn's Early Light* [1990] and *12:01* [1993].

The film is well acted and you achieved so much given the small budget.
Yes we did. I can tell you it was a very difficult shoot. The last scene we shot was the opening scene at the diner, which was about two or three hours north of New York City. The producer, who I would say was rather parsimonious, was the kind of guy who kept a roll of toilet paper in his car instead of a box of tissues because it was cheaper. Not a good sign! Anyway, he said, "I've got the perfect diner for you and it looks just right." It was out in the middle of nowhere and we got there and there was about a foot of snow on the ground. I said, "There's a foot of snow," and he said, "It's all right, it's a dream. What's the difference?" The funny thing is, when the film was done we had a big screening in New York at the National Theater on Broadway and Robert Shaye was sitting in the middle of the audience next to a couple of kids who like horror movies. As the film opens up, you see this guy—who wasn't even Landau, it was a double—trudging through the snow and entering the diner. The kid sitting next to Robert Shaye turns to his friend and says, "This film is bullshit. He just walked through the snow and there's no snow on his shoes when he walks in!" So there you go.

I really liked the opening scene. It is very stylized.
Yes it was, but the snow was not exactly what we expected. But we were there with the film crew at this diner. It was difficult. When the film was over, I slept for about three days straight. I would wake up for an hour or two, then go back to sleep. The schedule was tough and by the end of it I was psychologically and physically exhausted in every possible way. There was an awful lot of night shooting. And everyone was working one category higher than they normally worked. It wasn't a great crew but we had a very good and experienced director of photography in Joseph Mangine. But most of the crew were not that experienced so everything took that little bit longer to set up.

But that lack of experience doesn't show in the final film.
No, you're right.

One of the intriguing aspects of the film is that you present a world that is deeply psychotic and you cleverly blur the lines between those who are incarcerated and those who are not. You seem to be asking, "Who is really crazy?"
That's especially true of the final scene, with the girl and Palance. I have always thought of myself as an auteur. I wanted to have a style. I used to think that all my films were about outsiders, which in fact they are, but if you watch *Alone in the Dark* and *A Nightmare on Elm Street 2* and *The Hidden*, which I had less to do with in terms of its creation, they are all social commentaries. That's what I was trying to do. Unlike Wes Craven, who really expressed himself through the horror genre, I felt I expressed myself

in spite of the horror genre. I have a very ironic outlook on life. So all my films have irony and humor in them and they have a skewed view of the world. That's how I see the world. People don't act very rational. What's normal? That's what the subtext of the film is.

There's another insightful commentary on society during the blackout and law and order breaks down. You imply that when boundaries break down, or are pushed to the limit, we are all capable of "crazy acts."

Right. And the idea that when they go to the store they are looting, they fit right in, because the whole world is crazy now. That was supposed to be a more extensive sequence. However, the scene in the disco was scheduled for only one day of shooting and I said to the producer, "I don't think you can shoot this in a day. There is too much to do." We had to shoot the blackout, a light change, the riot and a whole bunch of other things. The producer said that we could shoot it in a day. I challenged him and he replied, "How many feature films have you made?!" I said, "None." He retorted, "I have made six." So we left it at a day with the promise of shooting another day if we needed it. Of course that was one big lie because once it is on the schedule for a day, you are responsible for shooting it in that timeframe. I think we started about noon, prepping the nightclub, and by the time we finished it was about ten o'clock the following morning. Palance, who had been told that there would be no night shooting, did his first shot about four in the morning.

The following day we were scheduled to do the scene in the parking lot of the department store. So instead of getting there at three o'clock and getting everything ready, like the fires, we couldn't get there until ten. So we only got a portion of the footage that I wanted. I had to drastically cut it down. There was an elaborate sequence that I wanted to film but I had to reduce that to almost nothing. I felt bad about it. I think the scene still works. However, I wanted to play around more with the idea. Here you have these psychotic killers and put them into contact with a normal crowd of people in society who have become psychotic. Once you release these boundaries, then everybody goes crazy. That is the default state of humankind.

One of the interesting aspects of Alone in the Dark *is that the character Bleeder wears a hockey mask during one of his kills. Some viewers will assume that that is a nod to the* Friday the 13th *films, but the iconic mask didn't appear in the series until the third one, which was made a year after* Alone in the Dark. *Did you influence the filmmakers?*

I have no idea. I actually know Sean Cunningham but I have never asked him. We had to have something to cover up Bleeder's face. I figured, "What do they sell in a department store that covers up someone's face?" and I chose the hockey mask because it seemed more interesting and a little scarier. We actually came first!

Were you pleased with the way you filmed and executed the death scenes?

Yes, they were the best that I could do under the circumstances. I thought they worked out pretty well. The only thing that I was really disappointed with, in that I wasn't able to do it in the way that I wanted, was the whole looting sequence. Other than that, I did everything else pretty much the way I wanted to film it. I think I had about 30 days to shoot the film.

Makeup effects artist Tom Savini worked on the film. Were you pleased with the monstrous apparition that he created for the film?

I had met Savini when we worked on *The Burning*. They were shooting in a summer camp in Buffalo, New York. They had hired Savini and in a way he was the star of the film. The Weinsteins didn't seem to have a whole lot of respect for the director, Tony Maylam. I couldn't understand why they hired him as he had mostly done films on motor car racing and Formula 1. He was more of a non-fiction director. The Weinsteins always seemed to rely on Savini and he was almost like the second unit director. So I got to know him quite well as he would come into the editing room and we'd look at the dailies together.

On *Alone in the Dark* we had hired another guy. He was a character, funny, and I kind of liked him. He also claimed he was a special effects makeup artist. He was supposed to make the zombie monster creature for the film and he was sculpting the head of this thing. No one had seen it and he told us it was a work in progress. Anyway, we found out two things. Firstly, he was an alcoholic and secondly he hadn't done the head! It was supposed to be shot the next day and he had produced nothing. So I called Tom Savini! He was available and came to the set on the afternoon we were filming the scene when the monster pops up. He had his kit with him and he said that he needed someone to take him to the supermarket. He came back with soap and Rice Krispies and he literally used this stuff to create this hideous-looking creature! It was so ugly I couldn't even look at it. It was very effective! Fortunately he stuck around and did other effects for the movie.

What was the reaction to the film by critics and audiences?
　　The critical response was very underwhelming. It didn't do particularly well. Nobody was particularly impressed with the film. The critics weren't impressed. The audiences weren't impressed. The studio wasn't impressed. If *A Nightmare on Elm Street 2* hadn't come along, I don't think I would have made another film. It didn't set the world on fire. I was with a good agency and they saw me as a writer. They felt they could promote me more as a writer than a director, after *Alone in the Dark*. When *A Nightmare on Elm Street 2* opened up, it was the top movie of the week. It opened on a Friday and by Monday the head of the agency called and said "Jack, Dino De Laurentiis is going to call you from his car in about 15 minutes." I thought, "Wow, my life has just changed."

Do you think over time the reaction to the film has changed?
　　Yes. A lot of people have had time to reconsider the film. The people who have rediscovered it really like it. I had mixed feeling about the film initially. But now I think it is a really good film. I think it has a lot going for it. It is more than a slasher film. It has a lot going on and it has a great cast. It plays very well. It is one my favorites and I am very proud of it. It is the only film that I have done that came 100 percent out of me. *The Hidden* is probably my best film. There is nothing in that I want to change. It was somebody else's script yet it fit me like a glove. Unlike *A Nightmare on Elm Street 2* where I was hired six weeks before the shoot, and on that film I just tried to keep my head above water. *Alone in the Dark* is all me as I was in 1981 when it was made.

You have frequently said that The Hidden *is your favorite film, out of all the movies that you have directed.*
　　I was looking for a film to follow up working on *A Nightmare on Elm Street 2*. I didn't want to do another horror film. I was getting offered all sorts of horror films and most of the scripts were really bad. I wanted to do something better. I had been turning things down and then the head of production at New Line Cinema said that they had a

project which they thought I would be perfect for. The project at that time was called *Hidden*, without the *The*. The head of production sent over the script and I read it and loved it. It was a really great script. It is not a horror film, but a science fiction film or a buddy-cop movie. It was really well written and the perfect film for me to do. They had another director attached at the time, who in my opinion was a hack. He basically would have done it as a simple shoot-'em-up or chase-'em-up kind of movie. So I said, "I really want to do this." However, the other director was a friend of Robert Shaye, like I was. So I managed to convince Shaye to hire me and to ditch the other guy. That's how I got involved.

By accepting the project, I also wanted to do some work on the script. The original script had been written by Jim Kouf [under the *nom de screen* Bob Hunt], who is a terrific writer. However, he had written it under his own name because he wanted to direct it. New Line Cinema disagreed. They had seen some of his work and didn't think he was suitable for this film. They told him they wanted someone else to direct the picture so he took his name off the film. He didn't disassociate himself from the film, he just said that he didn't want to do any more work on it. I felt the script still needed some work. I felt that the concept, the action, the clever dialogue, all of that worked great. However, I thought there were things missing. I thought, "What is this film really about?" Whenever I make a movie, I always ask, "What is the subtext?" That is what you're directing. If you are the director, the plot is the plot. The plot takes care of itself. Of course you have to understand it and you have to make sure that you tell the story properly, but it's what's underneath the story that is important. For example, *Citizen Kane* is about loss of innocence. What is Rosebud? It represents the loss of innocence. Everything in that story adds up to that. Look at Spielberg, a lot of his movies are about "home." Take *E.T.* [1982], for example. The one word the alien says is "home."

So I felt with *The Hidden*, the subtext was what it meant to be human. So we had a

Promotional Artwork of the horror/sci-fi classic *The Hidden*.

good alien and a bad alien, with the alien representing what it is like to be a bad human and the good alien representing a good human. The bad alien worked great. However, I felt with the good alien, there needed to be more going on. There needed to be more substance between the two cops, Gallagher and Beck. For example, Gallagher does get invited to Beck's house for dinner but the relationship between Beck and his wife was too breezy. There was no depth and I thought the script needed a stronger connection between the two of them. I figured I can't spend very much time on this relationship, as it wasn't that kind of movie. The key scene is when they have dinner. So I thought, "How could I strengthen the relationship between Beck and his wife quickly?" So I gave them a child. It immediately gave them something to bond over. Then I thought, "Why don't I add that Gallagher also has a child but that his child was killed by the alien?" So that gives him a connection. So I added the child and rewrote the scenes with the wife at the dinner table. I also rewrote the ending, when Gallagher looks at the little girl after he has transferred into Beck's body and she senses it is not her daddy and nobody else can. That's basically what I put in.

Your use of mirrors in the film is very well done. The characters always seem to be questioning, "Are they human?"

Yes, there are a number of scenes when both characters look at themselves in a mirror. When you look in a mirror, you see you, but what would happen if you looked in the mirror and saw somebody else? Then you would try to examine who you are. There's a really good moment when Gallagher goes to dinner and is left alone in the living room and he looks at himself in the mirror. I thought that was a great moment. I thought Kyle played that scene beautifully. Also, the biggest laugh in the entire film is when the dog looks at himself in the mirror. The same also when the stripper looks at herself in the mirror and thinks, "Hey, I've got tits!"

The car chase sequences at the start of the film were brilliantly realized.

When I was planning the film and the car chases, Robert Shaye said, "It's just another car chase, who cares? We've all seen a million car chases." I said, "I'm going to make the best car chase you've ever seen." So I got my assistant to get the video tapes of all the films that we could think of that had great car chases in them. So I watched and studied them so I could work out what constituted a really good chase sequence. The one I felt was the best was *The French Connection* [1971], which is fantastic. When I looked at it, I wondered why it worked so well. I realized that it worked so well because most of the footage was shot car to car and the action was always moving. When it wasn't moving, you would either have a shot to give you a bit of geography or the camera was close to the car, so it really put you into the chase. *Bullitt* [1968] also had a very famous chase sequence. But if you look at *Bullitt*, the camera is watching the cars whereas in *The French Connection*, the camera puts you in the car. I realized that the key to doing a good car chase was to basically put you in the car.

My basic philosophy is to use three cameras on the car—and I have shot car chases in similar fashion on other movies that I have done since, like *Renegades* which had an even bigger chase sequence. I basically stick one camera on the bumper of the car, with a wide angle lens so that you get this feeling of speed and being close to the road. I stick one camera which would be the driver's point of view and I have a third camera looking over the driver's shoulder. So that car, with the stunt driver, runs through every part of the chase. Then the other cameras I have, I try to position them near where the cars are going to go, and again I stick wide angle lenses on them. If you look at the film *Driver* [1978] by Walter Hill, he uses long lenses which tend to slow things down and flattens things out. In contrast, a wide angle lens shot down low sucks until the car is around ten feet away and suddenly it looms up and gets really big. The stunt drivers were instructed to get as close as they could to the cameras without actually hitting them. Sometimes we would have the cameras in a crash box, which is used in scenes when the car drives over the camera or crashes. The camera would be put in a crash box and operated remotely. The camera tends to be cheap and put into a steel enclosure. The other times, when the camera was being operated, we would have a rope tied to the camera and the operator. If it looked like they were going to get hit, then we could yank them out of the way. So using these techniques, this is how we shot most of that car chase in *The Hidden*.

The other thing about the chase is that if the other guy had directed the film, it would have been a good film, because of the script, but it would have been just another film. For me, because I am a reluctant horror film director, I am always interested in the characters and the story. What I found interesting was that the car was being driven by a man who can't be killed. He's an alien. So he would drive a car differently than you would. He doesn't care what happens to him. He's just having fun. In most car chases, the character is trying to get away and survive, while in *The Hidden*, the alien is thinking, "How can I get away and have a great time, and I don't care if I get killed?" That changed the dynamic of how you do the chase sequence. So that's one of the reasons why I think that chase sequence works. Also, in most chase scenes you wouldn't have a guy hitting someone in a wheelchair and smiling! [*Laughs*]

What makes that scene even more effective is that you open the film with the scene in the bank. At first we see the mundane goings-on for a minute or so before the normality is shattered as the robbery quickly and violently unfolds before leading us straight into that exhilarating car chase. I thought that opening was expertly edited and realized.

The story opened up with an elaborate bank robbery scene in the script. Again Robert Shaye said, "We've got to keep the budget down, this bank robbery is going to be expensive to do." It would have added another day to the schedule and been expensive. Also, we have all seen bank robberies. In this instance, I thought he was right. There was going to be nothing special about the bank robbery. The car chase was going to be special, in that it is driven by a guy with a different motive than in most car chases, which would make it unique. But the bank robbery itself wouldn't be. So I thought it would be cool to just start the film off with the alien exiting the bank with a bag of money. So that's what we did. We eliminated the bank robbery completely. I thought it would be an interesting way to start the film. In fact, the film opens in black-and-white and then shifts to color as he walks out of the bank. That was actually where the film started. But when we looked at the film when it was cut together, it didn't have any impact. It didn't make sense. It felt like something was missing. So New Line said we needed to go back and do something with the bank robbery.

So I had an idea where we could do the robbery on the cheap, in that we set up one camera as if it's a security camera and film the whole thing as if it is happening in real time. The producers said, "Fine!" as we didn't need a big crew or cast. All we needed was one shot. We rehearsed the scene and we then filmed it on a camera that was mounted high with a wide angle lens. As it turned out, it worked really well for the film. I especially like it when the bank robber looks at the camera, smiles, then shoots out the camera.

I understand that casting for the film proved to be very difficult.

We didn't finish casting for the film until a week before we started shooting. Michael Nouri initially came into read for the part of Gallagher in the movie. His big claim to fame had been his performance in *Flashdance* (1983). At that stage, I was interested in another actor reading for the role of Gallagher—which Kyle ended up playing—so when Nouri came into read for the part I wasn't interested in him at all.

Normally when you do these auditions, the casting director or the assistant to the casting director reads against all the actors, and usually they are not very good. They are not trained actors and don't generally give actors much to go on. However, Michael was coming in at the same time as this other actor was due in for his audition. So I thought that I would use Nouri to read against this other actor, so it will give the actor the best chance to do well. Nouri did a good job. We brought in lots of actors to read for the part of Gallagher. Obviously they weren't big names, as New Line wasn't that big a deal at the time. They were known primarily for *A Nightmare on Elm Street*. I wasn't that big a deal, either. I was known for *A Nightmare on Elm Street 2* [*laughs*]! So it was the last week before shooting before we found anyone. The actor I really wanted for the role wasn't available, we weren't able to get him. So I got the casting director to round up every possible person she could think of who would be good for this role and bring them in. So I saw a lot of actors that week.

We were also still trying to cast for Beck, and we brought in everyone we possibly could to audition for that role. However, none were better than Nouri. So we brought Nouri back in and again he was really, really good. So we all agreed on Nouri to play Beck. Then it came down to Kyle and one other actor to play Gallagher. New Line preferred the other actor who had auditioned for the part of Gallagher. They didn't want Kyle for that part because they felt he was too frail for the role and not strong enough. I liked Kyle and he had just had his breakout role in David Lynch's *Blue Velvet* (1986). So I was able to persuade them to use Kyle instead of the other actor. So Nouri ended up playing Beck and Kyle ended up playing Gallagher.

So that's how we cast the two main roles. We started filming on the Monday and we cast Kyle on the Thursday before.

The chemistry between the two actors is exceptional. They worked well off each other.

Yes, they did. The interesting thing is that when I was shooting the picture, I felt that Nouri was completely stealing the film. He had all the big stuff. He was very good and he knew how to play everything while Kyle, in himself, and in his role, was more reserved or reactive. He didn't say as much. His role was much more low-key. I thought that Nouri was stealing every single scene that they did together. It wasn't until I began cutting the film together that I started to realize just how strong Kyle was. He had this amazing presence and quietude and calm and focus. I really think it is his film.

I agree. I think his character is the most interesting and mysterious ...

Yes, you are right. I thought also that Nouri was very good but a little more obvious, whereas Kyle was not. Kyle was perfect for that role and again it was one of those lucky moments in filmmaking.

Kyle was very quiet and very easy to work with. Nouri, as you may have heard, was not. Nouri was very, very difficult. Basically, if I said to him, "Enter the room and walk over to the window on the right," he would say, "My character would enter the room and sit on the chair to the left." Whatever I said, he wanted to do something else. I think he didn't trust me as a director and maybe he felt after *Flashdance* that he should have been an A-list star. And here he is in this low-budget scifi–horror film with a director whose main credit was *A Nightmare on Elm Street 2*! I think he thought that he had to protect himself and make sure that the whole thing didn't drag him down too much. That's where he was coming from.

Having worked with Jack Palance, did you feel you could manage Nouri?

Palance was different. Palance came across as a jerk who was going to bust your balls. I'll tell you a story about Palance. I mentioned earlier about the shopping center scene in *Alone in the Dark*. When filming, instead of having two whole days I had four or five hours. So we were setting up and setting up, and Robert Shaye was there. This was the first film New Line produced on their own and they always had money problems. Robert was getting more and more antsy, and at one point he thought we weren't going fast enough. We had the camera set up but we were tweaking and tweaking, and finally he said, "Light everything up," as a way of forcing us to shoot. So when the cars and buildings were set on fire we weren't ready. By the time we filmed the fires they were dying down. At the end of that night, I slept for almost 18 hours straight. The night before I had only two hours sleep and I tried to do this enormous scene. I felt I had the rug pulled out from under me. I think I had to film the interior and exterior shots on the same night. I had all these elaborate plans and there was no time for me to do it. I had 10 or 15 shots and I had time to do about six. We had this one extra who I thought I would film looting and that would serve to illustrate the whole thing as opposed to hordes of people running through looting the store. Then I found out that Robert Shaye had sent all the extras home because he wanted to save money. So I had no extras! And at that point I was completely, utterly physically, mentally and psychologically exhausted and I basically crashed. I had gone to all this effort to figure out how to film this scene with six extras and not 60, or 100, and now I have none. I was totally out of ideas.

Landau, Palance and Erland van Lidth, the escapees, were waiting in a room that we were using as a lounge. A couple of nights before when we shot in the mental hospital, there was this scene where the guys are lying in bed plotting. When it came time to do that scene, Palance wanted to get up and walk around. I said no, no, no. I really need you all to be lying in your beds. I had this really clear vision when I wrote it that these three inmates were like peas in a pod, all lined up in their beds. Each of them still, but plotting. And Palance walking around would have ruined what I had in mind. So I said "no," and that I wanted him to do it lying down. So he argued with me and said that it was a stupid idea. Then Landau intervened and said, "Hey, Jack. Let the kid do it his way." Palance said, "All right," and we shot it the way I wanted. So we were at the shopping center, inside this department store, and I had completely crashed and had no idea how to get out of this thing. So I walked into the room where the actors were waiting and I said, "Listen, I want to apologize as there is going to be a bit of a pause here. I had one way to do this scene and they've sent the extras home. I'm totally out of ideas." You could tell that I was in really bad shape. I turned to walk out and Palance said to me, "Jack, remember the other night. The scene with the beds?" "Yes," I said. And Palance said, "You were right." And he turned and walked out. [*Laughs*] He just gave me that moment. It was fantastic. That's the kind of guy that he was. He would come across as a big asshole but ultimately he was a good guy. I learned a lot from him.

In contrast, Nouri came across as a good guy but was ultimately an asshole. He acted like an asshole. He would come across as nice, then he would do everything he could to fuck me up. Usually, if you read anything on the Internet about the film, you will read that I had problems with Michael Nouri. I was angry. I was really pissed off with him. I thought that he made my life hell. He made me look like an idiot in front of everybody. I had to use an enormous amount of mental energy to figure out how I could get him to do what I wanted. If I wanted him to go in and turn left, I would have to direct him to go in and turn right, and he would say, "No, I turn left." [*Laughs*] So I had to expend a lot of energy getting him to do what I wanted.

The first day of filming, the scene outside the record shop after the murder, was a key scene that established the relationship between Gallagher and Beck. I wanted Beck to be pissed off with Gallagher because Gallagher doesn't seem to be respecting him. So I wanted to shoot the scene so that Kyle [Gallagher] was walking in front of Beck and that Beck had to catch up with him. Nouri didn't want to do that. Nouri wanted to walk in front of Kyle. Part of it had to do with his idea of the role and part of it his own ego. He didn't want to be catching up with this guy, he wanted Kyle to be catching up with him. And we kept doing it and doing it and doing it until finally Nouri was behind Kyle. So that was day one and that's how it went for the rest of the shoot!

On day two we shot a scene where they are driving in the car and Gallagher talks about his family and how they were killed by the alien they are chasing. That was one of the scenes we used to audition for the roles in the film. In fact, that was the scene that got Nouri the role in the film because he and Kyle had done it so well. Whenever you shoot somebody in a car, they are not driving. The insurance company won't let them drive. It's dangerous. If you think driving while on your cell phone is dangerous, imagine trying to drive while acting in a movie! The car is always being pulled by a camera car. If you are shooting through the side windows, you have to mount the cameras on these special mounts that you attach to the door and they take about an hour to set up. The camera is worth a couple of hundred thousand dollars and you have to ensure it is on tight and weighted. So it is very time-consuming.

Eventually we shot this scene from one side of the car and it just wasn't working. We did take after take and for some reason it just wasn't gelling. We were going to shoot the other side but we ran out of daylight. The angle we started out on favored Nouri. The next day we shot the angle that favored Kyle and the scene was better. Nouri was disappointed because he thought it was an important scene. I said, "You know what, we will re-shoot your side." So the shooting went on and periodically we would say, "Can we fix this in?" The re-shoot would take us at least a couple of hours. So we tried to fit it into the schedule and then tell Nouri that we would shoot on that day. Then we would run out of time as we had to get the work done that was scheduled for that particular day. All this time, our relationship was deteriorating. I had promised that we would re-shoot that scene and I felt it would be dishonorable to not do it. So on the very last day of the shoot we scheduled it in, because we were doing a bunch of car stuff. I said we would film it first thing and I got the grips to come in an hour early to rig the car so that it was all set to go. I said to Nouri that this is the last day of the shoot and we can do the scene. However, he proceeded to tell me that it was not a good scene and that it was badly written and that he wanted to change the dialogue! He wanted to change stuff around. So we re-shot the scene and it sucked and I never used it. Basically, all actors are nervous to some degree. So now looking back at it, Nouri realized all the pressure was on him, as we had gone to a huge amount of trouble to get him to re-do his part of the scene, so he tried to take the pressure off himself by denigrating the whole thing by saying that the scene was no good and that he was going to cut out and change certain lines because they don't make sense.

There is a second car chase where they are chasing Claudia Christian and that is what we shot on the final day. We finished shooting all the footage on the actors in the car at lunchtime. Lunch, if you start at five in the afternoon, is at 11 in the evening. We finished the shot. We were all being towed in the camera car and we drove back to the base camp, which was somewhere in downtown L.A. We when arrived, everyone then got out of the camera truck and went to lunch, including me. Now normally when it is the actor's last day, or last scene, on a movie, everybody usually comes over and congratulates them and hug and make a big fuss. However, everyone just walked away. Not just me, the entire crew. They walked away and left Nouri in the car.

It sounds like he was a destructive influence on the film!
Yes he was!

However, that doesn't reflect in the final film.
Yes. Well, a lot of times films turn out pretty well even though they had various problems with this and that. Then there are movies where everyone gets on great and everything goes well and the movie sucks! That isn't to say there is a direct correlation but what it does mean is that there is *no* correlation. There is another scene when Beck and Gallagher go into the warehouse. That was another scene that Nouri caused problems. He didn't like the scene and we had to keep shooting and shooting it until finally Nouri said, "This is stupid." In the last take, Nouri said, "Cover me," and Kyle said, "I'd rather not." "Okay," and Nouri then runs in. I thought, "Fuck it, cut, and move on." So I didn't put it in the film and when I showed the cut to the New Line people, they asked, "Where is that great scene?" I said that Nouri refused to do this scene. They said, "That was such a good scene, why don't you go back and look at it again?" So we went back and found one take that was pretty good and again it gets a big laugh with audiences. But it was one of the takes that I didn't think was that good. It could have been better but at least we have the shot in the movie and it works.

It does work. I particularly like that scene in the warehouse.
Actually, in Kouf's original script it was a shoe warehouse and I thought, "A shoe warehouse? Why a shoe warehouse?" I was thinking about one of my favorite B-movies of all time, *Gun Crazy* [1950] by Joseph H. Lewis. And there is a great scene toward the end when they are being pursued and they go through a meat-packing plant and there are all these carcasses hanging up. I thought about that scene and I thought, "We have a film about what it means to be human and what it means to be an alien in a human's body. Why don't we make it a mannequin factory?" That way, it would tie in with the theme of the movie. So everyone in the art department had to come in and make over 100 mannequins! They were expensive so we created some molds and make them out of foam.

The scene was visually effective and it leads nicely into that spectacular stunt where Claudia's character jumps off the building.
That was easy to film. It was actually a guy in a wig. He jumped off the building into a giant air-filled foam pad. That is not something I would like to do, but stunt guys are crazy and he couldn't wait to jump off the roof!

You really underplayed the alien element in the film. You hint towards the creature, with some good special effects, but generally you didn't overdo it. It was very subtle.

The other big thing that I brought to the film, which another director might not have, was that there are six or seven different characters—DeVries, the guy who robs the bank, the old guy, Claudia, the chief, the dog and the detective and finally the guy running for Senator—and I thought, "These are all the same character; they are all the same person. They are just wearing different outfits." So I rehearsed the actors together for that one role. We all got together at my house one afternoon, the night before we started shooting the movie, and I said, "We should develop the character together, including the dog." We had the dog and trainer there as well! I started off doing some theater exercises to get everyone relaxed and then we started talking about what the alien is like. I then told everyone to ingest the alien and stand up and feel this thing in your body. I want it to take them over. I then got them all to walk around and I noticed some common characteristics in their aliens. They all had a certain way of walking and stiffness and a similar way of looking around that everyone shared. And Bob Shaye wanted this one characteristic or quirk that each of the aliens shared. We tried to figure out what to do, knowing that we were limited with the dog. I thought we could imitate something weird the dog does. I talked to the trainer and he said, "When he gets to the point where he is really going to lose it, he will bare his teeth and stick his tongue out a bit." So he got the dog to do it and then I got the others to copy it. If you watch the movie, you will see each of the aliens will have a moment where they do that with their tongues.

How was the film received critically upon release?

Very well. And we went to the Avoriaz Fantastic Film Festival, which at the time was in a ski resort in France. It was considered the premier festival in the world for film fantastique. It was the same year as *RoboCop* [1987], which was also in competition. The French papers all said that this was a very dull year for the festival because we all know *RoboCop* was going to win. And the jury was headed by Sidney Lumet. I have thought about *The Hidden* in that it was similar to Lumet's work, because I have always loved his cop films *Serpico* [1973] and *Dog Day Afternoon* [1975], nobody does New York cop movies better than Lumet. And to me, *The Hidden* was a cop-thriller. It just happened to have aliens in it. So I was influenced by Lumet's films. So here he was as the president of the jury. Lumet worked primarily out of New York and I had worked as an editor in New York for 14 years. New Yorkers are a very cynical crowd; however, whenever anyone mentions Lumet, no filmmaker said a bad word about him. He was like God. He was the ultimate film director and he was good at everything. So I got to have lunch with him and discuss the problems I had with Nouri, as it was still upsetting for me. I wanted to learn how to deal with actors like Nouri, because Lumet was a master of working with actors. So Lumet picked my film and we ended up winning, which was a huge upset! For about three weeks, I was a celebrity.

I wanted to touch briefly on Wishmaster 2, *which I have a soft spot for.*

Alone in the Dark and *Wishmaster 2* are the two films that I have directed where I wrote the script. *Alone in the Dark* came completely out of my head and with *Wishmaster 2* there was a format that needed to be followed. Interestingly enough, they tried to get me to direct the original *Wishmaster* [1997]. Honestly, I didn't think the script was very good and I wasn't interested. At the same time, Disney had wanted me to direct *Arachnophobia* [1990]. It was actually a good script, but I thought, "Who wants to do a movie about a spider? I don't want to do a spider movie." It was a $40 million budget, with a good cast, but I said no. I was hoping to get *Saving Private Ryan* [1998], or something great. Then ten years later I make *Arachnid* [2001] for a tenth of the budget and with a lousy script. So I turned down *Wishmaster* and several years later I did the sequel. The fact is that I am a working director. I had a family. I had a mortgage. I had to earn a living. I couldn't go back to editing, especially having been a director. No director will hire another director to edit their movie. So my agent called up and said that the producers of *Wishmaster* wanted to churn out a sequel. "They don't care what you do; as long as you can write a hundred pages, you can do what you want." So I figured it was an interesting premise. What if you could have any wish come true? I thought about situations where people would wish for things to happen, like in a casino, a prison, etc. So the idea was interesting to me and I incorporated the religious aspect into the film.

I honestly haven't seen the film since the cast and crew screening. I wrote the script and it does reflect my sensibility in that it is similar to *Alone in the Dark*. Again there is a social commentary that crops up in my films that this world is just a crazy, absurd and somewhat arbitrary place. *Wishmaster 2* got really bad reviews when it opened. Sequels used to mean less. When I did *A Nightmare on Elm Street 2*, they hoped to make 70 percent of what the original film had made. At that point, a sequel was a way of squeezing more money out of something. When it came to *Wishmaster 2,* that was what they were trying to do. They didn't have this giant franchise like *Batman*.

I thought you improved on the original.
That was my feeling. I didn't think the original was terribly good.

I thought the script and overall production design was much better. I noticed you worked with Alfred Sole.
Yes, I worked with him on two movies, the other being a TV movie called *Dark Reflection* [1994]. He is a terrific guy. I really enjoyed working with him. Alfred has an interesting background. He studied as an architect and lived in Rome. He and I got along really well. He understood my sensibility.

I also thought Andrew Divoff was fantastic in the role of the djinn.
I had worked with him before when doing *By Dawn's Early Light*. It would be nice if people go back and revisit the film and re-evaluate it. Horror films tend to reflect and critique the period. One of my all-time favorite horror movies is the original *Invasion of the Body Snatchers* [1956]. I remember seeing it as a kid and being absolutely terrified by it. The film was about Communism and that they would take you over and turn you into a soulless and mindless zombie. Zombie movies were also part of the Red Scare.

8

Sleepwalker

AN INTERVIEW WITH SAXON LOGAN

Saxon Logan's *Sleepwalker* (1984) is a film so obscure that many film historians assumed it didn't exist at all. Some people within the cinematic community accused respected horror writer and journalist Kim Newman of concocting a ruse to fool film fans when he wrote about it in the seminal tome *Ten Years of Terror: British Films of the 1970s*. On the contrary, Newman's recollections of seeing *Sleepwalker* at a press screening set in motion a chain of events whereby the film was discovered in the British Film Institute's vaults and re-released on DVD in the U.K., much to the benefit of fans of British horror cinema.

Intended as a short featurette to accompany the feature presentation at cinemas across the U.K., *Sleepwalker* is an atmospheric slice of English gothic horror with touches of the Italian *giallo* included for good measure. Yet the film is much more than a simple, cheaply produced horror flick. It's a study of class warfare and a damning indictment of British society during this era. With its Mike Leigh realism mixing with the surreal nightmarish visual palettes of Bava and Argento, it's a very bizarre film that is richly rewarding and gripping, with a nasty and freaky dénouement.

The basic premise sees warring siblings Marion (Heather Page) and Alex Britains (Bill Douglas) eking out a hand-to-mouth existence in a dilapidated house called the Albion, somewhere in England. Their run-down family estate with its broken windows, power cuts, leakages and all-around malaise is a mirror of their own broken, tired relationship and divulging political positions, as well as a metaphor for the country on the whole—a country in crisis since the demise of the Empire, a country divided by Thatcherism and Socialism, a country that needs to "wake up" from its somnambulistic state. These differences come to the fore when yuppie hipsters Richard (Nickolas Grace) and Angela Paradise (Joanna David) visit Marion. Alex and Richard take an instant dislike to one another, as their moral and political views are complete opposites. Goading each other at the house, and during dinner, the pair's antics turn nasty as the resentment and hostility grows and the booze is consumed by our foursome. Even Marion is cruel to her awkward, and slightly strange, brother, as she tries to impress Richard, to whom she is clearly attracted. (Later in the film, Marion sleepwalks into his room where Richard, equally comatose, begins undressing her and kissing her shoulder and breasts.) Embarrassing Alex, she recites a story where Alex strangled her while sleepwalking, much to the mirth of the others. Returning to Albion, the four retire for the evening. The film shifts gears and we are thrown into *giallo* territory when a deranged killer begins murdering the inhabitants of the home. In this nightmarish world, all shot with neon blues, we are treated to a bloody finale where the identity of the killer is revealed but not before those around them have been crudely sliced and dispatched.

On the face of it, the film is more than a horror film, and in many respects a critique of the nation: a country sleepwalking into oblivion unless it can "wake up." Yet the horror label is aptly applied here, for there is much in the film that makes it one of the great unsung British horror films of the 1980s. Director Saxon Logan paints an ominous picture from the get-go with the use of horror tropes to maximize his film's effect. First, we see the rain lashing the old, musky ruin of a cottage and herein lies a household riven with resentment and simmering hatred as our protagonists quietly display their disgust for one another. As this tension boils, the style of the film mirrors the impending horror. As the lightning flashes, the rooms are awash with strange blue tones. Logan hints towards the pending violence with images (shards of broken glass, a man chopping wood). As the slaughter begins, Logan ups the ante and fractures the narrative by infusing dreams into the plot. Is this real? Is this the twisted desires of the loathsome protagonists? Or is the truth far more macabre and sinister?

In January 2016 I interviewed Mr. Logan about his brilliant lost entry in British horror cinema.

Matthew Edwards: *How did you get involved in film and working with Lindsay Anderson on* O Lucky Man! *[1973]?*

Saxon Logan: I grew up in an African colony called Southern Rhodesia and going to the cinema was one of the great joys of life and I knew from a very early age I wanted to be part of making movies. So much so, I wrote at age eight to Warner Brothers offering my services; I still have the letter, as my mother never posted it for me. I loved *The Crimson Pirate* and *Robin Hood* and especially, when old enough, Hammer horror films although the *Carry On* series represented a truer Britain. Films were largely British (financed by the U.S.) and I got to see *Lawrence of Arabia* and *Zulu*. The latter is perfect filmmaking: from its wonderful score to the epic tale told with economy of expression (Great screenplay, too).

Then I saw Antonioni's *Blow Up* and Lindsay Anderson's *If...* and knew there was a special creative presence involved in making the film. *If...* created such an impression on me, I wrote the filmmaker's name on the ticket stub, so I wouldn't forget him. Little did I realize what fate had in store for me.

I objected to compulsory conscription in to the Rhodesian Army and instead faced a mandatory jail term, but my mother had me spirited out of the country. I was not allowed to return for ten years when Rhodesia became Zimbabwe (in itself an epic historical horror story!).

I arrived in Britain—a country held up as a truly great example of civilization. From day one, I realized this was propaganda and Britain would never live up to its pretensions. I refused to accept dole, which many of my contemporaries encouraged me do. Instead I took on menial work. Selling jewelry, carpets, even fish and chips. In my free time I wrote to the "greats" of British cinema: Attenborough, Forbes, Lean. None designed to reply—that is, all but one: Lindsay Anderson. He liked what he called my "idealistic ambition." I began work with him at the Royal Court as his assistant. He became my mentor in every sense: passing on his love of actors, his exacting approach to everything,

Saxon Logan writing the cult British horror *Sleepwalker* (courtesy Saxon Logan).

he made sure I never starved and would equally scold me for any flabby remark I might make. I owe everything to this great talent and person. One day he remarked that he'd raised the money for his next film *O Lucky Man!* To be honest, I could not make heads or tails of the script. I just said quickly enough, "It is unique." Not fooled, he laughed and said I was the proverbial Lucky Man and he asked, did I want to assist him on it? My answer was apparent even though working at the Royal Court had been some of my happiest days.

It was to be my baptism of fire. Lindsay was so exacting intellectually and emotionally. I was callow, with all these nonsense ideas—none impressed him. Except he saw I had a natural aptitude for blocking out scenes and editing. I knew I was a filmmaker and that I must make films; he realized that too!

Your film Sleepwalker *is now considered one of the "lost" and "forgotten" classics of British horror cinema.*

"Overlooked" is probably the best term. Lindsay Anderson was my greatest influence. I loved the way he used *If....* as a metaphor for [upper-class] Britain. I loved horror and was determined to make a metaphorical Grand Guignol film that somehow would be a satire on the United Kingdom. Not much has changed since I made it. I can see a well-meaning Jeremy Corbyn in Bill Douglas' character and you can take your pick from the Tory front benches, with regard to Richard's character. Of course the house is inherited but its infrastructure ill maintained. Marion is this frustrated Britannia while Angela represents the politely curious middle class.

Was the film always intended as a supporting feature?
It was intended as a support but Thatcher put an end to that (and probably a great deal of talent too). I was just lucky. I met wealthy young man Robert Breare who wanted to meet Lindsay. He said to send the script and if he could get a handle on it, he would finance it. Mercifully he did and was true to his word.

How involved were you in the scouting of locations?
Entirely. The location was sheer luck too. I saw the outside of a house, which I liked and rang the doorbell. The lady who had lived there sadly passed on. Her family was very accommodating and said the house would be cleared within days. I asked if they wouldn't mind leaving everything as is. It was perfect.

How did you set about casting for the film?
Socially, I met Nic Grace at a dinner party and he was game enough to give me a week. Joanna, David and I were very close and her best friend was Heather Page. Bill Douglas was a friend and had appeared in a short film of mine. Had he lived, I would have cast him in any film I was lucky enough to get going. He was a brilliant man and companion—and truly great filmmaker.

What was the budget on Sleepwalker? *Did the budget hinder you in any way?*
The film was shot for 60,000 GBP in seven days. I thought I was fortunate with the budget so, no, I didn't find the lack of a budget a hindrance at all.

There is a wonderful scene in the restaurant where the quartet share an uncomfortable meal as the hostilities between yuppie Thatcherite Richard and Socialite Alex deepen. You set up the tension well in this scene as you create a sense of distrust between the characters which feeds in well to the murderous, and bloody, finale. What are your recollections on filming this scene and was this your intention?
We shot the entire scene in a day; I guess this "gift of knowing" was what Lindsay recognized in me. I had a brilliant supporting cast in Fulton Mackay and Raymond Huntley. Lindsay Anderson was going to play one of the waiters but he slipped on ice and broke his wrist, so he couldn't take part in the film. Michael Medwin stepped in for him. He thought the film was truly courageous. It was just up his street as a movie: "a great punch between the eyes!"

There is a startling moment when Richard makes an inappropriate joke about AIDS, and Alex rightly points out that it is a disease that is not exclusive to homosexuals. Did this comment cause any controversy in the early '80s, as attitudes towards HIV and AIDS issues were quite prejudicial and ignorant at the time?
I co-wrote the script with Michael Keenan, a gay activist. He openly believed the line appropriate as it heightened the bourgeois tension. People still make remarks about Jews in this day and age … the British, when drunk, are insensitive, some would say even when they are sober. Nonetheless, it was in keeping with Grand Guignol approach: "The Great Punch"!

What marks the film as a real cinematic joy is the sublime visual style. Alongside the numerous surrealist images, it seems to tap into the best of British horror as it is rich in atmosphere and a sense of the gothic. Equally, you seem to eschew these conventions with the cold blue tones and haunting synths that hint towards the Italian giallo *slasher films of Bava and Argento. Did these filmmakers influence your visual signature or were you simply trying to conjure up your own nightmarish vision?*

My cinematographer had just seen Win Wenders' *The American Friend* and was influenced by Robert Müller's lighting. This suited me as Mario Bava and Dario Argento were who I had in mind; so style-wise, there was no argument.

The somnambulist sleepwalkers remind me of Cesare in The Cabinet of Dr. Caligari. *Would it be fair to suggest that the work of German Expressionists like Robert Wiene had a certain influence on* Sleepwalker?

You are very perceptive. Dr. Caligari and a hint of Klaus Kinski courtesy of Bill Douglas. German Expressionist cinema influenced me greatly. I was greatly pleased when Fulton McKay recognized this. He said, "I feel I can climb into every frame of yours."

There is quite a surreal nude scene between Marion [Heather Page] and Richard [Nickolas Grace] when she appears naked at his bed in a somnambulistic state and he begins kissing her breasts. Was that a difficult shoot for her? It is a very haunting and surreal scene.

Heather was utterly uninhibited. She and Nic Grace got along just fine. It was my mini-homage to [Luis] Buñuel. He licks her armpit first. I found that erotic.

One of the film's most striking elements is that you forgo conventional storytelling devices and opt for a non-linear narrative infused with metaphor and a degree of surrealism. Did you deliberately eschew these conventions in order to create a film that was fresh, raw and challenging? Were you given full license by the producers to realize your cinematic vision?

My producer never interfered. He invested in me rather than the film. Perhaps this is why I have not been so prolific as I won't have a producer tell me how to make my film. Such hands-off producers are rare but they are out there. I am still grappling with Godard—who I view as an outstanding innovative filmmaker and I suppose his influence came into play. Of course, Luis Buñuel is outstanding—always coherent but provocative. My greatest influence apart from Lindsay. What is it that Buñuel said? "In a world as mad as ours the only solution is revolt!"

Bloody horror befalls Angela Paradise (Joanna David) in the shocking ending of this cult British shocker, *Sleepwalker* **(courtesy Saxon Logan).**

The death scenes are well-handled, in particular Angela's [Joanna David], which lingers in the mind long after the credits roll. Richard's death is equally memorable. Were you satisfied with the way they turned out?

I was. They are perfect—quietly horrifying. Joanna was game throughout and Nic dying from a thousand cuts is out of a Tunnel of Horror. The effect was produced by making the knife blunt and dipping it in "ox-blood" paint for each shot. The rest is down to editing and Nic Grace's superlative performance of agony.

The editing by Michael Crozier is outstanding. As the film descends into the madness, the editing becomes frenzied and wild which serves to heighten the tension and horror. Were you pleased with how the film was edited, in particular the final ten minutes?

It sounds immodest but I am a hands-on editor. Michael and I have collaborated many times on documentaries. But I like to cut my own films. This does not subtract from his hard work or suggestions and opinions. I do listen. But I more or less know how every shot should be played. Michael is there as an objective collaborator. I think he is also a fine editor.

The decrepit mansion—aptly called Albion—seems to represent the eroding of British values and the state of the nation under Margaret Thatcher. When Alex and Richard shout, "Wake up, wake up," they seem to be calling out to a somnolent nation. The subtext implies that you were disturbed with the direction the U.K. was moving.

I still am. Britain is not a democracy but a liberal bureaucracy. The British are fine people but lack curiosity. Art is for a certain type, and politicians are really toffs largely. I think as a monarchy, little will change. I will eat the queen's crown, gladly, if Jeremy gets elected. I find it bizarre that my life began with an Etonian as prime minister and there we still have an Etonian in power. Little has changed, but that is no reason to not shout, "Wake up!"

History shows that Thatcher's government was particularly hostile to the British film industry, ultimately quashing preview featurettes like your own. How did Thatcher's reign affect filmmakers like you?

She was a market obsessed philistine. I don't think she cared about cinema. It certainly wasn't a threat with Alan Parker and Ridley Scott making films. After all, they were in it for the money. Those working class lads would have dropped on one knee had the queen picked up a butter knife. Hugh Hudson is old Etonian so he wouldn't mind either way. Look, one fights on regardless. I feel an inverse sympathy with the Soviet directors. As Elem Klimov said he is a master of patience. So am I.

The film received a Special Jury Prize at the Berlin Film Festival, and Nicholas Winding Refn has been influential in its restoration.

Its reception at Berlin was magnificent. They asked to show it every night. I thought I was made. Nicholas Winding Refn is an extraordinary altruist—and good filmmaker. I owe him a huge debt of gratitude.

Despite the accolades on the festival circuit, the film was treated with disdain by distributors and consigned to the cinematic abyss. What happened?

I was told by Britain's leading producer, "Saxon, I can see you can make films but why this one?" I guess he summed it up.

It has been over a decade now since Sleepwalker *was re-introduced to audiences. What kind of reaction has it gotten?*

Amazing, thanks ironically to the BFI. However, you do get some people—purists perhaps—who feel satire and horror don't mix. Well, I say to those people, "Talk to Tobe Hooper, George Romero and Wes Craven."

Revaluating Sleepwalker, *one is left with the notion that during this era, Britain has a tendency to ignore and marginalize singular talents like yourself, instead of allowing them to flourish, like in the U.S. Do you have a sense of regret that you never had the chance to fulfill your cinematic potential?*

Look, to be honest, you must network. I am no good at that. Become safe and part of the establishment. I adore Stephen Frears but he is a gun for hire. And as for Mike Leigh, it's a miracle anyone backs his films.

Are you pleased that Sleepwalker *is getting the recognition it so richly deserves?*

I have always said one should make a film as if it is your last. Not in a negative sense but that you put your whole life into it. Some great filmmakers are only known for a few films; Cervantes, one book. If you don't like the smell of sawdust, leave the circus.

I understand you are working on a couple of new films.

My war movie is in its development stage, so early days yet; I am tackling the Rhodesian Bush War but from the intimacy of four close friends who initially resist but are corrupted by the brutality and shape-shifting, mind-altering process the army puts you through. It is a largely poetical piece with poignant yet brutal close quarter fighting. The other film is more fully developed and could soon go into production. It is entitled *At the Gates of Thunder* and it tells the story of Dr. Livingstone's failed Zambezi expedition. I have just completed my latest film *Sylvia—Tracing Blood*, a documentary about Sylvia Raphael, one of Mossad's most effective agents.

9

Gritty Streets

AN INTERVIEW WITH BUDDY GIOVINAZZO BY JOHANNES SCHÖNHERR

Much to the disgust of the mainstream media, a new cinematic subculture spread through West Germany in the late 1980s: violent nihilist movies made by American independent directors who didn't give a damn about any "horror," "crime" or "action" genre conventions. The films were dirty and bloody and offered no way out for their characters nor for the viewer.

Festivals sprung up to show these films, like the Weekend of Fear in Nuremberg and Horror Bizarre in Regensburg. Fanzines popped up to provide information on the films; *Howl* from Munich and *Splatting Image* from Berlin were the most prominent.

All that interest was geared towards the bleak and raw wave of killer flicks and gore comedies of the day: John McNaughton's *Henry: Portrait of a Serial Killer* (1986), Jim Muro's junkyard bum and killer booze comedy *Street Trash* (1987), Jim Van Bebber's gangland splatter actioner *Deadbeat at Dawn* (1986), Stuart Gordon's *Reanimator* (1985), New Zealander Peter Jackson's *Bad Taste* (1987) ... and Buddy Giovinazzo's *Combat Shock* (1984).

Combat Shock made its way into the German horror scene first via a variety of bootleg video versions. None of them lived up to what we had read about the movie in *Films That Bite*, a groundbreaking text written by Steve Bissette and included in Chas Balun's *Deep Red Horror Handbook*. Bissette's description made this film sound like the *real thing*—but the videos were not. The gore footage was edited out to various degrees; one version even ended the film before Frankie, the main character, goes on his final rampage.

Eventually, a 35mm film version became available via an independent movie theater in Hamburg. It was just as disappointing: Frankie, sitting on a chair, puts a gun to his head and fires it, standing next to the table after a cut. Thus cutting out him killing all of his family—the central scene of the film.

The film remained a mystery. At every horror festival, rumors spread about what was included in the original version and what was not. Buddy Giovinazzo seemed to be out of reach to even the most dedicated festival organizer. Peter Jackson got flown in to Nuremberg, newly discovered gore veteran Herschell Gordon Lewis made the rounds, but nobody seemed to be able to locate Buddy Giovinazzo.

Meeting Buddy Giovinazzo

I first met Buddy Giovinazzo at Cinema Village in New York City in early 1994. I was screening Jim Van Bebber's *Deadbeat at Dawn* in a special midnight series and it turned out to be the first screening of the film in a real movie theater in New York. Jim made it to the screening all the way from his home town, Dayton, Ohio, traveling on the cheapest bus available through a blizzard. After the show, Jim introduced me to one of his New York friends who simply said: "Glad to meet you. I'm Buddy Giovinazzo."

Now, I could finally find out about all those old mysteries … about the original cut of *Combat Shock* and about the man behind the movie.

I soon arranged a few shows for the original cut of *Combat Shock*, which had originally been titled *American Nightmare*. The print came from the director. Slowly, I got to learn more about the director, his background and his other productions.

Buddy Giovinazzo's Background

Buddy Giovinazzo was born in 1957 as Carmine Giovinazzo in Port Richmond, a mixed Italian-black neighborhood on Staten Island, New York, to a family of Italian descent. His father ran a music school and his sons Ricky and Buddy started out in their teens as musicians. They played in a studio band—jazz and rock, *King Crimson* style. Buddy went to study music at Staten Island College. His family wasn't wealthy enough to pay for all of his studies, so he needed to depend on financial aid which was only available to full-time students. He had to enroll for 12 credit points per semester to be considered studying full-time. Being at a loss what additional classes to enroll in to receive the 12 credits, Buddy enlisted in a film class. They were working with Super 8 and he was suddenly in charge of doing the work of a film director—creating short movies and having the responsibility to get all actors, technicians, etc., to do what they were supposed to do. He loved it!

But music was still his main interest and he formed a new band with his brother Ricky, Circus 2000 A.D., this time playing underground venues like CBGB in Manhattan. Heavy rock was their agenda, Buddy being the drummer. But music alone didn't provide kicks enough and, true to the fashion of the day, Buddy arranged for violent film footage screened as wallpaper behind the band while they performed. It was footage that Buddy shot himself, but more often than not, it was grisly true crime magazine photos filmed with a 16mm camera. Like a Charles Manson spread from various magazines filmed and projected behind the band when they played their song "Return of Charlie." That being the age of MTV starting, Buddy did also a couple of "music videos" (all shot on 16mm) for the band, to be projected during intermissions.

But playing in the band proved to be a major problem in the long run. Several of the band members had regular jobs on Staten Island and complained about having to play CBGB on Wednesday night at one a.m. They had to get back to Staten Island the same night and be at work at six in the morning. Meanwhile, Buddy got more and more interested in directing films. He thought he had more talent doing that—and when being the director of a movie, he could dictate all details on the set.

In this period, while still playing with the band, he made his first "real" film, the 15-minute short *Subconscious Realities*, based on Ken Russell's *Altered States* (1980). Russell's film may be considered a drug movie but Giovinazzo wasn't interested in drug hallucinations as such; he was more interested in visions. Visions in an old Italian Catholic style where you see Madonnas while you're sober—not on acid. I haven't seen this movie and can't comment on it but for Giovinazzo it was a departure.

American Nightmare *aka* Combat Shock *(1984)*

That next feature was to be *American Nightmare*. According to Giovinazzo, the original inspiration came from being around Staten Island's swamps and having the thought, "Hey, those swamps look like Vietnam in the movies!" It was initially conceived as a short jungle piece with his brother Ricky accidentally killing a Viet Cong girl, then being captured and tortured by the Viet Cong. The footage was all shot in the Staten Island swamps, with Giovinazzo's Asian students standing in as Viet Cong fighters.

Right at that point, Giovinazzo was offered a paying job teaching film at his own college. It would relieve him of some financial pressures and set a new goal for his life: film director. He quit the fledgling band and put all his money into the Vietnam movie which he changed into a Vietnam veteran movie with the "jungle scenes" serving as intro and flashbacks. That film, later known as *Combat Shock*, features all the obsessions that would recur in most of Giovinazzo's later work: a cast of characters who are all desperate, hopeless and see violence as their only option to react to their situation, torturing flashbacks that give a reason why the main character acts the way he does, and a slow build-up to an explosive ending that "solves" all problems by exterminating everyone in sight.

Ricky Giovinazzo plays Frankie, a Vietnam veteran in the dilapidated streets of Buddy's own old Staten Island neighborhood. Everything goes wrong for him: the carton of milk in the fridge, the only food in the run-down apartment, is sour, his shoelace breaks, his wife is complaining, his baby, crippled by Agent Orange, cries constantly. Add an eviction notice from the landlord and you know Frankie is having a bad day. He's *just* stepped out of his apartment when Paco, the leader of a small gang of thugs, chases him down, demanding that Frankie pay back a loan. After a few threatening words, Paco lets him go, insisting on payment later the same day. Frankie tries to find work. But for a troubled character like Frankie with no special skills, no job is available. The employment office case worker is apologetic but what are his apologies worth on a day like that?

Frankie is not the only down-and-outer in the neighborhood. One derelict fishes rotten meat out of a maggot-infested garbage can, and Frankie's old friend Mike (Michael Tierno) robs a woman at gunpoint to buy heroin from Paco. Frankie would never resort to this kind of low-life crime. Or would he?

For Mike, it was the last dope purchase. Lacking a needle, he rips his vein open with a coat hanger—a coat hanger previously used for an illegal abortion (there is still a fetus dangling from it)—and simply rubs the bag of smack into his vein. Despite wasting most of the precious dope that way, he O.D.s. (It's later revealed that the drug had been poisoned by Paco to kill Mike.)

Frankie eventually calls his millionaire father. But his father, in poor health and living in a special care facility, refuses to consider Frankie's situation. Frankie had married a woman the father didn't approve of. The father remains unforgiving. (The desperate characters coming from a wealthy background and having to suffer for their choices in life is a recurrent theme in much of Buddy's work.)

Frankie does what he thought he would never do: He snatches a woman's handbag.

She runs after him. Paco and his two henchmen witness the crime and chase him down to the abandoned warehouse where Mike had died. The handbag doesn't contain any valuables—but it does contain a gun. Cornered by the thugs, Frankie uses the gun to shoot all three. Then, walking into an impressive sunset over a decayed industrial landscape, Frankie tells himself, "Now, I know what to do!"

He returns home. His wife scolds him for not bringing any money. He looks at the eviction notice she doesn't know about. The crippled baby cries. Frankie sits down in the kitchen, goes to the dripping water faucet. Frankie puts the gun to his head. The baby cries. Frankie loves his wife and kid—and he is going take them with him. He tells his wife, "I love you" and shoots her. But, unlike in mainstream movies, she doesn't die, but pukes up blood and moans in pain. He shoots her over and over again and screams "Die, why don't you die!" until she is finally dead. He shoots the baby in its basket and to make sure, puts it into the oven with the heat on. While some brown fluid is leaking out of the oven, Frankie tries to get a glass of water, but the water is suddenly off. He looks into the fridge—only that rotten milk is sitting in there. He pours himself a glass of that milk—and gulps it down. The water faucet is dripping again. Frankie sits at the kitchen table, gulping down more of the bad milk. Police pound on the door. Frankie raises the gun to his head, blows a bullet through it, and slides down the wall with blood spurting out of his head. End of the story.

Ricky Giovinazzo in the final scene of *American Nightmare/Combat Shock* (courtesy Buddy Giovinazzo).

It took Buddy Giovinazzo two years to shoot the film and you can see the financial problems that hampered the project throughout right on the screen: Most of the "actors" are not actors but just friends who happened to have time on the afternoon a certain scene was shot. While Ricky Giovinazzo is convincing throughout as Frankie, many of the supporting actors are not.

One of the least convincing is the third member of Paco's gang. Paco and his sidekick give a somewhat convincing performance as mean-spirited Latinos while the one white

Troma poster for *Combat Shock* (courtesy Buddy Giovinazzo).

gang member wears a karate bandana, chains and leather clothes. Actually, he was a last-minute choice after another friend of Buddy backed out and sent this replacement, who wore the outfit he wore when appearing on stage as a heavy metal musician. He comes off as a cartoon character, not a menacing criminal.

American Nightmare (as the film was still known when it was completed) does have many flaws: very slow pacing in the middle and poor acting from the minor characters. The swamps of Staten Island do not resemble Vietnam.

However, the hopelessness of Frankie's situation, the violence of the neighborhood and the bloody end of the main character are quite convincing. Giovinazzo definitely did the best he could do under the circumstances. If Giovinazzo had made an independent film like *Combat Shock* in the 1960s, he might have attracted the attention of Roger Corman. Given another shot at directing a cheap violent film may have been a stepping-stone to making it big in Hollywood.

That was on Giovinazzo's mind when finishing the movie. He didn't want to be part of any "underground scene" (of which he had actually no knowledge at the time), he wanted to use the film to break into the mainstream movie business—his way. But times had changed. A film that showed gritty, desperate scenes, conveyed no hope and ended in bloodshed was a product Hollywood producers didn't see as a recommendation.

Giovinazzo, showing the film around, met Rick Sullivan of the horror fanzine *Gore Gazette*. Sullivan was running a screening series at a Lower East Side bar called The Dive. It was a central meeting point for the horror and splatter crowd. Some nights, Dianne Thorne would proudly present the *Ilsa* movies she had acted in, with director Don Edmonds attending as well. These cheap, scandalous, hair-raising productions became cult favorites.

The crowd at The Dive celebrated Giovinazzo's film. The bloody, relentless psycho picture made in true punk spirit—the "just do it" spirit—was exactly their taste. Exploitation movie distributor Troma got word of it and bought the movie—changing the title to *Combat Shock* and cutting out several scenes (most noticeably the coat hanger scene) to secure an "R" rating.

Horror writer Steve Bissette checked the film out, and the rest is history. In Bissette's article "Films That Bite" in the *Deep Red Horror Handbook*, he wrote about *American Nightmare* alongside Jörg Buttgereit's *Nekromantik* (1987) and *Street Trash* (1987), Soon there was world-wide interest in the film. Mutilated versions began to wash up on Europe's shores.

Maniac 2 *(1986)*

While completing *American Nightmare*, a friend of Giovinazzo told him that Joe Spinell, the star of William Lustig's 1980 gore classic *Maniac*, was looking for a director to shoot a sequel. In *Maniac*, Spinell played a frighteningly convincing serial killer who hunts down and kills women to cut their scalps off and place them onto the heads of a big array of mannequins stored in his filthy flat. Giovinazzo got the phone number of a bar on 82nd Street and the advice that Spinell would be there every night. He called and reached Spinell, who told him to come to the bar at midnight. They quickly became friends and Spinell agreed with Giovinazzo's film ideas. They shot a truly grisly trailer for *Maniac 2* in which Spinell cooks a human head on the stove of a filthy kitchen.

Buddy Giovinazzo (left) and Joe Spinell on the set of *Maniac 2* (courtesy Buddy Giovinazzo).

With the help of this trailer, Buddy and Spinell now went out to raise money for the final film. Producers were shocked to see the atrocious images and didn't want to have anything to do with it. However, Giovinazzo was hopeful until the news came that Joe Spinell had died of a heart attack. The project died with it. No actor could have played the lead in *Maniac 2* but Joe Spinell.

Slice of Life *(circa 1990)*

Troma kept exploiting *Combat Shock* but there seemed to be no way into the film world for Giovinazzo. The only picture he made in the ensuing years was a short video entitled *Slice of Life*. It features his friend Steven Oddo doing what he loved most—cutting himself up with a razor.

There are a lot of rumors surrounding the shooting of this picture, including one that Giovinazzo encountered Oddo and his girlfriend on a rooftop while actually planning to shoot something else—and then just filmed what he saw. "Rumors" is what they are. *Slice of Life* was a preconceived, though not exactly scripted, shoot. But it does look very accidental: Oddo is on the rooftop of a building next to Tompkins Square Park in the East Village and you can clearly make out the noise that the homeless in their tent city below are making. Oddo's girlfriend tells him that she can't stand him any more and that she wants him to back off. Oddo tries to hold onto her via the powers of masochism: He starts cutting his skin. She is not interested and insults him even more. The more she insults him, the more he cries and begs her not to leave him and cuts himself more to prove how much pain she is inflicting on him. In the end, he is a just a bleeding bundle on the tar paper–covered roof. She looks at him with all the disgust she can muster and leaves. End of the movie.

It doesn't look like role play—it looks like a couple caught in the middle of a terrible situation. But of course, it was role play. You can see Oddo proudly cutting WAR into his chest in the opening credits of Nick Zedd's *War Is Menstrual Envy* (1992) if you want to see an example of Oddo's mastership in the use of the blade. But most likely, you will not be able to see *Slice of Life*. Oddo gave his life a new spin shortly after the completion of the film. He quit his girlfriend and his habit of cutting himself and didn't want to have his self-mutilations seen on screen any more. He actively tried to suppress all films featuring them. Giovinazzo agreed to protect Oddo's privacy, kept his promise and has not shown his film to anyone since Oddo made his request. (Nick Zedd did not listen to Oddo's pleas.)

Slice of Life was the closest Giovinazzo ever got to being part of the New York underground's then-fading Cinema of Transgression—by applying the same *cinema vérité* aesthetics as the underground and by employing underground figure Oddo. But Giovinazzo had no intention of becoming a Lower East Side underground celebrity living in poverty.

Life Is Hot in Cracktown—*The Book (1993)*

Giovinazzo next turned to writing. Writing needs no budget. Just a laptop computer, ideas and a quiet space. Giovinazzo had all of that—especially the ideas. His first book *Life Is Hot in Cracktown* (New York: Thunder's Mouth Press, 1993) was advertised by the publisher: "Not since *Last Exit to Brooklyn* has there been a book as shocking and emotionally riveting as *Life Is Hot in Cracktown*." *Cracktown* is strongly reminiscent of Hubert Selby's *Last Exit to Brooklyn* (1964). Both books deal intimately with the life of criminal outcasts, talk a rough language and consist of loosely connected stories that portray a neighborhood rather than telling a stringent narrative.

Selby's classic depicts the life of outlaws, living on the very margins in the fairly quaint and safe New York of the 1950s. By the late 1980s and early 1990s, however, crime was at its peak in New York City and gang members, drug dealers and prostitutes were not some strange outsiders but stood on the street corners of the respectable neighborhoods—and they ruled the streets in the less respectable ones.

Giovinazzo did not hang out with those folks but he encountered them every day, by then living on the Lower East Side. He started to wonder what they might do all day long—what their lives were like and what made them what they were. *The New York Post*, New York's cheapest and bloodiest daily, had all the great crime reports and provided plenty of insight into what was happening out there. No shooting went unmentioned in the paper, and reporters were sent out immediately to the crime scene once the paper smelled blood. Giovinazzo read all of it.

Vincent Musetto (1941–2015) was one of the main *New York Post*

Book cover of the first edition of *Life is Hot in Cracktown* (courtesy Buddy Giovinazzo).

headline poets at the time. He became famous in 1983 for thinking up the title "Headless Body in Topless Bar" for a story about a kidnapping and murder at a Queens stripper bar. Musetto was later put in charge of the *Post*'s film section where he championed gritty independent films. In 1996, he chose the headline "It's rated G, for gross" for a review of the original cut of Giovinazzo's *American Nightmare*.

Life Is Hot in Cracktown is fiction but daily occurrences—personal encounters with gang members and tabloid reports enriched by Giovinazzo's vivid imagination—were the source material. The book is a dense collection of short stories taking place in a fictional neighborhood somewhere in the South Bronx, then the center of New York crime. A neighborhood inhabited by violent hard-drinking fathers, careless crack-smoking mothers, pre-teen prostitutes, crack smokers and hardened criminals from an ethnic spectrum. At least the young ones have dreams and hope—and even some of the older ones do—but it wouldn't be a Giovinazzo book if all those hopes weren't shattered within a few pages.

In *Combat Shock*, it was one character, Frankie, who had all the bad luck—and he was a likable character. People around him were even more down-on-their-luck than he was, though he is the one running amok in the end. *Cracktown* offers a large variety of characters, from innocent but trapped in a bad situation to extremely depraved.

Characters include poor girl Londa in "Londa Fries Her Egg" who has to endure a violent father and finds her only solace in smoking crack (for which she gives blow jobs); Manny, who works the late night shift in a bodega to support his family (his retarded toddler screams endlessly) and ends up shooting a robber with an illegal gun; a washed-up prostitute sold to a sadistic killer by her pimp; a rich white housewife who visits the area to buy crack (it relieves her boredom), and Romeo and his gang who terrorize old people in their own apartments. That last story, "Bullets and Brutality," has such a violent intensity that some readers might find it hard to endure.

Immediately after the publication of the book, Giovinazzo turned the story collection into a film scenario with Manny's bodega in the center and the other stories taking place around it. It took many years, but Giovinazzo was able to make *Life Is Hot in Cracktown* into a movie.

Poetry and Purgatory *(1996)*

Giovinazzo's grim novel *Poetry and Purgatory* was published by Thunder's Mouth Press in 1996. He tells the story from the perspective of Eddie, a Times Square lowlife who has discontinued the treatment of his brain tumor and fights the constant pain by swallowing large amounts of illegally obtained prescription drugs. The drugs keep him in a whacked- out state most of the time, and in his mind, reality, visions and imaginations blur. In many cases, the reader doesn't know what is real and what isn't—though for Eddie, of course, everything happens as told.

Eddie's lesbian sister works as a dominatrix in need of additional income. She turns to blackmail and involves Eddie in her scam to have some of her customers photographed while undergoing sadistic treatment. She employs Eddie to do the photo work. He bungles it by being too unstable to even stand straight behind his cover. The customer (who had just eaten a plate full of feces) starts screaming and runs out. Soon after, the sister is brutally murdered and her S&M studio ransacked. Eddie is sure the customer was the killer and starts to look for him, but his unstable mindset hampers his efforts. At the same time, Eddie is getting involved with Kaval, an HIV-infected shoplifter with an explosive temper. They move in together, on the corner of Avenue B and 11th Street.

The intersection of Avenue B and 11th Street was quite a happening area in 1994 and '95. It had two bodegas, whose real business wasn't in old-fashioned groceries. The bodega on the East Side of Avenue B sold crack, the bodega on the West Side sold vodka without a license. In New York City, licensed liquor stores have to close at 11 p.m. and are not allowed to open on Sundays. Thus, that bodega had long lines of winos late at night and on Sundays.

In the end, Kaval is dead. Did Eddie kill her? Did the gas stove really explode? Eddie is back on treatment and off the pills ... or is that just a vision, too?

The story makes little sense but it succeeds in convincingly portraying a truly disturbed mind. Giovinazzo felt "constantly depressive" those days—a state of mind that certainly had its influence on the way he describes Eddie's view of the world.

Moving to Los Angeles and trying to get film projects off the ground didn't help. Nothing came of those efforts.

No Way Home *(1997)*

It was money from Europe that made his next film possible. A representative of Goldcrest Films from London saw *American Nightmare* (the uncut original of *Combat Shock*) at an underground show at Limbo Café in the East Village in 1994, liked it and arranged the realization of Giovinazzo's next film *No Way Home*.

This time, there was a real budget and real actors; it was shot in Giovinazzo's old and quite dilapidated Staten Island neighborhood. Tim Roth plays Joey, an ex-convict just arriving home after a six-year prison stint. Having no other place to go, he moves in with his brother Tommy (James Russo) who is now married to a gorgeous blonde (Deborah Unger). Joey's main goal is to start a new and honest life. But Tommy, a small-time drug dealer, is in trouble with the mob. He wants to enlist Joey in his business. Joey declines—and we learn that he took the rap and went to prison for crimes actually committed by Tommy. Joey becomes more and more friendly with Tommy's wife. Tommy doesn't like that. Tensions simmer and explode in one big bloody finale ... much bloodier and detailed than Goldcrest had bargained for.

Another gritty story of hopelessness and despair—though this time the actors really knew how to pull it off. It's simply great to see them interact.

First Success in Germany

American distributors didn't think that way. Despite the big names of the actors, the film went straight to video with no U.S. theatrical release. It was the same story in the U.K., Goldcrest's home turf. The only country where *No Way Home* received a theatrical release (limited to art houses) was Germany. There, the film was re-titled *Unter Brüdern* (*Among Brothers*) and dubbed into German by Munich independent distributor TiMe.

Germany seemed a place particularly open to Buddy Giovinazzo's way of looking at things. Americans weren't "into" Giovinzzo's dark views; Germans loved them. The novel *Life Is Hot in Cracktown* was translated and published by the small Maas Verlag. *Poetry and Purgatory* was re-titled *Poesie der Hölle* (*Poetry of Hell*), and initially published by Maas Verlag but in 1998 picked up by major pocket book publisher Droemer-Knaur. The national news magazines *Der Spiegel* gave the latter a rave review as most of the quality dailies of the country did. Germany seemed like a place to go for Buddy Giovinazzo.

Meeting Buddy in Berlin

In late spring 1998, I toured Europe with a package of Japanese underground and cyberpunk movies. I hadn't heard from Buddy for quite a while, though I had read the *Der Spiegel* review of *Poesie der Hölle* and had seen *No Way Home* at a theater.

I was sitting at an outdoor cafe in the Kreuzberg neighborhood in Berlin, having a late breakfast, when someone came walking down the street who looked strikingly familiar. I thought, "If this would be New York, this would be Buddy Giovinazzo." But in Berlin—that would be hard to believe. He walked straight up to me and said: "Hi. Remember me? Buddy from New York."

He was in town, he told me, because he had received a DAAD grant to write a book. [The DAAD, or Deutscher Akademischer Austauschdienst German Academic Exchange Service, is a study and research program in Germany for foreign students.] And he was teaching film at the Dffb [Deutsche Film-und Fernsehakademie Berlin is the German Film and Television Academy in Berlin]on a temporary basis. He said he was glad to be away from Los Angeles, but he didn't know what he would be doing after the current time-limited support program he had gotten from the German sponsoring agencies.

We lost contact again after this short meeting, only to meet another time by coincidence in Berlin in early 2000. I went to a party given by Berlin independent cinemas at the WFM club in conjunction with the Berlin Film Festival and ran into Buddy there. Over the loud techno music, he told me that he was in the middle of making a movie in Berlin.

The Unscarred *(2000)*

TiMe, the distributor of *No Way Home*, had learned that it could be more profitable to produce movies than to buy distribution rights. A whole lot of German state subsidies could be cashed producing movies—and TiMe would have a product to sell in the end. They liked *No Way Home* and thought Giovinazzo would be the right person to make a movie for them. He agreed.

But he didn't have a script ready for any story taking place in Berlin. He had already written a good part of his new book *Potsdamer Platz* but it wasn't finished yet and TiMe did not want to use the story. So they went for a screenplay written by American Todd Komarnicky. It took place in Prague but it could be easily adapted to Berlin. To secure German government funding, a German co-writer was invented, "Karl Junghans." Under the working title *Everybody Dies,* Giovinazzo began shooting. The story is about a complicated staged-death plot by several Stanford University graduates who want to scare off the man who constantly blackmails them. Not really Giovinazzo material.

Back in 1979, as the film story goes, they were all on a Stanford student exchange in Berlin: Mickey, Johann, Rafaella and Travis. Mickey and Travis get in a drinking competition over who wins Rafaella. Travis loses and, in a violent fit, pushes Mickey over the balcony of the dormitory. Mickey survives but his sports career is finished and Travis has to pay him damages for the rest of their lives.

Fast-forward to 1999: Mickey (now played by James Russo) has a manual job at a metal workshop in Newark, New Jersey, and he has gambled away all his money. A Mafia money-lender wants his cash back *or else*. He shows Mickey a corpse in the trunk of his car. That same night, Mickey gets a call from Johann in Berlin, inviting him over to a reunion of old friends. Mickey accepts. Cut to Berlin. Johann (Heino Ferch) and Travis (Stave Waddington) pick Mickey up and drive him to Johann's house. Johann has become a successful architect, married to Rafaella (Ornella Muti) and living in very spacious quarters he installed in an abandoned East Berlin metal factory.

They all enjoy their reunion, going out drinking to a techno club at night. Travis picks up a girl and takes her to Johann's house. Suddenly, in the middle of the night—a scream, glass shattering. Mickey goes to check. Travis stands there, devastated, pointing at the girl, apparently dead in the midst of a broken glass table. The upstairs railing broke when Travis pressed the girl against it, kissing her, he explains. Who is calling the cops? "Nobody," Johann intervenes. He has built the place without a permit … and who is going to believe the story that the girl just fell down anyway? They have to get rid of the corpse and also prevent the momentarily absent Rafaella from learning of the incident.

The next morning, Mickey and Travis drive downtown to buy a new glass table. On their way back, they drive down a one-way street, the wrong way, and are signaled to stop by police. A rather well-done car chase through East Berlin follows. They manage to escape the cop car. (Convincing car chases are a rarity in German-made movies. Here Giovinazzo's direction really stood out.) Eventually Mickey stops and reveals the real reason he came to Berlin: He demands a large sum of cash from Travis, to be paid right there and then. After getting it, he says, he'll leave Travis alone for good. Travis balks.

Later that day, the dead girl's brother shows up, looking for her. Johann shoots him. Now they have two corpses to take care of. Johann and Travis go to dispose of the corpses. Rafaella and Mickey have a tense encounter—they were lovers for a while and now Mickey wants cash from her. She declines.

Johann and Travis come back. All have an uneasy dinner, poorly faking they are having a great time. Rafaella asks a few clever questions—and the men reveal what has happened. Surprisingly, she is all for covering the killings up, but insists on doing it the right way. They all drive to the secluded river area where Johann and Travis had thrown the corpses into the water, ready to fish the floating bodies out again and to make sure they sink. Suddenly, they all turn against Mickey, telling him that he was the one to blame. His fingerprints were all over the crime. If police ever get nosy, the other three will join forces and blame it all on him. They hand him a ticket back to New York, drive him to the airport and tell him never to contact them again.

Cut to the house: Johann, Raffaela and Travis are celebrating, and the "dead" girl and her "brother" are with them. They discuss how great it all went, that their game worked perfectly well and that they finally got rid of bothersome Mickey.

Not so. Mickey suddenly stands in the door … you can imagine the rest. It's bloody.

The Unscarred (the film's final title) did not fare well with the few critics who saw it and or with film buyers. It does look more like a TV play than a big-screen film (despite being shot with a Steadicam all the way through). There isn't one likable character in the picture and the acting is a problem, too. James Russo is great, but that serves only to show how poor the acting is from the other actors. The film played a few festivals and was eventually released on DVD.

Potsdamer Platz

Buddy Giovinazzo went on writing *Potsdamer Platz*. For the last couple of years, Berlin's Potsdamer Platz has been the biggest construction area in Europe. Berlin wants to recreate its famous center of the 1920s in a futuristic style. In the 1920s, Potsdamer Platz was the busiest business district in all of Europe. Bombed to smithereens in World War II, it was divided by the Berlin Wall up to 1989. You can get a good view of the Potsdamer Platz of this period in Wim Wenders' *Wings of Desire* (1987).

In Giovinazzo's story, the New Jersey Mafia, always active in the construction business, send their henchmen to try to get a foot in the door. But the Russian Mafia, having good connections to enforcers from the former East German Stasi secret police, has the same plans. Of course, the Stasi folks know how things in Germany and in its construction business work while the New Jersey folks know nothing but killing. Until one of them falls in love with an East German girl.

The book was published in the U.S. by No Exit Press in 2004.

Interview with Buddy Giovinazzo (2015)

I followed the later developments of Buddy Giovinazzo's career in the succeeding years from a distance. While I was staying in Japan, Buddy was living in Berlin, mostly working for German TV, it seemed. In 2009, he finished and successfully released a film adaptation of *Life Is Hot in Cracktown* as an American independent movie.

I did the following e-mail interview with Giovinazzo in the summer of 2015 to find out about his more recent activities.

Johannes Schönherr: *In the last couple of days, I went through some of your recent productions. You are active in a lot of different cinematic fields both in Germany and in the U.S. Maybe the best starting point for this interview would be your* Genre Showreel. *It's only three minutes long but I suppose it features exactly the type of movies that you are most interested in.*

Buddy Giovinazzo: I can't deny that I must be interested in those films, because I made them all. But I'm interested in many types of films: drama, history, comedy, just about everything. But I feel my heart belongs to the characters who are outside of the mainstream, characters who fall through the cracks of society. Those characters speak to me intimately; for some reason I can see their lives clearly in my imagination. Also, I felt there weren't very many people telling these stories, so I felt I had something to offer in that regard.

The Genre Showreel *shows almost exclusively violent scenes.*

The reason for the violence in the *Genre Showreel* is that it was made as a showreel for the Frontiere's Film Market during the Fantasia Film Festival [in Montreal]. For this audience, I put together what I felt would excite a horror audience. But I could never show this reel to producers and people I know in L.A. I would never work again, and I'd probably be barred from their offices. My wife viewed the reel (and she's seen some pretty hard stuff; she's married to me, after all) and she said it was like being hit over the head with a lead pipe. I was very flattered.

The scenes in the Genre Showreel *all come from your more or less independent productions. No German TV crime drama is included.*

There are actually a couple short clips from German TV, the

Buddy Giovinazzo (right) and Udo Kier of *Polizeiruf 110* (courtesy Buddy Giovinazzo).

Polizeiruf 110 [*Police Dial 110*, an East German TV crime series] with Udo Kier. I've done some of my best work as far as character scenes in German TV but those films aren't really Buddy Giovinazzo films. They're made for a specific audience; a German TV audience. And I don't really feel an authorship to those films. They're not my scripts or my stories, I'm a director for hire on those productions and I have to stay within the boundaries of German TV standards, which means no blood, or not much blood anyway. Not too much violence, most of it has to take place off-camera. It's sort of against my vision as an artist, where I believe violence should be shocking and horrifying, disgusting, just the way it is in real life.

How did you get involved with German TV?

I moved to Berlin in 1998 having won a DAAD grant that allowed me to live for six months rent-free in Berlin. I was living in L.A. at the time and was going through a horrible time, emotionally and financially. I thought I would come to Berlin for a few months, clear out my head, then come back to L.A. to work on my career. Well, after three weeks I was happy in Berlin, fell in love with the city, and decided to stay. Shortly after, a German TV station, Bayerischer Rundfunk, contacted me about working for them. They loved my film *No Way Home*, it was quite successful here in Germany. That's how I got my start. I only had to learn German first.

How is working for German TV different from your own work?

It's completely different in that it's not written by me. The stories are already developed and written before I come onto the production. I've had to rewrite nearly all the scripts I've directed for production reasons and dialogue, so I try to slip in my own thoughts and ideas. I bring a lot of humor to the crime genre here in Germany. I always look for personal moments that have nothing to do with the crime story and present them as part of the drama. So far, it's worked for me and the German audience seems to like it.

Did you ever write your own script for a German TV crime drama?

No. I don't think I ever will either. If I'm going to write something to direct, I'd rather write my own film and not have it be part of a TV production. I don't think I could write for German TV. I find the parameters and limitations of staying in a traditional "crime genre" too confining.

The German TV work gave you some great opportunities. In one crime drama episode you got to work with Udo Kier.

Working with Udo Kier was a true pleasure. I've grown up watching Udo Kier films, notably *Mark of the Devil* [1970], *Andy Warhol's Frankenstein* [1973] and *Dracula* [1974], Lars von Trier films, etc. I've been a fan of Udo's for decades. He's a natural talent and a pleasure to be with on set. I met him at a film festival in 2000 in Vancouver and we became friends. Then when I could work with him in a *Polizeiruf 110* in 2004, I jumped at the chance.

You have also directed a few Tatort [Crime Scene] *TV crime drama episodes. It seems that in Germany,* Tatort *is a national obsession. In fact, reading a bunch of recent weekly* Tatort *reviews gave me the impression that* Tatort *has become a sort of focus point where the state of the nation is debated.* Tatort *doesn't simply show a crime and an investigation. The crime on hand seems to represent a certain topic that is under heated debate among the Germans. Like, say, neo-Nazis, organized crime, child abuse, criminal foreigners, etc. How do you feel about that situation as an American director shooting* Tatort *episodes?*

I have a good life in Germany shooting these episodes, but they're not what I normally watch. Some of them are really well made and the actors are generally first rate, but I much prefer shows like *The Sopranos*, or *Breaking Bad*, or *Mad Men*, or *The Wire*. The *Tatort* series has been on [West] German TV for over 45 years, it's an institution and a tradition, and it's great that this show has been running for so long and still has the popularity that it has. I'm privileged to be able to direct it, but at the same time, I find it difficult to try and bring something new to it because the structure is so firmly set by tradition: There's a murder, an investigation, and at the end the killer gets caught and must pay. Good must win out over evil. The bad guy can never win. That's too bad because sometimes the bad guy should win. But I guess that's the challenge of making *Tatort*: To find something new to bring to it. That's why a lot of the newer shows follow the news. They'll do a show about something taking place now in the news, whether it be child abuse, or Internet fraud, etc.

You've also worked for SOKO Leipzig. *I'm from Leipzig myself, lived there in the Communist era and worked as a gravedigger in Leipzig for a time back then. Leipzig was an absolutely run-down town at that time, the early 1980s … pretty much resembling Staten Island as you show it in* Combat Shock. *Your thoughts on the city and the series.*

I love Leipzig. My wife too. I rarely shoot in Berlin. My films are always shot in other cities, and I like all the different cities in Germany, they all have their own character and qualities. They all have their own beer, too! But Leipzig is very special to me. I love the rundown nature of the neighborhoods, the mentality is still somewhat of a DDR [old East German] mentality. When I work in Leipzig, we're all comrades working together, we're a family, with everything a family is, both good and bad. Shooting in Leipzig is the next best thing to shooting in Berlin.

Let's make a big jump and go to the run-down American inner city area portrayed in your 2009 film Life Is Hot in Cracktown, *a project you had planned for a long time.*

I had tried to make *Cracktown* for 13 years. I adapted the book shortly after it came out in 1993, then spent the rest of these 13 years trying to find a producer and a financier. People loved the script but always felt it was just too damn dark. Today, looking at it, it seems pretty light compared to what's on U.S. TV, but in the '90s and early 2000s, people were pretty horrified by the project.

Aside from the movie's child characters (basically Willie and his sister), it's hard to have any sympathy for anyone on screen. Ricky in Combat Shock *was a character a viewer could relate to; but watching* Life Is Hot in Cracktown, *I just wished pretty much everyone on screen a sudden death.*

    I find the characters, all of them actually, very sympathetic. But I guess as an author and filmmaker, you have to feel that way about your characters. My favorite characters are Marybeth and Benny, the transgender woman and her boyfriend. The more I think about it, I even love the worst character in the film, the most evil, Romeo, the young gang leader who rapes and murders. I find he has a sympathetic streak in that he's also a victim of his environment. If you remember when we both lived on the Lower East Side in the '80s and '90s, a lot of the people we knew from the neighborhood were low-lives and criminals, and yet they had a certain charm about them, they were likable in a crazy sort of way. We didn't trust them, or spend too much time with them—they were also dangerous characters—but for a short amount of time, it was fun being with them. That's how I feel about the characters in *Cracktown*.

Yes, it's a funny thing that we were both living on the Lower East Side in the early 1990s, a neighborhood that was very much like the one depicted in the movie. We both chose to live there on our own account and basically, we had a great life there. Plenty of weird freaks on the streets but actually, I felt rather safe there. We knew how to handle the neighborhood crazies.

    Yes, I miss those times and that neighborhood. I can't believe what's happened to New York City today. It's not my city any more, I just don't feel safe there with all the millionaires and gentrification. That to me is more dangerous than the drugs and criminals. Back then, you could live as an artist. Money wasn't so important because no one had it, and you felt a certain togetherness with the neighborhood. I miss that terribly.

Your most recent independent production A Night of Nightmares *[2012] is a horror film involving supernatural powers. To my knowledge, it was your first film in that genre. I thought it worked very well as a horror film. I suppose showing the violence of gritty inner city streets and making a well-paced horror movie need very different approaches.*

    A Night of Nightmares came to me from a producer friend who was looking to do this very low-budget film and wanted to know what I thought of the script. It wasn't something I wanted to do, or even thought about doing. But once I read the script, the character of Ginger really spoke to me. I loved her! I felt with some careful direction, this could be a really cool character piece with some good and creepy scares. I then jumped into doing it. It wasn't that different from my other films in that this was also a character piece. For me, it always begins with the character; once I fall in love with a character, then I can direct them and bring out the story. At the end of the day, the producers didn't want character development and we had some hard disagreements on the finished film. But it was their money and they were entitled to do what they wanted with it. They actually didn't like horror films, and it's very strange to make a horror film for producers who don't like horror films. It's a minor film in my career but I'm proud of it, especially the actors Marc Senter and Elissa Dowling, who I think are terrific.

Do you have any other projects in the works?

I'm working on a very dark TV series for U.S. TV. *The Fourth Nail* is a dark crime family drama taking place in Pittsburgh. It's got dark humor and violence, but the main character has a secret life that he keeps from his family and his friends. I'm meeting now with cable networks in L.A. about producing it early next year. It's something very close to my heart, criminals in a small city trapped by their environment and just trying to survive. It makes them do some desperate and horrible things. Should be interesting.

10

The Death King

An Interview with Jörg Buttgereit

Loathed by the authorities and a scourge to the censors and the morally righteous, German filmmaker Jörg Buttgereit has carved himself out a career as provocateur and director of a number of controversial films that have achieved infamy across the globe. Employing punk ethics and startlingly visionary visuals, his films have focused on such subjects as necrophilia (*Nekromantik*, 1987, and Nekromantik *II*, 1991), mediations on suicide (*Der Todesking*, 1989) and the warped psychosis of serial killers (*Schramm*, 1993). In essence, Buttgereit is a horror filmmaker who is drawn to the macabre and mankind's most perverse and violent tendencies and desires while commenting on the fragility of life. His artistic approach to his visual signature has alienated his work from some in the horror fraternity who deem it "too arty," despite the copious amount of blood-letting on screen and extreme imagery, like the genital mutilation in *Schramm* and the excessive finale of *Nekromantik II*.

Over 35 years later, his films are still culturally relevant and are being reassessed with a new critical keenness by audiences and critics to the extent that they are now lauded as underground classics in the mainstream press both in Europe and in America. Once vilified and refused classification in Britain and Germany, Buttgereit's notorious necrophilia films *Nekromantik I* and *II* are now uncut and available on home video. Clearly no longer a threat to world stability, Buttgereit's *Nekromantik* films are enjoying a renaissance and his work at last finding legitimacy in the cinematic world, instead of censorship and suppression. Cult film icon John Waters best summed up Buttgereit's *Nekromantik* as "the first ever erotic film for necrophiliacs."

Following on from this filthy classic, Buttgereit directed the acclaimed *Der Todesking* (1990), an episodic film split into seven parts to depict different days of the week, as we witness the violent and tragic demise of seven different individuals, generally by suicide. Buttgereit links these vignettes with the sight of a decomposing corpse, underlining that none of us can escape death's grasp. Death is shown to encompass many things: death as a reliever, death as a violent entity, death as the final act in our decomposition. The film is Buttgereit's best realization of horror as an art form while juxtaposing scenes of excessive and unflinching violence with moments that are profoundly moving.

Here, Buttgereit has made an anti-suicide film, asking the audience why these people have chosen death over life. Though on the surface Death ultimately reigns supreme, Buttgereit's message is equally about regeneration as while we see the body decompose, we

Iconic image from *Der Todesking* (1989) (courtesy Jörg Buttgereit).

notice that life replenishes itself, as maggots hatch from the corpse. From death comes life. While *Der Todesking* is repellent, it is still a fascinating exploration of the nature of death and those who decide to embrace it wantonly, while simultaneously asking you to question yourself about death and its inevitability.

Buttgereit seemed to stray into more conventional horror territory with *Schramm*, a serial killer flick that looked into the unbalanced psychosis of Lothar Schramm. Yet this deliriously insane descent into one man's heart of darkness is anything but conventional. With its non-linear plot and fragmented images, the film is the final memories of the protagonist as he lies dying in a pool of his own blood. As scattershot images of Schramm's psychopathic tendencies and fears and paranoia parade the screen, and his explosive impulses into the realms of sadistic violence and perversity, Buttgereit pieces together the warped mindset of an individual who has lost touch with reality and is consumed by a primal desire to murder. Buttgereit paints Schramm as a complex man with a serious personality disorder. One moment he is shown as friendly and helpful, the next he is murdering visitors and photographing their naked bodies for his sexual gratification. His extreme inability to relate to women has him fantasizing about toothed vaginas and drugging his prostitute neighbor and jerking off over her, while "the dirty whore," is passed out. Over the course of the film Buttgereit slowly scraps away the veneer of Schramm's psychosis to reveal the traumas that have led to his descent into madness.

I caught up with Jörg Buttgereit in September 2015 and did a career-spanning interview about his notorious films.

Matthew Edwards: *Do you consider yourself a horror filmmaker?*
Jörg Buttgereit: I'm a horror film director in your opinion?

Essentially, yes.
I'm happy with that. The thing is that horror fans buy *Nekromantik* DVDs but they consider my films too "arty," and the art house audiences consider my films too gruesome. So I'm stuck in the middle.

Your films are very artistic and well-shot but in a way that does alienate some horror audiences.
You are right, especially now with the release of *Der Todesking* [*The Death King*] in the U.S. It is the first time the film has been released in America on DVD and Blu-ray. It was released on VHS in the '90s by Film Threat. You can see when you read the reviews that people were puzzled by the film because it is an underground experimental film. But now horror film fans have to deal with it. They have problems with it, but they seem to like and appreciate the film, finally, after 25 years [*laughs*]. They recognize that these films are different.

That's right, your films are different. I think that's what has set you apart in the first place.
I was a horror and monster film fan but those films were made at a time when I was heavily involved in the punk rock movement in Germany. There had been an underground film scene in Germany but that was basically experimental movies. My first short movies were screened together with Derek Jarman's *In the Shadow of the Sun* [1974], which was scored by Robert Gristle. It was mainly colors and music, real experimental stuff. It was a strange combination of Jarman's films and my own. So even in the underground-experimental film scene in Germany and Europe, my films were unique because I was

doing films with a plot and not, on the first look, very political films. At the time, there were a lot of political films.

It is cited that your short film Bloody Excess in the Leaders Bunker *[1982] caused controversy.*
   The film itself didn't cause much problem because it was so small but at the premiere in a small punk club called the Risiko, where Blixa Bargeld of Einstürzende Neubauten used to be behind the bar and Nick Cave was hanging around there. I screened the film a few days after I went to a concert of the Dead Kennedys, the American punk band. At that gig, there was a lot of trouble because it was a noisy concert. The concert received lots of complaints because the whole audience was making a big fuss on the street. So the police came and searched me. They found fliers on me for the premiere of my film *Bloody Excess in the Leaders Bunker*. So at the premiere, a few days later, we had secret police in attendance at the club [*laughs*]! It was fun, but they realized it wasn't a neo-Nazi club or place, so they left and nothing happened. That film didn't cause too many problems. That came later with *Nekromantik II*.

The controversy, as I understand it, was over the use of concentration camp footage from another film shown alongside yours.
   Yes, that was strange. I had bought a 8mm film roll from a German flea market a few weeks earlier called *Nazi Death Camps*. It must have been from America because there was a swastika on it. So I bought it for a few bucks. Of course, it was very shocking. It was real concentration camp footage from 1945. I was so amazed that someone would release material like this for the home market. This Super 8 film roll had a colorful cover and on the back they had advertisements for cartoons. This was very alienating to me so I bought it and I presented it that evening in this context. I found this strange film at the flea market and I couldn't imagine what was on it and I screened it as a supporting film! Everyone was very puzzled by the film but the club was a tough place, full of drug users and alcoholics. People would never had admitted they were shocked by it.

Prior to directing Nekromantik, *you made the violent and dark short film* Hot Love *[1985] about a guy who rapes his former girlfriend and impregnates her with a monster baby. It is an extreme and shocking film. What are your memories working on that film?*
   That was my first step in the direction of a feature film. It was nearly 30 minutes long. I consider it still an amateur movie. It was my first attempt at doing something that would survive. When I made those films, including *Nekromantik*, I never thought I would be talking about those films 30 years later. I wasn't even sure that the film prints would survive all these showings and film clubs because very often I used the original prints. Only later did I meet Manfred Jelinski, the producer of *Nekromantik*, who was able to do film prints of my Super 8 films, so I was able to use copies instead of the original camera negatives in these clubs.
   Hot Love was also the first film that I tried to show not in clubs but in cinemas. So the first step to do this was to blow up the Super 8 films into 16mm. It was also presented for the first time in a big movie theater, here in Germany. It was an old cinema that was handled during that time by a punk collective. So we had our first splatter festival in that theater and *Hot Love* was the opening movie, I recall.

What was the reaction?
   During that time I had a reputation in Germany for doing gory films that were funny

and enjoyable. I think this film was the last film that was not particularly serious. How does it look today? I really can't judge these films. The plan was to do a clichéd horror comedy.

That definitely comes across, especially at the end with the monster baby. I also liked the creature effects. How did you achieve this on such a small budget?

I was unable to get into film school as they had rejected me. So I went to get an education as a decorator of windows for huge department stores. During this education, I learned to work with new materials and with wood, etc. So all the special effects and material that we used for *Hot Love* came from this education. A lot of stuff I learned on the job. I did silk screen printing so I was able to do my own stickers. This was my beginning in how to do special effects! A lot of stuff just came from the kitchen! I would say there was no real special effect equipment in that movie. It was all made from the kitchen or things that I stole from work.

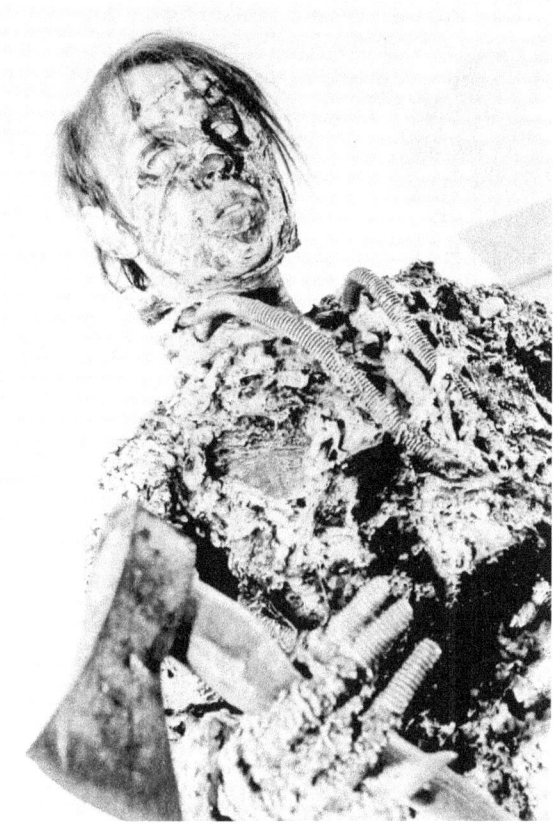

The boy monster ready to extract revenge on the girl/mother in Buttgereit's outrageous short film *Hot Love* (1985) (courtesy Jörg Buttgereit).

What I like about Hot Love *is that it is not intended to be taken seriously.*

The fact is that I wouldn't have been able to make a serious film because I was only working with friends. There were no actors. The same in *Nekromantik*. There are no professional actors in that movie. It is really hard to do something serious if you can only work with your friends. Also, no one would take me seriously at that time.

The same applies to Nekromantik. *Despite the subject matter, I feel it is a film that shouldn't be taken seriously.*

Interestingly, when the first *Nekromantik* reviews came out, I was surprised how positive they were and how seriously the film was taken. If I see the film, I wonder how seriously they were taking the film. The first review that I read, in a gay magazine, said that this was the first movie about AIDS, because people were going to bed with death. So I was surprised by this reaction and I wasn't prepared for the fact that people were taking it seriously because it has a lot of comedy aspects as well.

Both Nekromantik *and* Nekromantik II *are unflinching in their depiction of visual horror and pushing the envelope. They both seem like a finger up to the establishment as they force the audience to face up to imagery and horrors they would rather not look at.*

The will to provoke was part of the punk rock culture and that stayed close with me during the movie, I think. During that time, a lot of bands like Throbbing Gristle, SPK and early industrial bands came to Berlin and played in the same club where Dead Kennedys played in, SO36. It is a club that I did a documentary on in 1984, together with Manfred Jelinski. I saw these industrial bands on stage and next to the concert they also screened movies. Throbbing Gristle screened a movie called *After You Cease to Exist*, about a castration, and a friend of mine, standing next to me, was falling down after seeing this film. It was a combination of art and strong images and this was very impressive to me at the time.

There was a concert by the Australian band SPK and they screened footage they shot in a morgue in Australia. That was footage of cut-off dicks and heads and real corpses. So when I did *Nekromantik*, I had experiences in my head that were very impressive to me. So I never felt I was doing something really strong because what I saw on stage with SPK, because what they showed was much stronger and they were using the real thing.

However, in terms of the rabbit slaughter in *Nekromantik*, I wasn't really aware of how powerful these images would be. A lot of people had problems with that scene. People shouted at me when they left the cinema. When I screened the film in normal film festivals, in Berlin, or at special genre festivals, everything was fine. However, when I went to serious film festivals, the film was received very controversially.

Did you encounter any difficulties during the making of Nekromantik?

The production of all four feature films I did at that time was really exhausting. When you watch the making-of, which we produced at the time, it looks like fun. But

Disturbing imagery from Buttgereit's controversial *Nekromantik* (courtesy Jörg Buttgereit).

there was no real film crew, so I was really suffering from the fact that I had to do everything on my own. Manfred Jelinski, the producer, gave me the equipment and I could use his editing facility and his camera, but I had to make the film happen. I had to phone everyone, write the script and do the special effects. So often I was on set directing and I was already tired [*laughs*].

We could only shoot on weekends because people had to work during the week. So the film was like a big puzzle and the script was always evolving. From the beginning to the end, the film took two years to complete. That was the case with *Der Todesking* as well. *Der Todesking* was an episodic movie and again that did not have a main actor or a main plot. This was partly due to the hassle I had with *Nekromantik*. It was hard to convince the main actor to have the same haircut for two years! Small things like that became a big problem and made things difficult during shooting.

Both Nekromantik *and* Nekromantik II *have endured suppression and censorship in West Germany, with the latter seized by authorities in a move unprecedented since the Nazi era. What was your response to such a direct attack on your work?*
I already knew that the German authorities were very sensitive about horror movies. One of the reasons for doing *Nekromantik* was a protest against the censorship movement. Even ordinary horror movies like *Friday the 13th* were banned or heavily cut in Germany. You know about this in Great Britain as well, where you had the "Video Nasties" films. So the same thing happened in Germany. So I was kind of prepared that something would happen because it was a protest, but I was surprised that it took so long because *Nekromantik* was released in 1988 and *Nekromantik II* was released in 1991. As you can see, it took a while for the authorities to take me seriously as well.

After that, they tried to get rid of the first *Nekromantik* as well. So we had to go to court. Not only were the authorities trying to suppress the movie, they accused me of being a criminal. There's a term in Germany that says if you glorify violence, it is against the law. So they didn't just accuse me of doing a "wrong movie," they also accused me of doing a crime by doing the movie. I had to go to court to get the film back. We were lucky that the film was considered art by a film historian and they gave the film back to us. In the first place, the order of one judge was to destroy the negative of the movie.

What was so offensive about Nekromantik *and* Nekromantik II *in the government's eyes?*
I think the main problem was that we dared not to show the film to the classification board. We had the Do It Yourself spirit that we had taken from the punk rock movement. I decided to do everything on my own. I did the distribution on my own. Along with Manfred Jelinski, we set up our own distribution company to sell the film on VHS. I did my own film prints and went with the prints to the cinema and presented the film. It was all self-made and there was no way for the authorities to control it. That, I think, was the authorities' main concern.

Why are Nekromantik *and* Nekromantik II *now considered legitimate films and now available uncut in Germany, England and across Europe and America? Do you think we have become desensitized to violence, through mainstream media and Hollywood cinema?*
I think one of the effects might be that mainstream cinema is very gory today, too. They do big-budget remakes of old '70s or '80s horror movies. So it is more established, I think. On the other hand, I think that the fact that my films look very "arty," and the fact that they were made on Super 8 and 16mm, does make them look more like Warhol

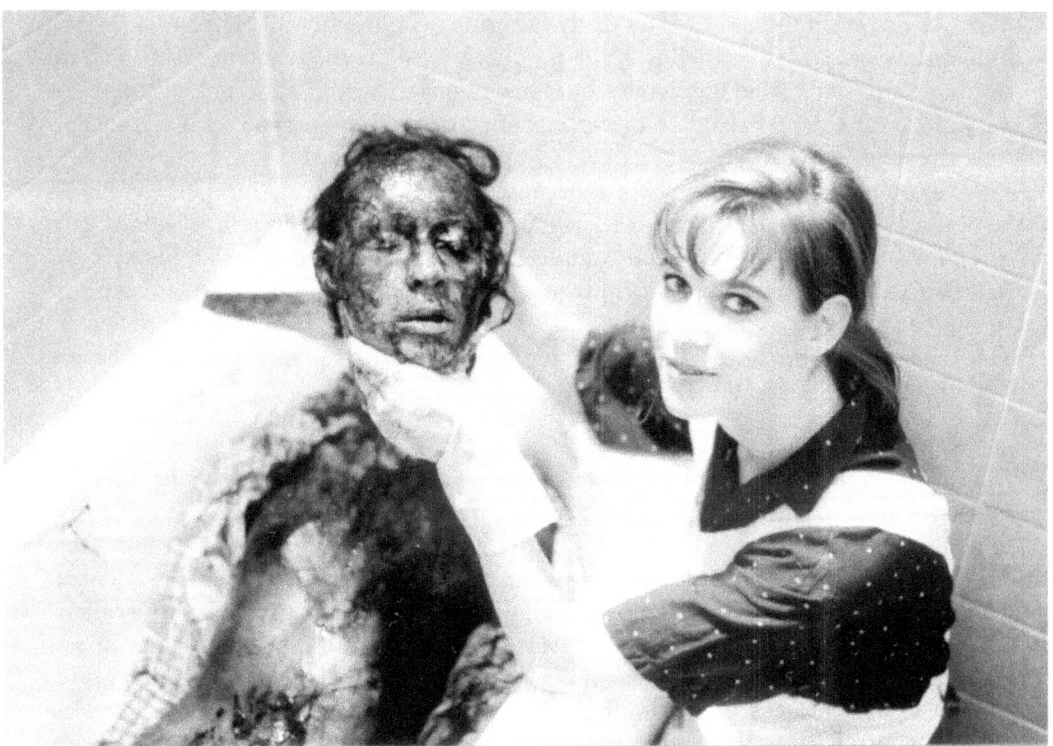

Monika M, as the woman, who digs up a corpse and hauls it home in gross out classic *Nekromantik 2* **(courtesy Jörg Buttgereit).**

movies and not so much like *Grindhouse* movies. This helped as well. You could also tell that I had serious subplots in the films as well. You could also see that these films were not made with big budgets or to make money. The films I made had no commercial value to them, and there wasn't at the time. We only started to make money years later. Now we make some money because the films are more available—in the U.S. they are selling so many copies that I could have only dreamed about during the '80s and '90s when we made them.

It is the art aspect and that the mainstream has gotten stronger. Also, the whole idea of censorship is not working any more. Even the censor knows that. If the BBFC think, "If we don't give *Nekromantik* or *Nekromantik II* an 18 certificate, what's the deal? They will just order the movie from Germany, the U.S. or elsewhere." You see, censorship doesn't work in the digital world.

Long ago I stopped buying DVDs from Britain if they were cut. I would get the complete films imported from elsewhere.

That's exactly what happened in Germany. You really harm your own country by not allowing the film industry to earn money. So it wasn't just a matter of not letting the films through because the films will be there anyway. The whole concept of censorship is pointless today.

Talk me through the production history of Der Todesking.

The idea stemmed from the concept of doing an episodic movie as I wasn't prepared to do another movie with one actor again. It took such a long time to do, over two years of production.

In the beginning we had a few ideas that wouldn't stick together as a whole movie. When Franz Rodenkirchen, the co-author of the movie, did an outline with me, we looked for a main theme and that theme was suicide. *Nekromantik* could have been a short story in *Der Todesking*, because that film is also about suicide. So it was a natural process that took the film in this direction. During *Nekromantik* and *Der Todesking*, I was having a lot of experiences with death. A lot of my family members passed away during that time. So I was having death in my head, you could say, all of the time. I lost my parents and at the same time I was doing corpse-rotting scenes. It was a way for me to deal with all the problems I had during that time. So it was cathartic. It was a way of getting it out of my system.

The film is a brilliant, bleak and disturbing meditation on death and suicide. In the film, death does rule as king as it is seen as an enemy, a reliever and something that is inescapable for all of us. Yet oddly, I found the film strangely uplifting. I know that sounds strange...

No, no, no. I know what you mean. I tell everyone that this is a movie against suicide. During the production of the movie, my mother died of cancer. I had the question, "How can anyone kill themselves when other people die and they don't want to die?" For me, this was the essence of the movie. The decomposing body was a way of getting away from these romanticized notions of suicide. You know, people killing themselves and going to Heaven and everything will be fine. I just wanted to show the plain basic truth that I experienced when I lost my mother. For example, that she is not there any more and her body is falling to pieces. When someone has cancer you can see that the person is fading away. For me, that is what I see in those images from *Der Todesking*.

The most moving segment is on the German bridge with the names of people who had committed suicide there.

That was something that just happened by accident, actually. That was shot in Bavaria in a small town. We found this place where we could shoot the decomposing corpse. The special effect guys, Sammy Balkas and Alois Vollert, were living there. We were there for about three weeks shooting the decomposing corpse with a time-lapse. During our time there, one of the guys told us about this bridge where people jumped off. So, while we were killing time waiting for the corpse to decompose, we took a trip to that bridge and shot these scenes. We made one episode out of it. It was an accident because we were bored [*laughs*]!

But it is so profoundly moving having those names appear on screen, their ages and occupations. You wonder who those people were and what drove them to that sad end.

It seems to work. I am continuingly surprised. When we looked at the material, we had the idea of coming up with people's names and professions that would inspire the viewer to have an idea about why they chose to die. That is an example of experimental filmmaking, right? So why do you think I am a horror film director [*laughs*]?

Well, you can be both!

I'm fine with that.

I do think though that art and horror can go hand in hand.

For me in Germany, it was essential for me to be labeled as an artist, otherwise my movies would have been destroyed. It was a way to survive and point out the fact that I am an artist. That is the only way I will get away with the stuff that I do. That is the same today when I do stage plays.

I find that some people can be very condescending to the horror genre and imply that it is not art. In my mind, Halloween *[1978] and* Texas Chain Saw Massacre *[1974] are just as valid as a piece of art.*

But it doesn't work this way in Germany. That is why I started doing film reviews, so that I could have my point of view on this kind of "art."

In Der Todesking *there is a homage to Abel Ferrara's* Ms. 45 *[1981]. Why did you reference and recreate a* Ms. 45 *scene in your film?*

During that time I was also working in a cinema, doing film festivals. We used to screen *Ms. 45*. I liked the film so it was very natural for me to pay homage to the film and to films that I like. I don't know if Abel Ferrara ever saw my movie or if he knows it has a homage to *Ms. 45* in it.

Your next film was the stylized serial killer flick Schramm. *I understand that inspiration came from real-life killer Carl Panzram.*

Well, there's a quote from him at the beginning of the movie. He was a mean guy—he raped and murdered children—but that isn't the guy that Schramm is. Schramm is a totally different character. For me, what was totally absent from Panzram was that he was able to relate to things that he had done. What I was trying to explore in *Schramm* was how you could live with the fact that you had killed somebody. That was interesting to me, as I was frustrated with movies about serial killers, like *Silence of the Lambs* [1991]. These movies were always mystifying the killers, making these big monsters out of them. I wanted trying to explore something more down-to-earth. I wanted to work on the psychology of these killers and notions of guilt. How does a serial killer deal with questions of guilt?

The film is enhanced by Florian Koerner von Gustorf's brilliant, brave performance as Lothar Schramm.

He is a very successful film producer in Germany. He has produced films by Christian Petzold and Thomas Arslan that get big awards in Germany.

Florian Koerner von Gustorf plays warped serial killer Lothar Schramm.

He is a friend of mine. He plays in a band from the punk days. It was very nice of him to do this film, because he always told me that he was doing "real movies" at the time, and that I should consider myself lucky that although I work with no money, I do have artistic freedom.

He gives a convincing performance as the crazed sexual psychopath and seems prepared to take on whatever you asked of him—including making love to a plastic doll and nailing his foreskin to a table.

Coming from this punk rock background, being a drummer in a noise band for ages called Mutter, there was no question that if you asked him to do one of the scenes in movie, there was no possibility that he wouldn't do it. He was ready for everything all of the time. We were there to provoke; to do something different and something new. We shot *Schramm* during the time that *Nekromantik II* was confiscated in Germany. So *Schramm* was filmed [at a time when] it would be dangerous to do this movie. So we rented a flat under a false name and in that flat we hid our film prints because we were afraid the authorities would take them away and destroy them. And in that flat, we also shot *Schramm*. So we had this flat where we could hide and shoot these films and make our art.

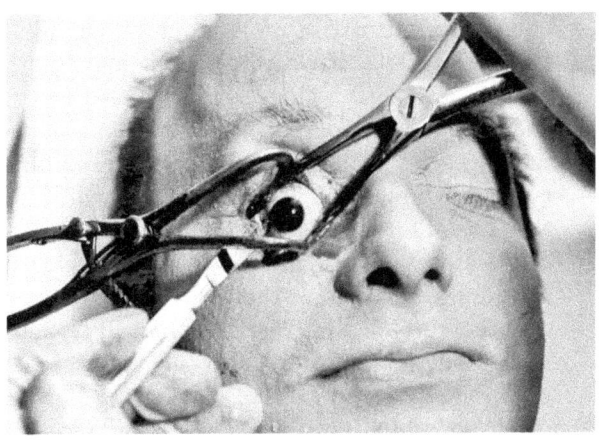

Eye, eye, what's happening here in *Schramm*?! (courtesy Jörg Buttgereit).

It sounds funny, but at the time it was really depressing. We were treated like criminals. For example, if the police came to your house today demanding the film print of the film you had just completed in order to destroy the negatives, you would feel really depressed.

How did Schramm *go down with audiences?*

Schramm was the first film of mine that was nominated for a film prize in Germany. It didn't win the prize, but with that film you could see that the mood was changing in Germany. Established film festivals were taking my films seriously and I got a lot of support because my films had been taken down by the authorities. People considered *Schramm* a serious movie. There was no question that this was not an art movie. I was very tired working on that movie, we had no money but we managed to achieve a lot of the effects that were in my head. Also, I had a lot of ideas that I wasn't able to achieve. That was frustrating.

I found the problem was if I went on making films like this because no producer, no production company, no television company would work with me, because I was having trouble with censorship. Every producer was running away from me because they knew they wouldn't be able to earn their money back as I made films the authorities didn't like.

Is this what prompted you to move into documentary filmmaking?

Yes, in one way. Also, I started writing radio dramas for national radio. That was considered not so dangerous and it was paid well. I found I could transfer my film ideas into radio dramas. Then I did documentary films like *Monsterland* [2009] and some documentaries for television. I did special effects and second unit director work on films such as *Killer Condom* (1996), a Swiss film. That was where all the experience I had made with my films finally paid off. I had my own film crew doing all the special effects and I could hire all the people who worked for free for me on my own films.

I went to Canada to shoot two episodes for the series *Lexx: The Dark Zone* [1998]. So I was doing normal director's work which was good but not very satisfying in an artistic way. I could see that I could earn money this way but I was not having control over the stuff I did on *Killer Condom* and *Lexx*, because other people were deciding what to leave in the film and what to cut out. That was very frustrating. So I stopped working on this level because I was used to having complete artistic freedom. The solution to this was to do writing, music clips and to start writing and directing for the stage. In Germany, working for the stage is considered art and I have never had problems doing stuff on stage, like in *Captain Berlin versus Hitler*. I did the first Ramones punk rock musical, which played here in Berlin and went down very well. Today I am still working for the stage in Dortmund. I am doing my fifth production. I have done a stage version of *The Elephant Man* and *Nosferatu*. My plays stem from inspiration from the '20s. It has a lot to do with my love of film and my upbringing, with me being a horror film fan. I just don't do it on film any more. I do it on stage. I told someone recently that I think I have invented genre stage plays [*laughs*]!

You recently adapted your stage play Captain Berlin versus Hitler *into a film. It is a brilliant satire of the absurdity of war and the feel of old B-movies. What were you hoping to convey with the play and film?*

That's out on DVD, too, but it is mainly a stage play that we filmed. After the Ramones stage play, I was frustrated that when the play was over, there is no permanent record of it. Being a film director, you are used to your work surviving. However, if you do something for the stage it is normal that you don't have a permanent record of it. It is the live event and that counts. The work is then lost. I made sure that *Captain Berlin* was shot on camera and we released it on DVD. It was important for Germans to be proud of their country and have a superhero like Captain America. The whole concept is very subversive for the German audience. We are going so far with Captain Berlin now that we have our own comic series which is on the newsstands. I am doing the concept stories and other people do the drawing. A small company [Weissblech Comics] is publishing the comic so I have complete control over the project. It is basically the same punk rock spirit that I work with. We did the first issue just for fun and now we have done a third printing of the comic. In the latest episode, Captain Berlin is off to North Korea! In comic books, you do not have to care about budgets. So if you want to go to North Korea or meet the Elephant Man in London, which we did in the last issue, we can put it on paper and there's no need for special effects or a big budget. That is something I really enjoy.

Do you plan an English-language version of Captain Berlin?

There is one story in English, because it was written in English and drawn by Martin Trafford, a British comic book artist who lives in Australia. That was part of issue #1. We have had requests from Berlin comic shops to do the magazines in English because a lot of tourists ask for them.

You have recently returned to filmmaking with a segment in the film German Angst.

This was mainly a favor to Andreas Marschall, one of the directors of *German Angst*, who had the idea for this anthology movie. He is the artist who did the posters for *Hot Love*, *Nekromantik* and *Nekormantik II* for me. As you know, no one was paid well on my films [*laughs*] so I couldn't say no when he asked me to use my name to collect money

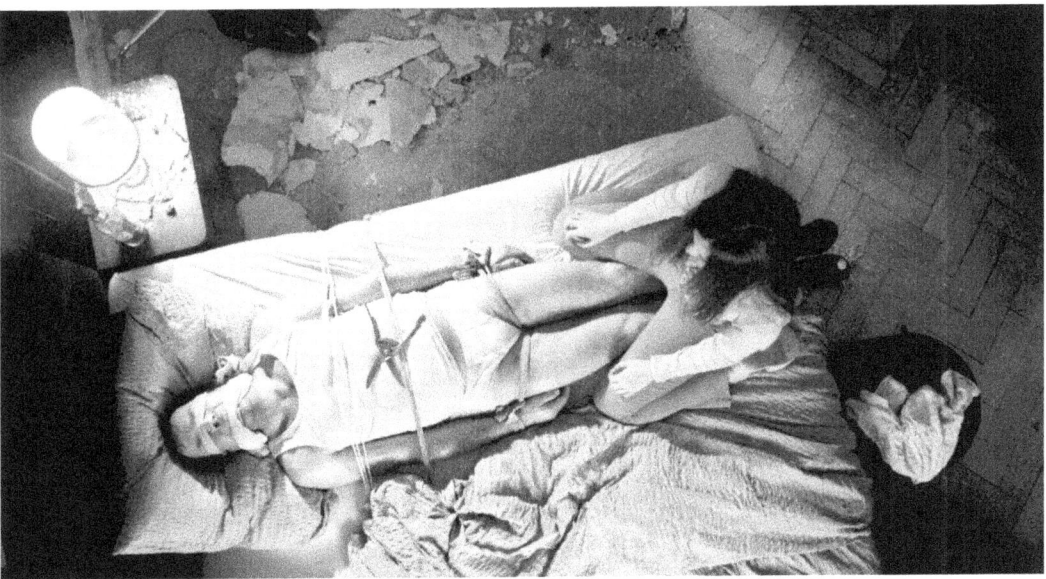

Top: Jörg Buttgereit with actor Lola Gave of *German Angst* (courtesy Jörg Buttgereit). *Bottom:* Scene from *Final Girl* in *German Angst*, which marks Buttgereit's return to filmmaking (courtesy Jörg Buttgereit).

for a new film. So I have made a little comeback! I was never away but I was merely working on different media, writing, radio plays, stage and comics. Going back to filmmaking was fun but I am not too eager to make more films on a regular basis because, especially in Germany, it doesn't really pay. Horror films are not considered art over here. I also find working on films very tiring. You only film for a few seconds and it is like a puzzle. It is not so interesting for me any more because you have to film all these little bits and pieces and you can only manipulate it in the editing stage. That is boring. I find it much more satisfying to see things developing on stage in front of me and have the feeling that it could go wrong because someone could stumble or forget their lines.

The film is very close to *Schramm*. Again it tries to find images that are in the head of the protagonist. In *Final Girl*, the main actress is an abused little girl. I tried to find images for the pain she has suffered. One reviewer has said that it is less a segment in a film but more a visual poem. That was a description I really liked, as I do a lot of abstract stuff for the stage. Not very linear. Working on film only interests me when I don't have to stick to the film rules. When I work for the stage, I don't allocate much time for rehearsal. The normal timeframe would be six weeks of rehearsals before the premiere. What I do is only four weeks so that the actors are not too well prepared. I think it is important that the actors are still afraid on top of the stage. That might be something left over from my old days as a filmmaker and watching punk and industrial concerts. Everything is possible.

11

Born of Fire

An Interview with Jamil Dehlavi

Prior from being dug up from obscurity by British DVD label Mondo Macabro, Jamil Dehlavi's surreal head-bending supernatural horror had been left languishing to rot in the cinematic graveyard. Deservedly re-released, this bizarre hybrid of art house symbolism and aesthetics gives way to scenes of nightmarish horror, as displayed in the opening credits when a skull head blocks out the sun's magna and crimson glow which is awash on screen, as if doused in blood. Dubbed by critics as the first Islamic horror film, *Born of Fire* (1984) is a film that revels in poetic and surreal imagery as opposed to narrative cohesion, as the hallucinatory visuals and non-linear plot take on a greater importance than the plotline.

In essence, the film can be described as follows: When an astronomer (Suzan Crowley) notices a strange occurrence resulting in volcanic activity in Turkey, she enlists the help of a brilliant flutist, Paul Bergson (Peter Firth), who is plagued by visions of fire and destruction. The pair attempts to solve the cosmic crisis that is drawing the sun's fire towards Earth, threatening the survival of the planet. Further complicating matters is the mystery surrounding the death of Paul's father, who also was an acclaimed flutist. The astronomer cryptically informs Paul that his father's music possessed an uncanny quality, as if inspired by some unseen power. Lured to Turkey to find master musician Oh-Tee, who knows the secret of his father's demise, Paul must battle a seductive djinn and a naked, wrinkly devil named Iblis, who is waiting for him inside his cave. In the bizarre finale, set against burning calcified rock pools, Paul must use his musical prowess, and the help of a strange deformed dwarf called the Silent One (who turns out to be Paul's half-brother), to defeat the demons and save the Earth.

Born of Fire is positively baffling at times; the mysticism and symbolism will leave some viewers scratching their heads. That said, there is so much to enjoy in this twisted horror film that packs a number of jumps and scares into its taut 80-minute running time. The sublime locations also add to the picture's unearthly feel, from the tropical water pools (which are the graveyards of the djinn) to the strange rock formations and rock pools that ooze an aura of strangeness.

Suzan Crowley is perfectly cast as the alluring djinn; there is an unnerving quality about her character that makes you question which side she is really on. Nabil Shaban is a revelation as the Silent One, scuttling and slithering across the craggy landscape as he helps mastermind the defeat of Iblis. He does so by stealing the flute, which Paul uses in the final showdown, and by chanting maniacally as he pounds his chest like a deranged gorilla.

Boasting sublime cinematography and imagery, *Born of Fire* is a surrealist masterpiece akin to the cinema of Jodorowsky. There is enough to enjoy just marveling at the striking imagery, while horror fans will find the naked djinn positively scary and creepy, especially when he shoots jets of fire from his eyes as he wanders amidst the stalactites and stalagmites of his eerie lair. Logic has been parked outside the door, yet those who tap into this film's strangeness will be rewarded with startling imagery and a terrifying battle of light vs. darkness.

In late 2014, I had the pleasure of interviewing Jamil Dehlavi via email.

Matthew Edwards: *Talk a little about your background and how you became involved in filmmaking.*

Jamil Dehlavi: I was born in Calcutta to an Indian father and a French mother. My father was in the Indian Civil Service and after partition he migrated to Pakistan where he joined the Foreign Service. I grew up between Karachi and a number of European cities where he was posted. At the age of 14 I was sent to Rugby School in England and then gained admission to Oxford University where I studied law. I was then called to the Bar at Lincoln's Inn in London. My interests had always been in the arts but my background prevented me from following my true passion. After qualifying as a barrister, I decided to follow my own dream. I went to New York and gained admission to Columbia University where I studied film in their graduate program and made my first short film. I then worked as an assistant director in French Television and a cameraman in the Radio & Visual Services at the United Nations. But that didn't last long and I decided to continue making my own films. I went back to Pakistan where I shot my first feature *Towers of Silence* [1975], an experimental film in black and white about a young boy's obsession with death. The towers of silence are the burial grounds of the Zoroastrians where the dead are left to be devoured by vultures.

Your film The Blood of Hussain *[1980] caused controversy in Pakistan.*

The National Film Development Corporation had just been formed by the Pakistan Government and they agreed to finance *The Blood of Hussain* in which I transposed the martyrdom of Imam Hussain, Prophet Mohammed's grandson, to the context of modern Pakistan. When he refused to swear allegiance to a usurper caliph, he was martyred by the caliph's army with his family and followers in Kerbala, which is in present-day Iraq. This incident cre-

Eyes of fire! The evil djinn in Jamil Dehlavi's *Born of Fire* (courtesy Jamil Dehlavi).

ated a schism in Islam and was the beginning of the Shiite sect. *The Blood of Hussain* got me into a considerable amount of trouble. Just after I finished shooting, there was a military coup in Pakistan and the film was considered to be anti-army. The government of General Zia-ul-Haq [who had seized power] was determined to destroy it. Luckily the negative was in a laboratory in London and I refused to hand it over. My passport was impounded and I was accused of subversive activities. After stagnating in Pakistan for two years, I managed to escape the country through the Khyber Pass into Afghanistan, then on to Paris and London. I was completely broke but somehow managed to finish the film and submit it to the Director's Fortnight at the Cannes Film Festival where it had its premiere.

How did Film Four get involved in financing Born of Fire?

Channel Four had just been set up and I was told that David Rose, the Drama Commissioning Editor, was looking for independent films to finance. I arranged a screening of *The Blood of Hussain* which he really liked and he then asked me if I had any new films in development. I told him about *Born of Fire*, a story which had been brewing in my mind for a while, and he commissioned the script. The film was then fully financed by Channel Four. Raficq Abdulla was an old friend of mine from university days, very knowledgeable about Islam, so I decided to involve him in the writing of the screenplay.

What was your intention with Born of Fire? *Was it the notion of Iblis and the Djinn? The film is essentially an exploration of the forces of good vs. evil, and a cinematic rendition of Iblis [the Devil].*

As a child we were told stories about djinns, creatures of fire that can assume human or animal shape and are capable of good or evil. In Islamic belief, Iblis, one of the djinns, was expelled from Heaven when he disobeyed God's command and refused to bow down before Adam. He claimed that man was made out of potter's clay and the djinn from fire. Why should he bow down before a mere mortal? I incorporated these ideas into a story which eventually became *Born of Fire* with the Master Musician as a manifestation of Iblis.

Did the Islamic community have any objections to the violence and nudity in the film?

I'm not sure how much the Islamic community is aware of this film. I have never had any really negative feedback from most quarters. When it showed at the Cairo Film Festival, viewers were somewhat nonplussed and were unable to categorize the film.

How did Peter Firth and Suzan Crowley become attached to the film?

Peter Firth was a young actor who I'd seen in *Equus* and Polanski's *Tess*. He had a nice fresh quality about him and I admired his work. We couldn't really afford him because our budget was so small. But then we came to an arrangement. The part of the woman was more difficult to cast. I saw lots of actresses before I met Suzan Crowley. She was a really gutsy actress, prepared to stop at nothing. Not many actors would have jumped stark naked off a cliff into a lake. And that wasn't a stunt double.

The film was partly shot in London and in Turkey, where you utilized some stunning locations.

To begin with, I went looking for locations in Morocco. But they didn't quite work for me. Then my brother told me about certain areas of Turkey he'd visited which sounded interesting so I went there and travelled around the country. I found some of the most incredibly surreal locations which fitted the film perfectly. We shot all over the country, although in the film it's made to look like one place.

It has been stated that you had issues with the special effects crew and that the actor Oh-Tee almost went up in flames.

At times the special effects guys were a little over-zealous and on one occasion their pyrotechnics went out of control during a shot we were doing with Oh-Tee. Luckily we were shooting behind a waterfall and they managed to quell the flames. On another occasion we were filming in Pamukkale in southwestern Turkey. I wanted a ring of fire around one of the hot springs formed by travertine calcium carbonate deposits which started interacting with the flames. They began to explode and we almost destroyed a world heritage site!

Born of Fire *has been described as the first Islamic horror film. It has numerous horror elements and motifs with horrifying, dark moments, especially when Suzan Crowley gives birth to a giant insect while screaming hysterically. Do you consider the film part of the horror genre?*

If I had to, I would categorize *Born of Fire* as surrealist cinema, although it seems to have found its way into the horror genre.

Viewers immediately compare Born of Fire *with the work of Alejandro Jodorowsky. Was he a reference to you during the filmmaking, or have critics made such a comparison due to the difficulty in classifying the film?*

Alejandro Jodorowsky was not a reference to me although both our films contain surrealistic elements. I met him at the Taormina Film Festival in 1980 when he was on the jury and my film *The Blood of Hussain* was awarded the Grand Prize. He obviously liked my work.

Oh-Tee is haunting as the Master Musician. His twisted skin seems to complement the catacombs and stalagmites. How did you direct him in the film?

With his extraordinary looks, Oh-Tee didn't need much directing. He was a great presence in the film. Every morning we had to subject him to two hours of prosthetic makeup before shooting.

How did you cast Nabil Shaban? He is brilliant as the Silent One.

I had seen Nabil Shaban in a Stephen Frears film with Ian McKellen [*Walter*, 1982]. I asked to see him and we immediately connected. He's a wonderful actor who has completely overcome his physical disabilities. He doesn't speak a word through most of the film and yet you can't take your eyes off him. And when he finds his voice in the battle of the flutes, he gives a magnificent performance. That was a scene which turned out way beyond my expectations.

You have directed a number of critically acclaimed films: Immaculate Conception *[1992],* Jinnah *[1999],* Infinite Justice *[2006] and the supernatural thriller* Godforsaken *[2010]. Your films deal with spiritual themes connected to Islam. Is that what inspires you as a filmmaker?*

I'm interested in spiritual and political themes but not all are connected to Islam. My latest film *Seven Lucky Gods* [2014] is a psychological thriller about an illegal Albanian immigrant who infiltrates the lives of a group of Londoners with disastrous consequences.

How was Born of Fire *received commercially?*

It received good reviews after it was shown on Channel 4 and then it had a theatrical release all over the U.S. before it went to VHS. It was sold to a number of other territories and won a few international awards. It has recently been released on DVD in the States under the Mondo Macabro label.

Are you proud that Born of Fire *has a reputation as a cult classic in the same league as films by Roeg and Zulawski?*

Yes, I suppose I am to some extent, but as the creator it's hard to feel proud as you tend to magnify the flaws in your work.

12

Noisy Requiem

AN INTERVIEW WITH YOSHIHIKO MATSUI

Unconventional, nihilistic, grotesque, twisted. These are just some of the words that describe the extreme violent images presented on screen in Yoshihiko Matsui's wonderful experimental nightmare film *Noisy Requiem* (1988). Filmed in grainy black and white, with a mainly non-professional cast, Matsui's tale of doomed love is shot through the warped perspectives of a number of misfits and violent inhabitants of Japan's biggest homeless area. This dirty and grimy landscape is matched by the perverse and cruel inhabitants who populate the dark underbelly of Japanese society, a place where many already have one foot in the grave. They live lives where they are merely existing in an unforgiving world, clinging on to, or searching for, love no matter how fleeting or unobtainable it may be.

Utilizing punk ethics and guerrilla filmmaking, Matsui's radical film centers on a series of outcasts. First we are introduced to Makoto (Kazuhiro Sano), who enjoys murdering women, ripping out their organs and stuffing them into a vagina he has hollowed out between the legs of a mannequin. Makoto keeps the mannequin, who he hopes to impregnate, on the rooftop of the abandoned warehouse where he lives. When he is not savagely killing defenseless women, he feeds pigeons before dispatching them with a claw hammer. Clearly deeply disturbed, Makoto soon finds employment as a sewage line cleaner for a couple of incestuous midgets. Both are trying to survive in a hostile world, dealing with the daily slurs and prejudices which have seen them pushed to the outer fringes of society, to the slums with the other misfits and gutter trash of Osaka. The sister, severely burned as a child, masturbates with an electric dildo and makes out with her brother, a service her brother provides as it was requested of him by his late mother in her will (her mother's insistence that her daughter will know what it is like to bed a man). The sister terrorizes local junior high school girls, her howls almost a jealous reaction to their appearance and lifestyle.

We continue to trawl through the slums, meeting shell-shocked World War II veterans and a bum who drags behind him a log in a shape of a woman's ass and vagina. We meet a silent young couple who, just when you think they offer the viewer a sense of salvation from the degradation on screen, meet a shocking demise. While all the characters in Matsui's film are vile, he get us to feel empathy for them all. They have been brutalized and traumatized and they live without hope, discarded like the litter around them. Matsui asks us the viewer to look past their repulsive ways and to take a closer look as they, like all of us, search for happiness and contentment. Whether that happiness is sought through sex with a log, or the tender embrace of a mannequin, we are made to feel a sense of compassion for these human beings and to recognize that they are merely products of the scummy post-industrial hell that they reside in.

Visually arresting and methodically paced, Matsui's transgressive feature does a marvelous job of capturing the real-life horrors of Osaka's slum areas and its down-and-outs and beggars. Clocking in at 150 minutes, it is a raw, challenging and experimental work, akin to the visual horrors and aesthetics of Shozin Fukui and Shinya Tsukamoto. The subject matter and art house aesthetics demand a sympathetic but tough audience. It's a truly original underground classic that deserves to be better known in the West.

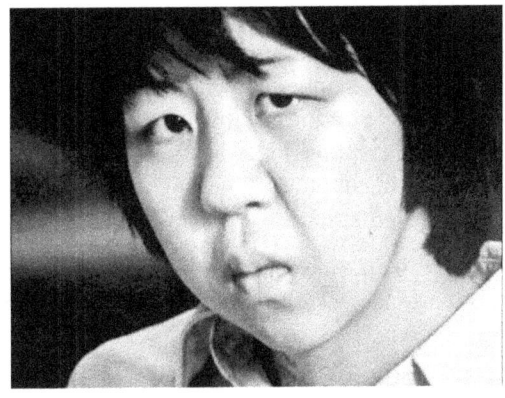

The scarred midget sister in *Noisy Requiem* (courtesy Yoshihiko Matsui).

In 2015, I was granted an interview with the legendary director. Rarely interviewed outside Japan about his work, Matsui was a joy to interview, a true gentleman. I would also like to express my sincere thanks to David Geevanathan for the brilliant job he did translating this interview from Japanese into English.

Matthew Edwards: *How did you get involved in filmmaking?*

Yoshihiko Matsui: I've liked movies since I was a child. At that time, there was a cinema near my house and I would often watch Japanese or mainstream Hollywood movies there. As a junior high school student, I started reading movie novelizations, with the names of famous art film directors such as Shuji Terayama, Oshima Nagisa, Fellini, Pasolini, Buñuel and Kubrick. This led to me going to watch my first art film, Shuji Terayama's *Denen ni shisu* [*To die in the country*, 1974]. Up until this point, I had only watched mainstream films so it was a real eye-opener. I realized that films could be a means of freely expressing one's ideas and thoughts and thus I started to watch as many art films as I could.

However, there was very little opportunity to watch art films in my hometown, so I decided to move to Tokyo. In Tokyo, I would go to the cinema every day and watch as many films as I could, new films, old films, Japanese films, foreign films, mainstream films and art films. This would continue for a few years and somewhere along the way I came to the realization that I wanted to be involved in the filmmaking process. It was at this time that I met Sogo Ishii, who was a college student. I became a member of his film crew and learned about filmmaking. Mr. Ishii and I would meet every day and discuss the films that we had seen or the films that we would like to make. Those days were really fun.

I then made my debut with the film *Rusty Empty Can* [1979]. This film was greatly praised by Oshima Nagisa and I was then able to meet Mr. Nagisa, a man I respected from the bottom of my heart. This film also provided me with the chance to meet Shuji Terayama. I was overjoyed and these events strengthened my resolve to become a genuine film director.

I was a member of the Kyo-eisha group, comprised of college students aspiring to be film directors. At the time of graduation, most would give up this dream but Mr. Ishii and I continued down the road to becoming film directors. Financially, it was a real struggle for me but my daily discussions with Mr. Ishii took me away from that harshness and I can now look back on those days with fondness. Looking back, meeting Mr. Ishii, learning about filmmaking and receiving praise from Mr. Oshima and Mr. Terayama are all events that I will never forget.

You worked as an editor on Sogo Ishii's Panic in the High School *[Koko dai panikku, 1976] and* Crazy Thunder Road *[Kuruizaki sanda rodo, 1980]. What did you learn from these experiences?*

I learned so many things from Mr. Ishii. One of those things is what you call "guerrilla filmmaking." In other words, in order to make the film that you want to make, you have to be greedy (you have to want it all), but of course within a range that doesn't cause trouble for others.

Sogo Ishii was the director of photography on your first film production, the 8mm film Rusty Empty Can *[Sabita Kankara]? And what are your recollections of making the film?*

During one of our daily film discussions, Mr. Ishii remarked that it was about time that I made my own film. He asked me if I had any ideas and I responded that I was thinking about making a film about homosexuality. I proceeded to give him a summary of the plot and he complimented the idea. I wrote the script quickly and had Mr. Ishii look it over. He called the script interesting and proposed directing the film himself. I thanked him humbly and accepted his proposal.

As I was in charge of writing the continuity from the opening to the ending, Mr. Ishii was able to stay faithful to the images that I wanted to portray. Mr. Ishii also gave his ideas and, if interesting, they were filmed as well. In other words, in his role as a director, Mr. Ishii felt it was important to create a film that respected the director's ideas and was filmed in a way in which his imagery was not compromised. In order to make a good movie, Mr. Ishii gave his ideas and we were able to work well together while creating this film. This is what led to Mr. Ishii directing this film.

As for recollections, well, what I remember clearly is that while filming a homosexual sex scene, Mr. Ishii, who was supposed to be directing the scene, closed the viewfinder of the camera because he felt it was distasteful. After the film was completed, Mr. Ishii mentioned this and we all had a good laugh about it. Although I forgot my anger and laughed along with them, inside I was just glad that it didn't cause any problems in filming. This one memory of Mr. Ishii left an indelible mark on me.

Was tackling the subject of homosexuality a difficult topic during that time in Japan?

In Japan, even now, homosexuals face discrimination and lead isolated lives. But even if I were a homosexual, as long as I found love, then that would be an amazing thing and that is what I tried to show in the film. At that time, the subject of homosexuality was not difficult for an independent filmmaker such as myself to touch but the same could not be said for mainstream films and television.

Your second feature is the gloriously titled Pig-Chicken Suicide *[Tonkei Shinju, 1981]. What themes were you looking to explore in the film?*

With *Pig-Chicken Suicide* and as in all my films, minority groups in Japan are featured. In particular, North and South Koreans appear in all my films, but in this film,

Burakumin are also present. Why did I choose to portray Burakumin? Well, I had been friendly with them since I was a child. The people around me would ask, "Why are you friends with them?" and I would reply that being with them was fun and interesting and I like them more than anything. At that time I was surprised at why the people around me would ask such a question and I came to realize that South and North Koreans and the Burakumin were subject to discrimination in Japan. This made me angry and that anger has been a constant throughout my life, which is why they are featured in all my films.

I'm glad that you like the title that I chose for the film. Let me tell you why I came up with this title. *Chicken* is used as a metaphor for the childhood of the two main characters who experience discrimination while *Pig* is used as a metaphor for their adulthood. The words pig and chicken are often used to depict a negative example in Japanese society. The theme being that people are all the same no matter if they are North or South Korean, Burakumin or Japanese. Ancient Japanese culture and arts were taken from North Korea but instead of feeling gratitude towards them, Japanese people would persecute them. This is absolutely ridiculous. In my mind, as humans there is nothing more disgraceful than discrimination. Why can't we all just get along? My anger towards that issue is what led to the theme of this movie.

Pig-Chicken Suicide *touches on the notion of zainichi Koreans in Japan. The film goes a long way to dispel prejudices against minority groups and I understand you grew up with many Korean-Japanese friends. At its heart, the film seems to suggest that there are no distinctions between race and color.*

Thank you for saying "This film goes a long way to dispel prejudices against minority groups." These words really made me feel happy. Currently there are certain politicians and cultured people who are vilifying not only Koreans living in Japan but the country itself. This is also happening with China. I feel that the stance of these people will only negatively affect relations and lead to future conflict with Korea and China. We cannot find a solution to this problem soon enough.

You say "There are no distinctions between race and color." To depict this *was* the intention of my film and I am glad that you were able to understand that.

Pig-Chicken Suicide *has some wonderfully striking imagery. I love the scene where the procession of bandage figures walks ominously out of their dwellings down to the river.*

The image of the bandaged Koreans is used to show how they used to hide who they really were. If they didn't do this, life in Japan would be very difficult for them.

You are best known in the west for your controversial third film, Noisy Requiem. *Where did the idea stem from?*

As I said before, the original idea stemmed from my interest in minority groups living in Japan. Why? Because these groups faced discrimination and poverty. To put it another way, all the problems of present-day Japan were concentrated in these groups. I thought that to depict the reality of their lives, within such extreme circumstances, would help in understanding humanity. I was also interested in complexes that form due to discrimination. I believe that people all over the world suffer from complexes be they large or small. To put it yet another way, I think that complexes are common points for people all over the world. By showing this in the film, I felt that many people would be able to relate and understand the theme.

On top of that, I was also interested in love. Whether it be heterosexual, homosexual, physical, parental, in my mind there is no difference. If people live by taking responsibility for the people who love them, then a praiseworthy love is born. Up until this point, I had made various films depicting love and all of their origins stem from this idea that love in all forms is the same and worthy of respect. I used the inheritance that I received from my father to finance *Noisy Requiem*.

It was filmed in the homeless ghettos of Shinsekai, in Osaka's Kamagasaki district. Can you tell readers a little bit about its history?
During the Edo period, over 200 years ago, there were many cargo ships hauling freight in the Kamagasaki district and accordingly there were many laborers living in the area. Being a city for dockworkers, there were cheap hotels, gambling joints, brothels and yakuza. At the start of the Meiji period, the number of cheap hotels was reduced and many laborers were forced to leave the area but at the start of the Showa period, due to the growth of the Japanese economy, laborers started living in the area once again. That is the origin of the Kamagasaki we see today.

But at the start of World War II, many laborers were conscripted into the army and the once enormous city was left as a shell of itself. A few years after World War II, the Korean War began and this led to the strengthening of the Japanese economy and laborers from all over the country started gathering again in the area, restoring vitality to the district. Even now it is known as a laborers' town but it is not the same existence that it once was. Currently a certain percentage of the laborers are working near the Fukushima nuclear plant incident. They are exposed to radiation but as there is no other work for them, they are left with no other choice but to accept their fate. I think that this situation also arises from discrimination. This is the Kamagasaki that I know.

As I mentioned before, I chose Kamagasaki as the location because I was interested in minority groups. Of course there are other labor towns such as Tokyo's Sanya and Yokohama's Kotobukicho, but Kamagasaki was the closest fit to the script that I had written. I think there is a unique atmosphere in this area because the city itself has a complex and the people living within it also have complexes; a certain kind of power can be felt in such areas. Usually having a complex leads to a loss of power but this was not the case for Kamagasaki and this is why the town was so attractive to me. Japanese directors often use the phrase "to become a picture" and with that in mind, I chose Kamagasaki.

Your friend Shuji Terayama stated that your Noisy Requiem *script was un-filmable. Clearly that didn't deter you. Did his comments spur you on even more?*
Yes, you are correct. "If this movie is made, it is going to cause a major incident" is what Mr. Terayama said to me. But I think he said that intentionally to spur me on. Knowing my personality well, he felt that those comments would make me create the film. At least that is how I understand it. Unfortunately Mr. Terayama passed away before filming began and so I couldn't get his impressions on the final product. That is one of my biggest regrets regarding this film. I am eternally grateful to him for his words which resulted in the film being made.

What prompted you to shoot Noisy Requiem *in black and white? As an aesthetic choice, it lends itself brilliantly to the depraved characters we see on screen and the hellish nightmare and squalor these characters live with.*
I chose black and white because for the process of writing the script, while walking

Director Yoshihiko Matsui directing the nihilistic experimental Japanese film *Noisy Requiem* (courtesy Yoshihiko Matsui).

around Kamagasaki, the idea of black and white popped into my head. At first, I was using color film to take pictures but when I looked at the final pictures, I felt that there was no appeal to the color at all. So I started taking pictures in black and white and found that there was a fascination with color even though it was in black and white. In other words, my imagination was stoked and thus I chose this style.

I was glad to hear your opinion that it lends itself brilliantly to the depraved characters and hellish nightmare and squalor these characters live with. Thank you very much. In regards to these words, I would say the following. Since I was a child, I have enjoyed watching people. And from that time onwards, I have been talking, hanging out with and becoming friends with all kinds of people—rich and poor, healthy and disabled, good and bad. Learning about different ways of living allowed me to imagine various things.

And above all else, I have watched a lot of movies. Even now when I have time, I go to the cinema or watch DVDs and imagine different things about the characters. I also love the theater, art, sports and cooking. At any rate, I watch people and use my imagination. If what I see impresses me, then that is the pinnacle of happiness for me. I believe that the more we are moved, the more abundant our emotions become.

What was the atmosphere on set like during the incestuous scene between the midgets? It is a brilliantly acted scene.

The male midget was a professional actor but the female midget was an amateur. When choosing actors, I always look for whether or not they have a sense of presence. Thus the female midget was not a skilled actress and I tried to give her acting directions in such a way that she could appear charming. But in actuality I didn't give her specific orders regarding acting because at any rate her expressions fit the part even more than I had imagined and without much hardship I could film the scene to my liking.

As you can imagine, the scene being what it is, it was very entertaining to film. If she performed strangely, her entire role would come to nothing and that would result in a heavy and painful filming atmosphere. As I believe that the filming atmosphere is always reflected in the film, I did everything I could to ensure that this did not happen. You commented that the scene was brilliantly acted. This is because the presence of the actors made you feel that way. No matter how good their acting may be, if they don't fit the role, then it amounts to nothing. Furthermore, to put it into perspective, 95 percent of the actors in this film were amateurs without acting experience.

Regarding the casting of people with presence, the importance of this is something that I have come to clearly recognize. I am proud of all the scenes in this film. If I wasn't, I wouldn't feel right about customers paying the entry fee to watch the film.

The homeless man is played by renowned butō dancer Isamu Ōsuga. How did he get the role?

I was friends with one of the young dancers in Mr. Ōsuga's group Byakko-sha. That dancer brought Mr. Ōsuga to one of my parties and introduced him to me. That was our first meeting. Mr. Ōsuga was a big fan of films and had seen *Pig-Chicken Suicide*. At the instant that I met him, I decided that I wanted him in the new film and he was happy to accept the part. He was amazing during filming, his presence and his movements were enchanting, and to this day I am glad that I was able to get him to appear in the film.

Many critics have labeled Noisy Requiem *a radical and nihilistic film. In part that is true, but I consider your films are ultimately about love, albeit taken to extreme levels.*

I agree with your opinion. Not only this film but all my films deal with the topic of love.

I don't expect everybody to understand the content of my films. But to the extent of my knowledge, critics, especially Japanese critics, tend to touch upon only the surface of the film, without even trying to discern what is portrayed underneath. If they don't understand the film, then they use negative words to describe it. Although it is easy for them to ask for clarification, they act as though they have understood the film even when this is not the case. They are embarrassed to admit to their lack of understanding and so they won't even ask for an interview with me wherein I could explain things to them in an easier way.

Let me tell you about something that actually happened. The Japanese critics who

Famed butō dancer Isamu Ōsuga as the homeless bum who drags around a piece of wood sculpted into the shape of a female's buttocks and vagina in *Noisy Requiem* (courtesy Yoshihiko Matsui).

panned *Noisy Requiem* quickly changed their tune when the film became a hit overseas, especially in Europe. When Europeans used the tag "A film about love," they shamelessly started using the same tag. What a bunch of idiots!

The scene where Natsuko terrorizes the junior high school girls is brilliant. They looked absolutely petrified. Was that staged or is that the genuine reactions of the students?

It seems as though you are a fan of that scene and that makes me happy. Thank you very much. That film was an example of guerrilla filmmaking and so the junior high school students' expressions of fear are real. In order to ensure that no one was arrested, I had to prepare for these scenes thoroughly. As this scene could only be filmed once, I looked into the timing as for when the most number of students would be gathered around the school gates and then let Natsuko loose at that time. After the panic scene was filmed, we had to hurriedly bundle Natsuko into a car and get the hell out of there.

The film features several such scenes where bystanders become part of your film. I am thinking of the scene of Natsuko in the Pachinko parlor and running crazily through a department store and when Makoto rips out pages of magazines from a bookstore. I am guessing those scenes were not staged. Was this a deliberate goal of yours, to blur the lines between what is staged and what is real in cinema? The film feels like a warped documentary at times.

The scenes you mention are all examples of guerrilla filmmaking and thus are used to show a higher level of realism and tension and that's probably why these scenes come across as a documentary.

I love the scene where you set fire to the rooftop and then film the emergency services battling to put out the fire and investigating the blaze. Was that filmed without permission?

Yes, it was. At that time, it was very difficult in Japan to get permission for filming. Even for a mainstream film, getting permission to film a conversation between a man and a woman on a street corner was difficult. Even if we had obtained permission, the time from the application to approval stage would have been very long. Now, there are film commissions all over Japan and so obtaining permission has become a lot easier but I think getting permission to burn the roof of a building would still be nigh on impossible. We shamelessly filmed the emergency services. Perhaps they thought that we were with new media services.

The opening of Noisy Requiem *is violently shocking, in that we see Makoto randomly murdering women, claw hammering pigeons and abusing and physically attacking Korean War veterans. Yet by the end of the film you've elicited a degree of empathy for Makoto. What were you looking to express through Makoto's character?*

First of all, not just with Makoto but with the men who appear in the film, the young man, Makoto and the homeless man, I used the Oriental cycle of birth and death as follows: In childhood, he unfortunately murdered his young love and was unable to love a human woman. In adolescence, [Makoto] fell in love with the mannequin but ended up burning it and thus was not able to love the mannequin either. As a middle-aged man [homeless man], the tree shaped like the female groin area of the woman he loved also ended up in misery. In other words, through the three lives of childhood, adolescence and middle age, the cycle of life and the immortality of love is depicted. This may be hard for an English man such as yourself to understand. So I will answer your question in regards to Makoto only.

Makoto is a Korean residing in Japan and for that reason only he was subjected to discrimination and ended up falling in love with a mannequin and took action under the delusion of having a child with it. He killed a woman, attached her womb to the mannequin and had sex with her. Looking at his actions from the point of view of modern society, it is clear that he is crazy. But he was crazily in love with the mannequin and all his actions came out of that love. In other words, his love was boundless but even though his actions started with love, they cannot be forgiven and that he is fated to die. I imagine that the reason that you could sympathize with him is because you could realize that this film is about love.

Love has been cheapened in our current society. People are getting married because of wealth, fame, position and power. In some ways, I feel that Makoto's love was more innocent. Of course his actions were criminal and unforgiveable but looking just at the concentrated feeling of his love, I can't help but feel that way. Makoto's life raised problems regarding love.

How was Noisy Requiem *received? Did it provoke strong reactions from both sides of the spectrum? Do you think the film's subject matter is controversial?*

First of all, please allow me to say that I am grateful that this film was seen by many people all over Japan. There was a clear divide between the people who liked this film and those who didn't, not only with the audience but with the critics as well. And of course the film was controversial. As I said before, the Japanese critics were greatly surprised that this film became a hit and the fact that it is still shown year after year even now has left them speechless and unable to criticize the film. Looking at them now, I can't help but wonder why they made such a big deal about the film. In addition, when the film was praised in Europe, many of the Japanese critics did an about face which has left me skeptical of Japanese critics since then. I cannot judge whether the film's content is controversial or not. In my opinion, it is only a love story and I didn't think that it would cause the ruckus that it did.

When the film was completed, we were thinking about showing the film at a foreign festival and showed the film to a number of festival curators who praised it. But the film was not allowed to be shown at any of these festivals for reasons unknown to me. However, ten years later [in 1998], the film was shown for the first time overseas in Germany.

You returned to filming after a 23-year hiatus with Where Are We Going? *[Doko ni iku no?, 2008]. Was the intervening years a period of frustration for you, in that you were not able to realize a number of cinematic projects?*

Yes, I did return to filmmaking after a 23-year gap, but I don't feel frustrated thinking about those years because every year there are many films made but most of them are forgotten over the years. However, *Rusty Empty Can* has been shown every year for the last 36 years, while *Noisy Requiem* has been shown for the last 27 years. My other films are also shown every few years and thus my films are still being viewed by new audiences even now.

In addition, I am meeting people. I made films because I wanted to meet people and as a film director this has been a great honor for me. There are also interviewers like yourself, film writers and journalists who continue to interview me, which leaves me with a sense of happiness and fulfillment as a director.

As you said, there have been a number of projects that I haven't been able to actualize, mainly because the subject matter has been considered taboo in Japan. In addition, I am very honest in my films and I speak very frankly in my daily life but those kind of people are feared in Japan, although I cannot understand why. I think that artists and expressionists should always be honest in their work. Unfortunately, as the majority of Japanese fit the above category, it was very difficult for me to make films. I don't think it could be helped and I feel that it will continue in the future too. Why? Because I feel that over the last 23 years, Japan and Japanese people have become more close-minded and unable to express their opinions in this era. You, who are interested in Japan, probably can understand what I am saying.

Where Are We Going? again deals with marginalized characters and focuses on discrimination in Japan. Discrimination is a theme that preoccupies your work. Do you think modern Japan is more tolerant to notions of race, homosexuality and disability, or do you think these prejudices are still prevalent?

When talking about race issues, as far as I know, modern Japan is currently being propelled towards patriotism by the extreme words used by politicians, bureaucrats, scholars and culture snobs. I think this is foolish. Ordinary citizens seem to have few race issues with cultural, arts, sports and sightseeing exchange happening frequently. I can't understand why the government wants to create unnecessary problems. Regarding homosexuality and the disabled, things seem to have gotten better over the last few years but I think that is probably just a surface change.

In the 23 years that lapsed since the making of Noisy Requiem, *do you think your directing style has evolved in any way? Aesthetically, do you consider* Where Are We Going? *a more mature piece of filmmaking?*

The type of movie you like changes over time and that was true for me too. Honestly, when I was in my twenties, I thought that Yasujiro Ozu's movies were boring but in my thirties and forties I came to love his movies. A person's thoughts and likes change over time. For that reason, the person that I am today would not be able to write the script for *Noisy Requiem*. People change on a daily basis and looking back at my experiences and the changes that have occurred in me gives me confidence to state this fact. The evolution you talk about is not something that I can recognize. I am only creating the film that I want to make at that time. I think this evolution is something that the people who watch my films should evaluate. As for aesthetics, people's ideas regarding this notion are constantly changing too. Although both *Where Are We going?* and *Noisy Requiem* were directed by me, the films are different and I cannot compare them.

Actor-director Kazuhiro Sano has appeared in all your films. What qualities does he bring to your films? Does he understand your vision and what you are trying to achieve?

Mr. Sano was introduced to me by a mutual friend while I was making *Rusty Empty Can*. At that time he was a university student. From that time onward, we would meet often outside of work and we shared many great times together. His acting skill, as I'm sure you'll agree, was top-notch. This is not only due to his hard work but to an innate talent. I believe that he was born with abundant creative talent. His ability to read scripts and create inspirational acting in moments was completely in tune with my vision. I was extremely fortunate to have met him and I cannot even consider the thought of making a film without him.

What does the future hold? Do you still intend making feature films?

First of all, I want to continue being a sincere person. Someone who doesn't tell lies or keep up appearances, who keeps their promises and doesn't pretend to be knowledgeable about things he knows nothing about. I want to understand other people's pain and I feel it as though it is my own. I want to keep being kind to others. Of course I want to keep directing films but nobody knows what the future holds. I want to continue living true to my feelings so in the future I may be doing something different but for now I would like to continue making films.

13

Dark Waters

An Interview with Mariano Baino

Italian filmmaker Mariano Baino burst onto the horror screen in the early '90s with a number of striking short horror films and his critically acclaimed *Dark Waters* (a.k.a. *Dead Waters*). Oozing with visual flair, Lovecraftian undertones, a sense of the baroque and gothic, the film overcame a production from Hell in the Ukraine that was beset with problems and disasters, and it seemed that a major new talent had arrived on the horror scene. Film critics lapped up *Dark Waters*: *The Daily Star* enthused, "*Dark Waters* is like looking at someone else's nightmare. Someone with a vivid and savage imagination that Bram Stoker would envy." *Sight and Sound* recognized Baino's talent by declaring that *Dark Waters* was an "ambitious tale of horror with lofty aspirations and little sense of conformity.... Signs of a talent worth nurturing." *The American Cinematheque* declared, "Director Mariano Baino conjures up a supernatural world of half-glimpsed madness, painting a waking nightmare...."

Dark Waters tells the story of a girl named Elizabeth who, after the death of her father, leaves London to investigate a convent her late father had been making secret payments to, in hopes of remembering her own blanked-out childhood. She uncovers strange practices from the nuns who are seemingly part of a demonic cult murdering all who stand in their way. Elizabeth begins to understand that the answer to both her lost childhood and the cult lies in an amulet that is a conduit for a horrifying demonic force that lies deep in the catacombs beneath the church. In the film, Baino stunningly utilizes light and shadow to make the nuns seem more otherworldly and sinister as they creep out of the darkness into the glowing light of the catacombs.

It seemed that Baino had a healthy film career ahead of him. But despite the numerous plaudits of *Dark Waters*, Baino slinked out of the limelight, and is yet to make a follow-up to his cult classic.

Matthew Edwards: *You first came to the attention of the horror fraternity with two striking short features,* Dream Car [1989] *and* Caruncula [1991].

Mariano Baino: I consider *Dream Car* to be the completion of the first chapter of a journey which started when I was eight years old. At that age, I started making films using my father's Super 8 camera and my brother Elio was the lead actor in every film I made during our childhood. He played Tarzan, Sinbad, Sandokan [a Malaysian pirate fighting the British Empire]. He played cowboys and Indians, sometimes he played both the cowboy and the Indian in the same movie and, because I had not discovered editing yet, many times that meant a quick change of costume in between takes.

Anyway, when it came to shoot *Dream Car*, it was the logical choice that he would be my lead. As for *Dream Car*'s genesis, I wrote six treatments for six short films on spec, because I knew some executives at RAI, the Italian State Broadcaster, from my brief stint as a production assistant, and I was trying to convince them to make a TV series which was going to be my homage to *The Twilight Zone*. *Dream Car* was supposed to be some sort of demo for the television series. Considering the story unfolding in the film takes place over a period of weeks, with changes from day to night, quite a few locations—including a car junkyard—and a character who grows a beard and starts to waste away as we progress, I am very proud of the fact we managed to shoot the whole thing in two days!

Your second short film Caruncula *was a big success on the festival circuit.*
Yes, *Caruncula* did very well and it's still being seen and discovered all the time. I'd had the basic idea swirling around my brain for a few years. Then, soon after I moved to London, I found myself working in a cinema and I thought it would be great if I could use it as one of the locations for a short film. In the end, as it always seems to happen, it turned into some sort of mini-epic production with many more locations than just the cinema and we even managed to build two sets in a garage that was attached to the house we used as one of the locations! We actually created our own mini–sound stage and it was very effective.

Original poster of the acclaimed short film *Caruncula* (courtesy Mariano Baino).

When it comes to influences, over the years, I have come to think that influence, like beauty, is in the eye of the beholder. People bring their own baggage when they watch a movie and often the influences they read in other people's work is more to do with their own life and the movies they have watched than with the work itself.

Caruncula has received excellent reviews from audiences and critics, most notably author Ramsey Campbell. Were you surprised at the response the film generated?
I was certainly very pleased!

Caruncula has enjoyed considerable success world-wide, which is rare for a short film.
I have been very lucky that the film seems to connect with audiences and that the film has been sold to television and been released on DVD as part of the wonderful *NoShame* limited edition box set and now as part of a stand-alone French release of my short films.

How important was it for you to start off making short films?
Very important. Making movies, even short ones, is such a massive undertaking that it is important to have something you can start and finish without having to wait for financing and all the things you need to wait for to get a feature film made. These days, the tools are more accessible, but when we made *Caruncula*, making a short film was still a rare achievement. It was before digital and YouTube. Before the age of incredible cameras that cost only a few hundred dollars. One had to secure and deal with a lot of equipment and labs and film and renting all sorts of things. Short films definitely were extremely important, I would say vital, for someone starting out in the '90s and still are important even now. They still have a reason to exist, even in an age when one can make a feature film with the same amount of money it took to make a short a few years ago. Short films are their own beast, and are to feature films what short stories are to novels.

Would you explain how Dark Waters *came about?*
Caruncula was shown at a film festival in Siberia, of all places, and that's how Victor Zuev saw it, liked it and ended up producing *Dark Waters*. It sounds very straightforward when one puts it like that. It took a lot more than just him seeing the short and saying yes to the feature. I had to find some of the financing from the U.K. and Italy and it took a couple of years to get it going but, basically, *Caruncula* opened the doors for *Dark Waters* to get made.

The eerie locations add to the visual horror. Were you active in scouting the locations for the shoot?!
Yes, I had drawn some concept artwork of some of the locations I had in mind, which were used as a guide to identify possible locations. Subsequently, I went to the Ukraine for two weeks, three months before the shoot, to scout locations and set pre-production in motion. Anyway, most of our interiors were sets built expressly for the movie and even the convent on top of the hill and the village on the beach were a cinematic illusion.

I understand that it was filmed near Chernobyl.
When I went to Odessa in pre-production, the idea was that we were going to build all the sets on sound stages on the Odessa Film Studios lot but, due to some mysterious double booking of the space we had been promised, we ended up having to build some of the sets in a studio situated only a few miles from Chernobyl. Kiev, Ukraine's capital,

is very close to Chernobyl and I remember some stalls in Kiev's main square were selling souvenirs which celebrated the nuclear disaster!

It has been documented that the production of Dark Waters *was plagued with problems from the outset.*

Yes, the making of *Dark Waters* was a real adventure! We, meaning me and the core crew I brought from London and our lead actress, Louise Salter, were truly "strangers in a strange land" and you couldn't get stranger than the Ukraine and Russia, where we did part of the post-production, after the collapse of the Soviet Union. To begin with, we started our work in the Ukraine by having to wait around for two weeks instead of starting to shoot the film, because our cameras got stuck in a remote region of Siberia and it took weeks to get them to Odessa.

Then some sets that were supposed to be built on sound stages were built inside the Odessa catacombs instead, because our studio space was sold to a rival production behind our backs. I told you earlier that we had to move to a studio near Chernobyl, but I need to add that we only discovered they had not built the sets we needed when we turned up to shoot the movie, so the sets were built as we shot the rest of the movie and we ended up having to shoot half the movie, including the whole ending, in the final two weeks of shooting.

When we were shooting in the Odessa catacombs, we had to go up and down hundreds of steps every day carrying all the equipment. Of course, that took hours every day and it would have slowed down any production. But this was far from any production! On the first day, when we finally got our cameras and we could start shooting, I arrived on location, outside the catacombs, at 7:30 a.m. The local crew was supposed to turn up at nine a.m. but turned up at around one p.m. instead. By the time we carried (yes I was doing the carrying, too) the camera equipment, the tracks, the lights and all the things

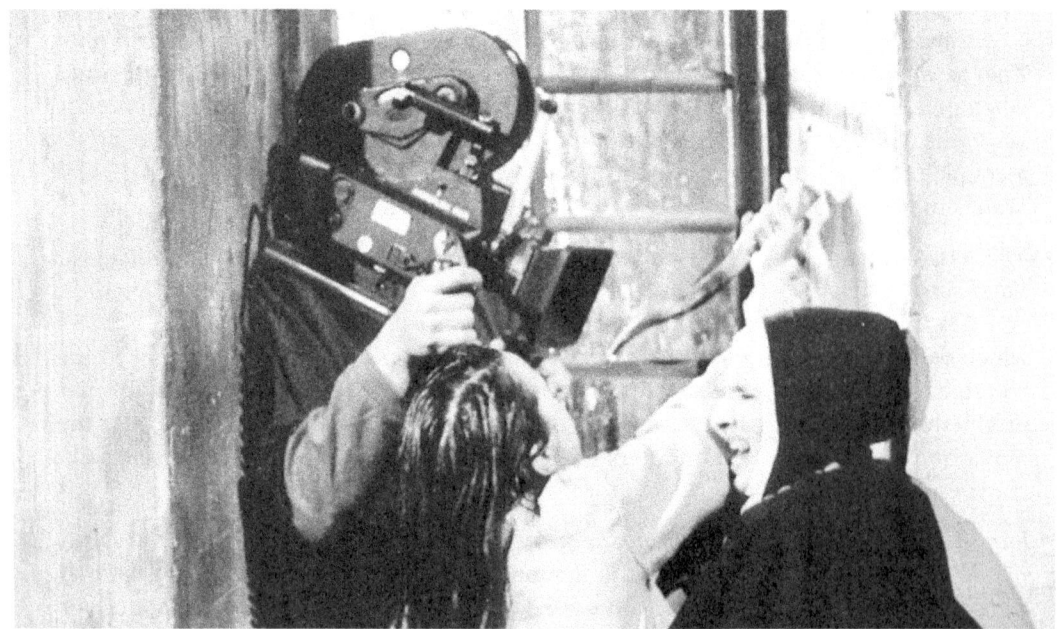

Behind the scenes shot of director Mariano Baino directing *Dark Waters* (courtesy Mariano Baino).

we needed down the steps and into the tunnel, dressed the set, lit all the candles, etc., it was seven p.m.! At ten p.m., just when I was ready to call action on a tricky jib shot that had taken a while to set up, the production manager announced that it was time to stop for the day. When I complained by pointing out that we'd only started three hours earlier, he didn't answer. He disappeared. I thought he'd granted us more time. Instead, he'd gone up and switched off the generators. So, as soon as I called action, all the lights went out and we were trapped in the catacombs in total darkness. Well, that definitely made us stop shooting for the night, I can tell you.

On the second day in the catacombs, I discovered that their way of making burning crosses was literally to soak a rag in petrol, wrap it around the cross and set it on fire. Needless, to say, after a few seconds the tunnel would fill with black smoke, making it impossible for us to breathe or for anything to be captured on film. We could only manage one take with the burning crosses, then we'd have to stop, wait for the smoke to clear and then do another take. As you can imagine, that didn't exactly help to speed up the shoot. And this was only the first couple of days. And they were relatively problem-free days!

Original poster for the Lovecraftian horror *Dark Waters* (courtesy Mariano Baino).

I could fill a book with all the problems that plagued our production. Mark Kermode, in his excellent book *It's Only a Movie*, dedicated a whole chapter, about 60 pages long, to his visit to the set of *Dark Waters* and to all the weirdness he witnessed. And he was only there for a few days. If anyone is interested, they should pick up his book, then watch the one-hour documentary *Deep Into* Dark Waters included on the NoShame special edition release of *Dark Waters* and on the new French release by The Ecstasy of Film, and, finally, listen to the audio commentary on the same discs. And even all that couldn't cover but a small part of the whole story.

The opening half-hour of Dark Waters *is extremely stylized and features minimal dialogue. Was this the effect you were looking for?*

Yes, it was all very deliberate. I strive to say as much as possible with images. I think, most of the time, for certain types of cinema, relying on dialogue is the easy way out. I am fascinated by the possibility of achieving a purely visual way of telling a story. I am intrigued by how many things one can say by juxtaposing two images and by choosing the right shot, the right angle, the right camera move, the right lens and so on. The short films I had made before *Dark Waters* were devoid of dialogue and I wanted to continue my exploration of that side of film language.

To me, Dark Waters *is one of the most underrated horror films of the modern era. In particular I like the visual style you employ and the many Lovecraftian references.*

I spent a lot of my teenage years reading Lovecraft. I really transitioned from science fiction to horror thanks to his work when, during a school trip to Rome, I bought a paperback of *The Dreams in The Witch House* and fell in love with Lovecraft's universe. Once again, there was no rational calculation involved while writing or making the film. Lovecraft's influence just happened. It was all swimming around in the dark recesses of my brain and it came out whenever it needed to come out. Andrew Bark, who co-wrote the movie with me, was also a fan of Lovecraft so there was no escaping it!

I love the scenes in the catacombs with the dead nuns.

Well, you already know about some of the difficulties we faced while shooting in the catacombs. Let me just add that we had nobody to light all those candles and very often our lead actress Louise Salter and I ended up lighting all the candles just before shooting a take! Also, because we couldn't find enough candles, we had to cut each candle into three parts, which meant that by the time we'd lit all of them, some of the ones we lit at the start of the ordeal had already melted down to nothing and gone out.

One of the interesting aspects of Dark Waters *is her performance as Elizabeth. How did you come to cast her?*

I had cast someone else but that ended up not working out. So I found myself without

Elizabeth (Louise Slater) in the catacombs in *Dark Waters* (courtesy Mariano Baino).

a lead actress about a week before departing for the Ukraine to shoot the movie! I started auditioning a lot of actresses who were still at drama school and that's how I found Louise. She was wonderful and I didn't even let her finish the audition. It was clear to me from the first second that she *was* Elizabeth! It was destiny. Once again, something that started as a potential disaster ended up being the best thing for the film. It often happens that way. I had the same experience when I was casting *Never Ever After* [2008]. Abby Leamon, who is exceptional, was the last actress I auditioned and it took only a few seconds to know she was perfect for the role. Once again, I didn't let her finish the audition and gave her the role there and then!

Louise Slater as Elizabeth in *Dark Waters* (courtesy Mariano Baino).

Maria Kapnist is memorable as Mother Superior. Speaking in whispers, she adds another layer to the horror that builds up in the film. Was that deliberate or improvisation while on the set?

Maria Kapnist was wonderful. A real legend and an absolute trooper. She was 87 years old at the time and *Dark Waters* ended up being her last movie. But she didn't speak a single word of English and her character was originally supposed to deliver all the dialogue now delivered by her "assistant." When I discovered she couldn't speak English, and that it would have taken her ages to memorize her lines, I thought I would make lemonade with the lemons I had been handed. I thought I would give her an assistant so that Mother Superior would speak in weird sounds and whispers which would then be "translated" by the younger nun who was her assistant. That character didn't exist in the script, it was basically invented on the spot. I asked for an actress who spoke at least some English and who would be ready to shoot the next day. Considering that scene works infinitely better as it is now than it would have worked the way it was scripted, I wish I could tell you it was all cleverly and deliberately planned, but it was pure improvisation and filmmaking by the seats of my pants.

Where did you find the creepy villagers who appear in the film? They send a shiver down the spine.

They were wonderful local extras. They were very nice in real life! It was makeup, acting and shot selection that made them look that shiver-inducing!

The late Mariya Kapnist as the creepy blind nun in *Dark Waters* (courtesy Mariano Baino).

The cinematography has stylistic nods to the work of Argento and Bava. Was that your intention? Alex Howe's?

I didn't set out to make any direct references, and Alex Howe, in truth, was not at all familiar with the work of Bava and Argento. I just storyboarded the shots. I always draw my own storyboards and concept art, and I wrote some instructions for the people working on the movie about the color scheme and the camera moves I wanted. I love warm colors, which also seemed to fit the subject matter. When I was in Moscow doing the color correction and the final picture grade, the colorist had printed a reference frame for each shot in the finished film and, as we were analyzing each frame, she would ask me, in Russian, "More orange or less orange?" and my answer invariably was, "More orange, please!" I also made the decision to use Kodak stock because, at least at the time, it tended to give results which looked warmer than other manufacturers' film stock.

Your creative and haunting sound design gives the film an unnerving quality that gets under the viewer's skin. Would you reveal how you achieved this?

I always wanted to layer the sound and include a lot of animal sounds. I thought it was important to complement the music by adding an unsettling soundscape which would not be too intrusive but would definitely be noticeable. Some sounds I wanted to keep almost subliminal. We did the sound post in Moscow and most of it was still done the old-fashioned way: listening to thousands of reel-to-reel tapes to find the right sound. Among the many sounds used, we used the sound of bear cubs crying, which seemed

Opposite: **Panels of *Dark Waters* storyboard artwork by Mariano Biano (courtesy Mariano Baino).**

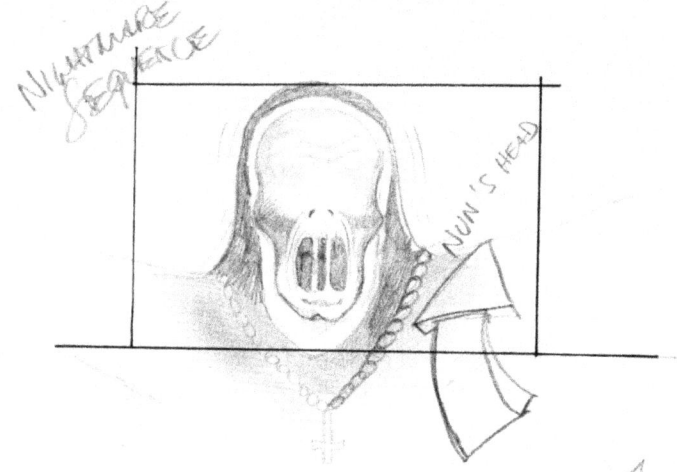

SC-62 PAGE 4

6B

6C

extremely haunting to me, layered with some tiger sounds, the sound of a Japanese tsunami, a particularly noisy donkey and even the sound of hundreds of sirens announcing the death of Brezhnev!

The scene of the nun crucified in front of the two young girls—did that inflame the religious masses? Were you deliberately trying to stoke up anger?

I definitely didn't set out to stoke up anger or controversy. It just seemed to fit the film perfectly and it made sense to me to include that scene.

*On that subject, the film is rich in Catholic imagery and iconology. Are you yourself Catholic or were you tapping into that strand of horror cinema—*The Exorcist *[1973],* Alice, Sweet Alice *[1976],* The Devils *[1971], etc.?*

I was born and spent my childhood in Naples, Italy. Enough said. It's a city where the living and the dead co-exist in a very matter-of-fact way and a city where one is surrounded by images of suffering and bleeding saints. Instead of a smiling Madonna, you're very likely to be faced with a statue of a suffering Virgin Mary, called the *Madonna Addolorata* [the Madonna in pain], veiled and dressed in black, holding her own bleeding heart, pierced by seven swords, in her hands. In souvenir shops they sell figurines representing the souls of the damned and one of the best sellers is a grinning representation of the local disruptive poltergeist, the Munaciello [the little monk]. So I didn't need to tap into any strand of horror cinema: I had all I needed all around me while I was growing up.

What have you been up to since Dark Waters?

I spent a few years trying to get *Ritual*, one of my passion projects, made. It's based on a fabulous novel by Graham Masterton and I wanted to make it into a film since I first read it in the early '90s. The project came very close to getting made a few times but hasn't happened yet. A lot of people who read the script I had written for *Ritual* really liked it and I started getting screenwriting jobs. So I spent a few years writing for other people, being commissioned to write, which was a great way to pay the rent and also practice the craft and allowed me to become a much better screenwriter. What some readers may be unaware of is the fact that it is totally possible to have some sort of career as a screenwriter and be commissioned to write all these scripts that never get made. You keep being commissioned, get paid, deliver the script and then the project never happens. That happens quite a lot!

Then I made the short *Never Ever After*, which has done very well, as a way of going back to directing because I ultimately want to write as a function of my directing. I also directed a few music videos and exhibited my artwork in New York and Italy.

You've said that you fear the dark. Is that what has drawn you to the horror genre and such vivid visuals in your films?

Yes, I am scared of the dark. In London I used to always go out with a pocket flashlight attached to my keychain because I was terrified of being stuck on the underground in the dark. Now I live in New York and I fear the same thing happening to me on the subway. I am drawn to fear because it's an emotion I know very well. Every time someone asks me why I chose the cinema of fear as my way of artistic expression, I am reminded of Clive Barker's brilliant answer when asked the same question: "I didn't choose horror. Horror chose me."

Anna Rose Phipps in Mariano Baino's *Dark Waters* (courtesy Mariano Baino).

How do you now view Dark Waters?

I am very proud of the film and I am very grateful for its very long life. It keeps being re-released around the world and keeps finding an audience. It was re-released in France in a marvelous new edition by the label The Ecstasy of Film. They did a wonderful job and even released, for the first time ever, some of my short films as a totally separate disc called "The Trinity of Darkness." They also commissioned original artwork for the covers of both discs and the result is absolutely stunning.

14

Aswang

AN INTERVIEW WITH BARRY POLTERMANN

In 1994, filmmakers Barry Poltermann and Wrye Martin embarked on their first cinematic venture with *Aswang*, a cult classic horror that would slip into obscurity as *The Unearthing* before being rescued and restored by the British DVD label Mondo Macabro. The film draws its inspiration from the mythic Filipino vampire that feeds on unborn children: Pregnant teenager Katrina signs over the rights to her child to the Null family, a rich clan of orchard growers. In exchange for payment, she must pose as Peter's wife to his creepy, wheelchair-bound mother (Flora Coker) and their odd housekeeper (Mildred Nierras) who constantly unnerves Katrina by frequently pressing her ear up to her bulge so she can hear the baby inside. The eccentric Dr. Harper, caught trespassing on the Null property, senses all is not what it seems with the family and that they might be hiding a dark secret. His fears are confirmed when he finds the cocooned remains of unborn fetuses in the woods, and that the Nulls are a clan of sadistic Filipino vampires. Peter, sensing that Dr. Harper will blow their cover, attacks the nosy professor in an outrageous scene that sees the vampire using his long slimy tongue to disable his victim before cocooning him. After the tension-filled and atmospheric build-up, the film goes into overdrive as Katrina realizes her life and her child's are in danger and the film descends into a wild ride of chainsaws, death by hoes, dismemberment and buckets of gore as the vampires do all that it takes to stop Katrina from escaping from their clutches. With cinematic nods to *Texas Chain Saw Massacre* and *Evil Dead*, and memorable moments (for instance, when Katrina brains Claire Null with a hoe), the film is one hell of a cinematic ride.

Norman Moses is wild as Peter Null, especially during the final quarter where he is positively insane as he wanders around the estate, holding an axe while covered in blood. Tina Ona Paukstelis delivers a fine performance as the troubled adolescent Katrina. The film can be read as an anti-abortion film, or pro-abortion film, depending on your viewpoint, and will no doubt cause heated discussion in the pub after viewing, especially in the U.S. where this sensitive topic is often debated. Of the other actors, Josh Kishline as Dr. Harper gives a wonderfully campy performance that is fitting with the overall nature of the film, while Flora Coker is menacing as Peter's deranged mother.

Despite its relatively low-budget, the film features an array of impressive effects, especially the vampires tongues which slither and crawl across the screen. Combine this with healthy doses of splatter sprayed across the screen and good visual effects during the dismemberment sequences, and we have a gripping and suspenseful horror yarn that will satisfy gore-hounds, schlocky horror fans and viewers who take their horror films with atmosphere. First-time helmers Martin and Poltermann deliver a film that stands up as one of the best to emerge from the '90s. This splatter-rific film deserves a wider audience. In January 2016 I had the pleasure of interviewing one-half of the directorial team, Barry Poltermann.

Matthew Edwards: *When did you decide to go into filmmaking?*
Barry Poltermann: I was a child of the '70s and inspired by the films and directors of that era, like Scorsese. I am old enough to remember the last of the classic John Wayne and John Ford films. I loved seeing them in the theaters. I grew up on a farm in Wisconsin, so there wasn't a lot of magic there. So movies were amazing. I used to enjoy watching the movie of the week and I wasn't really into horror films until I went to high school and college. I liked old school horror films like *Dementia 13* [1963]. I liked the Edgar Allan Poe films with Vincent Price and the Hammer films, but a lot of the contemporary horror films of the '70s I wasn't allowed to see! I did get to see films like *The Exorcist* [1973] and *The Omen* [1976] on television, but these were cut. Instead I got to read lots of horror literature. If a horror movie came out, I would get to read the novelization of the film. I was really into horror film books. So there is a mix of films, filmmakers and books that appealed to me but I would say that I wasn't a horror fanatic. I was more inspired by '70s movies in general.

Why did you choose to make a horror film as your debut film? Was shooting a genre film easier for you to make?
Yes, I suppose so. It was especially easier to make at that time before the era of DV and High Definition cameras. You can now make a movie for a thousand bucks and edit it on your laptop. But in those days, it was expensive to do anything. To even have everyone working for free and shooting for 24 days, you still had to light a scene with enough light that was bright enough to expose 16mm and then process the footage. To make a film like that would cost $70,000, $80,000. With the production costs much lower today, you can shoot a film for less than $1000.

At the time we were kids straight out of college and we didn't have any money. So you have to make a compelling financial argument to somebody in order for them to give you money. The direct-to-video horror market was huge, so we thought, "Let's make a horror film." We were big fans of *Night of the Living Dead* [1968], *Evil Dead* [1981] and all those scrappy filmmakers who came in from the outside and made a horror film in order to break into the business. These filmmakers, like George A. Romero, were models to us. He was from Pittsburgh. We thought it was crazy to make a film in Milwaukee, Wisconsin, but then Romero had made a film in Pittsburgh which was just as crazy [*laughs*]! So I thought, what the heck? Romero also built up his favor base in order to get people to work on his film. He did a lot of corporate work in order to pay the bills and to get credit accounts. So we followed the George A. Romero plan and said, "Let's do what he did and break into films that way." That was our strategy and after five years of doing a lot of local corporate TV commercials, we finally had enough people who trusted us, and access to cameras, lights, friends wanting to help us and other filmmakers who owed us favors, so we were able to pull it off.

You arrived on the cinematic scene with the brilliantly disturbing horror film Aswang. *What was it about the Aswang legend that inspired you to produce a horror movie about it? You have taken mythology from Asia and infused it with an American horror sensibility. How did an Aswang end up in Wisconsin?*

[*Laughs*] That's a good question! The person I made the film with, Wrye Martin, was looking to make a horror film. I had written another script and we showed it to a friend of ours, Frank L. Anderson, and he liked it, and thought it was fine. However, he suggested that if we were doing our first film that we had to do something crazy that was going to break through and get attention. He thought what we had written was a by-the-numbers horror film. In terms of tone, I am guessing it was similar to director John McNaughton's *Henry: Portrait of a Serial Killer* [1986]. He argued that there were a lot of these types of films out there and that people were trying to emulate them, because *Henry* had been a success. Frank had grown up in the Philippines and he told us about the legend of the Aswang. He started to tell us this story of a vampire that would sit on rooftops and drop down its tiny thread-like tongue to suck out the blood of fetuses. We later learned that it was impossible to recreate this thread-like tongue, so we turned it into a garden hose instead [*laughs*]! Now it would be easy to create using computer generated effects during post-production but then it was like, "How are we going to get a thread to dance about and do all this crazy stuff?!"

So he described the story and said we should make a film about that. I thought the story of the Aswang was totally screwed up, so we started to think of ideas, and within

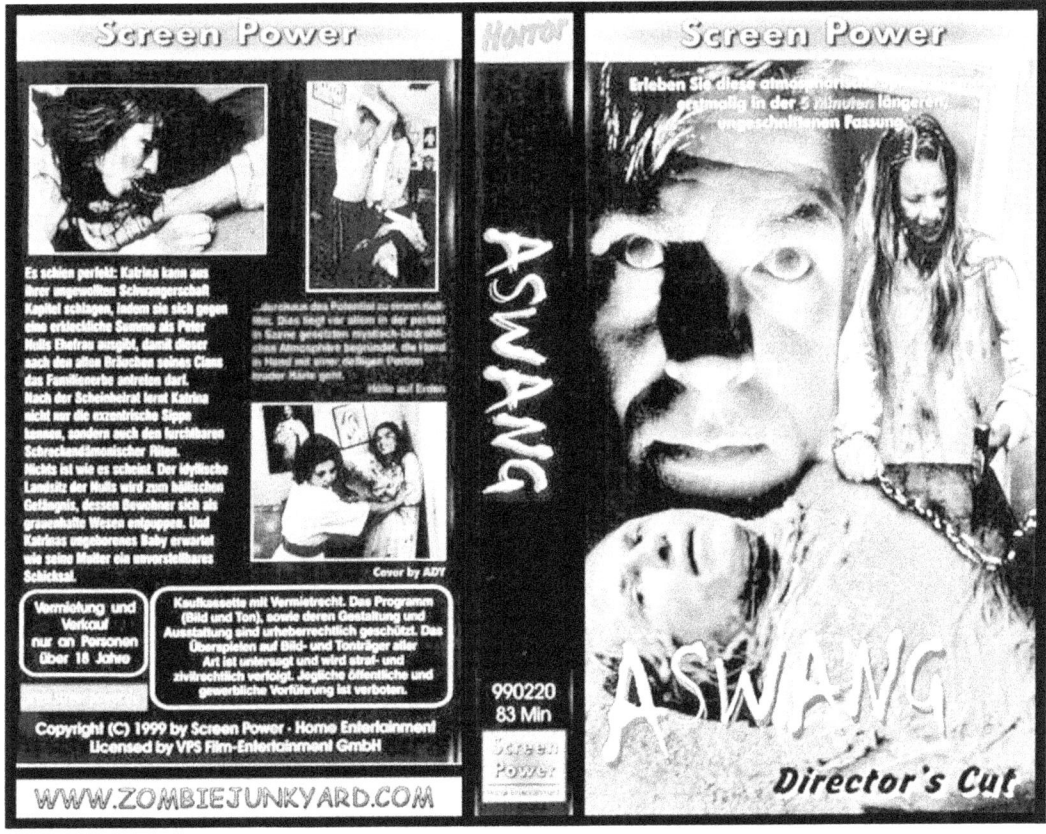

German VHS sleeve of the brutal and horrifying *Aswang*.

a week we had written a script. We literally bashed something out. We knew we couldn't afford to go to the Philippines so we thought, "Let's make it like Frank: a family that grew up in the Philippines and moved to Wisconsin, America. That is essentially Frank's story, right? So instead of knowing the story of the Aswang, what happens if he *was* the Aswang? He was infected by the Aswang and brought it to Wisconsin. They had been a wealthy family in the Philippines, owning a number of plantations. So we based it loosely on his background.

Did Anderson have any input in writing the script or was it just you and Martin?

When he read it, he thought it was ridiculous! I think he has a story credit because he told us the story, but when he read the script he was like, "Whatever." [*Laughs*] It was not what he envisioned when he told us the story. He thought it was an interesting take on the myth but not what he was expecting.

Did you think the subject matter—a story of fetus-eating vampires—may be controversial or too disgusting for some audiences in America?

It did cause us some problems, but not as much as I thought. Frankly, from my perspective, I thought the film was so ridiculous and campy and over-the-top that if you are going to deal with fetus-sucking vampires, you can't take it too seriously. It wouldn't be a fun movie to watch. I enjoy watching horror movies that are visceral but ridiculous enough to be a form of escapism. Wrye and I never took it too seriously. We were both film and writing majors and having more fun referencing other cult films, with small in-jokes for the audience. We had an early 1920s filmmaking mentality [*laughs*]!

We definitely talked about it. We wondered whether people would think the film was a metaphor for abortion, in one way or another. So we deliberately made it so whatever your perspective would be if you decided to go down that path, you would see something that would feed on that. We also added in the notion of dominant male figures controlling the bodies of women. It was also the Reagan era so Peter looked like former Vice-President Dan Quayle and did his hair just like him. We didn't expect *Aswang* to be a controversial film and it really wasn't ... because no one saw it! [*Laughs*]

I know that in the U.S., the abortion issue can be a very controversial topic with quite extreme views from both sides of the spectrum.

Yes, that was my hope. But then we had two directors working on the film with two differing views on the topic—myself and Wrye. It was interesting to think about the issue from our opposing perspectives and we did talk it through. I don't recall people writing about the abortion subtext at all. I do know there was a couple of screenings that received threatening phone calls about our film because it was perceived as being pro-abortion. Luckily nothing too serious happened. We spent $70,000 shooting the film and then another $40,000 finishing it.

How did you raise the money?

We originally tried to raise $125,000 but we could only raise $70,000. So we felt that either we don't make it or we do it at $70,000. At the time we running our own companies and over the course of a year or two we spent the extra money—from our own pocket—on completing the picture. We also had a better chance of selling the product, which made things easier. Once you have something to look at, it is easier to put money into. For example, when the production company Dimension returned my calls or when I was talking to New Line. Wow, Bob Shaye left a message. So it got a little easier towards the end.

Were the cabin and the estate situated in two different locations?

Yes. We have a friend named Peter Buffett, a successful musician, and son of American businessman and philanthropist Warren Buffett, whose family owned a large estate on Lake Michigan. It is right in Milwaukee. If you looked in either direction, there would be houses. It is similar to Beverly Hills, which looks like it is out in the country. So everything around it had to be shot, including the cabin, in locations other than the lake! We could aim towards the lake, but all other shots had to be in a different location, otherwise you would see other houses. Dr. Harper's cabin, which gets burned down, was an hour away from the estate.

I thought the locations added to the atmosphere of the film.

Well, we wanted the start of the film to feel like a Hammer picture, almost as if you are going to a secluded estate. We used lots of static shots and dollies, but then as the movie went along we moved into more handheld and chaotic filmmaking, akin to *Evil Dead* or *Texas Chain Saw Massacre*. The film is almost a chronological history of horror cinema, in terms of how we approached it stylistically.

I can see that. At the start of the film you build up the tension well and then as the film progresses it becomes more stylized and frenzied as displayed through the camerawork.

That is true. What is funny is that Wrye and I have always liked films that are uneven in tone. We see a review and it says, "It is uneven in tone," and we would want to see it because a lot of the time they are really interesting movies. In this case, we set out to make a film where, with each passing reel, the tone would change from the last and that it would feel more disturbing. We wanted the film, no matter how ridiculous the goings-on are on screen, to take itself more serious as it went along as a contemporary horror film. But a lot of people didn't like that. One of the biggest problems we had, and a lot of criticism the film received, was due to this uneven tone. Some people liked the beginning of the movie and not the end, while others loved the end but not the beginning. They didn't like both. Some reviewers said, "The movie started out great but then falls apart," or "It's a drag until stuff starts happening a third of the way through." Some viewers complained it was a slog to get through the first half-hour. So it polarized audiences. We thought it was going to be really fun, the way the movie changes, but the audiences and critics didn't agree.

I must be in the minority, as I loved the shift in tone! I loved the way you build up the tension and then turn everything loose!

That was our hope. And some people do feel that way. Usually the people who gave us good reviews cite that they enjoyed the twists in tone. It is unusual for a film to change style so much, don't you think? Some films change tone but don't usually change from static dolly shots to all handheld shots after an hour. It is also obviously our first film because it has a sense of "Let's try this, let's try that." As a first-time director, you don't really know what is going to work and what you are doing yet. So it affords you the opportunity to take risks. If I had a chance to make a second film, then perhaps I would be more disciplined stylistically. It was deliberately shot like that. We just thought that looked cool and went with it. Everything was like an adventure.

The film is visually brilliant right from the outset with that memorable sequence involving Asian shadow puppets.

That sequence was pretty much stolen from *The Year of Living Dangerously* [1982], which I was a big fan of. Frank was also an animator so we asked him to come up with something using shadow puppets. I recall someone else made the puppets [Bill Johnson] while Frank was in charge of the art direction. We shot the fire in a friend's fireplace and superimposed it over the animation. That was it, really. I just wanted to do something similar to *The Year of Living Dangerously.*

Along with the animation, and the fire, a nude scene is also superimposed over the credits sequence. There is an amusing story about that scene and the actor Tina Ona Paukstelis, who plays Katrina? By all accounts the male actor got over-excited!

Right! [*Laughs*] You know, we will leave that to Tina's commentary! The actor involved was rather embarrassed by it. He basically came during the scene. They had a towel between them, so they weren't really having sex. He was so embarrassed that he finished the scene and got up and left and none of us ever saw him again. He didn't come to the premiere or anything. He was horrified. We felt bad about that. It's funny, but funny at his expense.

I like the performances of Flora as Olive Null and I quite like Norman Moses' performance as Peter Null. He is like a campy Jack Torrance from The Shining *[1980].*

I love his performance in the film. Some people have said to me that they think his performance is too theatrical, but I say he is acting the character, till he starts breaking down and going mad when he realizes his life is falling apart. I think it is very well modulated. I think the part that people think is theatrical is the beginning where he is doing all these pretentious lines but that to me is perfectly in sync with what the character is doing at the time.

The casting of Norman was also interesting. In our minds, that was not how we envisaged Norman's character, Peter. But then he showed up and did this audition and he basically redefined the character. We hadn't envisaged a singing and dancing version of him. One that skips, sings, hums and whistles and then tries to kills people [*laughs*]. He brought most of those elements to the character himself. The rest of the cast were from a group here in Milwaukee called Theatre X which was really helpful because we didn't know where we would get a 50- or 60-year old person to hang out of a window by their tongue! We also wrote that the characters were always nude, which we didn't really intend to do! We just wrote it that way. "Olive hanging from her tongue nude." "Norman is nude as he runs through the house." We figured that if people were okay with that, then they would feel relieved that they were hanging from their tongues but with their clothes on. All the weird stuff in the movie, they were fine with as they were allowed to have their clothes on! So it basically boiled down to "Who can we get to do this script?" As we went through the process, it was mainly Theatre X actors that we chose because they were risk-takers. They also thought it would be fun to be in a movie. At that point, no one had made a movie in Milwaukee for almost ever! So the idea of someone making a movie was fun for the actors. I liked the performance of John Kishline as Dr. Roger Harper. [*Affecting Dr. Harper's accent:*] "I don't know much about … art." "Where are these from Mr. Null?" [*Laughs*]

I love the scenes with the rubber tongues. How did you film those? Did you reverse the footage to give the effect it was slithering up to its victim?

We shot some of it using reverse footage, but not all of it. We made a tongue. We did have an effects guy on the film from Los Angeles that we paid $5000 for. So that took up a large part of the budget. The tongue did lots of complicated things through the use of levers and buttons. It was actually quite cool. When it was on the ground, it looked like a garden hose going crazy. Within the first five minutes of its first scene, it broke! All the cables kept breaking and nothing worked. The tongue went limp on one side, as only one cable was working. So we thought, "What the hell are we going to do?" So you can see in some scenes that it only does small twitches. That was about all it could do! So then we tried to do everything in reverse and drive it through the scenes and then run the footage backwards.

I liked the effects when the professor is in his cocoon.
   That was achieved by two guys, Bill Yunker and Tim Brown. They were like these Monster Kids who were just amazing. My favorite effect by them was the tongue in the arm. That still grosses me out. When I wrote that, I put, "Dr. Harper is encased in a cocoon." What does that look like? These guys came in with all this crazy stuff. They get the credit for that.

It reminds me of Abel Ferrara's Body Snatchers *[1993].*
   I think that came out after *Aswang*. I love that look in *Body Snatchers*. I don't think we ripped it off. I doubt they ripped us off! Coincidently, they both had a similar look. We shot our movie in the fall of 1992 and the film premiered at Sundance in 1994.

I love the scene when Null's wife attacks Katrina with a chainsaw before she brains her with a hoe! What with the cabin, and frenzied camerawork, and chainsaw-wielding lunatic, one recalls Evil Dead. *Was that scene partly a homage to Sam Raimi's film?*
   That was definitely a homage to *Evil Dead*. It is funny because with chainsaw scenes, they always seem to be horrifying. *Texas Chain Saw Massacre, Last House on the Left* [1972], all these movies have horrifying chainsaw sequences, but they always tend to be the funniest scenes in the movie. There is something funny about someone running around with a chainsaw above their head. It is not necessarily funny when they are chopping someone's leg off, or they are killing someone, but the process of running around with a chainsaw is ludicrous!
   So we had scripted that scene pretty much as a fight. Katrina comes in and tries to help Dr. Harper, then Claire comes in and the pair start fighting—or two women brawling, as we had scripted it. Then Peter comes in and breaks it up, and they begin throwing each other around. That's how we wrote that scene in the script. However, a week before we were due to shoot that scene, we had still not found the cabin location. We didn't have a cabin. We couldn't find one that we could trash. People were not excited by the prospect of us destroying their house for our movie! Then I got a call from my brother, who is in the fire department, and he said that they would be burning down a house in two weeks and suggested we shoot there. They were going to burn down the property in a training exercise. So I thought that was awesome and I thought we could film the burning-down of the house and use that in the film. We walked into that house and that is exactly like it is in the movie. We did virtually no art direction in that house.
   However, there was nothing to have a fight with. There was no furniture, nothing! It kind of looked cool like that. So we had to think how we would utilize that space. So the night before the shoot, and I kid you not, Wyre suggested a chainsaw scene. He said, "Why doesn't Claire have a chainsaw and chase Katrina around the room?" We felt we could actually do that and survive the next couple of days, because we didn't know how to shoot this scene. So it was a kind of cop-out in the end. We thought, "Well, you are

going to have someone running around with a chainsaw so it is going to be ridiculous, but at least it will have energy." So that's how that scene came out.

I especially like the bit when Katrina just happens to find a hoe in the cabin!
[*Laughs*] When we got to those scenes, it was the last week of shooting, so we were just like, "Oh, there's a hoe there." But why does Claire have a chainsaw?! [*Laughs*]

But that's the beauty of horror films, they don't always have to follow logic or make sense!
Exactly.

Another great sequence is when the mother uses her Aswang tongue to violate Katrina but ends up dangling from the window! How did you film that?
There is a back story to that scene. The idea was suggested to us by one of our producers, David Dahlman, who had read an earlier version of our script. He suggested it would be cool if Olive's character was hanging by her tongue. So we fleshed out the idea, because I thought it would be funny as I've never seen that before in a film. Then we had to think of a scenario where she was falling and hanging by her tongue. So we had to figure that out, because the reality is that the window she gets caught in, it actually opens the other way, so her tongue wouldn't actually get caught like that. So it was a total cheat, but it just seemed too funny not to do. That effect with Flora was mainly shot on the ground, because we didn't film Olive's character fall. We cut to a shot of Katrina inside watching. Then we used one of our grips, Joseph Slagerman, who put on a dress and wig, in the shot where Olive's character is dangling. So that was Joe there flailing his arms and legs! If you look on the U.S. DVD release, there is an image of Flora and Joseph together in their dresses and wigs. Everything is off-screen in that sequence. Most of it is just sound effects and editing. You don't see anyone fall … we worked it out in the editing. It was a fun scene to work out, because it was one of the parts in the script that we had to figure out how to conceive on screen. We realized that through the use of sound effects, cutting and implying things, we could make it work. And that is the fun part of moviemaking where you can construct these pieces of narrative using bits of footage and creating the impression in the audience that they are seeing stuff that isn't there.

In another memorable scene, Katrina is chained and cannot break free so she cuts off her hand! How have audiences reacted to that scene?
I think by that time, the people who hadn't walked out [were okay with it]. At Sundance, a lot of people walked out when the blood started flying. They were fine 'til the blood started flowing. There was a bit of a gasp, but I think the effect it is a little cheesy. Some people reacted to it in a way that they thought it was silly, but some audience members were shocked. By that stage, the film is moving along so fast that I don't think you have time to process it.

I didn't expect it! I wrongly assumed she would cut herself loose from the chain.
That was one of Wyre's ideas. That came from his mum, who used to work at a zoological society. Wyre knew a lot about animals and his mum had talked about how when certain animals get stuck in a trap, they would chew off their own arms or legs in order to get away. They would do anything to escape. So we were going with that idea. So if you knew you would not be able to cut the chain, what else can you do? It is a bit like Danny Boyle's *127 Hours* [2010]. So we wanted to put Katrina's character in a situation where there was no way out.

How did you and Wyre Martin collaborate? Did you encounter any creative differences?

No, not really. We got along really well. We are not very close now. We don't really talk now. Time has moved our lives in very different directions. During the filming, and years after, we got on great. We both had a very similar sense of humor. We both brought different things to the table when we made the film. I am certainly more of an editor in terms of editorial structure. Wyre is smarter than I am, in terms of film referencing. He has more depth in his film background and education. I'm a little bit more technical.

The film debuted at Sundance in 1994. How did it get selected?

We actually didn't expect it to get selected. We used to joke that we thought *Aswang* was the first GenX film. *Clerks* [1994] hadn't come out yet. We used to say to friends that we were making the first Gen X movie because we thought the sense of humor was the first post–Boomer sense of humor. We played it at a couple of places, including the New York Independent Film Market. You pay $100 to show your film to buyers. We had a room of about six people and no buyers. We thought, there you go, we just wasted $70,000. But then there was someone there who suggested that we do a second screening as there had been a mix-up in a guide and they had wrongly advertised the time slot. So we were given a second slot and we ran into indie filmmaker John Pierson, who represented Spike Lee and Richard Linklater and who we had sent a copy of our film to, but assumed he had never watched it. He said he really liked the film. We were like, "Wow, you watched it?" He said that though horror wasn't his bag, he really liked it. So he said if we needed any help with the festivals, let him know. So he gave a tip to Sundance people to watch our film and consider it and then it came down to the wire whether we would be programmed or not, then we got the call and it was shown in the midnight section. Holy shit! Then we ended selling the film to Prism.

Prism cut the movie. They submitted it to the MPAA and it got a NC-17 rating. They suggested three or four cuts to obtain an R rating. We had to make the cuts and submit the master back to Prism. It was stupid. The film should never have been given the NC-17 certificate. It is not that bad. I was quite shocked, though I did think it was cool. Then Prism released the film, though they had previously already made up copies of the unrated cut, but labeled R. So some cases had the uncut version, while others had the restricted version that was edited down. When it appeared on television, or in the local video stores, they were cut, though these unrated first copies were still knocking about. Later, Mondo Macabro restored the film and released it uncut.

What was cut from the Prism release?

When Dr. Harper's neck gets ripped and the tongue goes through it. The bit when the blood sprays the camera. That was cut out. They cut out the part when Katrina's hand is chopped off. They cut that but allowed us to keep the blood on her face. Having the hand chopped was too much! There was a third cut … it was all bloody stuff that had to be removed. To me, the film didn't seem any more violent than other R-rated movies. I think at that time the MPAA was beating up on smaller, independent films. They still do it. I am still trying to recall the third cut …

The part when Peter pulls the hoe out of Claire's head?

Yes, that was it. Actually, what is interesting is that there are so many uncut bootleg versions of the film around the world. We never licensed it in Spain but there is a version on DVD. The movie business is so corrupt. When you try to see what recourse you have, and try to hire a lawyer in that country and sue them, you will probably only win $2000 is which is less than the cost of the lawyer! So there is no point.

How did you feel about your work being censored?

This probably isn't the right answer but I thought it was cool! [*Laughs*] It was, "I have made it. We have an unrated version." Therefore I didn't care that much. We were disappointed with Prism, because we wanted to make a film like *The Texas Chain Saw Massacre* or *Evil Dead* that would attract that type of distributor. Instead we got a schlocky straight-to-video company. It wasn't cool to be on Prism. They were the ones who were willing to pay the most money for the film. The people who we thought were cool didn't really want the film. So we gave it to Prism and they changed the name of the film to *The Unearthing*. They changed the poster so it looked like it had nothing to do with the film. We got our money back and we made our first film and we moved on.

How did audiences react to the film outside of Sundance?

We played at a lot of film festivals, lots of weird little ones. We did a film community screening in Minneapolis. Those audiences loved the picture. These audiences understood the film's sense of humor. I remember one person telling me that the only film they could think of that made them laugh in the same way was the movie *Reuben and Ed* [1991]! Generally the audiences into these type of films, or got the humor, really enjoyed the flick and got the movie. Joe Bob gave us great review but we got trashed in *Variety*. Getting trashed in *Variety* was quite cool.

Since Pete Tombs re-released the film on his Mondo Macabro label, it has built up a strong cult following.

He called me because he was working on a book. Someone had told him about the movie and he called me and said he wanted to see the film. So I had to dig around in the basement, find the master, and send him a copy. A couple of weeks later, he called and said he loved the film and he was amazed that it wasn't out there. I told him that some countries had released it and that there were bootlegs swanning around and that it is available. He asked whether he could release it on his Mondo Macabro label. They didn't have a lot of money but they cared for the film and the filmmakers. They treated us well and he made all those great DVD extras. He brought all the pieces together and resurrected the film. We got paid a lot more money by Prism and were treated like crap while if it wasn't for Pete, no one would remember the film. I feel so fondly towards the Mondo Macabro experience. Because of the release, we finally got a review in *Film Threat*. For years it drove us crazy that we never got reviewed in *Film Threat*!

Are you proud of Aswang?

Oh, yes. I have the same print we showed at Sundance transferred to HD. I am doing a cleanup of the print. So I watched it recently and I thought it was pretty good. As years go by, you get the impression that it will be bad, but I am very proud of the film.

15

Uzumaki

An Interview with Higuchinsky

Higuchinsky's cult Japanese horror film *Uzumaki* (2000) is set in the small, close-knit community of Kurouzu. The film begins by presenting a perfect(?) town where everything seems peaceful and idyllic. Scrape beneath the picturesque veneer and things are not what they seem. Things are starting to change. Strange phenomena are afoot as the inhabitants have become obsessed with spirals in their environment. High school friends Kirie and Shuichi pick up on this peculiar fad when Shuichi's father becomes introspected and fascinated with videotaping snails. Further proof that Shuichi's father is mentally losing control: He commissions Kirie's father, an artist, to make a spiral-shaped pot and his insistence on only eating spiraled centered fish cakes, which he marvels at with manic glee.

As spirals appear randomly in the landscape, a series of tragedies begins. A student throws himself to his death off a spiral staircase; Shuichi's dad commits suicide in a washing machine; the locals begin to transform into mutant snails that slither up the school walls. As the correlation between landscape and the inhabitants converge, the community becomes stuck in a perpetual spiral.

A local news reporter discovers a link between the spirals and a dragonfly pond, yet his death puts an end to his investigation. Shuichi's mother descends into madness and is confined to a hospital ward. Overcome with fear of spirals, she cannot even look at the spirals on her own fingertips. Her only course of action is to cut off the tips of her fingers. The realization that there are spirals in your ears sends her over the edge. With the townsfolk spiraling into madness and the world around them literally morphing into a sea of spirals, can Kirie and Shuichi escape, or will they too be sucked into the vortex?

One of *Uzumaki*'s greatest strengths is its creative art design. Higuchinsky uses strange green tones and creepy visual effects to create a nightmarish landscape that recalls Jean-Pierre Jeunet and Marc Caro's *City of the Lost Children* (1995). *Uzumaki* is essential viewing for horror buffs interested in J-Horror. But it slipped under the radar during the J-Horror heyday.

In January 2016, I had the pleasure of interviewing the director of the film, Higuchinsky, about *Uzumaki* and his adaption of Junji Ito's *Long Dream* (2000). The latter was a project Higuchinsky worked on for Japanese television; although it isn't as successful as *Uzumaki*, it features a number of standout scenes reminiscent of the visual brilliance seen in *Uzumaki*. I am indebted to my friend David Geevanathan for the translation of the interview from Japanese into English. Without him, this interview would not have been possible.

Matthew Edwards: *I understand you were born in the Ukraine. Did this shape your upbringing and your career trajectory?*

Higuchinsky: I was only in the Ukraine until I was three years old so I really don't remember much about that time. My father drew pictures and this got me interested in the arts even as a child. I also enjoyed making handicrafts and presenting them in front of others. When I was in my second year of junior high school, *E.T.* [1982] was released in Japan and I went to see it right away. There was a huge line outside the theater and when I saw that line I thought, "Even though Spielberg is not here, there are so many people here to see his film—people from a completely different culture! Okay, I'm going to be a director too!"

At that time I was also reading *Starlog*'s Japanese edition and I wanted to enter Industrial Light and Magic in the future. In high school, I realized that physical fitness was essential for directing and so I joined the boat club and trained every day whilst also making films with my 8mm camera. At university I entered the Japanese Art and Film Directing course and learned the basics of filmmaking. I realized at that time that I was Japanese and so I couldn't direct *Star Wars*, because a Japanese person could not become Luke Skywalker. Figuring out what kind of film I could make as a Japanese person was very difficult for me.

In 2000, you directed for Japanese television an adaptation of Junji Ito's Manga Long Dream [Nagai Yume]. *Was it easy to get the project commissioned?*

Long Dream was a project I worked on after *Uzumaki* and it was the producer from *Uzumaki* that first brought *Long Dream* to my attention.

Can you talk about the production of Long Dream? *Were you given much scope to adapt Ito's work or were you constrained by the limits of working in television?*

There were no real restraints just because the medium was television but I do remember being asked to dilute the color of the blood a little.

In Long Dream, *you play with the idea that dreams offer a false pathway to immortality and salvation. Yet these paths ultimately lead us into the realms of horror, as displayed by Dr. Kuroda's gradual descent into madness as he obsessively searches for the path to immortality in his patient Mukoudo. Was this your intention?*

The Japanese translation was a little difficult to understand but in the dream world we can achieve immortality through the image of immortality. This is something that I can feel myself while dreaming. How amazing would it be to constantly live in the dream world? Therefore I felt that Dr. Kuroda becoming obsessed with the attraction of the dream world would not be strange or out of place.

Considering the budgetary restraints, your eye for detail is not diminished in terms of your visual style and the atmosphere that you conjure up. In terms of space, color and composition, you do a splendid job in translating Ito's pages to the screen.

Just as in *Uzumaki*, I wanted to capture, as much as possible, the mysterious atmosphere of Junji Ito's world. For me, images are tools not just to tell a story but more importantly to enable the viewer to sense the atmosphere of that world. As to whether or not I am satisfied with the final product or not, of course there are certain points where I think, "I should have done it [another] way" but at that time when the film was released, under my responsibility, I think I gave it my all and that it was the best that I could do.

How was the film received critically in Japan? In the West, it has received a number of positive reviews since its release on DVD in America.

I think that there were few viewers in Japan as I haven't really heard many opinions about the film. Although it seems as though the people who actually watched the film were taken by the link with *Uzumaki*.

The misconception is that you shot Long Dream *before you shot the acclaimed J-Horror* Uzumaki. *How did the opportunity to make* Uzumaki *arise?*

As mentioned previously, *Uzumaki* was actually shot first. The opportunity came about when I met Kengo Kaji while filming the TV series *Eko Eko Azarak* and I told him that I would like to try shooting a movie next. Coincidentally, at that time I was reading a manga magazine compilation that happened to feature *Uzumaki*. That episode was about two fighters but I thought it was brilliant and I wanted to shoot it so I called Kengo Kaji. I found out that the wheels were already turning regarding production and they were just in the process of looking for a director. So I was able to meet with the producer and was given the job. At first it was going to be an indie project in an omnibus style, but somewhere along the line, Toei Corporation decided to shoot a cinematic release and everything got bigger.

What is it about Junji Ito's work that you are attracted to, in particular his manga Uzumaki*?*

I'm attracted to Junji Ito's view of the world. The Japanese word *kikai* fits this view perfectly. The dictionary definition is strange and mysterious things or people. In addition, eerily shaped things or people. Rather than general horror which generates fear and surprise, this word evokes eerie and mysterious images. I'm not sure if this will translate well into English. The allure of *Uzumaki* is not that the uzumaki itself is scary but rather the changes in the people caught up in it. I think the image of the fictional town of Kurouzu being eroded by the uzumaki is very artistic. It's pretty damn cool.

How did you set about adapting Ito's seminal manga series?

Basically I decided that I wanted to stay as faithful to the original material as possible. Rather than tell a story, I was trying to recreate the world of Kurouzu as vividly as possible. The manga was not complete and instead of having the film complete the story I wanted the film itself to be a loop constituent. At that time, film was shown using a film reel, which was also circularly shaped. It was to be repeatedly shown—a never-ending nightmare!

If I am not mistaken, Ito appears on a wanted poster in the film!

That's right. The portrait was actually in the original material. I asked the artistic team to make it for me.

Where was the film shot and how long did you spend filming?

It was primarily shot in Ueda City, Nagano prefecture. A few locations in Tokyo were also used. I think filming was for about two weeks.

How did you achieve the surreal horror effects?

The VFX (visual and special effects) supervisor was my friend Issei Oda. He worked closely with the staff from Digital Frontier to prepare the CGI effects. In addition, there are also effects that I added myself during the editing process. Makeup and objects were supervised by Tomoo Haraguchi. With regards to the image as a whole, we were trying to replicate the original images as much as possible, with an analog feel and taste, like that of an old movie. With that in mind, the actor's makeup was also done in a less natural, more theatrical, heavy style. Although there was some time for post-production, the system hadn't yet caught up at that time so the editing process was very difficult.

One of the memorable scenes is when a schoolboy falls from the spiral staircase. Would you talk me through the filming of that set piece?
   We set up the camera using an optical axis rotary stand attached directly to the spiral staircase. We shot the scene, without using CGI, by rotating the camera while zooming in.

Are you pleased with Uzumaki *from a technical and creative standpoint?*
   As this was just before the digital camera and digital editing age, we used the methods that were commonly used in the music video industry, i.e., shooting in film, converting to negatelecine, editing in video and kaleidoscoping back to film, which was a challenging process and I do sometimes think that if we had waited a little longer…. But the technology just wasn't there at that time. Also, when the DVD was being prepared, using the video master would have resulted in extremely beautiful images but it was reproduced from the film irregardless.

Literally, Uzumaki *translates as spiral or whirlpool but to me the film is about madness as the community spirals into abnormal behavior as a result of the curse. As the curse takes hold, the community conforms to its power, leading to its collective downfall. Were you looking to explore this madness in the film?*
   Right at the start of the original work, there is a line of dialogue spoken by Kirie: "Kurouzu … the town where I was born and raised. What I'm about to tell you is about the numerous strange occurrences that happened here." These words allowed me to focus on the fact that the story was told in the past; in other words, it had already been seen. Kirie is telling numerous mysterious stories. That made me think that Kirie himself was looping in this world. As I mentioned before, the film used for movies is also spiral-shaped. The nightmare of Kurouzu trapped within the spiral film. That is the point of this movie. If you are going to consider this meaning, the slides that the reporter Ichiro Tamura looks at and the documents that he researches in the library reveal hints about the secrets of *Uzumaki*.

For me, one of the terrifying elements of the film is how the community conforms to the spiral. It reminded me a lot of my time teaching in Japan and witnessing how high school students and workers would conform in certain situations without resistance. Were you trying to make a comment on Japanese society and conformity?
   I believe that "movies exist as new works of art dependent on the number of viewers." If you felt that, then I think that is one truth. The fact that so many theories and explanations are born from one movie is one of the intriguing aspects about film.

The numbers 6 and 9 appear frequently throughout the film. These numbers have spiral qualities about them. Was this deliberate?
   Yes, all the numbers that appear in the film are spiral in shape.

I understand that the film was made prior to Ito completing his manga. Did this give you artistic license to take the project in an opposite direction from that of the comic book?

At first I was unsure about how to end the movie, but the realization that the movie itself was a spiral solved that problem for me.

What was the critical reaction to the film in Japan?

The Japanese critics were largely divided into two groups. The ones who belittled the movie by saying it was not horror and the ones who graciously accepted this mysterious world, discovering meaning themselves and enjoying the film. The first group had a fixed idea about what horror was and had no intention of defining it for themselves, only wanting the same simple, easy-to-understand content that they were used to. The manga fans were also divided into two groups. The ones who thought the manga was scarier than the movie and the ones who thought that the movie was realized as true to the manga as possible.

Aesthetically, your films have nods to the work of German horrors such as Nosferatu *[1922] and* The Cabinet of Dr. Caligari *[1920] and the work of David Lynch. Were these works influential in shaping your own nightmarish vision in the film, alongside Ito's manga?*

David Lynch is one of my favorite directors but as a Japanese I wanted to express Japanese strange phenomenon so at that time I had the staff watch *Akuma no temari uta* [The Demon's Nursery Rhyme]. I'm not sure how it translates in English but it is an eerie world.

I understand that Long Dream *and* Uzumaki *were shot on digital film. What were the advantages and disadvantages?*

Uzumaki was from 35mm film while *Long Dream* was shot by digital betacam. As much as possible, we would like to shoot in film but this is difficult considering costs. I was rather more focused on widening the possibilities in the editing process. From my days at university, I had already realized that editing in video allows for greater scope in editing. And so, filming in a music video–style awakened me even more so to these possibilities. If you can widen the areas that are under your control, you can get closer to the image that you desire.

Do you consider you films to be surrealist takes on the horror genre?

I feel that *Uzumaki* and *Long Dream* are works of fantasy. At the end of the day, movies are false worlds and so that makes them fantasy in my book.

Uzumaki is a sleeper film in the canon of the J-Horrors Ju-on *[2000] and* Ring *[1998]. Are you proud of what you achieved with the film and the acclaim it has received, especially in England and America?*

I sometimes receive mail from European fans. This makes me very happy as it was my dream to use film as a way to overcome national borders and have my movies watched by people all over the world. I think that these fans focus not on the story but on the simple images, they sense something through the visuals.

Do you have any intentions to return to the horror genre in the future, or adapt further Ito comics?

At the moment I am not particularly looking to return to the genre. My reputation isn't that great in Japan so making a film is not that easy but at the moment I am editing a short film called *The Bionic Girl*.

16

Late Bloomer

An Interview with Gō Shibata
by Johannes Schönherr

Meeting Gō Shibata

In early autumn 1999, I went to Osaka to show a program of silent black-and-white stag movies from the 1920s. Vintage era explicit porn. Only real underground places would show films like that in Japan at the time. The owner of the theater, the tiny Planet Studyo + 1 cinema, was Kunihiko Tomioka. He invited me to stay at his house for a few days. To my surprise, his apartment turned out to be the camping ground for a large number of renegade students from the Osaka University of Arts. Parties were going on day and night in the cramped space and yet the main focus point was not the fridge with the beer but the Steenbeck 16mm editing table in the living room. Everyone vied for their space at that editing machine.

The previous year, Kazuyoshi Kumakiri, a Osaka University of Arts student, had run into problems with his school. They refused to screen his graduation film *Kichiku* [*Kichiku Dai Enkai*, 1997], an ultra-violent feature based on a real-life incident where Japanese leftists killed each other at a mountain resort in the early 1970s. Kumakiri approached Tomioka, who premiered the film in his theater. At that time, Kumakiri learned about the editing table at Tomioka's house and about Tomioka's generally free-wheeling and open ways. He told his student friends and suddenly, Tomioka's apartment filled up with students who felt that they found a freedom there that the school could never provide. Many of them stayed on for long periods, rolling out their sleeping bags wherever they found a space.

When I arrived, one of those students, Nobuhiro Yamashita, had just left for the Vancouver Film Festival with his slacker drama *Hazy Life* [*Donten Seikatsu*, 1999]. Another promising young director, Gō Shibata, lived in Tomioka's apartment and was busy putting the final touches on the editing of his first feature *NN-891102*.

The film was his Osaka University of Arts graduation project though the school had banned him from entering their premises. I heard vague rumors that he had caused a big fire at the school: During an illegal film show accompanied by a live noise concert, the electric equipment malfunctioned which resulted in a blaze.

I didn't speak any Japanese, he didn't speak English. But we immediately connected. Shibata called the way we communicated "telepathy" but actually, it was quite basic. We would sit down with beers and takoyaki (fried octopus served in small dough balls) in

16. Gō Shibata (Schönherr)

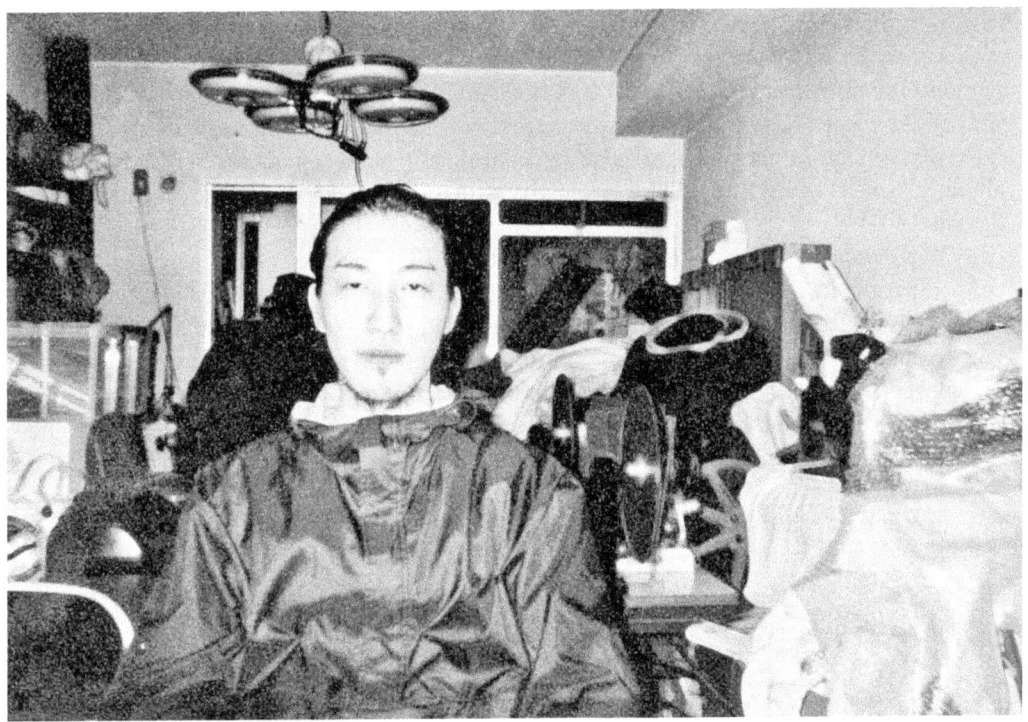

Gō Shibata in Osaka in 1999 (courtesy Johannes Schönherr).

the coolest tiny bar nearby, the Hatsubei, and would just throw band names at each other. Einstürzende Neubauten? Agreed. Merzbow? Agreed. Masonna? Agreed. We went through the whole inventory of extreme Japanese, American and European music just by name and titles—and could talk all night that way. Shibata clearly knew about bands on the furthest fringes of noise and punk. In fact, his personal background was in music rather than in film.

Whenever I went to Osaka in the subsequent years, I made sure to get in contact with Shibata. His *NN-891102* turned out to be quite an interesting film. It dealt with the sound of the atomic bomb that destroyed Nagasaki and focused on a character who tries to recreate that sound in music. The film was shown at international film festivals like Rotterdam as well as at avant-garde music events, including the Sónar Fest in Barcelona.

Soon Shibata began to show me raw footage of his next project, a film featuring a severely handicapped serial killer. Some of the footage was already scored with the techno-noise of Tokyo band World End's Girlfriend. It looked mesmerizing and deeply disturbing. Shibata eventually moved to Tokyo but continued to go back to Osaka to work on the project. He told me that all filming took place in Nishinomiya, a city between Osaka and Kobe. A rather faceless place, Nishinomiya is known to most Japanese only as the town where the Koshien Stadium is located, the home of the Hanshin Tigers baseball team.

Late Bloomer

In November 2004, Shibata's new film *Late Bloomer* (*Osoi Hito*) had its premiere at the Tokyo Filmex. It was a fast-paced, techno-music driven, black-and-white feature highlighting the emotional troubles of a wheelchair-bound middle-aged man suffering from cerebral palsy. Sumida (played by real-life sufferer Masakiyo Sumida, using his real name in the film) feels the limitations in his daily life: his electric wheelchair won't take him to the places he wants to go, he has to communicate via a sound computer device into which he types his messages as he can't speak, and he needs nurses to help him with all basic aspects of his life. Still he hasn't given up on life and tries to enjoy it as much as he can.

The Japanese health care system is good, tending to the needs of severely handicapped people like Sumida. He is issued two different helpers: an older lady who takes care of his household and a young, shaven-headed guy, Take (played by Naozo Hotta), who keeps him socially active in his community. The trouble starts when the old nurse is replaced by an attractive young girl, Nobuko (Mari Torii). Sumida interprets her close attention to be more than professionalism and falls in love with her, expecting her to be the first real woman in his life. But Take, playing in a noise rock band and versed in all the ways of life (Sumida is envious of him), is far more attractive to Atsuko. She falls for him.

In his bitterness, Sumida poisons Take and drowns him in a bathtub. Everyone thinks that Take died in an accident and Sumida gets away with the murder. Sumida's declaration of love to Nobuko is not appreciated; she quits immediately. The resulting emotional turmoil drives Sumida over the edge. He starts to kill randomly just to act out his rage. His favored targets are drunken businessmen, attacking them when they are at their most vulnerable, weakened by the booze. These drunks are made up of a cross-section of people who have either treated him badly in the past, or people who do what Sumida can only dream of: being successful in life and with girls.

The movie mixes psychological horror with the provocative decision to have a handicapped person playing a handicapped serial killer, and boasts beautiful black and white cinematography and fast but consistent pacing. The soundtrack by World End's Girlfriend is at times dream-like and at other times very aggressive. It is a small wonder that *Late Bloomer* turned into an international success.

Japanese flyer for *Late Bloomer* (courtesy Gō Shibata).

Interview with Go Shibata

In November 2004, just before Shibata's film took off, I met him for an interview at an Ainu restaurant in Tokyo. Over fried Hokkaido deer and salmon and a few Hokkaido microbrews, we started talking. Many thanks to Kayoko Nakanishi for translating the interview.

Johannes Schönherr: *So, how did you start out?*

Gō Shibata: An old friend of mine from college, Satoshi Naka, was the caretaker of Masakiyo Sumida and Toshihisa Fukunaga. They loved movies and watched a lot of movies together. They loved the movies so much, they wanted to make their own film and also be in this film. They looked for a director for that. When Naka told them that one of his friends was a movie director, they were very excited and said, "Let's meet him!" Naka contacted me and showed me a picture of Sumida. He somehow looked a bit like the singer of the [Osaka noise rock band] Boredoms. I got very interested. I went to meet Sumida. I had written a script based on some ideas of mine but I had to change that during the shooting to make it fit Sumida's acting.

You also used his own language machine in the film?

Yes, that's his machine. I observed Sumida and based the script on that.

That became then the love story with the caretaker girl and then you turned that into a tale of murder.

The story that Sumida would become a murderer was part of the original idea. That point has not changed. The main story has not changed but many details have.

You had written the original story before meeting Sumida?

No, I started with that after I had met him.

The guy in the hospital is a friend of Sumida in real life?

It's not a hospital. It's his home. He is Toshihisa Fukunaga. Fukunaga is really interesting. Fukunaga is the boss of the disabled people in Nishinomiya. Nishinomiya is the best city when it comes to taking care of handicapped people. *Why* is it the best city in Japan in that regard? It's because of Fukunaga. Fukunaga was a political activist in the 1980s. He went to town hall with his wheelchair, he did that three times and then he was arrested. Because these things happened, the town administration said, "Let's take care of the handicapped people."

What did he do in town hall?

He crashed right through a closed glass door with his wheelvchair. That brought him a lot of followers. Fukunaga was the driving force behind the movie. I met Fukunaga first. Fukunaga asked me if I like freaks. He likes freaks. He basically sent Sumida over to act in the movie. Sumida doesn't like violence,

Masakiyo Sumida in *Late Bloomer* (courtesy Gō Shibata).

he doesn't like war, he likes peace. He is into dealing with things with humor. He is very charming and he uses that charm to get people to help him. He is very smart.

At first, I was thinking about basing the story on something like *Taxi Driver* [1976]. But as I was working with Sumida, I discovered his loneliness. Sumida always wanted to have a girlfriend or a wife. So I thought that the story would become more interesting if I included Sumida's personality and his real concerns.

What did Sumida think about the murder scenes?

He didn't want to do it. But I told him that movies are about extreme situations and he could understand that. The murders belong to the story and he is an actor. I wanted Sumida to act out the frustrations of disabled people. That's the only thing I wanted to tell in the film. Sumida was to become a kind of anti-hero. I don't explain everything, though. I want the audience to think for themselves why Sumida commits his murders.

What about Naozo Hotta, who plays the caretaker Take?

Naozo plays in a noise punk band in Osaka. A lot of those punk musicians work as caretakers for disabled people. A lot of people around Naozo are caretakers. A friend of Naozo acted in my previous film *NN-891102*. He introduced me to Naozo after a concert of his band. We went drinking together. I found him a very interesting person because he has a very unique character. I asked him to watch *NN-891102*. After he watched the film, he understood what I was doing and decided to participate. What Naozo is doing with his band and his life is very much the same as what I am doing with my films. That's why I thought that he was right for the part. Naozo writes the lyrics and the music for his band. The first time Naozo and Sumida met, they immediately liked each other.

Where did Mari Torii come from?

She is part of a very famous Osaka stage theater group. They don't have a theater. They always build a set somewhere outside and after they finish their engagement, they always tear down the set. They destroy everything. Every time. The name of the group is Ishin-ha. They also toured Europe. They have about 40 actors and 60 on staff, about 100 people altogether.

What about the other actors? Did you have auditions?

No auditions. They are all my friends.

At the beginning of the making of the film, you had the main priest of the Nunose Shrine as producer.

That priest is Mister Terauchi of the Nunose Jinja. He is an artist himself, making iron objects. I knew Terauchi before I started the film, we sometimes went drinking together. He likes to support young artists. Like one young guy received financial support from Terauchi to go to New York and study art. I heard about that and asked him for support for my movie. He gave me 3,800,000 yen [about $38,000] as a first budget. I spent all that on drinking and for meals with the staff, for equipment. After all the money was spent, the shooting stopped.

So, after that, you had to find other resources?

In 2002, I met Toshiki Shima of Shima Films. A friend of mine, Yuge, played in a punk band. One night, I was drinking with the members of the band and Yuge asked me if I knew [film directors] Shinji Somai or Junji Sakamoto. I was surprised because I thought that he was only interested in music. But he told me that he had a friend, Toshiki Shima, and that this friend was supporting Japanese films. He told me that I should meet him and he introduced me to Shima. Before I moved to Tokyo, I went to meet Shima in Kyoto. About three months after our first meeting, Shima came to Tokyo on some matter related to his work. He stayed only three days in Tokyo. I wanted him to see *NN-891102* on film, not on video. I asked Kunihiko Tomioka in Osaka to send the print, and I asked Keiko Araki of the PIA Film Festival if I could use their screening room. I had no money right then and I asked her if I could pay later. She agreed and I did the screening just for Shima. I also showed him some footage of *Late Bloomer*. I asked him for his support. Two weeks later, Shima told me that he would produce the film.

What made you move to Tokyo from Osaka?
I couldn't find any creative work in Osaka. I worked some TV jobs there but I didn't like that. I needed to do some creative work for myself. I called my friends from Osaka who had already moved to Tokyo and who worked in film and I asked them for work. They told me that I had to be in Tokyo for that. Japanese like meetings, they don't like to depend on e-mail and so on. I hadn't finished my film yet and I couldn't face Sumida, Fukunaga and Terauchi.

Can you talk a bit about your background?
I'm from Wakabadai, a very new town near Yokohama. Although it is very close to Tokyo, the town is very much like countryside, very isolated. In that town, a lot of *bozosoku* [bikers] were around and my parents worried about me. So they asked me to go to a small junior high school in Tokyo. They wanted to keep me away from the *bozosoku*. All my friends from elementary school eventually became *bozosoku*. My life was very much divided between school in Tokyo where the students were very smart but once I went back to my home town, there were all these bad boys. I became a kind of therapist for them. Because in the world of those bad boys, they had many problems. I was listening to my friends in the hometown. I was not part of their group. That's why they could tell me their stories. At that time, I started to make movies. It was cheaper back then to use 8mm than video. Video cameras were still very expensive.

In middle school, I had a friend whose father was rich and he had a video camera. I liked to make miniature model tanks and to put them into stop-motion animated films. I was also very impressed by the Spielberg-produced film *The Goonies* [1985]. It's an adventure story about a group of boys who go out in search of a pirate treasure. I tried to make a remake of this movie with my friends. We never finished it but we were working on it for quite some while.

After I entered junior high school, I decided to make a new film. I shot my friends who went to play Pachinko. That was also on 8mm. I had a script but my friends didn't follow the lines. I said, "Okay, let's forget the script." I wanted to film a story ... but at last, it didn't work. I didn't have enough money to finish the film, so it didn't get finished. That was in Yokohama.

Which year was that?
About 1991, 1992. When I was in third grade in junior high school and first grade in high school, I was shooting so many things, shooting the nature, the scenery. At that time, I was very confused. Every weekend I went to go camping at that time, together with both my friends from Tokyo and the Yokohama *bozosoku*. With those people I shot the

Pachinko film that didn't get finished. I connected the footage I had with the music. Then I started my own band.

For that film, for the soundtrack, I started the band. We played all the music that I liked, Einstürzende Neubauten, Boredoms, Beastie Boys, and we made a cassette tape with our recordings. Masaya Nakahara of the noise band Violent Onsen Geisha listened to our tape and he found it very interesting. He had a record shop in Shibuya selling all kinds of independent music. Neither I nor Nakahara thought that the tapes would sell but they did. We made more than 80.000 yen with those tapes. 1.500 yen per piece. We made three tapes. I made the tapes at my house. This was when I was in second grade in high school.

What was the name of the band?
UNU. Just like the letters from the alphabet. [*He chants "Yu-En-Yu-En-Yu" like a Buddhist monk chanting.*] We named the band after a love hotel in Yokohama. Most of the tapes sold in Osaka. That's when I realized that Osaka might be a really interesting place. Like, they had the Ultra Fuckers in Osaka and all that scum culture. I very much like the Boredoms who are also from Osaka. I wanted to change my environment and in Osaka were all the bands I liked. So I decided to go there. There, I wanted to make my own film.

My family didn't have much money but I persuaded them anyway that they must send me to the Osaka University of Arts. In Osaka, I played then for two years in a band named Tochika Warmers Diary. I didn't and still don't really understand the meaning of the name of the band because it was named by other band members. It was a good name, though. We played regularly in all the clubs. The first three years I stayed in Osaka, I made music. During that time, Nobuhiro Yamashita and Kosuke Mukai were making 8mm films at the school and Kumakiri made *Kichiku*. I was living in a very big house. I could rent the whole house for only 10,000 yen a month, we could make any noise we wanted to make at that house. That's why Kumakiri and other friends from school came to the house to record sounds for their films. I started to get involved with those filmmakers and started to realize that I was just making music but that my reason for coming to Osaka was to make movies. So I said, "Okay, now I want to make my own film."

My first film was kind of work for the school, for the class. The school assignment was to make a film somehow related to a slope. I made the short film *All You Can Eat* [1996].

[The seven-minute punk rock short *All You Can Eat* shows two young guys and one girl eating and eating. They start with a table full of disgusting junk food, then hit the town and wolf down plants, insects and worms they find on the street. Finally resorting to cannibalism, they end up in jail where there is more junk to digest.]

I was poor at that time and with my friends, we went to McDonald's, Mister Donut, Kentucky Fried Chicken … all that junk food outlets. We went to their garbage cans outside the shops and we ate out of that. That was the inspiration for the film. All the people you see in the movie are real friends I did go to the garbage cans with, like Robin, the singer of the punk performance band Akainu.

Was it then that Kumakiri introduced you to Kunihiko Tomioka [of Planet Studyo + 1]?
Takashi Ujita, another friend from the university, introduced me to Tomioka. He later made the film *Ryoko in the Unfaithful Evening* [2001]. It showed at Tokyo Filmex two or three years ago.

You did all the editing of NN-891102 *at Planet Studyo + 1.*

I was on the blacklist in the school because I had so many troubles with my life. At the end of my sophomore year, I had to choose a major. The university didn't want to allow me to study directing, they didn't want me to use their facilities for editing. I had a lot of problems there … like, once my band played a concert in the school. Our equipment started a big fire in the school, so that got me into a lot of trouble. It was an accident but the school thought that I was just causing problems. We had a kind of guerrilla club there, without permission from the school. That's why I did all the editing for *NN-891102* at Tomioka's place. I lived at his house for ten months. Soon after *NN-891102* was finished, I met Sumida and started to work on *Late Bloomer*.

17

Outside Peering In

AN INTERVIEW WITH DANTE TOMASELLI

An outsider; a self-confessed loner: Horror filmmaker Dante Tomaselli is a unique anomaly in the field of American horror cinema. He is a filmmaker driven by his own artistic vision and a true independent of the underground U.S. horror scene. He has built up a résumé of accomplished, surrealist horror films which have been acclaimed in the horror media. Yet his unwillingness to compromise on his films and his surrealist and non-linear approach has alienated some audiences, leaving him at times on the outside fringes of the horror community. Those expecting a traditional narrative will find his gothic Hell rides too much to stomach. Yet those who adore his work tap into Tomaselli's surrealist palette where his films play out like a psychedelic funhouse, or a deranged maze of mirrors. His films are made up of striking images and laced with themes such as Catholic repression and iconography and the breakdown of the family unit. Tomaselli's films ooze with atmosphere and style and layered music that creates an audio-visual nightmare for the audience. Images such as a nun ravaged by freaky clowns, demonic masks and inventive death sequences linger in the mind long after the end of a film. One of Tomaselli's gifts is finding horror in unsuspecting sources, like transforming a childhood toy into something eerie. He is a horror filmmaker who feels more at home with the horror filmmakers of the '60s, '70s and early '80s as opposed to the new generation of horror filmmakers. He has refused to follow the new trend of torture porn films where explicit violence has come at the expense of producing genuine scares.

Born in Paterson, New Jersey, and cousin to legendary filmmaker Alfred Sole, of *Alice, Sweet Alice*, fame, Tomaselli has directed *Desecration* (1999), *Horror* (2003), *Satan's Playground* (2006) and the critically acclaimed *Torture Chamber* (2013), for which he finally received the respect and attention his films deserve. The latter film centers on a young boy who is institutionalized by his family, who believe he is demonically possessed. Escaping from the institution with the help of a group of cultists, he kidnaps his old art teacher and they wind up in a castle complete with a medieval torture chamber and eerie catacombs. Those who try to track him down, or mistakenly cross the boy's path, are subjected to cruel deaths. Featuring scream queen Lynn Lowry and *The Sporanos*' Vincent Pastore, the film is a must for fans of surrealist and gothic horror cinema.

In October 2014, I contacted Dante and he gave a career-spanning interview.

Matthew Edwards: *How did you get interested in the horror genre?*
Dante Tomaselli: Oh, God, I've been interested in it forever, since as long as I can

remember. In 1973, I was three years old and I can still remember imagery from *The Exorcist*, the newspaper ads, television commercials, the possessed sounds, even the cover of the book. Also *Don't Look Now*—same year—I was like, three. At that time I had a chalk board and I was constantly drawing ghosts coming out of haunted houses. I'd make these vast rolling hills and infinite horizons. Graveyards ... I loved drawing and painting graveyards for some reason. It was just an instinct. This kind of demonic artwork just poured out of me.

When I create these films, they're filtered through the child inside. Something needs to be exorcised, expressed. It's an involuntary reflex. There are images, scenes, embedded in my DNA that throb and these memories or impressions try to poke out. I follow through ... almost in a trance. I'm on an odd mission where my unconscious mind is leading the way. My childhood wasn't all bad. There was a lot of wonderment. I smiled a lot. I loved to laugh. I played games with my younger brother Michael, where I'd scare him and lock him down in the basement. Sometimes I'd hide a tape recorder in his closet with ghostly sounds echoing. I liked playing tricks. I wanted to be a magician. There was the woods, the beach, the ocean, riding my bike, riding the waves. I was happiest when I was one with nature. My grammar school years were pretty enjoy-

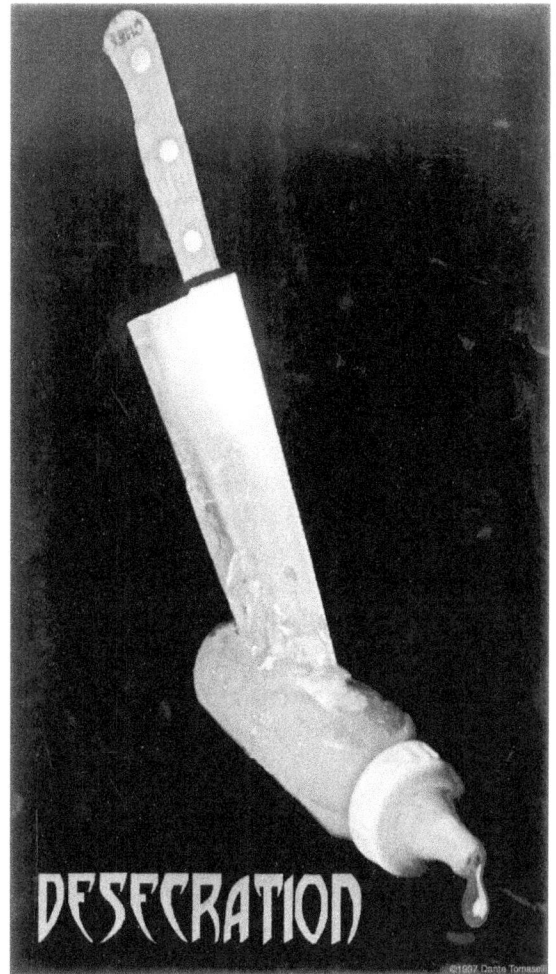

Desecration's original promotional poster. This great poster seems to be partly inspired by the iconic poster from *Alice, Sweet, Alice,* which was directed by Tomaselli's cousin Alfred Sole (courtesy Dante Tomaselli).

able but around sixth grade, something changed. At the age of 11, there was this start of a shift. Through that age until 17 I was definitely depressed. It was a period filled with a lot of emotional congestion. My school grades were fine but I was very somber and vibrating with anxiety. A kind of ... psychic torment. I was locking everything inside. And I didn't drink alcohol or take any drugs at all. I had no interest in that, I already felt like I was on drugs anyway. I guess I tried to be a good Catholic boy, imagining the pits of Hell opening under my feet. I felt very guilty about many things ... and would pay for them in my nightmares. While awake, I needed to be alone, I was always wandering off or getting lost. I'd go into woods, or anywhere, and suddenly my eyes were film cameras and I'd hear this electronic organ music. I felt safe ... in charge of the scene, the location, the action. I was totally in my fantasy. There was always a deep, low, throbbing baritone. Like something you'd hear in a John Carpenter movie or one of my films. I'd wander around, almost like a sleepwalker. I'd role-play the stalker and victim. There were dream symbols everywhere. I opened my eyes to the beauty of every living creature. But the bad feeling would pour in. I felt so trapped. School was depressing. I felt like cattle. I hated being younger … and couldn't wait to grow up. I always felt different than other kids, though not superior. Other kids scared me. Adults even more so, though I connected with a few. I had many issues … insecurities. I was too skinny, it made me feel insignificant. I tried very hard to gain weight but couldn't. I didn't like most social situations and played some sports and hated them. I was never a team player. I mostly retreated to my room and watched horror films or listened to Depeche Mode or Jean Michel Jarre. I was close with my mother and she took me to see every horror film, in drive-ins and theaters. Mom was an actress and president of a theater company in North Jersey. I enjoyed reading her lines … I guess it was my first taste of directing. I was very close to my grandmother, Rose Ruocco. My mother's mother. Rose made me feel so safe. If I have a guardian angel, it's her. I wasn't bullied at school, I kept a cool exterior but I wasn't what you'd categorize as a popular or well-liked kid. I was weird. Strange. No one knew the anxiety I kept hidden. I was locked in an invisible prison, I really needed to get out! So as soon as I got my license, I escaped to New York City as often as possible. I didn't need anyone around me to have an adventure. I didn't even need to travel out of my room. I'd fantasize. Or I'd listen to electronic music and experience a surreal audio light show projected right before my eyes. I preferred being alone. I still do.

You studied film at university. Did it prepare you for actually shooting a feature film?

Well, it was good that I went to Pratt Institute and School of Visual Arts, it helped to get an education in art. But even if for some reason I didn't go to college, it wouldn't have mattered. Actually I graduated from School of Visual Arts with a BFA in advertising—not film—I was only a film major my first two years at Pratt, when I was 18 and 19. So film school is fine, but it's not everything. I don't have a film degree. I know so many film majors who went absolutely nowhere, sorry to say. And believe me, they are the people who write things about me on message boards or at Amazon … hmmm. I sure made some enemies. There's a lot of back-stabbing and jealousy in this business. I've seen a lot of ugliness already … a lot of unhappiness. I try to stay completely on the outside while peering in. I want to be a pacifist. There's also an absolutely beautiful side, a magical side of the film business. When things work, they really work. Great pieces of art have been caught on film … it can be an almost supernatural experience. The crews on my feature-length films, *Desecration* and *Horror,* were out of this world. I've been blessed … connecting with the right people. Film is the ultimate medium. But getting back to your question, I don't think film school is that important. Sure, it's great to take some courses to get your feet wet. But the only way to become a filmmaker is to make films … on your own. Period.

Your debut film Desecration *started life as a short film. Why did you decide to expand it to feature length?*

It was always my intention to expand it into a feature. In fact, I told everyone it was more of a trailer than a normal short film. I had my mind set on a feature from the very start. I made it my goal to create the full-length version of *Desecration* before the time I turned 30. And I did it. I shot the feature-length *Desecration* when I was 28.

What attracted me to Desecration *was the interesting DVD cover artwork. My first reaction was that it reminded me of the work of Francis Bacon.*

Thanks. I like that comparison. Bacon is spectacular, so dreamy and macabre. The painter was Atmo Royce, another surrealist artist. I commissioned him to make those freaky nun paintings. My favorite one is the faceless nun, or maybe the skull nun. He also did the cover artwork for *Horror*. I met Atmo through Vincent Lamberti, who played Brother Nicolas in *Desecration*.

Going full circle, there is a nod to Bacon's surrealism and the freaky nun paintings in your film Torture Chamber. Desecration *and* Torture Chamber *seem like kindred spirits, especially when you consider the character Bobby is locked in a cage in* Desecration *and Jimmy is locked in a cage at the beginning of* Torture Chamber.

To be honest, I never really planned for that. I was never thinking of Bacon while concocting the hallucinatory nuns though I do hear that comparison a lot. Those nuns go back to a painting when I was 19 years old and attending Pratt Institute in Brooklyn. It was for a class called Light, Color & Design. I made a series of nun portraits. Stern Nun. Faceless Nun. Skull Nun. And Clown Nun. They all came together with an acrylic painting of floating faceless nuns. I was never a great painter, I'm a much better filmmaker, but this certain painting was somewhat well known at Pratt at the time. It was the best thing I'd ever done as a painter. Very weird and colorful, almost extra-terrestrial. It seemed to emanate a peculiar energy and I couldn't keep my eyes off it. One weekend, I took it to my family's home in New Jersey. At that time I was living in the dorms in New York and would visit New Jersey on weekends. Well, for some reason I felt compelled to destroy the painting. I don't know what came over me. First I tried to break it and I couldn't, it was too strong. Then I went to the kitchen refrigerator and threw all sorts of disgusting substances onto it. I desecrated the painting. It ended up in the trash outside. I guess deep down inside, I despised it. Or something came over me. I don't know what that was all about.

Considering the low budget of Desecration, *I was impressed with the cinematography and the stylized and atmospheric set pieces. Lots of low-budget horror films forget this aspect and instead opt purely for gore?*

Atmosphere is pretty much gone in most horror films. Well, it has been. It's making a comeback right now, and from what I hear there's some really good products coming out of Japan. But since the mid–80s, and especially in the '90s, horror films became lightweight, less subversive and I don't know … very safe. And everything has been too comedic. The reason why is because the people in power, the people who have the money, those producers who pay for movies, they are convinced that the public wants comedy in their horror films. I know this personally. They're delusional about what horror fans want. Horror fans want disturbing, scary horror movies. God, aren't we all sick of these horror-comedies? But yes, a lot of horror movies these days, ones that come out in theaters, focus too much on the special effects and not enough time on creating a serious, creepy atmosphere.

That said, Desecration *does feature some imaginative and gory deaths. My favorite is the death of the nun by a remote control model plane. It is so bizarre and offbeat that it borders on the comical. Was this intended?*

Yes, it was meant to be more offbeat, more weird than outright spooky. I kind of misjudged there. I purposely edited the sequence in a very fragmented way. But the critics savaged it; they said it was very bad editing. I purposely made it fake-looking as if saying,

"This can't be real ... this can't be happening." But I was wrong—nobody got it. I'd change it now if I had the chance. Just trim a few seconds.

But Desecration *received many plaudits upon its release. Were you surprised by its success?*

Definitely. I was hoping for it, but yes, it took me by surprise. I get emails from horror fanatics who enjoyed *Desecration* and who are excited when my films come out. You'd be surprised. These letters are almost better to read than reviews. Though I really love a well-thought out review. They're exciting to read because my movies have been puzzles so far ... totally interpretative. It's depressing reading some of the bad ones, and there are some, definitely. Some people can't stand my work. Hate it with a passion. Tomaselli sucks. And then I have the other way around, I have some people sending me gifts [*laughs*]. Seriously, there are different people I'm in touch with, online, from all around the world. People from Spain, Switzerland and California who have all contacted me through my website.

Some have even sent me different toys and memorabilia from my past, old Cars shirts and rare tracks, Depeche Mode re-mixes, Vincent Price's Shrunken Heads, articles on early John Carpenter and Alfred Sole, all sorts of things. Just this past year. The hate and love, for my work, hopefully they're the ingredients for a storm. No matter what anyone says, I plan for these films to get scarier and scarier.

As a filmmaker, how do you deal with people's criticism?

These days I mostly allow myself to be penetrated by criticism from actual critics and people who are good writers. I couldn't be bothered with haters. They can't hurt me any more. Explain why you despise my film with every fiber of your being. Don't just say, "It sucked" or "Worst movie ever." In the independent

Behind the scenes shot of Dante Tomaselli and Christie Sanford during the making of *Desecration* (courtesy Dante Tomaselli).

horror field, as far as opinions go, you can't visit the IMDb for guidance or you'd commit suicide. There are a lot of frustrated, would-be filmmakers, kids dominating the show. It's a cesspool. When I say kids ... I mean immature personalities. A lot of negative propaganda and my detractors have always taken a piss on me. There's nothing helpful for me there. Use your real name, don't hide behind 666whatever. Who are you? Do I know you personally? Are you a crew member I fired? Are you the crystal meth dealer who approached me about illegally funding my film? It could very well be propaganda. From critics, from actual critics, the reviews are mostly on the positive side. Sometimes the dreamlike feel annoys and I can understand that but usually it's understood that the budget is extremely low. Some mean-spirited whiner on the IMDb doesn't take that into consideration or blocks it out. Not everyone is going to like my work. It's like letting go, allowing yourself to be hypnotized. Just the idea of that can turn someone off. Maybe it simply doesn't agree with you at all, that's okay. This is not the usual $100 million plus production you see at the theaters. And on the other end of the spectrum, it's definitely not a shot on camcorder, shaky camera kind of experience like *The Blair Witch Project* [1999] or *Paranormal Activity* [2007]. This is a low-budget, intimate, surreal horror ride. You won't be spoon-fed. You won't know what's happening until the pieces coalesce ... until possibly the very end of the film and even then you still might not be sure. I notice there is extreme hate and love about my films, especially on message boards. In one enthusiastic post I'll hear someone saying something so flattering about me that I'll blush, and in the next instant, I'll cringe ... there's someone else saying that I'm a horrible filmmaker. A zero. The lowest. But wait, the last guy was just describing me as an independent horror maestro? It's very disorienting and I find it best to block it out and trust the inner voice commanding me to create these films.

Your second feature Horror *was shot again on a tight budget, yet the production values look a lot higher. How did you overcome the obvious financial limitations to deliver such an accomplished film?*

I think it's all about synergy. A bunch of passionate people all wanting something to work, trying their best. I'm more of a composer, or a cook. I gather all the right ingredients and put them together. The key is to treat each element with respect. It's just really about synergy. And some kind of karma ... what you put out, you get back.

Horror *is even more hallucinogenic and surreal than* Desecration. *Was that a conscious decision, to push the boundaries even further?*

Yeah, I thought *Desecration* was a little too mannered, a little too controlled. I wanted *Horror* to be wilder. It's completely off the hinges. I wanted the film to have a kind of epic exuberance.

I loved the performance of Kreskin as Grandfather Salo.

Ah, Kreskin. Well, he wasn't my first choice for the Reverend Salo. I was all ready to go with another actor—a cripple—a haunted-looking, wizard-like character actor named Wayne Bolton, but I got a letter from Kreskin's agent just two months before the production, asking if I was interested in casting him as Grace's grandfather. The letter came out of nowhere and I was like ... *what*? So we met, hit it off and he got the part. After our first meeting, I was inspired by some videotapes he sent me, of him hypnotizing people. I told Kreskin to inject the spirit of those performances into the film. He rewrote many of his lines—only for the performance pieces—the mentalism stunts—always within the context of the character—and it worked out beautifully.

Horror is such a visually arresting film. Your use of vibrant colors here and in Desecration *recalls the work of Dario Argento.*

I love Argento and Bava but I must say that I'm getting more and more annoyed when I read reviews of *Desecration* and *Horror* saying that I obviously study them. That's just not true. What comes out of me is instinctual, it has nothing to do with other Italian horror films. Maybe it's because I'm Italian-American. I don't know … I'm not even influenced by Italian horror films, since I didn't grow up on them. I wasn't even exposed to those films at all until I was in my twenties. The vibrant colors—like aura emanations—that's something I've been into forever. I used to see multi-colored streaks in the atmosphere. My style of filmmaking was developing when I was in grammar school; it has nothing to do with Argento or Bava. Don't get me wrong, I enjoy Italian horror. I'm now discovering these films, and I think Argento and Bava are incredibly talented but I don't sit around and study them. I don't really study any films. My filmmaking style is instinctual and comes from old images in my mind … color-saturated childhood nightmares … things around me I absorbed, and horror movies I watched before I was 17.

Are you proud of what you achieved on Horror?

For what I set out to do and its tiny budget, I'm pretty proud of the icy *Horror*. It's a bizarre little film that marches to the beat of its own drummer. Like all my independent movies, it really needs to be experienced in stereo … with the volume up. It's all about the journey … the ride. After creating *Desecration* and having some success … critically at least … Image Entertainment released it on DVD and VHS in the States. I felt empowered on *Horror* to allow my imagination to run free. I didn't listen to the *Desecration* pundits who wanted me to create a more easily understandable horror film. I went the other way. Aggressively non-linear and irrational. And by casting Kreskin, a world-renowned mentalist, who came out of the blue and asked to audition for the part … I

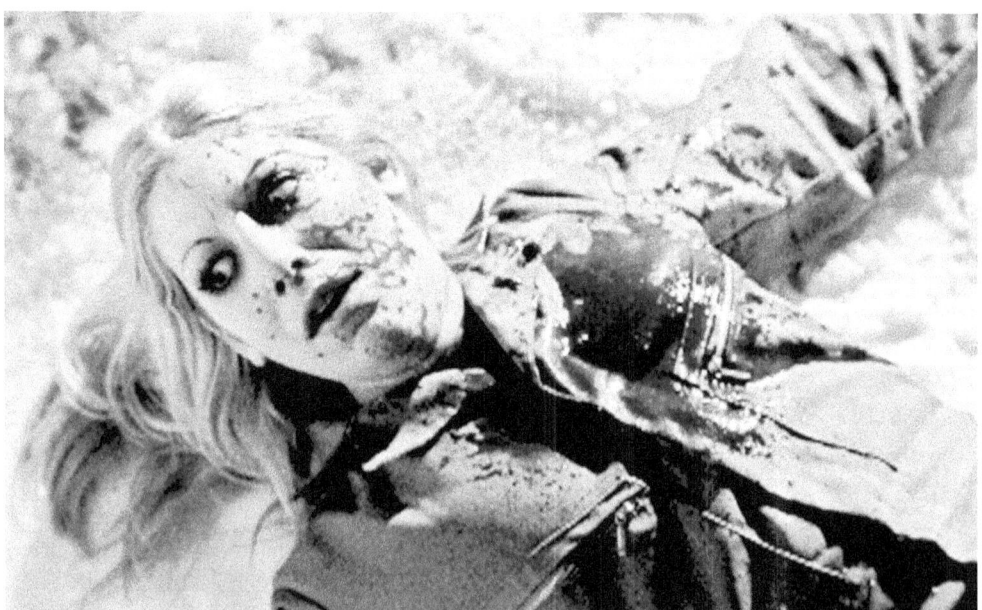

Scream Queen Raine Brown comes to a bloody end in Dante Tomaselli's *Horror* (courtesy Dante Tomaselli).

was tapping into the power of the mind, the power of suggestion. *Horror* is about being dominated by forces that we have no control over. That's what the film stands for. The movie is a mind-fuck. On the downside, although the dislocated feel was intentional, some of the acting and dialogue was a bit clunky. Some of my supporting actors were very inexperienced and I was probably more concerned with the visuals. Also there were many scenes that I wanted to shoot but didn't have enough time. And it lacks the heart of *Desecration*. *Horror* is a very cold movie. Very cruel. Still, the design works. I constructed it like a maze with many ways out. It's a labyrinth and pulls the viewer in and out of reality. You really have absolutely no idea what is coming next. Not a clue. There are secret doors leading to foggy torture chambers. Symbols, shapes, colors and sounds are pristine. Ambiguity is the essence of the skeletal plot. It's interpretive cinema. Film as out-of-body experience. Very non-linear.

I consider your next film, the excellent Satan's Playground, *your most fluid and visually accomplished.*

Thanks. I kind of have mixed feelings about *Satan's Playground*. In the beginning, before shooting, I was planning for it to be a very scary film and I don't think I was successful in that regard. When I got on set and actually saw the actors in their environment, in the moment, I realized it was going to be a kind of a colorful, fairy tale–like horror film, not necessarily a grim, frightening one. All the black humor was really more about how the characters fell into place with the locales. It's pretty comedic in parts and that wasn't really planned. Sometimes I guess playing gleefully sadistic comes across not as expected. Occasionally in the back of my mind, while shooting, I was humming, "Hmmm. This is not how I envisioned it." I knew the performances of Irma St. Paule and Christie

The sadists are on the loose in *Satan's Playground*. Actress Felissa Rose, of *Sleepaway Camp* fame, finds herself in a tight spot in Dante Tomaselli's gothic nightmare (courtesy Dante Tomaselli).

Sanford were gold. They were so engaging and entertaining. So the film kind of morphed into a whimsical horror film as I was shooting. I'm happy with the mood and atmosphere. And Irma St. Paule was born to play the witch-like Mrs. Leeds.

I contacted [actress] Ellen Sandweiss after we were both featured on the cover of an issue of *Rue Morgue* magazine. It had that famous shot from *The Evil Dead* of Ellen rising from the basement with her possessed eyes and mouth full of blood. The same image that I had plastered above my bed when I was a young teen. I called her and asked her and she said yes. I had Ellen flown from Michigan to the film production in the Jersey Pine Barrens. I loved working with her and we remain friends. She's a solid actress and we plan to work together again. Her daughter Jessy was in *Satan's Playground* too, and they share a scene together. We shot *Satan's Playground* during one of the coldest winters in New Jersey's history.

Having grown up in New Jersey, was it only a natural to make a film about the Jersey Devil?

Yes, I used to go to the Jersey Shore each summer, and we were right near the Pine Barrens. The Jersey Devil is kind of an icon for the state. There's this one town called Smithville that really commercializes it. There are Jersey Devil Mugs and shirts, and I remember being like 11 years old and coming back from a Smithville visit. Something about the legend really got to me and I was so scared. I had this fear that he was out there in the woods … was waiting for me. I'll never forget this one illustration of the Jersey Devil on a Smithville brochure, this grinning, dragon-like beast. I couldn't look at it and was paralyzed with fear at the time. Something just struck a chord.

After Satan's Playground, *you were all set to shoot* The Ocean. *What went wrong?*

It all started out so right. I had Adrienne Barbeau attached as the lead. I was on cloud nine. My favorite actress was set to portray a psychic haunted by visions of a watery

The New Jersey devil claims another victim in *Satan's Playground* (courtesy Dante Tomaselli).

apocalypse. It was to be my most ambitious and expensive film. I hired a second unit daredevil cameraman, Mike Pricket, he's famous for his work shooting massive waves. I had him shoot giant waves in Hawaii to be incorporated as B roll footage. Adrienne visited my New Jersey apartment and we went over lines together. I was ecstatic. Then some time passed, much too much time ... and the producers still didn't have the funding. Adrienne, at that point, had other work, she was starring as Judy Garland in a play in New York City. So when I was told the funding was nearly there, I reached out to Dee Wallace-Stone, another one of my favorite actresses. Suddenly Dee was set to play the lead. And there was an ad in *Variety* from a production company stating that *The Ocean* was slated to start shooting soon. I had enthusiastic phone conversations with Dee Wallace-Stone about her character and the upcoming film shoot. Alas, the shoot never happened and it was a big disappointment and embarrassment for me. It forced me to re-evaluate everything. I didn't want to make movies any more. I didn't want to live. I shriveled up and closed shop. I felt like the drowning little boy in the beginning of the screenplay for *The Ocean*. I was drowning and no one was helping me.

You picked yourself up and returned with your most critically acclaimed film, Torture Chamber. *Did you inject all your frustrations and anger into that picture?*

You're right, it probably has received the best reviews of any of my films ... from critics. Audiences are always divided. When it was clear that *The Ocean* wasn't going to rise, I decided to choose life, so I needed to create another horror film. But I decided it would be even lower budgeted than *Satan's Playground*. I wanted to prove myself all over again, like it was my first film. In some ways, *Torture Chamber* felt like my debut and the other films were leading up to it. *Torture Chamber* does feel like a mutation of all my past works. There was an intense build-up to it and euphoria when I was able to let it all out during filming. Serotonin was released in my brain. I couldn't be more happy or more focused than when I'm filming. There was much anxiety and tension in pre-production. I don't get any sleep during filming but that adds to the experience. These films exist at the hazy intersection between life and death.

Stylistically, how did you approach the filming and editing of Torture Chamber? *The final result is an audio-visual nightmare. Was that your intention?*

Yes. *Torture Chamber* comes from my own personal audio-visual nightmares. I would compare it to listening to ambient music. It's a trance-like horror film. There was so much brewing inside of me over the years ... a lot of anger, sadness and confusion. I dipped into death. It all translated into images and sounds. And out of that came some peace and clarity. It was a 19-day shoot. I was in a kind of Zen-like state. I didn't want it to end. Suddenly, I was able to see things from a fresh perspective. I said to myself firmly, "This is really happening!" And I got a tingling in my stomach, a happy feeling. I was conscious in the unconscious, not just in my dreams like lucid dreaming but in everyday reality. Sitting in my director's chair, I was aligned with myself. It took a while to get there, to get to that alignment but it felt like home. By pulling this thick veiny nightmare out of my hat. To me, *Torture Chamber* is about the confusion of being alive. It's a portrait of a boy and his family in deep psychic pain. I needed for scenes to be perplexing and tranquil and emotionally violent.

Torture Chamber *is the closest you have come to making a slasher film.*

I never really thought of it. There are definitely more slashings in this film than any of my others. Yeah, I guess it is the closest I've come to a slasher. The beheading scene was very disturbing to shoot and very hard to get right. I think only one take worked. Overall it's not a very gory film. It's more psychological, more internal. I realized that just the name *Torture Chamber* set the mood and the film itself in some ways doesn't match the title. You'd likely imagine an ugly, extreme gore film but my picture is more of an experimental gothic horror, suggestive, lush ... painterly.

The torture scenes are most unsettling. These scenes stick vividly in the mind ... beautifully designed and filmed. Tell me a bit about the set design and how you achieved the look of the "torture chamber."

I was translating the look and feel of my nightmares. Transcribing. This is a film about eternal damnation. For the torture scenes ... I kept visiting the same places you see in the film. They were nightmares of being burned ... strapped and stretched. You name it ... every torture device. I've had sleep problems my whole life ... insomnia, nightmares ... sleepwalking ... and recently something else has been happening and I'm wondering if it might be simple sleep apnea. I keep waking up in the middle of the night ... bolting from my bed, gasping for breath. That's something I did a lot as a little boy with scary dreams attacking and they were probably sleep paralysis episodes. This is different. Something is suffocating me. To combat bad dreams, I sometimes use lucid dreaming techniques. They really do work. I stare at my hands before I go to bed, visualize my hands. I keep staring at them. I tell myself that I want to find my hands in my sleep. I command myself ... make it my intent. It doesn't always happen but when it does, I can navigate the dream, travel to any location I desire, past, present or future. The unconscious mind remembers everything.

After the settings on *Torture Chamber* were firm, I hired a model maker to construct the bed of nails and some other dungeon contraptions. Then I hired my production designer, J.T. Camp.... We both worked together on *Satan's Playground*. Very talented guy. For *Torture Chamber*, he created the rack, the stove, the head crusher, the Iron Maiden. I was going for authentic medieval torture devices ... realism ... and he really delivered. Lots of wood. Lots of natural materials. We originally had more cobwebs threading though the tunnels but it started to feel hokey so we stopped. It was all about balance. I

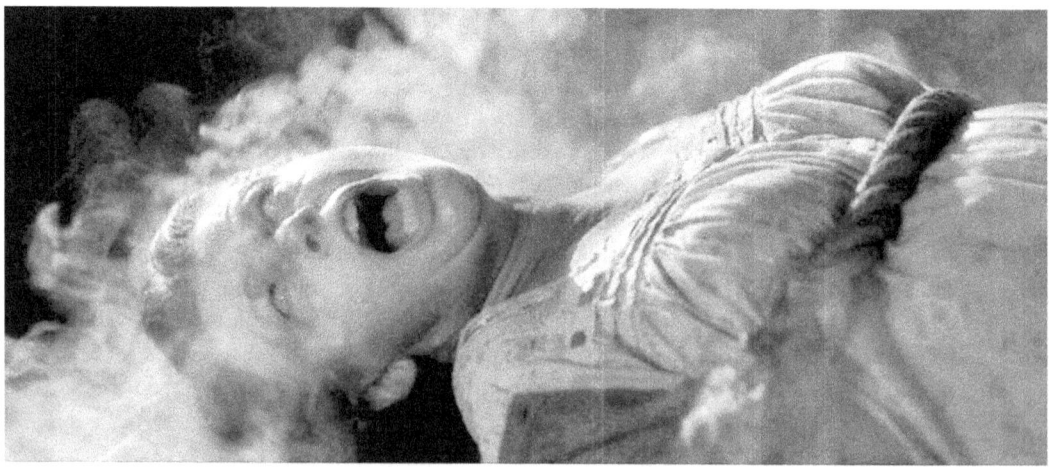

Dante Tomaselli regular Christie Sanford is subjected to the horrors of the torture chamber in *Torture Chamber* (courtesy Dante Tomaselli).

felt very in control of the visuals in *Torture Chamber*. I wanted Jimmy's room to have an oppressive religious feel and you'll absorb that almost subliminally. The room itself is designed like a little church. As with my other films, with the production designer, I employ haze, fog, diffusion. I love bringing props and sets together, forming a unique world. I work with really talented people on my film crews, the highest quality craftsmen that the New York non-union scene has to offer. For *Torture Chamber*, I collected props for many months before the actual production. It's part of my process. The visual design is always at the forefront of my mind or it's gestating. I'm obsessed with it to the point where it affects my health.

What about the iconic mask worn by the character Jimmy Morgan?

The mask was something I actually wrote into the script as we were close to shooting. I did it out of necessity. I learned very quickly that child labor laws would prevent me from shooting the lead actor, Carmen LoPorto, Jimmy, for the hours that I truly needed him. So I devised the mask idea. I got another actor to play him under the mask. That solved the problem and it fit with the demonology vibe. It was meant to be and added to the motor of the film. I went all the way through with it. I featured the odd mask throughout the show. It came out just the way I wanted! I couldn't keep my eyes off it. Jimmy was possessed by Baalberith … or maybe he was never possessed and it was just mental illness. Baalberith, the spirit possibly invading him is a demon … of blasphemy and murder. I envisioned an ancient tribal mask, mystical-looking with a cruel, off-kilter smile, and the effects artist delivered the mask to my specifications.

Promotional artwork for Dante Tomaselli's acclaimed horror film *Torture Chamber* (courtesy Dante Tomaselli).

What was it like working with scream queen Lynn Lowry?

I contacted Lynn and offered her the role of the art therapist and she flew from California to New Jersey. Lynn was at my New Jersey apartment a few years earlier, the same day Adrienne Barbeau visited. Lynn was very ethereal. It was a genuinely pleasing experience working with her on *Torture Chamber*. She's ego-free, genuinely good-natured and with just a touch of devilishness. Very sexy, bewitching. She fit the role of the art therapist, the vision in my mind. Lynn is like a wounded angel in the film. She gives a very interesting performance in *Torture Chamber* with her character being psychically stalked by a telepathic 13-year-old. She ends up on the torture rack.

Lynn's final scene was very intense. I'll never forget how effectively she portrayed death. The way she would leave her eyes opened, unmoving, totally expressionless.

On the blackboard in the school it says "The Devil Is in the Details." Do you believe in the Devil?

I do. I probably believe more in the concept of the Devil than God. But I vacillate. I'm not anti-religion, I just question it all. I'm skeptical. I wouldn't say that I'm an all-out atheist, though I definitely veer in that direction. I believe in God, I think … not in an organized religion, follow-the-sheep, cult-like kind of way. I believe in an entity, an all-knowing eye, an energy of wisdom. A bright light. It's there. Unfortunately, that energy of darkness that we refer to as the Devil seems more powerful and pervasive, more all-encompassing. It fuels my films. Religious conservatives in particular tend to focus on the Devil way more than God, consciously or unconsciously. Actually, their God is closer to the Devil … full of negativity and violence. I purposely made the mother in *Torture Chamber* a religious conservative. A puritanical religious fanatic. It's important to illustrate hypocrisy when it exists. Jimmy, her youngest son, is in some ways like a suicide bomber. A slave to his family and their religion.

How has the film been received in the U.S. and abroad?

Torture Chamber was released in the U.S. and Canada and in its first European territory, Germany. Critically … overall, the response has been good. I'm still an underground oddity when it comes to the general public. I'm always surprised when I show up on the occasional top then list from the mainstream critics. Most of my films are reviewed pretty favorably in *Variety*. Recently I was on a list of the top 13 indie directors to look out for. I divide audiences to such an extreme degree, and certain people who connect, *really* connect. They write me and they tell me. I think those are probably people who form an opinion on something and are not easily swayed. They probably don't care what others think too much. Who knows, though? Those who hate my work, really hate it with a deep passion and are very vocal. Those who like it, describe things in many ways that I never even considered. A lot of abused people write to me. Or people with conflicts, conflicts with their parents. Or … maybe they attended Catholic boarding school and still have issues with nuns and priests. I've gotten so many emails over the years. Some just enjoy the atmosphere, the visuals or the music, the sound design.

How do you go about casting for a film?

Sometimes I'll write a role with a particular performer in mind. Like Irma St. Paule, the old actress who portrayed the grandmother in *Desecration*. Rest in peace. I wrote *Satan's Playground* with her in mind while visualizing Mrs. Leeds. Usually I'll place an ad in *Backstage*. I write the ads myself and then I watch all the actors' head shots pour in. That's always fun. I usually go through them all. On *Torture Chamber* I did that but I also had a casting director, Pamela Kramer, wrangling all the child actors. She gave me a big group to choose from and then we'd have auditions. Carmen LoPorto, who plays Jimmy, was a great find. I have final choice in casting every actor on all my productions. And I realize this will change as budgets go up. My budgets have always under $500,000.

Torture Chamber, like all your films, utilizes a number of brilliant locations. Do you get actively involved in the scouting of these locations? Being a filmmaker driven by his strong visuals, I am assuming this a crucial stage in the development of your films.

The locations in my movies are the real stars. After I have a firm grip on the imagery,

I storyboard with an artist. On *Torture Chamber,* it was Mark Jones, an illustrator living in New York City. Storyboarding helps me to further visualize the film. I never want to draw the frames, I like someone else to do that. The illustrator is my cinematographer and I'm the director. It feels very much like that relationship. Once the storyboards are finished, the visions become more etched. I then search for the locations. The places trapped in my dream world. I have to find them. And it took six months or more to lock down all the right locations for *Torture Chamber*. The New Jersey Film Commission was very helpful. They assisted me on my other projects too. I always give them special thanks in the closing credits. I shot inside a mine in Ogdensberg, New Jersey. It looked like the caverns of hell. We also shot at an underground military base in Queens, New York, called Fort Totten. Lots of creepy, cold hallways and dungeon-like spaces. I love looking for locations. It can be a spiritual experience when it all clicks. Alfred Sole, my cousin, has a knack for locations. He actually helped secure the main location in *Desecration,* a big Paterson mansion that was used as the interior of the film's Catholic boarding school.

You have worked with actor Danny Lopes on Desecration, Horror, Satan's Playground *and* Torture Chamber.

Danny is kind of like my alter ego in these films. I can't really articulate why that is, I don't try to analyze it. When I was auditioning actors for the role of Bobby in *Desecration* back in October 1997, I was ready to go with this one other guy, I forgot his name, but he was like 26 or something. It didn't feel authentic because Bobby—the character—was supposed to be 15 going on 16. I felt a little queasy that I was making the wrong decision. At the time, I was getting tons of head shots through an ad I placed in *Backstage.* Then I got from a company in New Jersey called Talent Marketing a picture of Danny Lopes. I was like, wow, this looks like the Bobby I always envisioned in my mind when I was writing the script. I thought, "God, I hope he can act." This was like two weeks before actually shooting the film, so I knew I had to make a decision very quickly. He came to that audition with little actual on-film experience but lots of passion and an innocence that suited the role perfectly. And on top of it all, he really was 15 going on 16! It was also interesting that his father was a jeweler and owned a jewelry store. *My* father was a jeweler and owned a jewelry store. Strange as it sounds, his father actually knew my father. So we are both jewelers' sons. His dad is alive. Mine is not.

A lot of filmmakers tend to find it more comfortable working with actors and actresses they know. Looking at your cinematic overture, you too are an advocate of this.

Absolutely. I can see why John Carpenter did that with Jamie Lee Curtis and Tom Atkins and some others. Ulli Lommel did it with Suzanna Love in *The Boogeyman* [1980] and *The Devonsville Terror* [1983]. Not only does it feel comfortable and natural, but also the films of a director almost form a connective tissue that way. It's like the characters are shape-shifters, interchangeable, all part of one universe.

Dreams are a recurring motif in your work, especially Desecration. *How important are they to you as a source of artistic inspiration?*

I suffered from nasty, nasty nightmares in my childhood. Very vivid. Too vivid. In fact, there was a time when I couldn't tell if what was happening was real or a dream. And I didn't take drugs. I think I had something, a real condition, called sleep paralysis. These dreams were different, they were more like supernatural experiences. My films are my dreams—they look and sound and feel just like the weird nightmares I had growing up. I think I'm trying to replicate them.

The music increases the tension and horror in all your pictures. The soundtrack is equally important as the visuals when it comes to horror films. Take Dario Argento's Suspiria *[1977] or John Carpenter's* Halloween *[1978] as examples of this.*

Yes, the music is so important. I really love composing and designing the soundtracks. I used to play the organ at an insanely young age, like two or three, and I always would try to conjure some spacey, weird, ominous tone by pressing the low and high notes. I'd sit there in a trance and play for hours on end and my imagination would run wild. Then I bought one of those little Casio keyboards. I have released three horror-themed ambient CDs, *Scream in the Dark* and *The Doll*. I completed a third album, *Nightmare*. There will be more music coming from me in the future, without a doubt. I enjoy layering synth tones and strange sampled sounds more than anything else, it's my favorite thing to do. "Scream in the Dark" was the name of a funhouse in New Jersey in the mid--70s that I was way too young to enter but only imagined how terrifying it might be. It was spoken about in hushed tones by my older brother and sisters. The music on *Scream in the Dark* is the kind of stuff you'd hear in a funhouse. It has a haunted attraction feel. *The Doll* is a conceptual soundtrack. I created *Nightmare* during a long period of sleepwalking, nightmares and possible sleep apnea. One night I woke up, I came flying out of my bed, I couldn't breathe. Actually that happens a lot but on this night, in the darkness, I flung myself onto the sharp edge of a wooden crate located on the other side of the room. A very deep, painful wound and now an ugly scar. I should have gone to the hospital that night to get stitches. Instead … it was around 3:30 in the morning … instead I went into the other room and began sculpting tracks for *Nightmare*. It's like I was sleepwalking. I worked on it all the way until noon.

How much of an influence was your cousin, Alfred Sole, on you wanting to become a filmmaker?

Well, I was going to become a filmmaker no matter what. But it did give me a sense of, yes, this can happen, y'know: "If my own cousin can do this, then maybe I can." But *Alice, Sweet Alice*, or *Communion* as it was known at the time, definitely had a huge influence on me, no doubt about it. It's my favorite film. I remember, at an early age, walking around my house with a yellow rain slicker and wearing that translucent doll-like mask. We had a replica of it and I'd put it on a lot and scare people. It's a very scary mask. It's smiling and happy, yet so evil, so sinister. In my films, there's a lot of stuff like that: laughing sounds that are not cheerful, clown-like faces, Christmas gifts, sparkling holiday decorations and religious iconography—things that are meant to be soothing, comforting, but somehow end up being frightening. I'm intrigued by that.

Are you still slated to direct a remake of Alice, Sweet Alice *and would you clear up whether it will be a remake, sequel or a re-interpretation?*

It will be a remake and there will be some new scenes, new surprises. It's in development now. I've had a couple of false starts, where the funding was not there. People ask me about it all the time and I tell them that I'm not going to say a word any more. One day they'll look in the news and see it in production. The *Alice, Sweet Alice* remake is not like my other projects. This film can't be filmed for under $500,000. It's too multi-layered, too epic, and it would be short-changing it. Yes, the film's original budget was $340,000 but that was back in 1975. A budget like that in modern times equals about 1.2 million. So the kind of funding that it needs is out of my hands. We have a few offers right now and we'll see who really has the gold. Alfred Sole is my idol. I respect him so much. *Alice, Sweet Alice* is *The Godfather* of independent horror films. I can't think of a more complex, intriguing, visually dazzling low-budget film. I'm so proud of Alfred. I'm in awe. The film made its debut in Paterson, New Jersey. All my family and cousins were there, including all the actors from the movie: Brooke Shields and her mom Paula Sheppard, Mildred Clinton.... I was six years old in 1976, too young to attend. But I always heard stories about the premiere screening. My mother told me that some of my relatives from Italy, the older ones, ran out of the theater screaming, "No more, Alfred. No more." They couldn't take the terror. Many of these men and women were off the boat from Italy, very religious, and were not accustomed to watching horror films at all. They were shocked beyond belief. The remake script was co-written by Michael Gingold, ex–managing editor of *Fangoria* magazine, and myself. He's a huge fan of the original and we really tapped into the family sickness, the emotional violence that pervades *Alice, Sweet Alice*.

The disintegration of the family unit is a common theme in your work. Whether the threat is paternal or through a sibling, the family is portrayed as a vehicle for violence, as opposed to security and comfort. Did your own childhood experiences shape this view?

My damaged relationship with my father has affected me in all sorts of ways. I've been a people-pleaser for a long time. I'm also the complete opposite, I'm obstinate and need to get my way. I can block everyone out ... easily. I guess it might go back to the way my father dealt with me sometimes, or made me feel, the way he'd put me down. I find myself putting myself down. It's a dialogue inside. And I just have to steer from it. When I do, I'm in a better place. I guess I don't easily show it. As a director, I have to be in charge of many people. I've gone through ways of handling situations—being friendly but aggressive—being passive aggressive—never really finding the balance. Sometimes I'm too forceful and I don't realize it. I'm a Scorpio and my Moon is in Gemini which means my dark side, the side that I keep hidden is split in two opposites. Like a split personality. When it comes to making my films, I'm in a trance. On a mission. I expect a lot from others. I can be detached and aloof when I don't get my way. I know I need to stop that. I'm very intense when I really want something. My force of will is strong.... Usually it's for a good cause, like one of my films getting made. When I was a senior in high school, I had a telemarketing job where I did so well, sold so much, that it caused a sensation. There was a sales graph on the wall, and on my name the sales were going off the charts. I was surprised by it but went with it. It startled me that I could do this—persuade people—because I've always been so inside my shell. This new trait eventually helped me out when I started directing in my early film classes in college. My true nature is introverted but I was forced to step out in the light. I'm used to the darkness. I feel much safer there. I'd much rather not engage, I'd rather be in the background. You know, as I grow older, I don't candy-coat as much as I used to. I'm more comfortable in my own skin. I've always been a weird mixture of confidence and shyness. When it comes to my films, I do get my way.

Catholic iconography and symbolism is present in all your films. Would you consider yourself a Catholic? Is Catholicism simply used as a plot device to explore repressed feelings of guilt and suffering like other horror filmmakers have done?

I was raised a Catholic but would consider myself a questioning Catholic who veers to atheism. I surely don't go to church any more. I grew up in a world filled with Madonna statues on lawns. The neighborhoods in Paterson where my grandmothers lived were almost exclusively Italian-American and could have easily been the set of a Martin Scorsese film. I made my communion, my confirmation. I've been inside a confessional booth many times. My films are more about questioning faith in an abstract way … the psychic reverberations of a damaged childhood. I incorporate Catholicism, or any organized religion as a backdrop. Organized religion in general frightens me. Though both my grandmothers were very religious and they were top-notch human beings. I can't judge. My fear is when religion is warped. When there's a smiling priest who professes holiness yet there's an evil undercurrent of sadism to be revealed. I got the name, Sister Madeline, the possessed nun in my first film, *Desecration*, from a relative who told me stories of a Sister Madeline, who would pull the sharp needle out of her nun's habit and stab or prick children for discipline. That's evil. That's where I got the idea of a nun's floating scissors attacking an innocent in *Desecration*.

A refreshing aspect of your cinema is that your films are free of sexual violence towards women. Does your own sexuality play a part in this or do you find misogyny in horror films unsettling?

Usually violence in my films is directed towards both genders equally. I'm not sure if that has anything to do with me being gay or not. My relationship with women has always been solid. Growing up, I know I always felt uneasy when a sex scene would come on while watching a horror film with my mom. A sex scene that felt unnecessary would break the mood. It was a visceral feeling so maybe I project that now by not filming any scenes like that at all. I do find misogyny against women unsettling, yes. I avoid those kinds of films in general. Torture porn types. It makes me feel very uncomfortable. At the same time, I don't like the trend of some modern films featuring ultra-strong Rambo-like women. That's not realistic and it diminishes the horror. I don't like a superhero type protagonist in any horror film, male or female. It's more interesting to be vulnerable.

You talked earlier about turning familiar objects, toys, etc., into something horrifying. Do you deliberately set out to startle your viewers in this way?

I just do it naturally. I also work with a lot of talented artists who help me bring my vision to life. So many different artists and crew members throughout the years, too many to name. They work for very little pay and bring much to the table. I don't take it for granted. Scott Sliger, a phenomenal effect artist with heart and soul, is always on my radar. Maria Tassiello has been a producer on most of my films and recently executive producer on *Torture Chamber*. She's my rock. As far as the reason behind the imagery, I think maybe the idea of something smiling, innocent and childlike being perverted, desecrated. The deception. The shock. Also, I'm really interested in blurring dreams with reality. I want the viewer to travel through a maze. As a kid, I used to draw mazes all the time, intricate mazes that were very hard to get out of … and now I make films that are twisting, turning. Plus there's my lifelong love of funhouses. I think all my films are psychedelic funhouses. When I was growing up, a very exciting happy dream would be me owning my very own funhouse. It was called Dante's Inferno. That was the actual name of a funhouse at the Jersey Shore. There were some other giant funhouses in the late '70s and early '80s in New Jersey that were great, the Brigantine Castle and the Haunted Mansion at Long Branch. I loved the eerie commercials on TV. I would visualize designing and constructing my own funhouse.

How difficult is it for you to get your films funded and what avenues are open to you?

Well, I've learned that if I continue to work on low budgets, I can keep making horror movies. All my independent films have been made at low prices and were distributed. This track record alone assures me another one, at least a low-budget one. I tend to stick with the same investor on all my films although *Satan's Playground* had a different investor. I have my tentacles out there. There are more projects brewing. Right now I'm writing a screenplay to *The Doll*, a horror film centering on a family-owned wax museum in Salem. Michael Gingold is co-writer. And the *Alice, Sweet Alice* remake could go into production at any time.

Do you feel you are more accepted now in the horror community? You have stated that you have felt somewhat of an outsider and not always given the recognition that you feel you deserve. Has this attitude changed?

Yeah, I do feel differently now. I think *Torture Chamber* was the tipping point. The people who like my films really got it. The entities who matter in a film career. Distributors and critics. Audiences are divided ... or hate me but that will never change ... it will just happen at different levels. I do feel a different energy, a better one. I'm not in such a paranoid place, though my constant nightmares and jolting up in the middle of the night ... not breathing ... might say otherwise. If I'm at war with anyone, now I realize it's myself. I lead a more peaceful existence knowing this. I live in South Jersey in Ocean County, a very country area right on the edge of the Pine Barrens. I love the beach, the ocean. I love my English Springer Spaniel. His name is Trippy.

What are your future ambitions as both a filmmaker and a composer?

I just want to continue creating my films and music. As long as I can do that, I'll be okay. When I moved to South New Jersey a couple of years ago, I immediately started taking piano lessons. Now I have a mini–recording studio out of my house and my piano teacher became my sound engineer. It's just a tiny room but its got the computer software. I'm a sound editor now ... my Roland synthesizer, thousands of samples and two good speakers. It's all I need ... and my imagination ... and I'm off. I don't have to rent some expensive Manhattan studio. I create all my sound design right here now. Making films will always be crucial for me. I've risked my life for my films. I remember shooting a scene in *Desecration*, one of the last scenes in the film, where the boy is taken out of the hole and the priest says he's alive. That was shot on top of a deadly cliff in Garrett Mountain Reserve, New Jersey. In retrospect I can't believe I shot the scene there, on the edge of a cliff, a hole so deep I wince just thinking about it. As we were filming, I kept wavering, I was dangerously close to the ledge. I was wavering and imagining the headline "Dante Tomaselli falls to his death on the set of his horror film" and I was thinking that I couldn't imagine a better way to die.

For further information on the films of Dante Tomaselli and a detailed analysis of *Desecration, Horror* and *Satan's Playground* please see the chapter *The New Throwback: The Films of Dante Tomaselli* in Matthew Edwards' *Film Out of Bounds: Essays and Interviews on Non-Mainstream Cinema Worldwide* (McFarland and Co., 2007). The chapter also features an exclusive interview with Dante Tomaselli on *Satan's Playground*.

18

Horrific *Offspring*

An Interview with Andrew van den Houten

Award-winning producer Andrew van den Houten has unleashed a number of horror films that have been critically acclaimed by both critics and the horror community, most notably *The Girl Next Door* (2007) and the Lucky McKee vehicles *The Woman* (2011) and *All Cheerleaders Die* (2013, which McKee co-directed with Chris Sivertson). Aside from being a skilled producer, wringing out a number of excellent features on his own Moderncine label, van den Houten is an equally gifted and accomplished director with two horror cult classics to his name. His debut film *Headspace* (2005) is a brilliant indie-slice of psychological horror that marked the arrival of new talent in the field of horror. The film's narrative arc follows Alex, a troubled soul who lives on the edge of society trying to eke out a living in a number of mundane jobs. His only solace is going to the park and watching chess maestro Harry, who he longs to beat, which momentarily distracts him from the horrors of his childhood—where he witnessed his father shooting his mother dead. When Alex starts experiencing severe headaches, resulting in increased brainpower and bizarre hallucinations, his life is turned upside down as he is dragged further into his subconscious. A vicious creature kills those he comes into contact with. As the creature grows in strength, which mirrors his own heightening power, can he stop this monster from consuming him or is it merely a manifestation of his troubled psychosis? And just what is the connection between Alex and Harry, who is also a painter and seems to suffer from the same nightmarish visions?

Headspace is a psychological trawl through the horrors of the mind that nods to the work of David Cronenberg and features acting greats Dee Wallace Stone, Olivia Hussey and Udo Kier. Director van den Houten elicits a fantastic central performance from Christopher Denham; you always feel that his character Alex is dangling on the precipice between sanity and insanity. As he slips into madness, the kills begin to pile up; van den Houten intelligently only shows you glimpses of the beast at work. In one memorable sequence, the Rev. Karl Hartman (Kier) has his face clawed off in church. There's plenty of blood and female flesh. This creepily stylish film once again confirms that the real horrors are those that lurk deep within our own subconscious.

In 2009, van den Houten returned to the directorial chair with an adaptation of cult horror writer Jack Ketchum's novel *Offspring*, a sequel to his acclaimed novel *Off Season* (and made prior to *The Woman*, which was based on a novel by Ketchum and McKee).

18. Andrew van den Houten

The small, picturesque Maine community of Dead River is terrorized by the surviving members of a cannibalistic clan that pick off locals. Things start off ominously for a typical and wholesome American family, the Halbards, when David notices a feral girl in his backyard. Meanwhile, David's wife Amy has an unexpected visitor in Claire, who arrives to escape the brutal clutches of her viciously abusive husband Stephen. The family is brutally attacked by the flesh-eating clan and gorged upon by the bloodthirsty nutters in a truly grotesque home invasion scene that is one of the most disturbing aspects of the film. The wildlings take Claire and Amy back to their dwellings to mate with. The police enlist the help of a retired sheriff who had wiped out the clan ten years earlier ... or so he thought! Law enforcement tries to locate the cannibals' lair, and the plot threads converge to a violent and brutal finale that lays the seeds for the third installment, *The Woman*.

Filling the screen with a disturbing amount of splatter and gore, *Offspring*'s impressive effects capture the butchery employed by these savages where we witness the feral kids hacking adults limb from limb with an assortment of crude weapons. A thrill ride for fans of *The Hills Have Eyes* (1977) and films of this ilk, *Offspring* deserves plaudits for its excellent set design, in particular the clan's creepy cave that is shot in magma orange and decorated with dangling fur and strewn with bones so that it feels like a prehistoric torture chamber. In this cave we witness the social structure of the group and the lengths it will go to in order to preserve its way of life. Survival doesn't only depend on the food but procreating so that the clan can continue. *Offspring* is a fast-paced assault on the senses that is brutally shocking and a visually arresting nightmare. It's hard to shake off, even after the credits have rolled.

In October 2014 I had the pleasure of speaking to director Andrew van den Houten,

Hands of the ripper! The Rev. Karl Hartman (Udo Kier) comes to a ghastly end in *Headspace* (courtesy Andrew van den Houten).

Cannibalistic horror in *Offspring* (courtesy Andrew van den Houten).

modest, funny and a real gentleman. One hopes he will return to directorial duties in the near future as he is undoubtedly a talent in the making.

Matthew Edwards: *Talk about your background in the film industry.*

Andrew van den Houten: I grew up in New York City and got involved acting in commercials at a young age. In fact, I was "Baby Karen" in an Ivory Snow Baby commercial. That's right, I did the role in drag. In addition to commercials, I did a number of shows, including a pilot and some specials for Nickelodeon. As a teenager, I did a number of independent films. I continued acting in my teens and then I decided to do stand-up comedy. I figured it would be a great way to vent about my teen angst and divorced family.

Film school for me seemed to make a lot of sense when college time came. It honestly just sounded like a lot of fun. Who doesn't like movies, right? Plus, Boston seemed like a nice change from New York for a few years.

What sort of comedy did you do?

I did Jim Carrey impressions and cussed about being a youth in New York City. Celebrity impressions were fun but my favorite material I focused on being a kid and getting into trouble in the city. Talking about the benefits of divorce, like Christmas and other holidays, was also good material for me at the time.

What prompted you to set up the film production company Moderncinè?

I was in college at Emerson in Boston and in order to work with SAG actors on my thesis film, I needed to form a production company. I called my mother Carola, an art consultant in New York City, and she helped me brainstorm a few ideas. Her company was called Modern Art Consultants so after 30 minutes of brainstorming we came up with the name Moderncinè.

Your company is responsible for a number of critically acclaimed and controversial films and nurtured talent such as Lucky McKee and Gregory M. Wilson.

I attribute my abilities as a producer to having both produced and directed many shorts and a feature film first, before producing for other feature film directors.

Understanding the job and needs of a director come a lot easier when you have worked as producer and director under the constraints of low budget in the past. With directors like Gregory M. Wilson, Lucky McKee and Patrick Wang, I gained a far better understanding of the gentle balance between creativity and commerce. Furthermore, I learned better with each film how to support the director's creative vision. Knowing when to say no has to be an honest conversation based on a reason that is usually unavoidable.

Cult favorite Larry Fessenden in *Headspace* (courtesy Andrew van den Houten).

Running out of money tends to be a good reason. Also, being honest with both your director and crew about resources from the beginning is incredibly important. It's a team effort to get to the finish line and you ain't gonna do it by yourself.

In 2005, you directed the creepy Headspace. *Where did the inspiration come from? It feels like a hybrid between H.P. Lovecraft and the work of David Cronenberg. Is that a fair comparison?*

Hell, yeah! I'll take that. I have always loved Cronenberg, *Videodrome* [1983] being one of my favorite films growing up, and e*XistenZ* [1999] another. Cronenberg continues to make interesting films. Likewise, Lovecraftian storytelling is very, very engaging and dark. I find macabre subject matter very interesting to explore. In *Headspace* I got to play with many darker aspects of storytelling in addition to getting to play with lots of fun gore.

What was it like working Pollyanna McIntosh on Headspace *and* Offspring?

In *Offspring* she transformed herself from beautiful model to wild, untamed feral beast. She's really a chameleon and goes 100 percent into whatever character she plays. She got to further explore the character of the Woman in *The Woman*, which was a total treat to watch unfold as we got to go deeper into her character's head. Polly is so smart and when she works she always considers the story first and how her character's choices will strengthen what is happening in each scene. Even in *Headspace* we had long talks about the world of the creatures during the strange possession scene at the end of the film. Polly is never afraid to push the envelope and for me a fearless actress makes for real on-screen suspense, drama and horror.

What was your main reason for wanting to cast Lauren Ashley Carter in her first film Rising Stars *[2010]?*

She had these big expressive eyes and an amazing ability to connect with whomever she was reading with in the room. I thought if she did a good job in the family musical *Rising Stars* we were making, I would definitely want to cast her in a horror film. Her look, energy and talent you could not ignore so when *Jug Face* [2013] came around, I knew I had the right piece for the perfect actress.

Christopher Denham made his screen debut in the film Headspace. *He gives a convincing performance as a man teetering on the edge. The film is essentially about the darkness and violence that lurks deep in our subconscious.*

Chris is brilliant in *Headspace* indeed. I loved working with him on the film, particularly because he brought so much commitment to the role. He's so interesting to watch as the character peels away and descends into a complete state of insanity. Chris is intense and not for one minute do you question if he is living what is happening around him on screen. It was a true pleasure working with such a raw talent on his first feature project.

Our collaboration and friendship that developed on *Headspace* led to us working on a film Chris wrote called *Home Movie* [2008]. This was a fun journey into the nature vs. nurture debate as it relates to a couple of young kids and their almost too-perfect parents.

The ambiguity of Headspace *is one of its most interesting elements. Is it all in his head, or is there a dark demonic force at work? We never know if what is happening is real or not.*

Was that your intention to leave it to viewers to formulate their own interpretation?

I think leaving it open for interpretation was definitely the goal. The film is about the subconscious and the blurred line between two worlds as our character tries to make sense of what is happening around him. I wanted people to question Alex's reality and character as much as I wanted them to believe that he was the victim of something much larger and darker entering into his life. Certain paranoia builds with the film and hopefully with the suspense between the two brothers at the end of the movie, you feel Alex's subconscious completely taking over. He goes mad, no doubt. That said, I think the creatures could still be real.

Seeing Demons: Christopher Denham as Alex Borden in the psychological horror film *Headspace* (courtesy Andrew van den Houten).

Some reviewers have criticized you for this ambiguity.

That's fine. If they don't like it not being black and white, they should make their own damn little horror movie! This was my first film and I'm glad I did it my way. It was fun and I stuck to my guns. People who like the film have accepted it for what it is and enjoy multiple viewings to explore a deeper meaning. I'm sure some have found it.

The film has an impressive cast. How did you get so many famous names involved?

It started with William Atherton saying he'd be in the film. I reached out and made an offer to Dee Wallace Stone's people, who said she'd do the movie as she dug the script. The same happened when I reached out to Mark Margolis' team. As for Udo, I had met his lawyer after an L.A. screening for a short film I had produced. He introduced me to Udo, who said he would definitely work on my little movie. His manager also repped Olivia Hussey so that's how we got her. It all kinda just came together. Passion, persistence and following the path as life presented it.

The church scene with Udo Kier is fantastic. Talk me through the filming of that scene and how you achieved the visual effects.

Jamie Kelman is to thank for this scene. I haven't gotten to work with him since *Headspace* but look forward to working with him again one day. Our approach was to make something that looked atmospheric and just have the effect of the claw coming out of nowhere. Jamie was covered by black fabric with the creature claw on his arm and he was behind Udo. It was amazing how we pieced it together, actually, with the framing. We really worked to hide the details around the effect. Also, we only got one shot to do the torso breakthrough so it was good the first take was gold. The behind-the-scenes on the Blu-ray has all the details and is definitely worth a look.

The film has a sleek and atmospheric look. Was that easy to achieve on such a tight budget?

I credit cinematographer William M. Miller for the look of the film. He also shot Jack Ketchum's *The Girl Next Door* [2007], *Offspring* and many other Moderncíné films over the years. Bill really hit it out the park with *Headspace* and *The Girl Next Door*. He and I got to play with Super16 as the film stocks kept improving and we pushed everything as much as we could. At a time when digital filmmaking was still on the rise, Super16 was the only great low-budget alternative to achieving a theatrical feel without shooting on 35mm. I feel lucky to have shot so many of my early movies on film. That said, it didn't make it any easier on a budget…

I think what you achieved on such a low budget is great and I can understand why some people have marked you as a talent to watch.

Why, thank you. I love the horror genre and it is a really fun place to create in low-budget. My goal is to expand my producing to larger budgets in time and ultimately make a few studio movies. I think applying the scrappy low-budget mentality to larger budgets will yield incredible results. I asked David Mamet once, on the set of a film I was an extra on, what it was like to shoot a movie with so many people and resources. Shit, he had closed down Charles Street for the night. He said, "Not much different than when you are shooting a small movie. It's just a matter of scale but all the elements and rules still apply." It was a very encouraging statement. As it turned out, many of the crew working on this large set had worked with him in the early days on many of his smaller films.

With regard to the creature effects, were you satisfied with them?

Yes, though I think we could have lit them a bit darker in some of the scenes. There are things I would have done differently knowing what I know now. That said, there is something funny about the creatures that I do really love. For better or worse, they definitely lighten the tone of the film, which makes for good B-movie filmmaking.

I liked the scenes at the end when they were attacking Alex. There was definitely a comedic element to it.

You're right, but I think we could have made them much scarier in some scenes through the lighting. But again, the film works for me as it is and at the end of the day that's the most important thing to me on this first one. When people talk to me about *Headspace*, they usually don't go, "That movie was fun and scary but I hated the creatures." Why did you ask me that question? Do you not like my creatures?

[Laughs] I really like them. I was doing some research on the film and some reviewers had commented somewhat negatively on them and I wanted your reaction to that.

Ask Jamie Kelman his thoughts! I'm sure he thinks they were too over-lit.

Offspring was an adaption of acclaimed author Jack Ketchum's novel of the same name. What attracted you to this story?

I wanted to direct a Jack Ketchum movie as I had just produced *The Girl Next Door*. I read a bunch of his books over the years and I thought *Offspring* would be fun since *Off Season* was unavailable, due to the rights being tied up elsewhere.

For me, the idea of these middle-class people being accosted by this crazy cannibal clan with their feral kids was a fantastic idea. My favorite scene is the home invasion. It definitely shows too in terms of the energy and detail that is used in that sequence. The scenes in the cave were interesting, controversial and twisted; hardcore classic Ketchum.

Promotional poster of the cannibalistic horror film *Offspring* (courtesy Andrew van den Houten).

No doubt the Woman character in *Offspring* attracted me to the material as well. She certainly made for an interesting visual as the character pops right off the screen.

I think the movie works.

Thanks. I am happy it worked well enough that Sam Raimi's company bought the movie and Lionsgate released it. As much as I appreciate what we pulled off in making *Offspring*, I don't feel it is representative of the quality of the other films that we have done. There are some people who are obsessed and love this movie but I feel like the film is my bastard child. Ironically, it was one of the most fun films to make. I love Michigan in the summer!

The film is resolutely downbeat and grim and taps into mankind's primal savagery and how violence can explode anywhere, unexpectedly. This is one of the disturbing aspects of the film and Jack Ketchum's writing in general. Did you deliberately set out to make the film relentless and capture the spirit of Jack's writing?

It's Ketchum, so I don't think you ever have a choice. He is so intense and his writing is so psychologically and emotionally wrenching. It just grabs you and beats you over the head. That's why Ketchum and McKee are an interesting pair; McKee has this dark humor to him that he brings to his work. It lends itself to a Jack Ketchum adaptation or project and makes it more accessible. There is a good balance between the two of them. That being said, for me as a director, it was less about the humor and more about the shock in *Offspring*. I wanted to capture the visceral and hardcore horror; the Ketchum nature of it couldn't be avoided. When *The Woman* was made, the script was written by McKee and Ketchum, so it was a much different project and process altogether.

Some of the clan murders are unsettling and disturbing, including the brutal home invasion sequence. The disembowelment of one of the film's likable characters is most horrific. At the beginning of the film, audiences may have identified David Halbard as the hero of the flick.

David Halbard is such a nice guy and lives life perfectly. You feel terrible that this guy gets completely destroyed [*laughs*]. I decided to set him up as a nice middle-class, coffee-drinking suburban boy, with a nice family that we are going to completely rip up. And that's what I did. We tore the shit out of them and ultimately Mr. Halbard as well. Oh, well. You can't win 'em all.

Talk me through the scenes in the clan's den. How did you create the look and the feeling of a feral community?

We built that in a warehouse in Muskegon, Michigan, and we had a lot of control over the lighting and creating the right atmosphere for those scenes. At the time, I hadn't shot much on sets other than the basement set for *The Girl Next Door* so it was a lot of fun having so much control over the look and design for the cave scenes.

[For the exteriors,] I was involved scouting every location for the film with our local liaisons in Michigan. We shot the film there because of tax incentives that helped complete our budget. Our opening shots were taken in the Upper Peninsula close to Christmas, Michigan, at Pictured Rocks. It's truly gorgeous up there and we definitely achieved the look we were going for. People sometimes give me a hard time because there is an emblem of Michigan state on a police car door in the film instead of the state of Maine. To those people, I say, "Well done, you got me!" I don't think we were trying to make *Cannibal Holocaust* [1979] with this film either.

The violent demise of David Halbard (Andrew Elvis Miller) in *Offspring* (courtesy Andrew van den Houten).

That's a crazy film, isn't it?
 Yes, but it is so real and well done. The newsreels early on and the way it's set up. I'm definitely a fan and love that film. It's sick.

How has Offspring *been received?*
 When the film came out, I took a lot of shit for it. Now when I'm at conventions,

people actually come up to me and ask me to sign the DVD or Blu-ray. I suppose there are certain films that change with the seasons or look better or worse as time goes on. I think *Offspring* will be stuck in the middle. Not fully loved or hated over time … maybe mostly forgotten. Thankfully, however, it is because of *Offspring* that we have the timeless cult hit *The Woman* and we will have a sequel to that in the near future as well. One day we may try and make a huge film out of all of them and intercut and play with them as one piece. Then *Offspring* will live again and finally find more credit for what it is … or what it is not.

Between Headspace *and* Offspring, *do you think your directorial vision matured in any way?*

Absolutely not. *Offspring* was a step-back for me as a director. I was scattered and it came together far too quickly. I was doing the producing and directing at the same time and didn't give myself enough of a bubble to just be the creative visionary on the project.

Is that because Headspace *was a more personal film?*

No. Even though *Headspace* was more personal because it was my first film and I had intimately been involved with developing the script, I was excited to do a Ketchum film as a director. It was just the circumstances of how I had set the film up. I didn't give myself enough time or support in the producing department to allow me to play, create and develop a directorial vision for the film beyond Ketchum's script.

Do you allow for improvisation in your films?

Yes, it allows for spontaneity and many times coming up with something fresh and different. That said, it's a matter of knowing when to cut your losses when it comes to improvisation. Especially if you are using the technique to try and make something work that isn't working. In these types of cases, usually a re-write or re-working of a scene may be needed.

You had great reviews for Headspace. *With* Offspring, *was it hard to replicate that?*

Ketchum's movies tend to polarize. I wouldn't say a cannibal movie usually gets the best reviews in general. *Headspace* was definitely a more commercial concept that definitely got reviewed well, for which I was grateful.

What's next? Will you direct again?

Next up is a film I'm producing with one of the producers of *Paranormal Activity* [2007] called *Camera Obscura*. I'm pretty excited about the film and think the writer-director Aaron B. Koontz is going to be someone to watch. It's fun helping launch a new director's career, especially in a genre I know so well. This kids got skills so keep your eyes peeled for a 2016 premiere.

Yes, I will direct again. Give me another three, five years to find the right story. I'll be ready by then!

19

Jug Face

An Interview with Chad Crawford Kinkle

Not only is Andrew van den Houten a brilliantly accomplished director in his own right, but he has an uncanny knack of spotting raw talent for his indie studio Moderncineé, When young Tennessee filmmaker Chad Crawford Kinkle approached him with his award-winning script *Jug Face* and the short film *Organ Grinder*, van den Houten immediately saw a talent worth supporting. His faith in Kinkle was rewarded with one of the best indie horror films to emerge in the last ten years. Oozing with style and a foreboding sense of the macabre, *Jug Face* is an unsettling, repellent and grotesquely horrifying piece of cinema that gets under your skin from the get-go before it descends to the darkest pit of your stomach to unnerve and corrupt you.

In *Jug Face*, a small backwoods community worships a mysterious pit wherein dwells an unseen creature that seemingly protects the commune with its special healing powers. To appease the creature, the townsfolk perform a blood sacrifice, offering up a member of the community. The unfortunate is chosen when local hillbilly Dawai (Sean Bridgers), who sculptures jug faces from clay, goes into a frenzied trance and molds a face that resembles one of the inhabitants. The pregnant Ada (played with boggled-eyed brilliance by Lauren Ashley Carter) discovers that she is intended for the ritual slaughter and buries the jug face to prevent the community from discovering that she is the chosen one. With the creature angered, locals are slaughtered and disemboweled by the creature. Ada must escape her ritualistic family and friends before they and the pit consume her and her unborn child (the father is her brother, Bodey).

What is striking about the film is that its horror operates on many levels, tackling topics such as incest, paternal abuse and the nature of sacrifice. In many respects, it is the customs and practices of the community and Ada's family that are the most horrific as shown in the excruciating scene when Ada is forced by her mother to "inspect her" to ensure she is still a virgin and hasn't been fooling around. When she protests, her mother cruelly burns her thigh with her cigarette. When it's discovered that Ada is no longer pure, she is cut with a knife on her hand. Further punishment is prevented when Ada swears on the pit that she has not had intercourse but was merely "playing with herself."

No matter how backward the townsfolk are portrayed, it is the notion of sacrifice that drives the narrative. The commune is willing to sacrifice themselves in order to continue to prosper and to keep its god happy. In contrast, Ada's reluctance to accept the fate marked out for her by the pit results in the death of innocents, as the creature becomes angrier and more hostile. This conundrum forces Ada to assess whether her life is more valuable than those of the townsfolk. The salvation of the community rests on her self-sacrificing herself for the greater good, a terrifying notion for a teenage girl, and one she is not ready to accept. What is striking about the film is that it is deliberately paced so the tension can be wrung for maximum effect as Ada's journey reaches its grim and inevitable dénouement. Kinkle infuses the narrative with a number of gory sacrifices and explosions of violence that will satisfy horror fans looking for more visceral thrills. Add into the mix some fine turns by fan favorites Larry Fessenden as Sustin and Sean Bridgers, excellent cinematography and a fine musical score by Sean Spillane. Small wonder that *Jug Face* has been finding praise around the globe.

Kinkle's directorial debut placed him at the forefront of the new vanguard of American horror filmmakers. In October 2014 I had the pleasure of interviewing Mr. Kinkle about *Jug Face* and his career to date.

Matthew Edwards: *How did you get involved in filmmaking and directing the short film* Organ Grinder *[2011]?*

Chad Crawford Kinkle: I've been making films since I was in high school, during the early '90s. My parents had a VHS camcorder, so I was making horror movies and gangster movies with my friends. I was the art kid, so I went to art school and I didn't know what I was going to do or major at. I didn't know if I was going to do sculpturing or illustration. My roommate was in the film program at my school—I didn't even know they taught that there—and when I saw his project, I got really excited and I realized that I had been doing that and that I could make movies at this college. I went to school and got my masters and I started more film theory, especially horror movies, in New York; then I moved back to Tennessee and I wrote for eight years on a screenplay. I stopped making shorts during this time because once I moved back to Tennessee, I didn't know anybody in the industry or have any funding. So I tried writing shorts and screenplays. Once I wrote *Jug Face*, I thought, "To get money for this, to direct it myself, I need to make a professional short film." At the same time, I started to hear back from the screenplay competitions and *Jug Face* won the Slamdance Film Festivals screenwriting competition. That propelled me, and the week after I came back from Slamdance I tried looking for a producer. Most of the people who I talked to thought *Jug Face* was completely crazy, so I thought, "Who would make a crazy horror film like this?" I thought about Lucky McKee's *The Woman*, which I had seen, so I thought I would try and find that producer [Andrew van den Houten]. I sent him an email and eight minutes later I was talking to him. He said, "It sounds pretty cool but if you want to direct it, I want to see something." I told him that I was making a short film called *Organ Grinder* that very week, which I had been planning for months to make. Four weeks later I showed it to him and they came back and said that they were going to make this movie and that I was going to direct it. Five months later we were making it!

Talk about your Jug Face *screenplay winning best screenplay at the Slamdance Film Festival.*

Yes it did, in the horror category. It won the grand prize, too. That was first time a horror screenplay had won that. It was wild. When I won, Slamdance wanted to make the movie and had a producer all ready. However, they weren't saying anything about me directing it. I was asking people in L.A., "What should I do? Should I just give it to Slamdance and not direct it?" But I actually started writing *Jug Face* to direct, because I was in school making shorts and people were saying that if you want to direct your own features, it is best to write them yourself. The funny thing about it is that I was not a writer. I didn't write as a kid, hardly at all. I was terrible at English [*laughs*]! Two of my English teachers hated me. In ninth grade I actually failed English. Which wasn't completely my fault! So how I became this writer is somewhat absurd to me.

So then some people were saying that I should keep it and direct it and others were saying, "Give it away and at least you will have a credit which will help propel you to the next stage." I started reading the book *Shock Values* by John Waters, which had just come out. As I was reading it, I was getting so excited as I thought I was reading about

Original poster art of the creepy horror *Jug Face* (courtesy Chad Crawford Kinkle).

my own history, in a way, but 40 years ago with these guys. I thought, "There is no way that I am giving up this script." So I told Slamdance that I wanted to direct it and they went back to the investors and the investors said I had pulled out because I wanted to direct the film. They wanted a more experienced director on it. So I thought, "Oh, crap," and they tried to look for another investor but things started hurtling so fast when I started looking for a producer independently and that's how I hooked up with Moderncine.

Where did the idea for the screenplay originate from?

My wife's aunt and uncle live in North Georgia, which is a mountain region, and literally down the street from where they live, a pottery art museum was built. When we visited them, they said "Let's check out this museum," with folk pottery. I studied a lot of pottery in art school and it is boring as hell! So I was not excited to go down there. We went and that's where I saw a face jug for the first time. I was like, "What the hell are these things?" They are so dark and scary and I had to buy one of these things. So I was walking around the exhibit and there was this video of this potter describing the process and he was in overalls and you could barely understand what he was saying, and I really got this feeling that he was talking about backwoods black magic or something. So I stood there and had this vision of this possessed potter who is making a face jug and it is the face of someone in his community. In the initial idea, he was actually in the pit getting the clay out and was hearing voices from the pit. So that was the initial seed of the idea and I wrote it down and didn't do anything with it. I phoned a local company who wanted to make a horror film and I met them and they asked for a couple of ideas. I gave them three ideas and *Jug Face* was one of them. *Jug Face* was my personal favorite of the three and they said that sounded like a movie. This was totally on spec and they asked me to go ahead and write it and they would check it out. I don't think they actually expected me to come through but four months later I handed them a script. Of course, they didn't have any money at that time and they eventually went bankrupt because they spent a lot of money on a book option.

Did you draw inspiration for the human sacrificing element in the film from cultures such as the Aztecs? Were you inspired by films such as Texas Chain Saw Massacre *[1974] and* The Wicker Man *[1973]?*

Definitely *The Wicker Man*. I love that film. Like I said, it came from that initial inspiration that there was a pit and this thing wanted a sacrifice. I didn't think too much about it other than the fact I had written another story called *Fruit Farm* and it was a similar idea where these people were worshipping a creature in a cave and there was this whole idea of sacrificing children. I began writing that during the invasion of Iraq. In my mind I was thinking about how communities give up their children for war and how they come back scarred from that. That's what it was about and I think I was using those same thoughts when I began writing *Jug Face*. What does sacrifice mean? Not in the literal sense. At the same time, my wife and I had just had our first child and so I was feeling the shrinking of my time [*laughs*]! I now had to sacrifice time for my daughter. All these things wrapped around my brain.

What is interesting about the script is that the community—the inbred hillbillies—are as abhorrent as the entity in the pit. Their violent and perverse backwater ways are the most monstrous element in the film. Was that what you were striving for?

Yes, I find it way more interesting when the characters are creepier than the monster. The monsters are always just a metaphor. In my mind, I didn't want it to be these people who were just being attacked. I wanted the script to be more complex. I felt it would be far more interesting to have these characters that are really worse than the monster during the story. But I grew up in a small Southern town and the whole county has around 10,000 people. So it is fairly small. I knew people who went to snake-handling churches and other off-shoots of Christianity who made up their own rules on dress code and one of my best friends was in a church where when you turned 14 you had to stand up in church 'til she spoke in tongues, otherwise they wouldn't let you leave. She was there half a day 'til she faked it and she could go. So I lived in this community that had these extreme characters and extreme forms of religion that was just twisted. They took the bits that they liked and kind of created their own thing, so that played into the idea.

How did Moderncíné become involved in adapting your screenplay into a feature?

Andrew van den Houten produced the film and is the president of Moderncíné. He liked my idea and he got Sean Bridgers to read the script. He really liked it and wanted to be in the film for sure. He was really in love with the Dawai character. So that helped, having a seasoned actor saying that this was really good because Modernciné did send the script out to get coverage on it. That's when companies will score it for marketability. Actually, one of the reports was really glowing but some of them didn't like it very much. I don't think that deterred Andrew but there was enough positive movement with the script that he felt comfortable with it. Lucky McKee really liked it. So all these factors just added up to making him feel safe to make the movie. Andrew then pulled all the funds together to make the film. It was relatively low-budget film.

Sean Bridgers as the creepy potter Dawai in *Jug Face* (courtesy Chad Crawford Kinkle).

But that doesn't show in the final film. It looks very polished.

The D.P. Christopher Heinrich is really talented and this was his first feature. The rural locations were really cool. I found every location. I shot the film outside of Nashville, Tennessee and I didn't know any of the places. I knew a guy who I sit next to at a restaurant every week who I talk with and I was describing what I needed and he said, "Come and check out my land. Right next to it is this creepy looking garage thing." That ended up being Dawai's house. Actually, across the creek from there was that trailer where the family live. So all these things started lining up in this little area. We had to go to a different area to dig the pit because that area is full of limestone.

Christopher Heinrich's cinematography adds a new layer to the film, especially in capturing rural Tennessee.

The look of the film, I'm proud about. My first professional film, *Organ Grinder*, is not under the professional time of doing things, so when I started shooting *Jug Face* I was unsure how much we could get done in a day. We had an A.D. who did the schedule, but I didn't know how many scenes or shots I could do. So I did my shot list on how I envisioned the movie. We had to shoot under half of that, so a lot of times we had to shoot one shot for a whole scene which would just be a wide because we only had time for four takes. So that was wild. It is funny when you watch bigger movies like *Alien* and you start counting up the number of shots in a scene and there is at least ten in a very simple scene. But Chris and I tried to minimize things and we did the best we could. It worked out for the best part but there are still moments where I want to stab my eyeballs out.

I enjoyed watching the film with other people at film festivals, so I've seen it over and over again. You feel their emotions and it is always interesting to see the different crowds react to the film, like the incest. Some of the audiences knew there was brother-and-sister incest in it and some of the audiences didn't know and I could feel the tension in the air and how it was going to hit them. But it was always interesting watching the audiences that already knew.

If you're not paying attention you can almost miss the moment when they say to Ada's brother that her sister is getting married. People are always taken back at that moment and look at the person sitting next to them and say, "Did they just say that?!" So the audiences are surprised; I set them up, of course, by showing a sex scene. By then, they have already experienced that sex scene visually and half–"turned on" by that; then once you trip them and say it is brother and sister, then I've stuck the dagger into them. It's nice to trip people like that.

The opening credits, with the chalk animations, is phenomenal. It sets the tone perfectly and creates a surreal atmosphere.

Some people thought it was child art but it is actually inspired by Southern Primitive Art. What happened was, when we were editing the movie, we realized that when you start without the credit sequence, you see the pit for the first time and it just a damn hole in the ground! It has no gravity. And so I always had that backstory in my mind and so we thought we would create a credit sequence that would explain a bit more about the pit and its background, so when the audiences first see, it they will know, "That's the pit where people get sacrificed." I felt that would give it more gravity and that it would be creepier. So that's why we did that [chalk] sequence, and if we didn't have that, I would have had to structure the film differently.

Who was responsible for the animations?

The editor, Zach Passero. He actually got a lot of stuff dumped on him [*laughs*]. He of course edited the movie, he did all the effects in the movie himself and he did the credit sequence. So his hand was in the movie big-time. Most of that was due to budget reasons.

Did you encounter any problems during the shoot?

Yes, there was always a time problem. One day we were shooting at the pit location, a day of sacrifices and

Promotional poster for Chad Crawford Kinkle's fantastic debut film *Jug Face*. This poster is based on the stunning animated credit sequence that aptly sets the nightmarish tone of the film (courtesy Chad Crawford Kinkle).

all the grisly scenes. We started two hours late. Things like that happened and it really impacted on what we were trying to do. We had to shoot a lot of pick-up shots to edit into the scenes on different days because we couldn't get them when we wanted to. Time was the biggest problem—for me, at least. The only other major problem we had was when we lost a whole day's worth of footage on the data recorded on to a chip card. We had to go and reshoot but with hardly any time. I managed to get a few shots. So that kind of thing happened. Luckily, I didn't have any major issues with the actors. Everything else went fairly smoothly.

You shot the film digitally?

Yes, we shot on an Arri Alexa digital film camera. It is German-made and it is the best digital camera. It's huge and looks like a normal film camera but it doesn't shoot high resolution, 4K, but it shoots normal High Definition. The thing about it is the latitude and that's super-amazing, as during post-production we could fix lighting issues and the color correction.

The possession sequences were very well handled. Did you feel it was important to get this right?

Yes, as that is one of the key elements in the movie. I think the way I described it in the screenplay was that these scenes were going to be trippy and intense moments. They were super-important and the sound designer did a great job on it and Zach did the aftereffects to create that look during the editing. Actually, what was odd about the shoot was that a few days before we started shooting, we were told that we had a monster suit. And I was like, "Well, you don't see the monster in the movie!" But I thought "Okay, we can shoot it and see how it looks and whether we can use it." But of course it did not work in the actual cut, seeing this monster. You are supposed to see through the eyes of the creature during the possessions and kills. You are really seeing through Ada's eyes as the creature. So that's the concept and it didn't make any sense to ever see the creature. There's one scene that is really cool where Ada's head is back and if you pause the movie, you can see the creature's face over hers. It is a really cool shot but you don't notice it because it happens so quickly. But it is there. So I thought it was cool to put something subliminal into the film.

The scenes of family violence are disturbing, especially the scenes of sexual and physical abuse from Ada's parents, as a way of punishment for her "sins." Was they difficult to write and for the cast to perform?

Yes [*laughs*]. It was really hard for Sean Young to do those things. But the actors understood that it was this community based on control, ranging from a spiritual element to a physical element as well. Everyone was controlled in different ways. What was weird, as far as writing goes, was the scene where Ada has just been whipped, and her mother Lorris is cleaning her back in the bath, and she has a miscarriage. When I first consider the sequence of events, Ada was going to find out she was pregnant after that scene. But as I was writing the scene, I saw blood in the water and I realized she has had a miscarriage. When I was writing that scene, I was like "I'm done for the day! That is so heavy. I'm done." But that wasn't in the original outline.

Another unsettling moment is when Ada's mother finds out that she is not a virgin.

I don't have a story how I came up with that other than the fact that I didn't know any other way how someone would be able to figure that out, outside of an examination!

They don't go to doctors so I assumed that they would try and handle everything themselves in whatever way they knew how. The idea the mother checking the daughter to see if she was a virgin or not was a very practical thing, but in our society that would be seen as violating and not something parents do to their children.

That scene is very well-acted.

Yes it is, and that is definitely my favorite scene. When we premiered the movie at Slamdance, for some reason it was the most intense experience watching the movie. I felt when we were done that I had been run over by a truck. We were in a really small room and everyone was huddled together, and it was super-intense, and before that scene I could just feel everybody's emotions. And then I realized; "Oh my God, this is not going to get any better. That scene is coming up." Then the scene happened and it was super-powerful. I just love the shots in it.

How did you come to cast Lauren Ashley Carter in the role of Ada? She gives a brave and brilliant performance, especially as there were a few difficult scenes for her to act in.

A lot of the actors we had used had worked with Andrew van den Houten before. Sean Bridgers already wanted to work on the film and then it was suggested Larry Fessenden for one of the parts and my jaw dropped. I love Larry's movies, I've seen them all. So that was amazing. Then Larry said he could get Sean Young for the film and I was like, "No, you can't." And Larry said, "I know her, I worked with her on a movie." So when Sean Young first read the script, she called Andrew and said, "What is this?" She didn't get it at all. So I didn't think we were going to have her. Then she came around to the idea. With regard to Lauren, Andrew had given me a Blu-ray copy of Lucky McKee's *The Woman* and I remembered that she was really interesting looking. I did searches on the web to see what she looked like now and I literally became obsessed with her face and her eyes and how her face would translate to pottery. She has these huge eyes and an expressive face; such emotion in it. It felt so right for the film as the story has an overall fairy tale feel to it. So I spoke to Andrew and suggested her and he thought that was awesome. Andrew sent her the script and asked her to read it and asked her what she thought of it; he didn't mention any roles. Her boyfriend read it and said it was really

Lauren Ashley Carter as Ada in *Jug Face* (courtesy Chad Crawford Kinkle).

good. So she was asked to play the lead in it—her first leading performance in a feature—and she said she would love to. So that's how we got her. For the other parts, we did casting out of New York ... local actors. The girl who plays Pryer [Katie Groshong]—the second family mother, who dies and whose children are killed? She is the main actor in my short *Organ Grinder*.

Here in the U.K., the film was received well, especially in Empire *magazine.*
    They really liked it, which was cool. They devoted a whole page to the film. The reviews are pretty much across the board. When people really like it, they get it and see it for what it is. People who have problems with the film go into it expecting something totally different or they pick it apart for its flaws and do not think about the rest of the movie. The funny thing is, you don't remember the good ones. The ones you think about are the bad ones. Which is a shame, but that's the way it is. That's why people say, "Don't read reviews." But I came obsessed and addicted to them.

How do you deal with the criticism?
    I've had all kinds of crazy reviews. It definitely bothers me because you naturally want everyone to like what you do. It's human nature. I try to brush it off most of the time. They didn't get it, or I didn't write it for them, or it wasn't for them. I get really irritated when they make comments about the script, saying it is lazy writing. They have no idea about the process of writing a movie and that what you are seeing can be very far from what has been written [*laughs*]; or if they make a personal comment about me. There was one guy who went onto every place you could write a review of the film and slammed the film, me personally, and I thought, "What's this person's problem?" Most people I'm fine with, but if I found that guy I would probably beat him up [*laughs*].

You have received some very positive reviews.
    Totally. It took me a long time to realize that I had made a feature film. That sounds silly but before we started making the film, it didn't seem real. I spent so much time after college dreaming about the moment, waiting for it to happen and working hard on scripts; and then for it to finally happen was surreal. You are not in the moment. It wasn't until many months later during the festival run that I finally felt, "Oh, crap. I did something that is permanently out there." It was a weird feeling. That's when I realized that I had done something and that I had ideas which had worked.

And the film, in my opinion, does work. A lot of people are calling you a talent in the horror genre.
    I wish the money people agreed with you [*laughs*]. With the reviews, what you start seeing is patterns. I have collected over 200 reviews from anything that I would see on Twitter to a Google Alert. I would read most of them. You would seem patterns forming and someone would change the topic. Other patterns would keep on the same point and about halfway people would start commenting on me more that I'm a filmmaker to watch and, thankfully, this thread has continued.
    I have told people that my genuine desire is to be a horror writer-director and to add to the genre that I love. That has always been my goal. For a lot of other people who do horror movies, that is not always the case. They are using the genre as a stepping stone; they like it but they like other genres, too. They don't seem as invested in the horror genre as I am. I hope people see that.

Bob Kurtzman provided the makeup effects. Did you work with him closely to get the intended look?

His team did the makeup effects. Basically he had two people who came to the set and worked on the film. They were all fine. I thought the physical effects were pulled off pretty good, especially the throat slashings [*laughs*]! Actually, my two favorite effects are the two actual dead animals in the film. The deer and the possum are real. I contacted a taxidermy place a couple of months before the shoot, as there is always hit deer in Tennessee that you can use. I asked if they could keep one and they said of course. They kept it in a huge freezer where they keep the animals. What you don't see in the movie is that the deer is really extended because it was bloated and it had been hit by a car. In the script it says that Sustin [Larry Fassenden] is supposed to be field dressing it and cutting the deer open and pulling the guts out. But I said, "Don't even dare cutting that thing open. It will smell so bad and rancid." I was pretty sure that all the intestines had exploded. So everyone would have been throwing up and we wouldn't have been able to work. What is funny about that scene is that Larry is a vegan and he had to cut this back strap off the deer. I told him to just cut the tenderloin. He had to do that and handle the dead possum [*laughs*]. He was a sport about it.

Generally the effects were pretty good. I was never super-crazy about the digital effects in the movie, but what happened when we got into the editing was that the actual practical effects on the ghost boy didn't have any presence. It failed visually. He was the weakest thing in the movie. So during the editing, we added the digital effects and it made it miles better than what it was. Actually, that is one of the points that people hate about the movie, that some of the effects look hokey. I understand that, but sadly there was no money and this was the best that we could come up with. That is one thing I would go back and change, if I could. I would definitely do that differently. That was in general a big learning experience about how important it is to get the effect right on set, or before you are on set.

The effects reminded me of Japanese horror films or The Devil's Backbone *[2001].*

Actually, the film was bootlegged in Japan and someone wrote to me on Twitter and said that this film is so Asian. I was like, "Really?!" What was interesting was when it came out on iTunes here in the U.S., it was immediately pirated all over the place and I started seeing Tweets from Indonesia, every day. Maybe ten or twenty each day. One day I woke up and there were over 200 tweets about *Jug Face*. There were all these little Muslim girls having *Jug Face* parties. All these little Muslim girls taking selfies while watching *Jug Face*. It lasted seven months. I was like, "Wow, this is amazing." It became a cult little hit in the pirate realm. I am pleased it has played well in different cultures as I am interested in Asian horror films. I am not steeped in it but I like films like *Audition* [1999] and the Japanese ghost stories.

I actually wanted the shunned ghost to look like the ghosts in *The Devil's Backbone*. If we had those effects, then that would have been amazing, but we didn't [*laughs*]. But then some people just watch movies to find something wrong with them. Critique of movies is a very strange thing because people think that because they have seen so many, that they are experts, yet they know nothing about moviemaking. But then, it is subjective, like you say. That's great because I want to see all the different reactions people get from their subjective point of view. But then, some people become super-critical for the sake of being critical, to make themselves feel better [*laughs*]! But at the end of the day that doesn't matter because the film should be judged on what it is. The fact that people do like it means that I did well. So I am happy with that. But the movie is about 40 percent of what I wanted. Just from the lessons that I learned from that shoot that if I did a movie straight after, I could immediate increase what I was doing by another 30 or 40 percent.

Lucky McKee is listed as executive producer. How did he become involved, and what influence has his work had on your own?

I definitely admired him. He read the script—I can't remember the exact timeline of it—and at some point Andrew asked him to be an executive producer, and he said he would. We were shooting and he came down for about four days of the shoot. The first week of the shoot was the most stressful week of my life. We would shoot so much in a day that I couldn't think what we had shot in the morning. We had done so much. So to have him on set during my first week, [during] the big scenes, because we only had Sean Young for a week, all these scenes first and Lucky McKee watching the monitor, the pressure was just insane. He didn't offer too many comments, just one bit of advice when I was shooting. It wasn't until the editing that he played a bigger role. It's funny that people see his name attached and they think he had all these influences and none of that is true. He sat with the editor and me for a week and helped us with the structure and made suggestions to the various cuts of the films and gave us notes. It is funny how people make these parallels and connections when there wasn't any. But that week with him was amazing. I learned a lot from him. We stayed in Texas, where the editor lived, in his house, and it didn't have cable or the Internet, we had bad TV and a Blu-ray player, so we basically drank every night and stayed up late watching and talking about horror movies. It was the most amazing week of my life.

Some critics say the film is too short and the mythology around the pit could have been fleshed out more. Do you understand where they are coming from or are you happy with the final edit?

In terms of adding any mythology, well, I like the way it was handled. I cut the movie myself after I saw the simple edit, which was just all the wide shots and how it is in the script. And I was really worried at that point. I put all the dailies onto my computer and I cut it in a weekend and we started working back and forth. I would have liked a lot of shots to have lasted longer and had a slower pace, if I had edited exactly how I envisaged it. It wouldn't have worked to make the editor work that way, so you are seeing the editor's rhythm rather than mine. I would have stretched the scenes out a little longer or held onto a few shots longer. But I think it really works well. But to make the pace that I saw in my mind, I would have had to have shot the film differently.

Do you intend to keep working in the horror genre?

Yes, I want to make great horror films and make my mark in the genre and in the history books. I want to make more Southern horror, set in the region and country that I live in. It is the environment that I know and understand. There are lots of interesting opportunities there for the horror genre. I've been reading a bunch of scripts from people who are not Southern but trying to write Southern stories and most are horrible.

You want to remain true to yourself.

Yes, I want to write and direct my own films. Maybe occasionally take a bigger job and a larger commercial movie which has been written by someone else. But I still intend to do the smaller and personal movies.

20

The Last Will and Testament of Rosalind Leigh

An Interview with Rodrigo Gudiño

Rodrigo Gudiño is no stranger to the world of horror. Creator and founder of the seminal horror magazine *Rue Morgue*, Gudiño has for many years been one of the leading voices in the genre, delivering through *Rue Morgue* brilliant and insightful analysis of the genre for movie fans the world over. For some, it came as little surprise when Gudiño announced he would be branching out from the printed page to the cinematic realm. He has made a number of award-winning short films: *The Eyes of Edward James* (2006), *The Demonology of Desire* (2007) and *The Facts in the Case of Mister Hollow* (2008) have received plaudits from such luminaries as Guillermo del Toro. With each passing film, Gudiño has continued to display a growing maturity, an eye for detail and the ability to create cinematic shocks.

The year 2012 saw the release of Gudiño's magnificently frightening debut film *The Last Will and Testament of Rosalind Leigh*, a minimalistic and unnerving ghost story. He resisted the temptation to cover the screen in geysers of blood, instead opting to make an atmospheric and chilling shocker that was easily one of the year's best. The premise concerns a young antiques collector, Leon (Aaron Poole), who returns to the family home of his estranged mother after her death. Once inside the house, he discovers that his mum was part of a strange suicidal sect that worshipped angels. As the terror mounts, and as childhood memories of abuse resurface in Leon, he comes to realize that he might not be alone in the house as it seemingly watches his every move.

Employing inventive camera angles and a slow methodical pace, the film creates a sense that we are looking through the eyes of a sad, lonely entity that is spending eternity looking for what it has lost, yet can never retrieve. It is a film of quiet solitude, where eerie silence gives way to moments of startling terror. It is a film about loss of faith, loneliness and fractured relationships, with spooky narration by Rosalind Leigh (Vanessa Redgrave) as she longs to reconcile her differences with her son, who she drove away. An unconventional ghost story, the film tackles the question of religious oppression and superstition and how Rosalind Leigh's blind faith ruined her family. It laments the way the victims of child abuse must come to terms with the horrors to which they have been subjected. This haunting, sad film is made even more effective with the beautiful set design and camerawork.

In January 2015 I had the pleasure of interviewing the legendary Rodrigo Gudiño about his work and his film career.

Matthew Edwards: *Tell me a bit about your background and how you developed an interest in the horror genre.*

Rodrigo Gudiño: I've always been interested in horror even before I was aware that it was also a genre. One of my earliest childhood memories involves poring over an edition of Dante's *Inferno* from my parents' library that featured illustrations by Gustave Doré. Some of them were perfectly macabre and, even though I was terrified beyond belief, I could not stop looking at them. Much later, after I graduated from university and decided to start a magazine, I could think of no personal interest that felt more natural to pursue.

You are primary known for founding the brilliant and influential horror magazine Rue Morgue. *What prompted you to begin producing and directing your own cinematic output? Was it a reaction against the type of films you were seeing?*

Even though I am known as a publisher, I am an artist at heart and have always seen myself this way. I consider the magazine to be as much an artistic endeavor as a commercial one. Even in the beginning, I used to tell people I was launching a magazine to facilitate making movies. So you could say the movies were there before the magazine.

Your first film was The Eyes of Edward James. *The film is seemingly a hybrid of the work of Hitchcock and Lynch infused with your own distinct and unique style.*

Prior to *The Eyes of Edward James,* I had never made a movie—not even a home movie or a student film. It literally is the first time I picked up a camera. So the idea behind this movie was very pragmatic: How can I scare people in 15 minutes? I noticed at the time that most of the horror shorts that came through the *Rue Morgue* offices were better described as comedies, since they were written in the structure of a knock knock joke with a funny punchline at the end. I wanted to earnestly try to scare the audience.

Promotional poster of Rodrigo Gudiño's excellent short film *The Eyes of Edward James* (courtesy Rodrigo Gudiño).

Every decision I made in that movie was with the intent of getting into the audience's head and involve them in a scary story in record time.

One of its interesting elements is that it is shot from the POV of the protagonist. Why did you employ this method?

The premise of this movie came to me in a dream in which I saw a girl with a bag over her head and a guy with massive scissors, so that naturally led me to develop it in a psychological way. At some point I realized that if I placed a movie inside the mind of a person during hypnosis, I would be able to give the story a few extra layers. So the movie ended up being as much about someone's memory but also about how the doctor is interpreting this memory that he can only hear but not see. All of this seemed unique and fertile ground for a film.

You followed up with The Demonology of Desire. *To me, the film seems a slight departure from your other work. Was it a stab at a more conventional horror film?*

I have always believed that different films come from different places. *The Eyes of Edward James* was a product of trying to achieve something concrete within a period of time. *The Demonology of Desire* is completely different in that I ignored any practical considerations while writing and making this movie. It's a product of pure inspiration. Everything that happens in this film is just really just how it came out in the writing, there was no deliberate intent to be more conventional or even to tell a story with a beginning, a middle and an end. In the end, however, it certainly was more conventional, to a horror audience at least. That movie ended up being an audience favorite on the circuit and probably received the most enthusiastic response of all my short films.

How did you come to collaborate with animator Tomasz Dysinski and Vincent Marcone on the fantastic The Facts in the Case of Mister Hollow?

Vincent and I have been friends for a long time and I have always admired what he does. Among his many projects is a band called Johnny Hollow which he used to ask for my feedback on. At some point we started talking about the idea to shoot a video of one of their songs. Of course, I can't just shoot a music video, I need to write a story to go with it, so I wrote the script for *Facts in the Case of Mister Hollow* as a music video treatment with the band members as the protagonists in the film. But when it became apparent that we couldn't secure the funding for the video, I decided to rework it into a short film. This seemed to fare better and, once the project was green-lit, I really wanted it to be set in Vincent's world so we ended up collaborating on it and even had Johnny Hollow provide the score. So it still ended up being a video of sorts. Tomasz was Vincent's tech guy at the time and he was instrumental in bringing Vincent's world to life.

The film's style and visuals are splendid. How was it shot and put together?

The film is actually (technically) not a film since there is no motion camera involved. It began with a series of stills with the actors and props photographed against a green screen. All of this info was then assembled together and animated in the environment you see in the movie. The "movement" of the camera is an animation created by zooming into, panning across and transitioning from one photograph to the next.

The Facts in the Case of Mister Hollow *reminded me of Lovecraft and Poe. Was there a nod to "The Raven" in the film?*

I would say that Poe was definitely a big influence on this film—it's no happenstance that its title is a reference to a Poe story. But the influence is more a matter of feel and spirit and not to any specific story. As you can see, *The Facts in the Case of Mister Hollow* doesn't really resemble much of what happens in Poe's "The Facts in the Case of M. Valdemar." They're just two macabre stories that could have happened in the same world.

Your first feature film was the excellent The Last Will and Testament of Rosalind Leigh.

This idea came from necessity, after a film governing body in Canada asked me for a low-budget script. I had been working on something else and didn't really have something low-budget, so I locked myself up in a room for three weeks and hammered out the script for what ended up being *The Last Will and Testament of Rosalind Leigh*.

How difficult was it to raise money for it? Did your short films and association with Rue Morgue *help?*

It was remarkably easy, but I think that was partly luck! From the moment I turned the script in to the moment it was green-lit was probably a couple of months. I don't think I will ever get a project put together that fast ever again, even though I'll always keep my fingers crossed for that, of course. I think part of the

Poster from the creepy and atmospheric short film *The Facts in the Case of Mister Hollow* (courtesy Rodrigo Gudiño).

reason this happened was because the script I turned in was a surprise to them in that there was no blood, profanity or violence of a sort that they expect from horror movies. I think they were surprised by and became [enamored] with the poetry of the piece.

Did working on a tight budget hinder your aspirations and the production at all?

I can't say it really did since everything I wanted to shoot ended up on the screen. But making a movie is always difficult and there is always a lot of talk about money when you are making it. In this sense, my producers Marco Pecota and Lilia Deschamps were really great because they just figured out a way to give me everything I needed. Of course, it also helped that I shot a bunch of it at the Rue Morgue House of Horror which was a sprawling former funeral home that I used to own.

There are some great scares which really get under the viewer's skin, especially the scenes with the statuettes of angels. You manage to bring angels into the realm of horror. Were you pleased with the way these scenes turned out?

Mostly I am happy, though it's tough not to see the flaws in a movie you've made, every time you watch it. Guillermo del Toro once told me that you never finish a movie, you abandon it, and there's something very true about that. Every film can be tinkered with for a lifetime, you have to let it go at some point. But overall if I see the scene working for an audience, then I am happy with it. In the *Last Will* I was happy that the angels turned out to be as dreadful as they are beatific, since this captures one of the central dichotomies of the movie, which is what your relationship to faith is or, to put it a better way, what its relationship is to you. When you put an angel into a movie, you have to recognize it's a very charged image and people bring a lot to that image by themselves. So the idea was to simply let that happen.

The film is filled with religious symbolism and at its core seems to be a battle between the believer, Rosalind Leigh, and the non-believer, Leon. Ultimately, faith does not save Rosalind. Would you agree that the film could be interpreted as anti-religious?

Yes, but that is not the message of the film as I intended it. I have often said that *Last Will* is a religious horror film where religion is the horror, but that doesn't mean that I hold this view as a metaphysical statement in the sense that all religion is horror. The movie is just as much about alienation and loneliness which results when religious views are misapplied, especially to members of our own family. The movie is not supposed to side with either Leon or Rosalind in this respect. For Leon, his disbelief is enough to dispel the demon, so for him atheism is greater than faith. But in Rosalind's world we see that she is speaking from the reality of an afterlife, so the opposite is true. The movie is really about the meeting place between these two points of view, and especially about the consequences when there is no meeting.

The visual look and feel of the film is beautiful and one of its standout elements; the cinematography by Samy Inayeh is exceptional. It is almost as if the camera is a POV of a ghost. In terms of the visual style and approach to filmmaking, are you striving to capture a sense of the otherworldly in your films?

Absolutely in *Last Will*, the idea was to have the camera emulate the spirit of a ghost as she wandered throughout the house. Samy and I even made sure we kept the lens at Rosalind's height to keep this idea present in every scene. The roving camera is attractive to me for aesthetic reasons as well, however, since it allows the viewer to explore the scene independently of the cuts that tell him where to look and when. I find this makes for a far more enriching viewing experience. To me, the camera is the principal tool for telling stories in the format of a movie, so I like to be self-aware with it. I like the audience to be able to notice the camera if they care to notice. It's what makes cinema great.

Last Will *goes against the grain of current horror cinema, especially the explicit violence associated with genre. Was it your intention to make an atmospheric ghost story? Personally, I think this was a very brave and commendable move as readers of* Rue Morgue *may have expected something more akin to* The Demonology of Desire.

Thank you and yes I am aware that many people, and *Rue Morgue* readers especially, expected something far gorier or violent for my first movie. But every story has its style and I am interested in lots of stories, not just violent and gory ones. With *Last Will* I wanted to make an atmospheric, esoteric and spiritual horror film, one best seen alone and in the context of personal reflection. That's not what I think most people would expect from the publisher of *Rue Morgue* magazine but, I admit, there is great artistic freedom in going against people's expectations.

Horrifying hauntings in *The Last Will and Testament of Rosalind Leigh* (courtesy Rodrigo Gudiño).

How did Vanessa Redgrave get involved?

Once the movie was green-lit and I had begun casting, I was at a standstill with respect to who to cast in the role of Rosalind Leigh. I wanted someone who could carry a lot of weight using only their voice. I began looking at actors and had a few in mind—Glenn Close and Angelica Houston were two of them. Then I chanced on a BBC interview with Vanessa Redgrave and I was spellbound by her voice. I kept playing that interview over and over with my eyes closed. There was a lot of experience and pain and more than a few cigarettes in that voice. It was the voice of a lifetime of experience. From that moment I was convinced she needed to be in the movie. As luck would have it, the first person I reached out to was a casting agent I had been working with for another project, and he knew her quite well. So he was able to get her the script and she liked it. I didn't know it at the time, but she later told me that she was very impressed with the writing and she kept remarking on the lines in studio. Obviously, I was extremely flattered.

Her narration adds an eerie undertone to the film. Was it a difficult part for her to play—the sense of death, regret, loneliness—in light of the tragic death of her daughter Natasha Richardson?

We didn't really speak of her daughter when discussing the role, but her performance really carries the weight of some sad experiences and I am sure she drew significantly from that. Vanessa was a consummate professional; she was able to turn it on and off on a moment's notice. The first take of the first lines of the movie were absolutely perfect—I've never had that happen to me with an actor. That said, she was also quite feisty and we butted heads when we first met, but it was a necessary step for honest collaboration.

I am very thankful to her that she opened herself to this novice director on my first feature film.

Aaron Poole was excellent.

I am very happy you liked Aaron's performance; I was very pleased with him and, in fact, wrote large chunks of the script with him in mind specifically. Although he has little dialogue, there was a significant amount of choreography with the camera and this was new for him. I think in the beginning he was a little overwhelmed with the idea of carrying an entire movie, but he never let it show. Whenever I see the movie, I never see Aaron the actor, I only see Leon, and I can think of no greater testament to his talent than that.

How has the film been received critically?

The best compliment the film has received from festivals is the sheer amount that have invited it to screen—close to 40 by the end of the run. And also that it was invited by many non-horror-specific film festivals. But this advantage also turned out to be a disadvantage in the sense that many horror-specific festivals didn't think it was genre enough for their audiences. So it simultaneously narrowed my access to genre audiences and broadened it up to mainstream audiences. Overall I would say the film was critically received very well; among genre fans, it was definitely a polarizing movie.

There has been some criticism that the film is style over substance. Now that you are on the other side of the cinematic spectrum (no longer critiquing films but directing your own) how do you deal with criticism?

I have many criticisms of my film, but lack of substance is not one of them. The substance is there, but it's not obvious, you have to look for it. Unfortunately, this is not something that a lot of people want to do with movies—and I perfectly understand that. Ultimately, I think the film was too cerebral, too "art house" for a straight genre audience, but this is not something that was a surprise to me. I deliberately made the film this way.

Aaron Poole as Leon Leigh in The Last Will and Testament of Rosalind Leigh (courtesy Rodrigo Gudiño).

I figured that if I was going to have a small budget, then I may as well indulge myself artistically. So I happily accept if the film does not resonate with everybody. Criticism is a tricky thing: Now that I am a filmmaker, I put less importance on it than I previously did. This does not mean I tune bad reviews out, it means I tune out all reviews. Once you've read a few, you realize that everyone is coming at it from a personal place and the film belongs to them in whatever way they see it.

I believe the ending of the film is truly horrifying—the idea of perpetual loneliness, sadness and regret. Did you deliberately set out for a downbeat ending?

Thank you and yes I did, even though it was something that was discussed at the production level many times over. I felt that in dealing with the concept of a ghost, one has to presuppose a level of unhappiness; otherwise that entity would have moved on in the afterlife. Any ghost story, it seems to me, carries this idea with it in some form. Naturally I wanted to make the biggest impact with it and decided that the best way was to turn the tables on the audience at the last minute and suggest that, rather than a failed dialogue, the film was actually an empty monologue. There is no greater loneliness than that.

You recently directed an episode of Darknet.

Darknet was the first project I ever worked on that I did not personally write and I really felt this difference when I was working with the actors. When something doesn't pour out of you, it just never really feels your own, at least to me. But *Darknet* was a remarkably positive experience in that it is the first time I felt truly comfortable on set, so it was important for me to do from the perspective of being confident and able to achieve what I wanted. So I thank Vincenzo Natali and Steve Hoban for bringing me on, it was a real treat to work with those two.

What is the future for both yourself as a filmmaker and Rue Morgue Cinema?

Right now my future is Rue Morgue Cinema's future but that won't always be the case. I am currently neck-deep in several projects including a Spanish-language fantasy horror film which I hope to shoot in Mexico or in the U.S. close to the Mexican border. I am also really excited about a new project I am currently writing which has to do with witchcraft. I think it's the scariest thing I have ever written.

21

Off the Beaten Path

AN INTERVIEW WITH SCOTT SCHIRMER

Trawling through the dreck of modern horror cinema can be a chore, especially with the plethora of amateurishly made films clogging the distribution network. These films entice you with their fancy ads (that usually bear no resemblance to the actual movie) and quotes from horror blogs that you never knew existed. Yet it all seems worth it when you stumble across a film like the brilliantly twisted indie *Found*, funded by its director Scott Schirmer for a measly $8,000. It's a smart yet brutally graphic film that pays homage to the slasher films of yesteryear while tackling subjects such as bullying, racism, screen violence and the nature of murder.

Marty, a suburban 12-year-old, loves watching horror flicks, much to the disdain of his overbearing mother. Marty is being subjected to physical and psychological abuse by school bully Marcus. All these problems seem trivial when he discovers that his aloof brother Steve is a serial killer who keeps the decapitated heads of each victim (usually a black female) in a bowling bag. After Marty comes across a violent flick entitled *Headless*, he realizes that his brother is using it as inspiration for his murder spree. When Steve realizes that Marty knows his secret, there can only be one dreadful outcome for both him and his family.

What initially starts out as a strange coming-of-age tale, with a loving look back at the VHS home video era, the film then rushes headlong into a frenzied, relentlessly downbeat finale. Originally banned in Australia for its prolonged depiction of sexualized violence, and cut in the U.K. for the same reason, *Found* has received rave reviews from horror fans across the globe, not least because of the clever use of films within the film—snippets of supposedly lost '80s horror films. The snippets from *Headless* caused such a stir in the horror community that Schirmer funded and produced a 2015 film about the serial killer (see the next chapter's interview with director Arthur Cullipher). The *Headless* scenes are the most violent in *Found* with females being tortured and gutted in an abandoned warehouse by the deranged masked lunatic, who then slices off their heads and spoons out their eyes (which he then feasts on, as rivulets of white goo pour from his skeletal, blood-stained mouth). What makes these scenes particularly grotesque is that the females are sexually mutilated by the skull-faced freak with a machete, a horrifying image for the young adolescents watching the movie. Schirmer brilliantly captures the scummy-sleaziness of '70s and '80s slashers with *Headless* and you are at times led to believe you are watching a recently dug-up flick from yesteryear. The other film within the film is the campy romp *Deep Dwellers* which seems to be a cinematic nod to the likes of *Creature from the Black Lagoon* (1954), with its rubber-suited amphibious monster emerging from a lake to attack sex-crazed teenagers.

In March 2016 I had the pleasure of interviewing Schirmer about his work in the field of horror, from his early shorts to his recent feature films. A new and exciting voice in the genre, he is a talent worth following as shown by his horror-fantasy film *Harvest Lake* (2016) and the cannibalistic horror *Plank Face* (2016).

Matthew Edwards: *Prior to finding international fame with* Found, *you had been experimenting in video production and screenwriting for over a decade. Where did this passion stem from?*

Scott Schirmer: I made up my mind when I was six years old that I wanted to be a filmmaker. It was *The Empire Strikes Back* [1980] that did it. My mom took my brother and me to see that movie in the theater many, many times. We'd just sit there and watch it three times, back to back to back. It enthralled us. It still enthralls

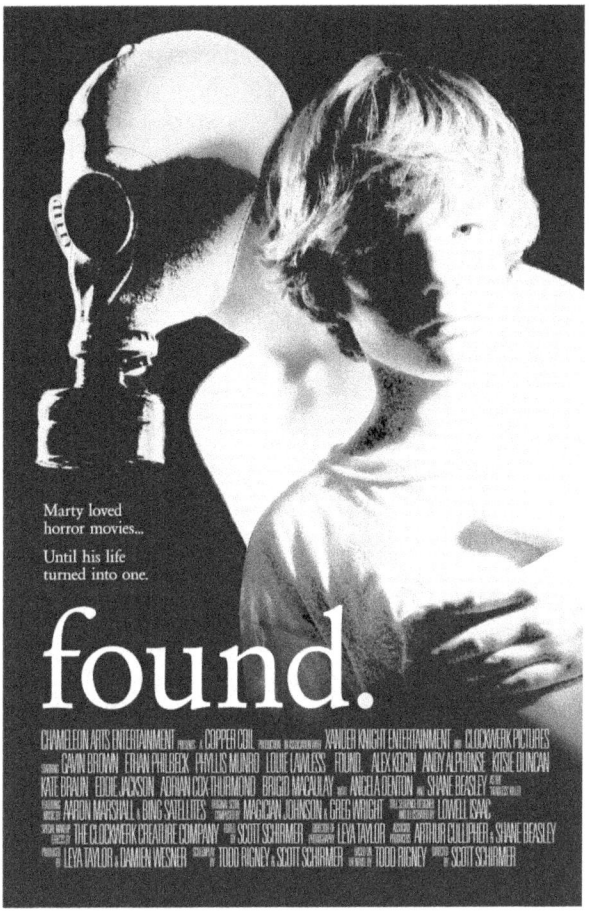

Promotional poster for the controversial horror film *Found* (courtesy Scott Schrimer).

me. My love for movies has only grown since then. I wrote short stories in grade school, and started illustrating those stories and recording narration soundtracks for them. Camcorders weren't easily accessibly back then, so up until late in high school, I was working on filmstrips and audio-visual presentations to tell stories every year. Then in my senior year, I finally got a chance to tell a live-action story on VHS tape. In college, I continued working in VHS and dabbled in some 16mm film. It's been a decades-long education, really, and I'm somewhat grateful for that. I think a lot of young people today see how easy it is to get the equipment to make a movie, but they haven't put any time at all into studying movies and practicing their storytelling techniques. I feel like DSLR cameras and digital editing caught up with me right as I was starting to find my voice and hone some skills.

Your first foray into the horror genre was the short film Full Moon Sonny, *which you wrote, produced, photographed and directed. What prompted you to go from drama-based films into horror territory?*

With unlimited resources, I would probably be telling larger-than-life stories like *Star Wars* and *Harry Potter*. I was always into world-building as a kid and through college, but there was absolutely no way to bring a stories like those to life without a lot of money. So I was forced, really, to fall in love with smaller stories. I drew upon my personal experiences to tell the first few, but at some point or another, it dawned on me what horror had to offer. It's visceral, it's marketable, it's stylish, it's provocative—it was great. I had never liked horror movies growing up. I thought they were just stupid slasher movies, because that's what Hollywood was putting out in the '80s. But once a few friends opened my eyes to how great horror films could be, I really saw it as an exciting challenge to make a horror movie. *House of Hope* was actually the first horror movie I shot, back in 2002, but it wasn't completed until much later. Immediately after *House of Hope*, I shot *Off the Beaten Path*, which was a gay-themed road trip movie. Then in 2003, I shot *The Day Joe Left*, which is sort of horror. And *Full Moon Sonny* was in 2005, when I moved back to Indiana after living two years in Los Angeles. I've had at least one foot in horror ever since, but you never know what might happen in the future.

In Full Moon Sonny, *two brothers lost in the woods have to make it home by nightfall, otherwise one of them turns into a werewolf. In that premise, you already create a tension and a sense of dread in the audience.*

I've always loved stories about kids growing up, brothers, stuff like that. So that seemed like an interesting way to spin a werewolf story. I was also—like always—writing with my resources in mind, so I needed to keep the number of cast members and locations to a minimum. That project was about 30 minutes long, and had four characters total. And it was all shot in the woods, which are easy to come by in Indiana.

A lot of *Full Moon Sonny* was shot day-for-night or just day. The scenes inside the tent were shot in a darkened basement. The scene where the main character transforms and attacks another character was shot outside at night, but it was literally in the back of my apartment complex, not far from civilization. It was still very hard to light. I intended to shoot it day-for-night, but I think we simply ran out of daylight that day. The makeup effects took too long. Makeup for a werewolf character was extremely time-consuming. I seem to remember Arthur Cullipher took over eight hours to get John Quick ready for filming that day. I was just biding my time until we could shoot, and by the time we could get started, night was already falling. Makeup effects can really make you pull your hair out sometimes.

For a film shot on a minuscule budget, I thought Cullipher's makeup effects were well done. Were you pleased with the final results?

Arthur and I were both pleased with the sculpting job he did. The paint and hair layering turned out pretty good, too. It wasn't the most expressive piece of makeup, but it looks good in a still picture. Arthur and I met back in around 2001 or 2002. He replied to a newspaper ad for auditions we were having for *House of Hope*. He came to the auditions and introduced himself. He was just up from Orlando, Florida, where we studied at the Joe Blasco school, and now he was living in Indiana. I hadn't thought of using makeup effects in *House of Hope*, really, but after meeting Arthur and his friend Kirk Chastain, we decided it might be fun to cast Kirk as the old man in that story and give him some grotesque old-age makeup. It turned out pretty well. Arthur and I have been working together ever since.

Do you feel that Full Moon Sonny *marked another step in your development as a filmmaker?*

Full Moon Sonny was one of the worst experiences of my life. It sent me into a years-long depression during which I made no movies at all. I received a small grant of maybe 300 or 500 dollars to make *Sonny*, but it was conditional on a precise release date that couldn't be moved. The movie had to play at a certain film festival where all the funded projects would premiere. And half the shooting days were rained out, putting *Sonny* way behind schedule. I had very little time to rehearse with the cast. The script had some really clunky parts to it. And I made some terrible on-the-fly decisions during the shooting of it. The score had to come together in, literally, a day or two. It was awful. I'm incredibly embarrassed by that movie. Also, it was the hardest movie to make. I was so alone during that shoot. I wasn't supposed to be the D.P., but my D.P. bailed the morning of the first day of filming. Most of the shoot was literally just me and the cast. I had to do everything and it sucked. The only good thing about that movie was that the cast really wanted to do a good job and they tried their very best. I feel like I failed them on that movie, though.

The whole experience of *Full Moon Sonny* was so damaging that I decided not to make any more movies. And from late 2005 until I started shooting *Found* in 2011, I didn't make anything. Those five years were really dark times. I'd lived my whole life knowing for certain what I wanted to be and what I wanted to do, and all of a sudden I felt like I had to give that all up; it was becoming too difficult and it just wasn't rewarding any more. But I kept watching movies, and the desire slowly built up inside me. Partway through that five-year exile, I decided maybe I could make a movie again. But if I did, it would have to be something very special—something that would fuel my passions through pre-production, production, post-production and promotion. Something I loved so much, my love for it would carry me through any kind of Hell that might come along. And that turned out to be Todd Rigney's *Found*.

You've directed the comedic drama Off the Beaten Path *and two other films that fit into the horror genre,* The Day Joe Left *and then* House of Hope. *Both marked an upping of the ante in terms of horror and the violence displayed on screen. Both films seems logical steps to the visceral horror that you would unleash in* Found. *What were you setting out to achieve in both films?*

House of Hope was my first horror movie, and I think it was primarily inspired by *The Texas Chain Saw Massacre*, but I put my own twists on it, I think, with the religious and sexual elements. I was just trying to go balls-to-the-wall on that one. My frustrations with religious zealots kinda fueled that story, and it was pretty well received at test screenings shortly after we shot it. The problem with that movie was that it took forever to get scored, and it just disappeared from existence for several years, really. Back in 2002, YouTube wasn't robust, and there wasn't really any viable avenue for indie movies shot on mini–DV cassette. But I was still cutting my teeth and it was a wonderful learning experience.

The Day Joe Left was shot a year later, in 2003, during a trip back to Indiana. I was living in Los Angeles from 2002 to 2004, but Dan Dixon and I were keen to make another movie together after *Three Animals One Stuffed* [2001] and *Boy in the Making* [2000]. So I quickly wrote *The Day Joe Left* and we were off to the races again. It's a pretentious script, but I like some of the imagery. It was an indulgent piece, probably. And another great learning experience. There were so many locations in that shoot, it went way over-schedule and really put a strain on my relationship with Dan. It was originally a 50-minute movie and, like *House of Hope*, we had trouble getting it scored. So it also languished for years without being seen. But around 2010 I cut it down to a ten-minute short and put some of Aaron Marshall's music to it, which really seemed to breathe new life into it. It was better as a short than a 50-minute piece, too. I entered in Triggerstreet.com's online festival that year, and it got really far! It was almost seen by Kevin Spacey and a panel of other celebrity judges. That kinda gave me a little hope, during that dark post–*Sonny* malaise, that I should give moviemaking another try. It was about that same time that I finally got some music in *House of Hope* and started showing both movies to people.

House of Hope is very stylized in terms of its visual palette and arresting visuals. Were you pleased with the way it turned out?

Of all my pre–*Found* movies, I like *House of Hope* the best. The shoot went pretty well. I think it's one of the best casts I've ever worked with. My D.P., Matt McDaniel, was very invested in the project and ready to work hard. My friends Dan Dixon and Jenn Handy were also on hand to help get it made. It took years to get it scored. I just didn't have a network of talent to go to, and I had no money to pay a composer. I actually did pay a composer in L.A. a little money to do the score, and he did a few minutes of it before we lost touch with one another. In 2010, eight years after it was shot, I ended up scoring it myself and putting it out on DVD-R through Amazon's Createspace to no fanfare whatsoever. That was pretty much my mentality before *Found*, though. That none of these movies were really good enough to properly release and promote, much less try to get paid for. No matter how good I was, I didn't think my production values would ever be good enough as long as I was working on mini-DV cassette. It was part of what caused the post–*Sonny* depression, and why the introduction of DSLR cameras was such a critical step toward *Found* getting made.

You found international fame on the festival circuit with your gut-wrenching horror classic Found. *How did you get involved in the project and adapting Tony Rigney's novel? It is a coming-of-age story fused with elements of '70s and '80s slasher films and* Henry: Portrait of a Serial Killer *[1986]!*

I worked in video marketing at the company where Todd published the book. From time to time, I would browse for book covers to use in some of my marketing assignments. And that's how I stumbled onto *Found*, which had a black cover with big, bold type, and a skull next to a bowling bag on the cover. It really stood out from all the poetry and recipe books that we published, so I looked the book up and read its description and I was immediately intrigued. I read it cover to cover in one sitting and was knocked on my ass. I wanted to make it into a movie more than I ever wanted anything in my life. So I looked up Todd on the Internet, contacted him and started a conversation to get it made. I had nothing to offer him, but he took a back-end percentage of the movie and gave me his blessing. I think a year or a year and a half later, we were filming.

We shot the film entirely in Indiana. Leya Taylor and Damien Wesner produced it and they helped me find all the locations. The main house in the movie is actually Leya's parents' house. The video store interior is a store where Damien worked. Locations can make or break a movie, so we put a lot of time and energy into finding the best ones, but at the same time we were also keenly aware of our own immediate resources. The *Headless* portion of *Found* was shot in an abandoned stone mill here in Bloomington. They were very cool about letting us film there, but after the movie came out, they were so appalled by the content that they wouldn't let us return to shoot the *Headless* feature film there.

That's probably the single biggest drawback making horror films in Indiana. The community loves to help make movies because there's a mystique about movies here. But they're also pretty prudish about sex and violence, and they look down on you if they find out you're making *those* kinds of movies.

How did you go about casting the role of Marty in the film? And did you do *the casting?*

At this micro-budget level of filmmaking, I have a hand in everything, including casting and location scouting. I would always want the final say in casting, though. We knew from the start that the casting of Marty was the single most important job on *Found*. The entire film would ride on his shoulders, and if the kid was bad, the movie would fail. Sheila Butler is the mother of two other young actors I've worked with on previous movies, and she knew a lot of child actors in town. She recommended I talk to Gavin Brown and his mom about Gavin possibly being in the movie. She just had a feeling he might be right for the role, even though he had never acted before. And she was right. I got that same feeling just from meeting Gavin. He seemed fearless, willing to do whatever it took to do the job, even though he'd never done anything like it before. And he was such a precocious 12-year-old that I knew he'd be okay with the material—the violence and sexual content. His mom knew he could handle it, too. I think we got tremendously lucky with Gavin. Any other kid would have lost interest in the project really quickly. They would have given up, gotten embarrassed and quit. But Gavin accepted the challenge and he was there for every day of filming, which turned out to be about 30 days spread out over the course of eight months. I pushed him, and he let me push him. It was hard to see it at the time, because I was so worried about getting a performance out of him, but he nailed it.

Was it a difficult film to shoot, considering the low budget?

I saved up $8000 to buy my first DSLR camera, some lights, sound equipment, makeup effects supplies and catering. No one was paid to work on *Found*. Micro-budget movies are always difficult to make, but when it's a passion project, that passion can become infectious and everybody gives it their best regardless. That's how *Found* went. The cast and crew were there for it, every day, and we all got along extraordinarily well. It was a dream, really. The difficulty of *Found* was in the length of the shoot, because 30 days is a long time. *Headless* was shot in about 14, and *Harvest Lake* was shot in about eight, I think—just to give you a comparison. Part of that is because last-minute casting changes pushed our shoot into the school year, and at that point we had to shoot on weekends and some weeknights, which really dragged things out several months. And part of the reason it took so long was for performance. I had to be patient with Gavin. Sometimes, he'd give his best performance on the very first take, and sometimes it'd be the fifteenth or twentieth take. We did a lot—a *lot*—of takes on *Found*. It took me six months to edit the movie. There was so much footage, and it was usually to get the best out of Gavin—to get him settled down into "the moment.." And it was beautiful when it happened.

The films-within-the-film are particularly striking, most notably Headless *which invokes the boundary-pushing slashers of the '80s. You did a fantastic job capturing these old VHS horrors and the grimy grindhouse feel of these pictures. How did you approach the filming of these movies within the context of the overall film?*

We shot *Deep Dwellers* and *Headless* first, before we shot anything with Gavin and the other *Found* cast members. We treated them like their own, self-contained short films, and we treated *Dwellers* like a '50s or '60s teen monster flick, and we treated *Headless* like a late '70s or early '80s slasher movie. I de-saturated the color and applied dirt and scratches in post-production to make them look more aged. Magician Johnson and Lito Velasco helped a lot with their music for those sequences. The two days we shot *Headless* were really great days. The actors and the crew were on top of their game and everyone would probably tell you those two days are their favorite from the entire *Found* shoot. We were in our element.

Headless is particularly violent and nasty with its decapitations and violence towards women. It is almost as if you were highlighting the misogyny apparent in these old films and magnifying it. Would you agree that your film successfully articulates the inherent misogyny in a lot of horror pictures of the '70s and '80s?

Absolutely. Much has been written about the relationship between misogyny and horror, and I think most of it is on-point. When you get right down to the very bottom of *Found*, the reason I most wanted to tell the story was to present the terrifying possibility that male sexuality is intrinsically frightening. The notion that men are biologically driven to plant their seed far and wide and are given penetrative genitalia to perform that function—that's scary stuff. In college, I was told over and over that rape is about power, and not at all about sex. But I disagree. I think some men are absolutely sexually aroused by violence. It turns them on. So how can it not be about sex? It's scary, but I think that's a very real thing that plays out all the time, all over the world. And I hadn't seen any movies broach that subject before. Some people have said that Steve's erection near the end of *Found* is a hollow shock moment, but I completely disagree. It's what the entire movie is about.

Ethan Philbeck in the violently disturbing finale of *Found*.

Heads in bowling bags, decapitations, torture and the grueling finale: Some audiences have found the violence hard to stomach, yet I believe the true horror comes in the underlying themes of teenage angst, racism, homophobia and bullying which are just as traumatic and sickening as the depictions of violence. I thought you married these elements well.

One of the things I loved the most about Todd's book was that it introduced so many thematic elements and visceral moments. I loved all of them individually, and I loved the way the book made me feel when I finished reading it. So I never really questioned how these elements functioned in the movie. I just wanted to preserve the balance that Todd had created with his story. Some people have responded that the racism is just "tacked on," but I think that's how racism plays a role in many of our lives: It's just another layer to our everyday experience, which makes it scarier, I think. And some people feel the middle of the movie is over the top, during the *Headless* sequence in particular. But I feel that part of the movie is justified by the thematic content dealing with children and horror, and whether or not people are impressionable enough to allow horror movies to incite violent tendencies within them. I decided several years ago that visceral moments are why people go to the movies, and I enjoy them as much as anyone. But the best visceral moments are ones that also have meaning. So I try not to cut a head off, or rape a character, or show gratuitous sex unless it serves some sort of story function. The more provocative the visceral moment, the more I try to earn it with the writing. I think reaching for meaning like that is what can distinguish movies like *Found* from pure exploitation cinema.

With Steve's character copycatting the crimes he sees in Headless, *you raise the question of the influence of violence in the media on young or damaged adolescents. What is your stand on this controversial issue? Do you think these old VHS slashers and grindhouse films were wrongly blamed in witch hunts by moralists who looked to blame these films for all of society's ills?*

A few people have been upset with *Found* because they thought the movie was anti-horror. But it's not, and I'm not. I think it's a fair question to raise and talk about, but I'm absolutely not for censorship of any kind. I think weak-minded people will always be inspired to do bad things when they see or hear certain movies and music. But that's not the fault of the movies and music. Art serves a vital function by making us question things, by drawing attention to aspects of ourselves we might not otherwise pay any attention to. And that is of more value, I think, than protecting a few bad apples from wrongdoing. If we whitewash our creativity and creative expression, we kill art. We stop growing. And bad people are going to do bad things anyway. If anything, I think the

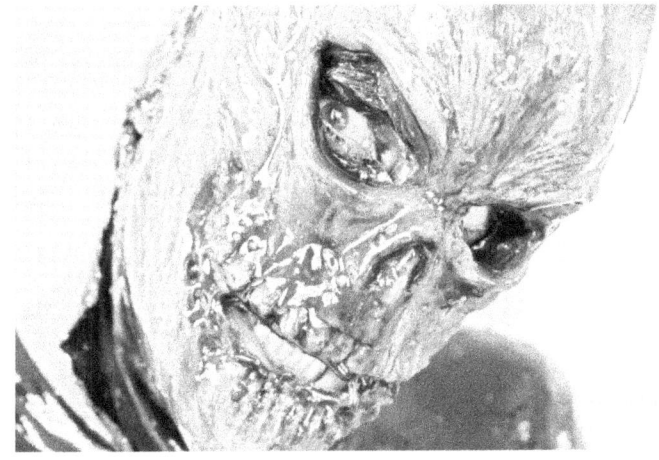

Shane Beasley as the warped killer *Headless* (courtesy Scott Schrimer).

lack of art and diminished creative expression will create more bad people and more bad deeds. Art is more therapeutic than people know.

In contrast to Headless, *I love the campy feel of the film-within-a-film* Deep Dweller. *It recalls films like* Creature from the Black Lagoon *and* It's Alive.

I originally wanted more of an oil-slick type creature for *Deep Dwellers*. Like the creature that killed Tasha Yar in *Star Trek: The Next Generation*. But Arthur was interested in doing a *Creature from the Black Lagoon* homage, and I love the Creature, so we went that way instead. The two days we shot *Deep Dwellers* were the first two days of filming on *Found*, and my first days making a movie in over five years. So they were pretty cool. The most challenging part of that shoot was Arthur's Dwelly costume. With all that latex on his body, the actor could never tell if he was submerged in the water or not, so it was a little scary for him not knowing for sure if it was safe to breathe, and also hard for him to get all the way under the water because air pockets in the costume kept making him float.

The Steve character is one of the most repellent psychopaths in recent cinematic history. The finale when he walks out into the street covered in blood recalls the finale of The Day Joe Left. *Was that deliberate?*

I think we can attribute those moments to me still being inspired by the ending of *The 400 Blows* [1959], when Jean-Pierre Leaud turns after a long run and stares directly into the camera. That moment makes the character's dilemma the audience's problem now. Since *The Day Joe Left* and *Found* both deal with male violence, maybe I thought it was worthwhile to put the problem in the audience's laps like Truffaut did. I think Joe actually looks into the lens, but Steve doesn't. I backed away from going that extra step of pretentiousness. Especially after seeing how that trick was used by Mel Gibson in *The Passion of the Christ* [2004]. That pissed me off when Mary looks in the lens accusingly.

You've called Harvest Lake *an "erotic creature feature." What can audiences expect? It seems to include a few nods to* Deep Dwellers.

It's really not much like *Deep Dwellers* at all, though it evolved from the same point of interest. *Harvest Lake* was born very quickly out of the desire for Brian Williams and me to make a movie together. We spent several days talking all day and night about story ideas until we hammered out a basic concept. Then I took a week to write the script, and a month later we were filming. It's the fastest I've ever made a movie, but it's also been the best experience making a movie. It was an experiment in that Brian and I wanted to make it for ourselves, and we just hoped that if we enjoyed it, maybe other people would, too. And even though it's not your traditional horror movie, and nor is it an exploitation movie, it seems to be resonating fairly well with people. We were a little nervous about stepping outside our comfort zones, but we couldn't be more pleased with the reception so far.

Where was it filmed? The cinematography is stunning.

It was shot in Indiana. Brown County and Morgan Monroe Forestry. A little bit was shot in Paragon. Brian was the D.P. on *Harvest Lake*, and he did a hell of a job. He decided around the time we met that he wanted to become the best cinematographer he could, so he did a ton of research and experimentation before we went into production. He knows more about it than I do, so I'm really glad to be collaborating with him.

Left to right Dan Nye, Jason Crowe, Ellie Church and Tristan Risk appear in *Harvest Lake* (courtesy Scott Schrimer).

The film is essentially about sexuality (which is very true for a lot of your work) and it features lots of erotic and sexual material. These scenes are tastefully done and show both gay and straight scenes. How did you handle the filming of these scenes?

Nude scenes and sex scenes have never been a problem to shoot. I always cast actors who are comfortable with what's involved, and I try to make sure they're comfortable with everyone in the crew as well. I'm sure everyone has their nervous moments, but if you don't make a big deal out of it, they usually don't make a big deal out of it. A lot of it is in creating a comfortable, respectful, inviting environment on the set. I feel like the cast and crew usually becomes a little family and everyone feels safe. As far as how audiences react to sexual content, I don't really know. I don't worry about it a whole lot—I just make sure I like my own reaction to the content, and then I hope the audience has a similar reaction. If we're making a serious gesture or telling a serious story, we obviously don't want laughs, so we're careful in those situations, but in a movie like *Harvest Lake*, I think the nudity and sex comes in and out of the story so naturally and fluidly that it never takes you out of the story. There will always be people who get uncomfortable seeing sex and nudity, and I think those people just need to get over it.

Did you have a hand in the design of the creature and work closely with the Clockwerk Creature Company?

My script described the creature as a blob with one eye and many tentacles. The execution of the creature was a challenge all the way up to the shoot. We were so nervous about it, because it was scheduled for the first day of filming, and on the night before, it still wasn't finished. We dropped most of the tentacles for time and practicality issues, though you may see one or two in some shots at the end. I think the creature works, but it's not one of my favorite creations. I should have been more involved with the Clockwerk Creature Company during pre-production, because they were being overly slavish to the screenplay when we should have dropped the script's description of things and come up with designs that could be better executed. I think the creature's eye, however, turned out very well—it's my favorite part. Fortunately, it's also the most important part.

What does the future hold for you? Will you continue making horror films that are off the beaten track?

Brian and I have recently formed Bandit Motion Pictures to produce films together. *Harvest Lake* was such a wonderful experience, we want to make more together. Our goal is to make two or three movies a year.

22

Headless

AN INTERVIEW WITH ARTHUR CULLIPHER

Unrelenting, sickening, vile, disturbing and perverse: These are just some of the words to describe Arthur Cullipher's fantastically brutal, off-the-wall horror flick *Headless* (2015). Based on the film-within-a-film in Scott Schrimer's unforgettable *Found*, *Headless* is a feature-length adaptation of the "lost slasher film" that informed part of *Found*'s narrative and left audiences horrified. If you thought the antics of the masked killer in *Found* pushed the cinematic envelope, then you are advised to stay away from this slaughter-tastic offering as we follow our warped protagonist on a killing spree that involves torture, cannibalism, necrophilia, and worse, while trying to stop his demons from his own abused past from consuming him. This time our nameless killer has a companion, Skull Boy, who may or may not be a figment of his deranged imagination.

Featuring a number of outrageous scenes that will make timid folks run from the theater screaming for their mommies, *Headless* is 80-odd minutes of mayhem from one twisted dude. Standout sequences include a grotesque corpse-filled pit, some surreal eye-chomping and a decapitated corpse being raped in the neck. Actually, this is a film that makes you feel kind of scummy and horrified from the first frame to the last. Director Arthur Cullipher goes for the jugular and in doing so has created a film that has the aesthetic feel of the slasher films he is trying to emulate. With the print smeared in scratches and blemishes, Cullipher captures the grimy feel of '70 and '80s horror cinema while displaying an artistic flair that is hard to deny. The onscreen savagery is expertly realized. Believe the hype, this is one of the goriest and bloodiest films to emerge for quite some time, laced with enough depravity and dirtiness that you will come away from the picture feeling unclean.

In July 2016 I had the pleasure of interviewing the director about *Headless* and the rest of his career.

Matthew Edwards: *Talk a bit about your background and how you got involved in cinema and directing the segment* Come on Down in Psycho Street *[2011]*.

Arthur Cullipher: I've been creating special effects since I was a kid. I had made a few shorts in school and with friends before I moved to Indiana, but nothing serious. I met Scott Schrimer in 2001 and did special effects on three of his films, with some help from Kirk Chastain. Kirk and I got involved with a filmmaking group called Cinephile, which is where we met Dave Pruett. Together, we created and maintained Atomic Age Cinema, every Saturday at midnight, for six years. It was initially a fundraiser for Cinephile, but that group sort of dissolved. After three moderately successful festivals open to all genres, we decided to head back to our true love: horror! We started a festival called Dark Carnival. In our first year, we were brought a film called *Beef* by one of its stars, Marv Blauvelt. He became part of the festival committee while continuing to act in indie horror. After making *Hypochondriac*, he decided he wanted to produce an anthology by different directors in the field, with *Hypo* included. The Clockwerk Creature Company, our special effects moniker, ended up doing the practical special effects for the rest of the stories. I had Marv act in my short film *Come* and, shortly after, he had me direct *Come on Down*. That's the short version.

Genre fans will recognize Headless *as the film-within-a-film in Scott Schirmer's* Found, *which left a big impression on moviegoers. What prompted you and Scott to want to make a standalone feature out of* Headless?

We really didn't intend to, but as we took *Found* around to festivals, it was the number one question: "When are we going to see a full version of *Headless*?" One night, Scott says to me, "Ya wanna direct *Headless*? Nathan Erde's gonna write it." It just seemed like the right thing to do.

The Headless *scenes are some of the most controversial and shocking scenes in* Found. *How did you and screenwriter Nathan Erdel approach adapting* Headless *into its own feature? Was it important to capture the feel and look of these '70s and '80s slashers in your own film?*

Scott and I sat and talked about what we wanted to see. Scott wanted to see someone in a cage. So we put the killer in a cage as a young boy and gave him an abusive mother figure. I had an image of Skull Boy crawling out of the woods while Mom was butchering a rabbit and feeding the caged boy only the head. That scene was transported nearly whole into the finished film. We approached the group with what we had and asked what they wanted to see. Everyone gave their contributions and Nathan cooked it all together into the story we all know today. Nathan and I have very similar tastes in movies, so I

Headless will leave you legless! Bloody goings-on in this violently deranged classic (courtesy Arthur Cullipher).

knew he grasped how important it was to me that this was, for all intents and purposes, a "lost" film from 1978.

You funded the film through fundraising on Kickstarter. Was it an easy process, as the idea already had a strong fan base that was ready to support it?

No, I would not say it was easy. I think we fretted over every instant of it. I'm grateful it was only for a month. People were very supportive, though, and, yes, because of *Found*, they really wanted to see this thing happen. But I'm not naïve enough to think that it would have been as supported if we had made it first. And we were lucky to get in just before the real negative attitude shift in the horror community against fundraising that way. Not that I blame them, really. A lot of people have been burned by contributing to projects that never get made. Still, it's a knee-jerk reaction to think, "Because I got swindled by someone unscrupulous, every project is a scam designed to separate me from my cash." I'll probably not do an Indiegogo or a GoFundMe campaign for that very reason. With Kickstarter, though, it's all or nothing. For a filmmaker like myself, it's one of very few options I have and the only one that will allow me to keep the project and make it as true to the original idea as possible. It's not only the amount of money, but where the money comes from, that dictates what you will be able to make. My next project, *Smut*, is very dear to me and has spent years in development. I'm looking at, at least, $25,000. Keep in mind, that's without paying anyone upfront, except the actors. Not a lot in movie terms, but there's no way for me, at this point, to reach that on my own. So, fingers crossed.

On a low budget, you did a remarkable job of giving the film a '70s vibe.

The wardrobe was all Emily Solt and she did an amazing job of pulling things together from a wide variety of sources. She even made a shirt for the punk chick for the "moon and three stars" bit. Kara Erdel found the roller rink after much deliberation. We were insanely lucky to find "Roller Bob," too! Most rinks are very family-oriented and don't want to be associated with horror movies at all, let alone something like *Headless*. But he had run the rink for years as a haunted attraction, so he was totally on board. Kara found the cars as well, I believe, and really was just totally invaluable. I was very fortunate to have the crew that I did.

Talk about the casting.

Shane Beasley originated the role of our killer. There was never anyone else I would have even considered. If he had said no, there wouldn't be a *Headless*. Aside from Shane, Ellie Church was the first to be cast. Really, I think everyone did a fantastic job. Mainly because they all did just what I needed them to do. I tend to think that 9.9998 times out of 10, if you're enchanted by an actor's performance, thank the actor. If you're not crazy about an actor's performance, blame the director. That's certainly true in this case. I got exactly what I wanted.

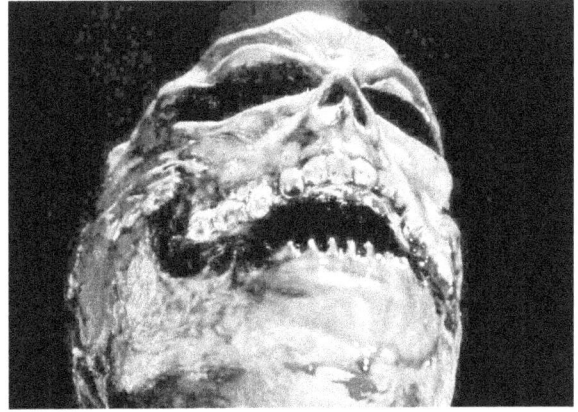

Shane Beasley as the warped killer *Headless* (courtesy Arthur Cullipher).

How did you cast actors who were willing to appear in the film naked, tied up, sexually violated, decapitated and worse?

It's not as difficult as it may seem. People love horror movies. For the most part, when someone has gone so far as to say, "I want to be in a horror movie," they already get what that means. Still, you should never just expect that from your actors. You need to speak with them honestly about the requirements of the role during casting. I'm very direct when it comes to that because that's what I respect. I need that understanding upfront because, on-set, I need them and I expect them to do their job.

One of the standout scenes in the film is the bloody pit sequence, which is truly frightening.

I was really excited about the pit scene when I read it. It was one of the things that Nathan added, I fell in love with it and we just had to make it work. There was a lot of healthy skepticism as to whether we would be able to do so, even up to the day before we shot it. I knew, though. For some reason, we always end up shooting the biggest effects scene on the first day. I can't say that's preferable, but it gives you some leeway when you're running short on pre-production time. We spent most of our allotted pre-pro making corpses for the pit, out of everything from latex, foam, and gelatin to PVC, Saran Wrap and duct tape. The actual pit was not really in the ground, by the way. We built it in Sam Sturgeon's old cattle corral. In the end, it was a bunch of heat-shrunk plastic over a frame, covered in mud, blood and slime. It was filthy, slippery and quite, quite cold.

You used snippets of the footage seen in Found *at the beginning of* Headless. *Was that to keep a sense of continuity with the movie, as a way of continuing the myth that this was indeed a lost slasher film of the '70s?*

Very much so. I wanted it to be the genuine article, as much as possible. I would've loved to have been able to have included everything that we saw in *Found*, but it just ended up bogging the movie down. The compromise was to just take the best parts and I think, ultimately, it was the most effective choice.

How did you play around with the image in post-production? The veneer of the film is coated in scratches and blemishes as to give the film a dirty and grungy feel that is similar to the films you were looking to emulate.

Between Scott's camerawork and Leya Taylor's excellent cinematography, we had a lot to work with. We talked a lot about what makes those films look the way they do. We put in the cigarette burns and reel changes, of course. The scratches are always worst around the reel changes. Scott also suggested that each reel should be a slightly different color as they always had development issues. I think that's a large part of what sells it. It's subtle and effected in magical correspondences. We blurred it all a bit, then gave it just enough grain and dust to hide the sigils.

Genital mutilations, decapitations, cannibalism, necrophilia, eyes plucked and buckets of gore sprayed across the screen. Was it your intention to make the film as grueling and unsettling as possible?

Sure. The whole film is a special effect. One big special effect. I wanted to give those who did grow up on these sort of films some things they hadn't seen before, but in ways that were reminiscent of things they had. That "Should I be watching this?" feeling. I think it does its job very well in that respect. I had an excellent effects crew and I encourage the audience to read each and every one of their credits and learn those names. You'll be seeing them again.

Promotional Artwork for the blood-soaked splatter-fest that is *Headless* **(courtesy Arthur Cullipher).**

Despite all the bloodshed, Headless *is ultimately a tragedy in a sense: The family violence and torture (being locked in a cage and systematically abused) inflicted on the killer is the catalyst for his violent impulses and depravity. In a sense, despite his despicable acts, you do elicit a sense of sympathy for the killer. Was that your intention?*

Absolutely. He is a tortured soul and his human self is even reluctant to kill. He doesn't seem to want to do it until the mask goes on. Then, as they say, give a man a mask and he will tell you the truth.

The Killer's imaginary friend, Skull Boy, who seemingly feeds his violent tendencies, further strengthens the notion that the killer is completely psychotic. I found this an effective device. What was your thinking about the inclusion of the Skull Boy [not present in Found*]?*

Skull Boy showed up pretty much fully formed during our initial talks. I'm not sure he's imaginary. The killer might have lost touch with reality. Or maybe reality betrayed him. Obviously, he never knew anything of what we would consider conventional reality. Maybe he's trying to create his own reality or bring the one he knows to ours. It's completely possible that Skull Boy is some type of demon that promised the boy a kind of solace in exchange for his servitude. Whatever goals anyone else may have had, it seems it's Skull Boy's that are executed. Even the killer couldn't stop him. I think that's up to the audience.

Taking this idea further, there are a lot of psychedelic, abstract scenes—eyes on the branches, the faceless woman he makes love to—that play with the notion that we are locked in the fragmented mind of the killer who is witnessing these strange hallucinations.

He may be searching for something he can hold as just one perfect moment where he feels a sense of what we would think of as "home," perhaps, loved. Or, perhaps, these things exist and only he can see them. Something may have switched in his brain that allows him, or curses him, to see further vistas of existence. He is haunted, certainly, but he may only be an agent, a damaged medium, one eye in this world and one in the next. It seems to be real to him.

The film is also a meditation on love, or in this case, the warped sexual desires of the protagonist which stems from the early abuse he suffered. While Found *hints at the notion that violent images or media can influence young, impressionable minds,* Headless *seems to suggest that violent traumas or sexual abuse experienced early in childhood shape these killers with their violent impulses in adulthood. A circle of violence that is perpetual.*

I would say that, with *Headless*, we weren't trying to speak for all killers, just this one. This is what happened to him. Like anyone, his life experiences and the choices he makes are unique to his situation. I have to say, though, I do really love reading people's interpretations of his reasoning. No one is living the same life and no one is ever watching the same movie. It's fascinating.

The ending is incredibly horrific and brutal. Did it feel like that when shooting?

Well, the actors really did give it their all and I assure you no one on set was unaffected. In the end, though, I think we'd all agree that the most depressing part during that scene was the amount of fake blood we lost. We were, also, really going for it and sometimes you get overzealous and things explode. Then, to protect the camera, Leya and the crew were behind glass and under a plastic tarp. It mostly worked, but I understand the heat under there was pretty brutal. Other than that, I think we all had a pretty good time.

You don't shy away from showing graphic decapitations and breast-slicing in the film. How did you achieve the effects?

I tried to keep our materials to things that were available in the late '70s. Silicone was really the only exception.

How have audiences reacted to the film, especially the head fornication sequences?

Lots of groans, good-natured and otherwise. Some people have walked out of screenings. One reviewer said he wanted to punch both Nathan and me in the face. It's really been a "love it or hate it" kind of thing.

Headless has been called an instant classic and garnered a lot of fanfare. What are your thoughts on this?

I think that's absolutely correct and everyone should buy a copy to preserve for posterity. On the other hand, I rarely think of it as something I made. I was only four when it came out.

What does the future hold for you as a filmmaker? Will you continue to marry your special effects work with directing?

Absolutely. I make horror movies. That's not stopping any time soon. I have stories to tell. My next directorial effort is the aforementioned *Smut*. The elevator pitch is that it's like a cross between *Gremlins* and *Videodrome* with a *Cemetery Man* vibe, a noir feel, sex as both the hero and the villain of the tale, and lots and lots of creatures, both great and small.

23

Visions of *German Angst*

An Interview with Michal Kosakowski by Marcus Stiglegger

The German-based director Michal Kosakowski creates films about a world you would not want to live in. And yet it *is* your world these films are about: a world of violent phantasies, of intolerance, harassment, murder and of history repeating itself. In *Zero Killed* (2011) he directed the violent imagination of average Austrian people. In *German Angst* (2015), the German capital becomes the home of living nightmares.

He is a director, writer, producer, director of photography and editor. CEO of the Berlin-based film production company Kosakowski Films. He started making films when he was ten. By 18 he had already directed and produced more than 30 shorts and developed his unique and controversial visual language with his first film production company Dark Productions.

Kosakowski studied film production at the Vienna Film Academy. From 1997 to 2000 he continued his studies as film director at the film department of Fabrica, Benetton's Artist School & Communication Research Center near Venice, Italy. He has produced and directed numerous short and experimental films, documentaries and video installations such as the critically acclaimed *Just Like the Movies* (2006) and *Fortynine* (2007).

Kosakowski's controversial *Zero Killed*, a hybrid of feature film and documentary on murder fantasies, has been shown at more than 40 international film festivals and has won numerous awards. In 2015, *German Angst* premiered at the 45th International Film Festival Rotterdam; this anthology feature was co-directed by Germany's best-known genre directors Jörg Buttgereit and Andreas Marschall.

Kosakowski was also lecturer at MD.H (Media Design Hochschule) in Munich, Germany, teaching Experimental Film & Theory. He regularly presents his films at international symposia and film seminars.

Marcus Stiglegger: *Can you please tell me how and where you grew up and about your first encounters with genre cinema?*

Michal Kosakowski: I grew up in Poland in the medium-sized city of Szczecin. The history of this city is special, since it was not clear after World War II whether the city belonged to Germany or Poland because the Oder river border was actually the border that was drawn between the victorious powers. And 80 percent of Szczecin was west of the river Oder. Therefore, many valuable buildings, such as the State Theatre, were dismantled in order to take construction materials, such as bricks, to the totally destroyed capital

Warsaw, to be reassembled. For about 400 years the city had been part of German territory and therefore after the end of World War II, all German citizens were expelled and many Poles were settled in the new territories. Even my maternal grandmother and my grandfather. You have to imagine this, a city that was completely empty and was easily repopulated with people who could choose their homes. However, the situation was not easy, because there were many assaults and rapes on civilians by Russian soldiers. There were quarters where simply no one wanted to go. My grandmother told me a lot of horror stories which stayed in my head, such as the German butcher who killed and dismembered children and threw them into a pond in the middle of the city. Until a few years ago, body parts were still being recovered from this pond.

Anyway, I was born in 1975, in the midst of Communist rule, in the period be-

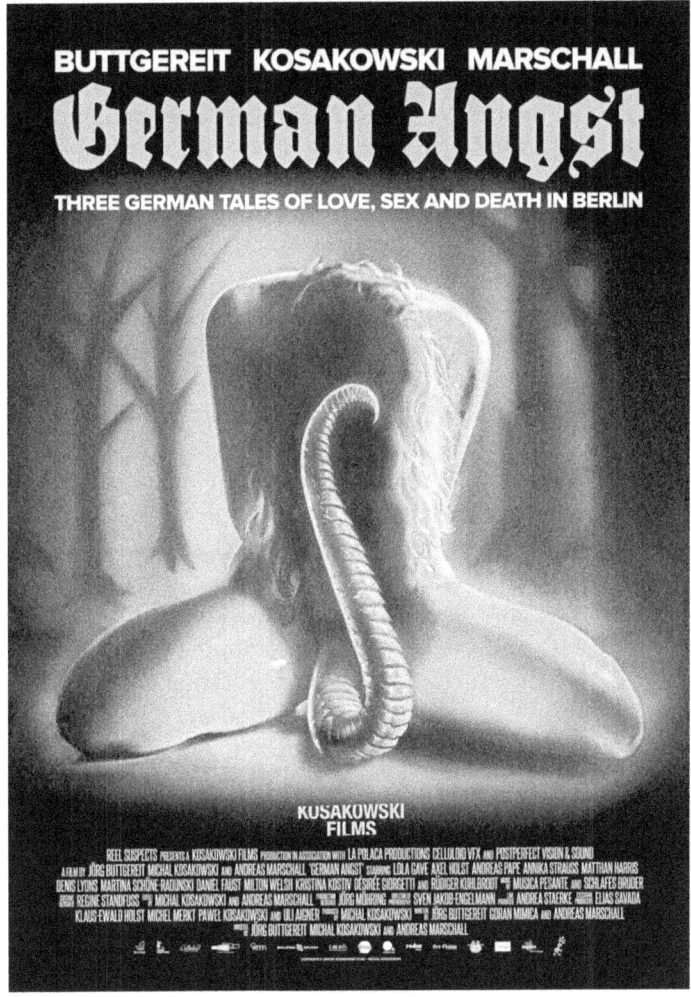

German Angst's poster proclaiming "Three German tales of Love, Sex and Death in Berlin" by three of Germany's most uncomprising filmmakers (courtesy Michal Kosakowski).

tween the two major strike periods 1970 and 1980, led by the Solidarity trade union under Lech Walesa. Szczecin was a port city, and there and in Gdansk the demonstrations started. In 1970, Szczecin saw a brutal suppression of the uprising, and there were many casualties. Martial law was imposed in Poland in December 1981, and that was certainly one of the most striking periods in my life. I was only six years old and I witnessed every day tanks on our doorstep. There was a curfew, arbitrary arrests were common and the whole situation was totally tense. As a child, you are not consciously aware of the threat, but it tends to come from the subconscious. However, despite all these bad things, I had a very nice and warm home, which kept me away from these experiences.

On Polish television there was only two channels, TVP 1 and TVP 2, which I watched on a black-and-white TV set. Besides Polish and Czech children's films and television productions, there was hardly any Western material. From time to time, Western content was shown from the mid–80s on. One day I saw a snippet of the music video *Thriller* by

Michael Jackson. These images of zombies scared me a lot and I immediately hid under my duvet. That was something I'd never seen before. Otherwise, there were many cinemas in Szczecin. When I look back now, I can think of the large number of theaters that the city had to offer. Very often, I went with my mother to the Pionier cinema, which is still the oldest theater in operation in the world. Strangely, we often saw Japanese monster movies like *Gamera* and *Godzilla* at Sunday matinees. My brother and I were fascinated by these films. Once we arrived home, we drew these monsters from memory.

When I was six, there was a special event: I saw *Star Wars: A New Hope* (1977) in the cinema with my father. This influenced me a lot. For the first time, I could immerse myself totally in a fantasy world that I had not known before. Another experience: My father used to travel abroad, so somewhere in West Germany he saw *Cat People* [1982] by Paul Schrader. One night, he told my mother about the film. I listened to them from my room and then crept slowly to their bedroom. Suddenly, I imitated the sound of a cat and my parents screamed. Their scream made me very scared and I ran back to my bed. We lived in Szczecin on a housing estate, and my brother and I played a lot outside with other children. There was something raw in these games. I remember that there was a covered hole near the train tracks and one day someone fell in and injured his foot. Or when we played with the dustbins, someone hurt a finger. Or there were twin brothers who were always up to no good, breaking into places, and sometimes they got arrested. Or we played with the elevators, stopping them while people were inside.

But the experience that made a lasting impression on me was when my brother and I went to the sixth floor of our building and started throwing water bags and other rubbish out of the window. Even bricks. A neighbor of ours, who was watching this spectacle from below, was struck by a brick and when we saw all the blood we thought we'd killed him. When we ran down, I saw a lot of blood and I will never forget the smell of it. Luckily he only had a bloody nose and needed some stitches. Thank God.

In school, corporal punishment was normal. I remember that our lifeguard would turn his ski stick into a weapon. While we were fooling around in the locker room, he would appear and start hitting us. Also, the school janitor had a small leather whip that he used arbitrarily, if anyone behaved stupidly.

At the age of ten, I moved with my family to Vienna, Austria. My father was appointed commercial attaché at the Polish Embassy. Thus, I came to the West. The first thing I noticed was the video stores. I found out quickly that you could watch movies there if you wanted. I suddenly had plenty of choice. This was new to me. Above all, I was overwhelmed by the large number of films and by all the colorful video cases. Thus my campaign began and I watched as many movies as possible. I was just fascinated by this medium. I was hungry for more.

You started making short films in your teens. What did you film?

I quickly understood that I had many possibilities to realize my own ideas. Inspired by my mass consumption of videos, I resorted to the VHS-C video camera that my father had bought soon after arrival in Vienna to film his tourist experiences. I was fascinated by the video system in which one could equally examine the movie on a TV. And so my first film experiments began. I met Christian Scharf who lived in the house opposite. He was also impressed by the fantasy and horror genre and so we founded our first underground company Dark Productions and began to implement our ideas for films. The first short films made were *The Legacy*, about a hammer murderer, *Frogman*, about the transformation of a human into a frogman, *Roboforce*, a variant of the film *RoboCop* [1987], *The Bread*, about a murderous cheese sandwich, *Death from Space*, about an alien creature that can possess a person and turn him into a zombie, *A Damned Videotape,* about a VHS tape that turns nightmares into reality, *The Ball,* about the transformation of a man into a football, *The Drill*, a revenge story, *After Death*, a story about zombies, *Face of the Death*, about antique masks which have sinister forces, *The Secrets of Grünbach*, a rape-revenge movie, etc.

In the period from 1985 to 1994, I made more than 30 short films. The films became more professional and expensive. I also read many books about other filmmakers. My school friends met in the evening to drink in a bar. But I used every free minute of my time to make movies and edit them on my analog editing system. My movies were always about dark themes, which have fascinated me since my childhood. How could I excite my neighbors and friends who watched my films, or scare them or make them panic? That gave me great fun and so I learned over time how the fear mechanisms in film work. Sometimes, I tried to introduce new ideas into my films and in 1996 I had a great idea, which turned out to be my biggest project so far, *Fortynine*: What if I interviewed ordinary people about their murder and violent fantasies in the form of short films shot with them as actors? The result is a total of 49 short films about killing, an elaborate video installation, and my first feature film *Zero Killed*. More on this later.

Your first step after school was into art school areas. Please tell me how you managed to end up in Italy and how this affected your later filmmaking.

After graduating from the commercial college in Vienna in 1994, I decided to apply to the Vienna Film Academy. After a very long entrance exam, I was finally accepted into the production class. However, I quickly found out that I had already acquired "too much" movie knowledge in my youth and I started to get bored there. I didn't want to produce "Heimatfilme" and TV crime. The fact that as a filmmaker you could grab the camera after six months was repulsive to me as an autodidact. With my ideas about human abysses, I had the feeling of being out of place in the most conservatively oriented film school.

Luckily, about that time, I found out by accident about a creative workshop in Northern Italy, Fabrica, which was founded and financed by the fashion group Benetton. I applied. I could see that only previous work was counted for the application. They didn't really care about your education, only your level of creativity. My own semi-skilled expertise and my existing filmography convinced the authorities in Fabrica to accept me in the video department.

Fabrica was overwhelming for me: It consisted of about eight or nine departments from all sorts of creative fields such as photography, graphic design, music, writing, comics, fashion, industrial design and film. Fabrica was headed by well-known photographer Oliviero Toscani, who in the '80s was in charge of all Benetton advertising campaigns. He then created a place for artists, which for me was perfect for its time: a place where the idea was in the foreground, a place where one had enough budget available to implement these ideas and a place where you could work free from constraints and conventions. The first principle of Fabrica was to promote creativity and find new ways of communicating. Thus, nothing stood in the way of my work. The place seemed to offer the perfect environment to put my own ideas into action with many other creative people from around the world. It was also a great inspiration to share ideas and to learn from each other. Multi-day workshops were held at regular intervals, in which world-renowned creative minds such as Issey Miyake, Godfrey Reggio and Marco Müller were invited to share their experiences with us. Between 1997 and 2000, great contacts arose with whom I still work today, such as the outstanding author Goran Mimica, who writes screenplays for my films. What I liked most was the fact that we learned there to complete projects as a team in a short time. The power of the image was always at the center, according to the principle that a picture tells a thousand words. This has accompanied me to this day and my film work would not be as it is today if I had not been at Fabrica.

When did your interest in violent interactions begin? Would you say violent conflict is a key element of your art?
Interest in violence certainly began in my childhood. As I have already mentioned, I had contact with the theme of violence in my childhood and youth. But just as these points of contact were different, so is the large thread of violence that interests me today. First, I must say that I have a terrible fear of real violence. I have been in several situations where I have seen outbreaks of violence on the street. I felt really bad, my feet went stiff and I immediately left the scene. So I couldn't look. When violence takes place in front of my eyes, I'm the first to run away. Even when it comes to real violence in the media, whether it is an ISIS video, where people are being beheaded or burned alive, films like *Faces of Death* [1978] or Mondo Films [pseudo-documentary exploitation films] or Gaddafi covered in blood being dragged on the road, I cannot and will not look at these images because I know that these are real moments and these do not interest me as such.

What fascinates me much more are the numerous forms of representation and iconography of fictional violence. Here I speak of visible violence and the violence that is hidden behind the things, that is the trigger for certain events or psychological interpersonal violence that is going on inside the individual. Abysses, crossing boundaries, just the dark soul that is inside each of us, is a mystery which I explore in my work. Moreover, I'm interested in the perception of images across all societies and the related media criticism and how this affects transversely through the history of the image on developments in all life situations.

I would like to mention two examples from my filmmaking to show my context for violent interaction. The short film *Just Like the Movies* [2012] re-constructs the events of 9/11 in New York by using footage from 52 Hollywood movies made before September 11, 2001. The instantaneous multimedia spread of the images of that catastrophe profoundly disturbed our perception apparatus. The images of the airplanes slamming into the Towers, and the Towers' subsequent collapse, seemed, at first glance, to be scenes from a disaster movie. "It's just like the movies!" was usually the first reaction of those watching the events unfolding on their TV screens, no doubt recalling the endless number of catastrophes that Hollywood has proposed over the years. Now confronted with the reality of one such scenario—of unprecedented destructive and symbolic resonance—a feeling of *déjà vu* arises while looking at these images. This paradoxical *déjà vu* presents a great challenge to our realism. The violent interaction happens within the image itself.

The other feature film project that I'm working on is called *The Glow*. In the autumn of 1938, a film crew of six goes into a forest near Berlin in defiance of the Nazis' ban on making horror films. They accidentally stumble upon a hidden house in which torturers inflict pain on artists and capture the expressions of their agonized, dying faces in a mysterious glow contained in a carved wooden box. *The Glow* is intended as a metaphor for our times in which "viewing" has become the essence of our existence. Does the reality make the image or does the image make the reality? Here I'm also following traces of the case of Lynndie England at Abu Ghraib prison during the Iraq War in 2003: Were they tortured in this way because of the photos, or were they photographed because of the cruelty and perversity of the torture? The glow from the carved wooden box is what the medium of film has been since the dawn of its existence: the ubiquity of the camera at all times in all places. To suffer and to see others suffering merges into one and the same.

You began with video art. When did you switch your attention to genre films?

For me personally, there is no distinction between video art and genre film. When I approach a substance, it is always the idea and the concept at the center. If the form of documentary is the best to communicate the idea, then I will select this form. But it can just as well be a video installation, a short film, a feature film, a series, or even photographs or some web movie. This is my freedom as an independent filmmaker, which I cherish. I try not to dwell on certain conventions and constructs, but to break them. Everything else bores me very quickly.

You also became a film producer.

Actually, I have always been a film producer. Since I produced my first movies when I was ten years old, producing and directing has been one thing for me. I'm a total control freak and I like it when I can keep a firm grip on things. Therefore, I often edit my films, or take the camera into my own hands. But when I realize major projects, it's important to have good people with the same energy, people who understand and appreciate me as a filmmaker. I'm interested in long-term friendships, arising from a working relationship. Only then can you successfully implement future projects, with people who share the same interests and who, just like me, display manic tendencies on the day.

Your cultural roots are Polish and Austrian. Now you live at Berlin.

I began living with my wife Uli Aigner and her three children in 2006 in Munich, where she was working as a curator at the Municipal Art Gallery of Munich, Lothringer 13. For me, as an artist and filmmaker, it is also very important to be constantly on the move. In Munich I worked a lot with my wife. Together we designed exhibitions, I produced many artists' documentaries and I also promoted my own projects. When our daughter Zoe was born in 2011, we decided to move to Berlin. Our Munich apartment simply became too small and we wanted to change location, and many of my friends were already working in Berlin. I quickly gained a foothold in Berlin. And for me as a filmmaker the city, with its unique history, was reason enough to pursue my filmmaking here. The available shooting locations and different people from other countries have enriched me. This city is an inspiration to me and my work, and the close proximity to my Polish hometown Szczecin brings me back to my childhood. In Berlin you have the tranquility to work on projects, but at the same time you have the necessary structures in order to realize these projects.

Please tell me about your project Fortynine *[1996–2007], how it was created and how it affected your later film* Zero Killed.

I've told you about experiencing tough times during the Communist regime in Poland, especially during the martial law between 1981 and 1983 in Poland, when I witnessed real violence on the streets and how easily ordinary people could turn into monsters. In 1996, I was wondering about asking only "normal" people from the street to tell me about their own violent fantasies. After what I had witnessed, I thought that anybody could be a potential killer under certain circumstances or at least could think about a scenario of killing somebody. So I ended up with this theory, this conclusion: If ordinary people fantasized about their own abyss or about plotting to get rid of somebody, these people must be the best actors in the world to act out their own personal crime fantasy.

So, I started meeting up with different people with no criminal backgrounds, and asked them to play killers or victims in a short film where the story was based on their own fantasies. I provided the necessary tools for them and I offered my skills as a director to realize their own murder fantasy as a fictitious scenario as realistic as possible. The more stories I shot throughout the following years, the more I found it interesting to delve deeper and deeper in the specific fantasies of the people I met. Finally, over 160 participants from 23 countries became part of this project.

But the original idea as to why I was shooting the short films was the video installation called Fortynine, which was shown in 2007 at the Lothringer 13 Kunsthalle in Munich, and was curated by my wife Uli Aigner. It was a $5 \times 4 \times 3$ meter mirror-walled "cube" that you could enter and look at 49 short films on murder. These homicidal fantasies were simultaneously back-projected on a screen. So basically, when you were standing in front of the projection wall, the reflections of the projection gave you the impression of being inside a room with infinite TV screens in which not the content, but an army of millions of TV screens was looking at you and you, as a spectator, become part of the installation, looking at the screens. The viewer was confronted with the unpleasant state of shock, only a closer view of the content revealed the short films on murder fantasies that were depicted on each screen. Firstly, this video installation was my attempt to criticize the violent images on television in itself that we were consuming without reflection every day. And secondly, to look at violent content in a surrounding that was far away from a safe home and a cozy couch where you can sit and relax in front of the TV.

Later, in 2008, I asked myself, "How would it be possible to bring the Fortynine short films to a big cinema screen? Just putting the short films one after another in a row, like an anthology film, wouldn't be enough. It would create more of a voyeuristic film rather than generating criticism of the depiction of violence as Fortynine did." I came up with the idea to meet the participants of the short films again and to create video interviews in which they were confronted with questions such as "If someone murdered a person you love, how would you feel about it? Should torture be legalized? How would you define good and evil? Are soldiers murderers? What causes rampages? Are you for or against the death penalty?" and so on. This juxtaposing with the fictitious murder fantasies and the real documentary style material allowed me to create similar criticism of the topic of violence as with the video installation Fortynine. Furthermore, the end product, which was the movie *Zero Killed*, turned out to be a self-reflective docu-drama which for me has a double effect on the audience: While being affected by the horror depicted in the dramatization of murder fantasies, we immediately have a direct or indirect "real" comment on the horror that had been presented to us by the same people who were the fictitious killers. At the same time, we question what is more horrifying: the murder fantasies of "normal" people or the comments that the participants are popping out at us. Inevitably, the dramaturgical structure of *Zero Killed* forces the audience to ask themselves "Do you have murder fantasies?" and regarding issues like revenge, good vs. evil, war, torture, rampage, media, domestic violence, etc. Maybe *Zero Killed* is not so much about understanding graphic violence, but more about feeling yourself and understanding your point of view through an unconventional approach.

23. Michal Kosakowski (Marcus Stiglegger)

Have you had real-life experiences with physical violence?

When I unexpectedly arrived in Vienna at the age of ten, I was often in risky situations where I experienced physical and psychological violence on my own body. Since I could not speak German, I was often beaten up by my classmates on racial grounds. I was then ashamed to tell my parents, so I kept it to myself. These events became important later because I have expressed myself more intensely with the issue of violence in my work.

During the conflicts, I often had the desire to switch roles between perpetrator and victim. I imagined how it would feel if someone who attacked me, had been in my body, how it would feel and how I would feel in the body of the offender. Would I just turn to violence if I was in this position of power? From this thought came the idea for my episode *Make a Wish* in my second feature film, the horror anthology *German Angst*.

What was the genre film situation in Germany when you tackled the German Angst *project?*

When I traveled to the world premiere of my first feature film *Zero Killed* at the Transylvania International Film Festival, I met the German director Andreas Marschall, who was showing his second feature film, *Masks* [2011], there. We understood each other at once and we also found out that we were neighbors in Berlin. We met several times and talked about our next film projects until finally Andreas had the idea to make an anthology horror movie and wondered if I would like to participate. The third member was the underground director Jörg Buttgereit, who caused a worldwide sensation with his *Nekromantik* movies in the '80s. We all met, I hadn't met Jörg not until then, but we

The talented trio (left to right) of Marschall, Buttgereit, and Kosakowski, the directorial team behind *German Angst* **(courtesy Michal Kosakowski).**

shared the same energy from the start. I was excited about this collaboration, and I also suggested producing the film with my production company Kosakowski Films. But I knew straight away that the situation in Germany, to produce a horror film, was not the best. We'd all had very bad experiences with public funding for cross-border films. Therefore, from the beginning we decided to finance through crowdfunding. Finally, this worked out, and in the process I was able to attract more private investors for *German Angst* which I had met during my festival travels with *Zero Killed*.

Within a very short time, I managed to come up with a budget which would allow me to produce the film. A big help was certainly the valuable support of our three different fan bases which we were able to win with our previous film works. Nevertheless, in Germany it is still very difficult to finance and to produce genre films because films here depend almost exclusively on public funding. To gain access to these funds, you need basically one or more German broadcast channels on board. Unfortunately, this is still a very difficult task for genre films in Germany. The genre film is regarded here as something "indecent," and it has a lot to do with the German past in World War II. This is a paradox, because actually the origins of horror films come from the Germany of the '20s. Films such as *The Golem* [1915], *The Cabinet of Dr. Caligari* [1920] and *Nosferatu* [1922] are genre milestones. When the Nazis came to power in 1933, many directors went into exile and this was also the end of the horror film productions. Under the leadership of the Propaganda Minister Joseph Goebbels, such productions were prohibited from then on. Every film or film project was subjected to censorship. The Reich's drama adviser could pre-censor any manuscript, deciding whether a film could be made at all. From 1934 on, any film which in the eyes of the Nazis was likely to "violate the Nazi, religious, moral or artistic sense, to brutalize or demoralize, to jeopardize the German reputation or Germany's relations with foreign states" was banned. To date, I have the feeling that the German film industry has not recovered yet from that period and therefore the German genre film pushes today on so much resistance and lack of understanding among public bodies.

The Nazi theme seems to be a constant element in your work. Why is that?
I would say it's more the subject of World War II that I'm very interested in, but of course not exclusively. It is even more my own analysis of past history, the work-up of my background that I'm interested in, the older I get. Coming from Poland, it is still a great mystery to me, how it could come to the terrible conditions in occupied Poland between 1939 and 1945. The stories of everyday life from my grandparents, the atrocities committed by the Nazis are difficult to understand, how the high civilization culture of Germans managed to produce barbaric states and to classify people in a system of racial fanaticism in the occupied territories—to divide people into categories worth living and not worth living and then treat them according to this. How did the German nation manage to completely switch off certain emotions like compassion? How could this happen? What tools and mechanisms were used to produce this condition? Genocide, crimes against humanity had already existed for thousands of years. But for me, the crimes of the National Socialists are a unique phenomenon in itself which was conducted with a perfidious and bureaucratic thoroughness, which is based on a complex, thoughtful construct of lies and still has no equal.

Therefore, I am always very skeptical of statements, claiming that enough has been said about Nazism and "Why should we do more movies about it?" Because once the

23. Michal Kosakowski (Marcus Stiglegger)

Nazi gun-toting madness in "*Make a Wish*" (courtesy Michal Kosakowski).

process of coming to terms with the past is finished, this past risks being forgotten and history could repeat itself.

I would not like to appear as a moralist, but this time concerns me greatly, also because of my background. There are still hundreds of exciting stories from this period that have not been told, but which I consider very important. And each generation has its own view of history; therefore, it needs to be told anew in contemporary garb every time.

Make a Wish—your segment of German Angst*—has a very up-to-date depiction of racist violence and bullying in Germany. How do you see this film in the context of actual events during the refugee crisis?*

When I shot *Make a Wish*, the refugee crisis had not yet assumed the gigantic proportions we have today. In this episode, it was primarily about showing how quickly and easily someone can become the "villain" once you are in a position where you have unlimited power to exercise control over another person. As an example, I wanted to introduce this to my own past, where the old conflict "Germany against Poland" is applied. However, it is alarming to see that the hatred and conflict that strongly comes to the fore in my episode can be felt today in some regions of Germany and generally in many European countries. East European countries, who vehemently defend themselves against the admission of refugees and who spread a populist tone in public, make me worry.

You showed German Angst *at many international festivals. How did audiences react?*

During the world premiere screening of *German Angst* at the Rotterdam International Film Festival, there was an incident which put me to some extent in a state of anxiety: A young spectator of Asian appearance stood up, came up to my seat near the exit and began to curse me. When he lunged at me, luckily he was restrained by the festival staff. He shouted "Fuck you!" to the audience, slammed the door and left. That was my first experience of audience reaction. Then the movie went around the world and the experiences were very different. For example, at the Brussels Fantastic Film Festival, the film was constantly commented on by the audience, there was laughter and applause, so at times we could not hear the movie soundtrack. Right after that, we went to the Night Visions Film Festival in Helsinki, where the audience was completely silent, no emotions were felt. Of course, the whole thing has to do with the mentality of different nations, but on the whole, the film was very well received by festival audiences, with no incidents similar to the one in Rotterdam.

Zero Killed *and* German Angst *are pretty graphic in their depiction of physical violence. Germany has the strictest youth protection laws in the E.U. Talk about getting a rating for these films.*

When *Zero Killed* was presented to the FSK (a German movie rating system)for inspection, I was very surprised that the film immediately scored a 16 rating, which is similar to PG-13 in the U.S. Although much graphic violence is shown in the film, it is the self-reflection of the individual performer, which is presented in documentary form as talking heads, that was decisive for the positive assessment of the inspector. Thereby the portrayal of violence is never an end in itself, but also expands the discourse on the reception of violence and the sensation associated with it.

It was different with *German Angst*. After the first presentation to the FSK, the film did not even get the 18 rating (rated R). I had two options: either to remove the offending depictions of violence or to appeal and to submit the film again uncut. Our German distributor and I decided to appeal, and luckily we succeeded in passing the film in its original length with an 18 rating. In its explanation, the Examination Board said:

> The message of the film is a clear rejection of violence as a way to solve conflicts. The violence shown is not an end in itself and is not formative for the design of the film. The protagonists who use violence do not develop attractive role models. The constant focus on the victim by the camera and the distance-creating visual use of other cinematic means, such as editing and music, promote an analytical discussion by the audience of the violent scenarios. Excessive emotional stress and a socio-ethical disorientation is a risk for children and youth because of their insufficient reflectivity has been determined. Starting points for further endangering effects have not been seen.

Just reading this, it is clear how serious and analytical the FSK is in inspections. However, I am critical of this institution because I rarely agree with the identification of the films. On one hand, some children's movies are not suitable for children while others with an 18 rating are actually harmless. Believe me, I speak from experience, since I have four children ages four to 17.

What does your future hold? What is in development?

As usual, I have several projects in the pipeline and I'm currently working intensively on two of them. One, a documentary called *Dark Tourism*, is currently in post-production. The film shows my personal journey as a so-called "dark tourist" to Poland's capital Warsaw to observe and examine the activities of the members of a Polish historical re-enactment group. This group re-enacts real historical situations from World War II in Poland, playing both Waffen—SS soldiers and Polish resistance groups. It's a journey full of contradictions and borderline experiences which motivates me to ask several questions: Who are these people? Why do Polish citizens dress up as German SS soldiers? What's going on inside these people? How does this kind of commemorative culture affect the young generations?

The film follows the protagonists and their world as closely as possible with particular focus on the practice of their ideologically charged rituals of remembrance. To feel it, to breathe the whiff of the street air of that time, perhaps only beginning to comprehend the incomprehensible events in the occupied Poland.

The other feature film project is called *Visit from Poland*. It's a story of a German-Jewish family protecting themselves and their apartment from an SS-mob in Berlin during the so-called Reichskristallnacht on November 9, 1938, which is also seen today as the beginning of the Holocaust. The story is based on one of the most incredible books I've ever read, *Pogrom: November 1938*. It's a 1000-page spine-chilling book with hundreds of reports from the Pogrom night in Germany and Austria. Alfred Wiener (1885–1964) was a German Jew who survived the Pogrom and escaped to the U.K., and who dedicated much of his life to documenting anti–Semitism in Germany.

Explicit blood-letting in "*Make a Wish*" (courtesy Michal Kosakowski).

I have taken out dozens of stories from the book and have created this story which fascinates me. The description of destruction, the fear and pain of the people, the tormenting perception of time, I have never ever been so close to the events of that night as with the book. So, there is a lot of work ahead of me!

Index

Alice, Sweet, Alice 28–38, 162, 188, 202–203, 205
All Cheerleaders Die 206
Allport, Christopher 47
Alone in the Dark 2, 82–89, 94, 97–98
American Nightmare see *Combat Shock*
Anderson, Lindsay 100–103
Arachnid 98
Argento, Dario 1, 35, 99, 103, 160, 194, 202
Aswang 165–174
Audition 227

Bad Taste 106
Baino, Mariano 2, 153–164
Bava, Mario 1, 35, 99, 103, 160, 194
Bazzoni, Luigi 8
Beasley, Shaun 249
BFI (British Film Institute) 18–19
Blind Fly 7
Blood and Black Lace 1, 35
The Blood of Hussain 138–139
Bloody Excess in the Leaders Bunker 126
Blue Velvet 93
Body Snatchers 171
The Bogeyman 201
Born of Fire 137–141
Bridgers, Sean 217–218, 220–221, 224
Bullitt 91
The Burning 83–84, 89
Buttgereit, Jörg 111, 123–136, 261

The Cabinet of Dr. Caligari 65–66, 103, 179, 261
Cannibal Holocaust 5, 214
Captain Berlin versus Hitler 134
Carpenter, John 1, 61, 189, 192, 201–202
Carpi, Fiorenzo 10–11
Carrie 75

Carter, Lauren Ashley 210, 217, 224
Caruncula 153–154
C.B. Hustlers 56, 58, 60
Chambers, Marilyn 56, 62
Clark, Lawrence Gordon 17–20
Clyde, Jeremy 17, 22
Combat Shock 106–111, 114, 120
Coppola, Francis Ford 28
Craven, Wes 61, 87, 104
Creature from the Black Lagoon 244
Cronenberg, David 206, 210
Crowley, Suzan 137, 139–140
Cullipher, Arthur 236, 238, 247–253
Cunningham, Sean 88

Dark Waters 2, 153–164
David, Joanna 99, 102–104
Deadbeat at Dawn 106–107
Deep Red 35
Deep Sleep 28
Dehlavi, Jamil 137–141
Deliverance 46
Dementia 13 166
The Demonology of Desire 228, 230, 232
Denham, Christopher 206, 210–11
Denham, Maurice 17, 22
DeNoble, Alphonso 32
Desecration 188, 190–195, 200–201, 204–205
The Devil and LeRoy Bassett 59
The Devils 25, 162
The Devil's Backbone 227
Les Diaboliques 35
Dickens, Charles 18, 26
Dog Day Afternoon 97
Don't Go in the House 2, 63–81
Don't Look Now 29, 189
Douglas, Bill 99, 102–104
Dream Car 153–154
The Dress Rehearsal 7
The Driller Killer 5, 29
Drive-in Massacre 2, 54–62

Ellison, Joseph 2, 63–81
Entonce 7
Evil Dead 1, 165–166, 169, 171, 174
eXistenZ 210
Exorcist 162, 166, 189
Eyeball 35
The Eyes of Edward James 228–230

Faces of Death 258
The Facts in the Case of Mister Hollow 228, 230–231
Ferrara, Abel 1, 29, 132, 171
Fessenden, Larry 209, 218, 224, 226
Firth, Peter 137, 139
The Fog 1
Footprints on the Moon 8
Found 236–237, 239–244, 247–248, 250–252
The French Connection 91
Freund, Karl 1
Friday the 13th 28, 36, 43–44, 63, 71, 75, 82, 88, 129
Fulci, Lucio 35
Full Moon Sonny 237–239

German Angst 134–135, 254–265
A Ghost Story for Christmas 17–19, 26
Giovinazzo, Buddy 106–122
Giovinazzo, Ricky 108–111, 121
The Girl Next Door 206, 212, 214
Globus, Yoram 52
Golan, Menahem 44, 48–52
The Golem 261
Grace, Nickolas 99, 102
Grant, David 11
Grimaldi, Dan 68, 76
Gudiño, Rodrigo 228–235

Halloween 1, 28, 36, 43, 82, 132, 202
Hammill, Ellen 63, 66–71, 76, 78

267

Index

Harvest Lake 237, 241, 244–246
Headless 236, 240–244
Headspace 206–211, 216
Henry: Portrait of a Serial Killer 2, 106, 167, 240
Herzog, Werner 1
The Hidden 2, 82, 87, 89–97
High Noon 51
Higuchinsky 175–179
Hill, Marianna 40–42, 49
The Hills Have Eyes 207
Hitchcock, Alfred 36, 73
Horror 188, 190–191, 193–195, 201, 205
Hot Love 126–127, 135
House of Hope 238–240
Hussey, Olivia 206

I Spit on Your Grave 5
Insatiable 56, 62
Ishii, Sogo 144
Ito, Junji 176–178

James, M.R. 18, 20, 26
Jarman, Derek 19
Jordan, Kathy 65, 68
Jug Face 217–227
Justin, John 22–23

Kapnist, Maria 159–160
Kennedy, Cheryl 17, 21, 25
Ketchum, Jack 206, 212, 214
Kichiku 180, 186
Kier, Udo 119–120, 206–207, 211
Killer Condom 134
Kinkle, Chad Crawford 217–227
Kinski, Klaus 39–43, 48–53
Kinski, Pola 42
Koerner von Gustorf, Florian 132–133
Kosakowski, Michal 254–265

Landau, Martin 82, 85–87, 94
Lang, Fritz 83
Last House on the Left 171
The Last Will and Testament of Rosalind Leigh 228–235
Late Bloomer 180–187
Lawrence, Flo 41–42, 50–51, 53
Le Fanu, Sheridan 17, 19, 25–26
Lenzi, Umberto 35
Lewis, Herschell Gordon 59, 106
Life Is Hot in Cracktown 113–114, 116, 118, 120–121
Lloyd, Christopher 40, 49, 51, 53
Logan, Saxon 99–105
Lommel, Ulli 201
Long Dream 175–177, 179
Lopes, Danny 201
Lovecraft, H.P. 153, 157–158, 210, 230

Lowry, Lynn 188, 199–200
Lumet, Sidney 97
Lustig, William 111–112
Lynch, David 1, 93, 179

M 83
MacLachlan, Kyle 82, 90–91, 93–97
Man Bites Dog 2
Maniac 2 111–112
Martin, Wrye 165–166, 168–169, 171–173
Matsui, Yoshihiko 2, 142–152
Maylam, Tony 83, 89
McIntosh, Pollyanna 210
McKee, Lucky 206, 209, 214, 218, 220, 224, 227
McNaughton, John 167
Megahey, Leslie 17–27
Meyer, Russ 56
Miller, Jonathan 18, 20
Miller, Linda 29, 31–33
Monsterland 134
Moses, Norman 165, 170
Ms. 45 132
The Mummy 1

Nekromantik 111, 123, 126–131, 135
Nekromantik 2 123, 126, 128–130, 133, 135
A Night of Nightmares 120
Night of the Living Dead 166
A Nightmare on Elm Street 2: Freddy's Revenge 82, 87, 89, 93–94, 98
Nightmares in a Damaged Brain 2, 5–8, 11–16
Nine Lives of a Wet Pussy 29
NN-891102 180–181, 185, 187
No Way Home 115–116
Noisy Requiem 2, 142–152
Nosferatu 65–66, 179, 261
Nouri, Michael 82, 90–91, 93–97

Off Season 206, 212
Off the Beaten Path 239
Offspring 206–210, 211–216
The Omen 166
Omnibus 18, 20–21
One Flew Over the Cuckoo's Nest 49

Page, Heather 99, 102–104
Palance, Jack 82, 85–88, 94
Pandemonium 37
Pastore, Vincent 188
Paukstelis, Tina Ona 165, 170
Paulsen, David 2, 39–53
Pearson, Robert E. 59–60
Pig-Chicken Suicide 145, 148
Pistilli, Luigi 6
Pleasence, Donald 82, 85–86

Poetry and Purgatory 114–115
Polanski, Roman 139
Poltermann, Barry 165–174
Poole, Aaron 228, 234
Price, Vincent 166, 192
Psycho 73

The Quiet Fever 7

Raimi, Sam 1, 171, 214
Rassimov, Ivan 6
The Ravaged One 7
Reanimator 106
Redgrave, Vanessa 228, 233–234
Reed, Carol 70, 74
The Renegades 82, 91
Rivto, Rosemary 29
Robinson, Shawn 10
Roeg, Nic 29, 141
Romero, George A. 166
Rose, Felissa 195
Rosenberg, Richard 33–34
Russell, Ken 18, 25, 107
Russo, James 115, 117
Rusty Empty Can 143–144, 150

Salter, Louise 156, 158–159
Sanderson, William 39, 47
Sandweiss, Ellen 195
Sanford, Christie 192, 195–196, 198
Satan's Playground 188, 195–198, 200–201, 205
Savage Weekend 2, 39–40, 43–48, 50
Savini, Tom 13–14, 16, 88–89
Scavolini, Romano 2, 5–16
Schalcken, Godfried 17–27
Schalcken the Painter 17–27
Schirmer, Scott 2, 236–248
Schizoid 2, 39–43, 48–53
Schramm 123, 125, 132–133, 136
Sebastiane 19
Segall, Stu 2, 54–62
Serpico 97
Shaban, Nabil 137, 140
Shaye, Bob 78–79, 82, 86–87, 90–92, 94, 97, 168
Sheppard, Paula E. 31–32
Shibata, Gō 180–187
Shields, Brooke 28, 30, 203
Sholder, Jack 2, 82–98
Sleepwalker 99–105
Slice of Life 112–113
Sole, Alfred 28–38, 188–189, 192, 201–203
Stafford, Baird 5
Stewart, Evelyn 6
Straw Dogs 83
Street Trash 106, 111
Sumida, Masakiyo 180–187
Sunrise 66
Suspiria 1, 202

Tanya's Island 37
Tarantino, Quentin 78
Tarkovsky, Andrei 1
Tarr, Béla 1
Terayama, Shuji 143–144, 146
Texas Chain Saw Massacre 132, 165, 168, 171, 174, 220, 239
The Third Man 70
Der Todesking 123–125, 129–132
Tomaselli, Dante 2, 37, 188–205
Torture Chamber 188, 191, 197–201, 204–205
Tsukamoto, Shinya 143

The Unscarred 116–118
Uzumaki 175–179

van Den Houten, Andrew 206–216, 218, 220, 224, 227
Videodrome 210, 253
Vidor, Zoli 45–46

Wallace Stone, Dee 197, 206, 211
Wang, Patrick 209
Wasson, Craig 39–41, 49–50, 52–53
Watkins, Peter 1

Wheldon, Huw 18
Where Are We Going? 150–151
Whistle and I'll Come to You 18, 20
A White Dress for Marialé 5–12, 13, 16
The Wicker Man 220
Wilkes, Donna 40–43, 50–53
Wilson, Gregory M. 209
Wishmaster 2 97–98
The Woman 206, 210, 218, 224

Zero Killed 254, 259, 264

www.ingramcontent.com/pod-product-compliance
Lightning Source LLC
Chambersburg PA
CBHW081546300426
44116CB00015B/2773